Cyberwarfare/Cyberattacks

Contents

Chapter 1

Cyber-attack

Cyber-attack is any type of offensive maneuver employed by individuals or whole organizations that targets computer information systems, infrastructures, computer networks, and/or personal computer devices by various means of malicious acts usually originating from an anonymous source that either steals, alters, or destroys a specified target by hacking into a susceptible system. These can be labeled as either a cyber campaign, cyberwarfare or cyberterrorism in different context. Cyber-attacks can range from installing spyware on a PC to attempts to destroy the infrastructure of entire nations. Cyber-attacks have become increasingly sophisticated and dangerous as the Stuxnet worm recently demonstrated.*[1] User behavior analytics and SIEM are used to prevent these attacks.

1.1 Cyberwarfare and cyberterrorism

Main articles: Cyberwarfare and Cyberterrorism

Cyberwarfare utilizes techniques of defending and attacking information and computer networks that inhabit cyberspace, often through a prolonged cyber campaign or series of related campaigns. It denies an opponent's ability to do the same, while employing technological instruments of war to attack an opponent's critical computer systems. Cyberterrorism, on the other hand, is "the use of computer network tools to shut down critical national infrastructures (such as energy, transportation, government operations) or to coerce or intimidate a government or civilian population." *[2] That means the end result of both cyberwarfare and cyberterrorism is the same, to damage critical infrastructures and computer systems linked together within the confines of cyberspace.

1.2 Factors

Three factors contribute to why cyber-attacks are launched against a state or an individual: the fear factor, spectacular factor, and vulnerability factor.

1.2.1 Fear factor

The most common, fear factor, a cyberterrorist will create fear amongst individuals, groups, or societies. The bombing of a Bali nightclub in 2002 created fear amongst the foreign tourists who frequently visited the venue. Once the bomb went off and casualties ensued, the influx of tourists to Bali significantly reduced due to fear of death.

1.2.2 Spectacular factor

With spectacular factors, it is the actual damage of the attack, meaning the attacks created direct losses and gained negative publicity. In 1999 a denial of service attack rendered Amazon.com unusable. Amazon experienced losses because of suspended trading and it was publicized worldwide.

1.2.3 Vulnerability factor

Vulnerability factor exploits how vulnerable an organization or government establishment is to cyber-attacks. An organization can be vulnerable to a denial of service attack, and a government establishment can be defaced on a web page. A computer network attack disrupts the integrity or authenticity of data, usually through malicious code that alters program logic that controls data, leading to errors in output.*[3]

1.3   Professional hackers to cyberterrorists

Professional hackers, either working on their own or employed by the government or military service, can find computer systems with vulnerabilities lacking the appropriate security software. Once found, they can infect systems with malicious code and then remotely control the system or computer by sending commands to view content or to disrupt other computers. There needs to be a pre-existing system flaw within the computer such as no antivirus protection or faulty system configuration for the viral code to work. Many professional hackers will promote themselves to cyberterrorists where a new set of rules govern their actions. Cyberterrorists have premeditated plans and their attacks are not born of rage. They need to develop their plans step-by-step and acquire the appropriate software to carry out an attack. They usually have political agendas, targeting political structures. Cyber terrorists are hackers with a political motivation, their attacks can impact political structure through this corruption and destruction.[4] They also target civilians, civilian interests and civilian installations. As previously stated cyberterrorists attack persons or property and cause enough harm to generate fear.

1.4   Sanctions

In response to cyber-attacks on April 1, 2015, President Obama issued an Executive Order establishing the first-ever economic sanctions. The Executive Order will impact individuals and entities ("designees") responsible for cyber-attacks that threaten the national security, foreign policy, economic health, or financial stability of the US. Specifically, the Executive Order authorizes the Treasury Department to freeze designees' assets.[5]

1.5   Syntactic attacks and semantic attacks

In detail, there are a number of techniques to utilize in cyber-attacks and a variety of ways to administer them to individuals or establishments on a broader scale. Attacks are broken down into two categories, Syntactic attacks and Semantic attacks. **Syntactic attacks** are straight forward; it is considered malicious software which includes viruses, worms, and Trojan horses.

Intrusion kill chain for information security[6]

1.5.1   Viruses

Viruses are a self-replicating program that can attach itself to another program or file in order to reproduce. The virus can hide in unlikely locations in the memory of a computer system and attach itself to whatever file it sees fit to execute its code. It can also change its digital footprint each time it reproduces making it even harder to track down in the computer.

1.5.2   Worms

Worms do not need another file or program to copy itself; it is a self-sustaining running program. Worms replicate over a network using protocols. The latest incarnation of worms make use of known vulnerabilities in systems to penetrate, execute their code, and replicate to other systems such as the Code Red II worm that infected more than 259 000 systems in less than 14 hours.[7] On a much larger scale, worms can be designed for industrial espionage to monitor and collect server and traffic activities then transmit it back to its creator.

1.5.3   Trojan horses

A Trojan horse is designed to perform legitimate tasks but it also performs unknown and unwanted activity. It can be the basis of many viruses and worms installing onto the computer as keyboard loggers and backdoor software. In a commercial sense, Trojans can be imbedded in trial versions of software and can gather additional intelligence about the target without the person even knowing it happening. All three of these are likely to attack an individual and establishment through emails, web browsers, chat clients, remote software, and updates.

Semantic attack is the modification and dissemination of correct and incorrect information. Information modified could have been done without the use of computers even though new opportunities can be found by using them. To set someone into the wrong direction or to cover your tracks, the dissemination of incorrect information can be utilized.

1.5.4 Israel and the Palestinian Authority

In the conflict between Israel and the Palestinian Authority cyber attacks were conducted in October 2000 when Israeli hackers launched DOS attacks on computers owned by Palestinian resistance organizations (Hamas) and Lebanese resistance organizations (Hezbullah). Anti-Israel hackers responded by crashing several Israeli web sites by flooding them with bogus traffic.*[4]

1.5.5 India and Pakistan

Main article: India–Pakistan relations

There were two such instances between India and Pakistan that involved cyberspace conflicts, started in 1990s. Earlier cyber attacks came to known as early as in 1999.*[4] Since then, India and Pakistan were engaged in a long-term dispute over Kashmir which moved into cyberspace. Historical accounts indicated that each country's hackers have been repeatedly involved in attacking each other's computing database system. The number of attacks has grown yearly: 45 in 1999, 133 in 2000, 275 by the end of August 2001.*[4] In 2010, Indian hackers laid a cyber attack at least 36 government database websites going by the name "Indian Cyber Army" .*[8] In 2013, Indian hackers hacked the official website of Election Commission of Pakistan in an attempt to retrieve sensitive database information.*[9] In retaliation, Pakistani hackers, calling themselves "True Cyber Army" hacked and defaced ~1,059 websites of Indian election bodies.*[9]

According to the media, Pakistan's has been working on effective cyber security system, in a program called the "Cyber Secure Pakistan" (CSP).*[10] The program was launched in April 2013 by Pakistan Information Security Association and the program as expanded to country's universities.

1.6 China, United States and others

Within cyberwarfare, the individual must recognize the state actors involved in committing these cyber-attacks against one another. The two predominant players that will be discussed is the age-old comparison of East versus West, China's cyber capabilities compared to United States' capabilities. There are many other state and non-state actors involved in cyberwarfare, such as Russia, Iran, Iraq, and Al Qaeda; since China and the U.S. are leading the foreground in cyberwarfare capabilities, they will be the only two state actors discussed.

But in Q2 2013, Akamai Technologies reported that Indonesia toppled China with portion 38 percent of cyber attack, a high increase from 21 percent portion in previous quarter. China set 33 percent and US set at 6.9 percent. 79 percent of attack came from Asia Pacific region. Indonesia dominated the attacking to ports 80 and 443 by about 90 percent.*[11]

1.6.1 China

Main article: Cyberwarfare in China

China's People's Liberation Army (PLA) has developed a strategy called "Integrated Network Electronic Warfare" which guides computer network operations and cyberwarfare tools. This strategy helps link together network warfare tools and electronic warfare weapons against an opponent's information systems during conflict. They believe the fundamentals for achieving success is about seizing control of an opponent's information flow and establishing information dominance. *The Science of Military* and *The Science of Campaigns* both identify enemy logistics systems networks as the highest priority for cyber-attacks and states that cyberwarfare must mark the start if a campaign, used properly, can enable overall operational success.*[12] Focusing on attacking the opponent's infrastructure to disrupt transmissions and processes of information that dictate decision-making operations, the PLA would secure cyber dominance over their adversary. The predominant techniques that would be utilized during a conflict to gain the upper hand are as follows, the PLA would strike with electronic jammers, electronic deception and suppression techniques to interrupt the transfer processes of information. They would launch virus attacks or hacking techniques to sabotage information processes, all in the hopes of destroying enemy information platforms and facilities. The PLA's *Science of Campaigns* noted that one role for cyberwarfare is to create windows of opportunity for other forces to operate without detection or with a lowered risk of counterattack by exploiting the enemy's periods of "blindness," "deafness" or "paralysis" created by cyber-attacks.*[12] That is one of the main focal points of cyberwarefare, to be able to weaken your enemy to the full extent possible so that your physical offensive will have a higher percentage of success.

The PLA conduct regular training exercises in a variety of environments emphasizing the use of cyberwarfare tactics and techniques in countering such tactics if it is employed against them. Faculty research has been focusing on designs for rootkit usage and detection for their Kylin Operating System which helps to further train these individuals' cyberwarfare techniques. China perceives cyberwarfare as a deterrent to nuclear weapons, possessing the ability for greater precision, leaving fewer casualties, and allowing for long ranged attacks.

1.6.2   United States

In the West, the United States provides a different "tone of voice" when cyberwarfare is on the tip of everyone's tongue. The United States provides security plans strictly in the response to cyberwarfare, basically going on the defensive when they are being attacked by devious cyber methods. In the U.S., the responsibility of cybersecurity is divided between the Department of Homeland Security, the Federal Bureau of Investigation, and the Department of Defense. In recent years, a new department was created to specifically tend to cyber threats, this department is known as Cyber Command. Cyber Command is a military subcommand under US Strategic Command and is responsible for dealing with threats to the military cyber infrastructure. Cyber Command's service elements include Army Forces Cyber Command, the Twenty-fourth Air Force, Fleet Cyber Command and Marine Forces Cyber Command.*[13] It ensures that the President can navigate and control information systems and that he also has military options available when defense of the nation needs to be enacted in cyberspace. Individuals at Cyber Command must pay attention to state and non-state actors who are developing cyberwarfare capabilities in conducting cyber espionage and other cyberattacks against the nation and its allies. Cyber Command seeks to be a deterrence factor to dissuade potential adversaries from attacking the U.S., while being a multi-faceted department in conducting cyber operations of its own.

Three prominent events took place which may have been catalysts in the creation of the idea of Cyber Command. There was a failure of critical infrastructure reported by the CIA where malicious activities against information technology systems disrupted electrical power capabilities overseas. This resulted in multi-city power outages across multiple regions. The second event was the exploitation of global financial services. In November 2008, an international bank had a compromised payment processor that allowed fraudulent transactions to be made at more than 130 automated teller machines in 49 cities within a 30-minute period.*[14] The last event was the systemic loss of U.S. economic value when an industry in 2008 estimated $1 trillion in losses of intellectual property to data theft. Even though all these

events were internal catastrophes, they were very real in nature, meaning nothing can stop state or non-state actors to do the same thing on an even grander scale. Other initiatives like the Cyber Training Advisory Council were created to improve the quality, efficiency, and sufficiency of training for computer network defense, attack, and exploitation of enemy cyber operations.

On both ends of the spectrum, East and West nations show a "sword and shield" contrast in ideals. The Chinese have a more offensive minded idea for cyberwarfare, trying to get the pre-emptive strike in the early stages of conflict to gain the upper-hand. In the U.S. there are more reactionary measures being taken at creating systems with impenetrable barriers to protect the nation and its civilians from cyberattacks.

According to *Homeland Preparedness News*, many mid-sized U.S. companies have a difficult time defending their systems against cyber attacks. Around 80 percent of assets vulnerable to a cyber attack are owned by private companies and organizations. Former New York State Deputy Secretary for Public Safety Michael Balboni said that private entities "do not have the type of capability, bandwidth, interest or experience to develop a proactive cyber analysis." *[15]

1.7   Infrastructures as targets

Once a cyber-attack has been initiated, there are certain targets that need to be attacked to cripple the opponent. Certain infrastructures as targets have been highlighted as critical infrastructures in time of conflict that can severely cripple a nation. Control systems, energy resources, finance, telecommunications, transportation, and water facilities are seen as critical infrastructure targets during conflict. A new report on the industrial cybersecurity problems, produced by the British Columbia Institute of Technology, and the PA Consulting Group, using data from as far back as 1981, reportedly has found a 10-fold increase in the number of successful cyber-attacks on infrastructure Supervisory Control and Data Acquisition (SCADA) systems since 2000.*[3] Cyber-attacks that have an adverse physical effect are known as cyber-physical attacks.*[16]

1.7.1   Control systems

Control systems are responsible for activating and monitoring industrial or mechanical controls. Many devices are integrated with computer platforms to control valves and gates to certain physical infrastructures. Control systems are usually designed as remote telemetry devices that link to other physical devices through internet access or modems. Little security can be offered when dealing with these devices, enabling many hackers or cyberterrorists to seek out systematic vulnerabilities. Paul Blomgren, manager of sales engineering at cybersecurity firm explained how his people drove to a remote substation, saw a wireless network antenna and immediately plugged in their wireless LAN cards. They took out their laptops and connected to the system because it wasn't using passwords. "Within 10 minutes, they had mapped every piece of equipment in the facility," Blomgren said. "Within 15 minutes, they mapped every piece of equipment in the operational control network. Within 20 minutes, they were talking to the business network and had pulled off several business reports. They never even left the vehicle." *[17]

1.7.2 Energy

Energy is seen as the second infrastructure that could be attacked. It is broken down into two categories, electricity and natural gas. **Electricity** also known as electric grids power cities, regions, and households; it powers machines and other mechanisms used in day-to-day life. Using U.S. as an example, in a conflict cyberterrorists can access data through the Daily Report of System Status that shows power flows throughout the system and can pinpoint the busiest sections of the grid. By shutting those grids down, they can cause mass hysteria, backlog, and confusion; also being able to locate critical areas of operation to further attacks in a more direct method. Cyberterrorists can access instructions on how to connect to the Bonneville Power Administration which helps direct them on how to not fault the system in the process. This is a major advantage that can be utilized when cyber-attacks are being made because foreign attackers with no prior knowledge of the system can attack with the highest accuracy without drawbacks. Cyber-attacks on **natural gas** installations go much the same way as it would with attacks on electrical grids. Cyberterrorists can shutdown these installations stopping the flow or they can even reroute gas flows to another section that can be occupied by one of their allies. There was a case in Russia with a gas supplier known as Gazprom, they lost control of their central switchboard which routes gas flow, after an inside operator and Trojan horse program bypassed security.*[17]

1.7.3 Finance

Financial infrastructures could be hit hard by cyber-attacks. There is constant money being exchanged in these institutions and if cyberterrorists were to attack and if transactions were rerouted and large amounts of money stolen, financial industries would collapse and civilians would be without jobs and security. Operations would stall from region to region causing nationwide economical degradation. In the U.S. alone, the average daily volume of transactions hit $3 trillion and 99% of it is non-cash flow.*[17] To be able to disrupt that amount of money for one day or for a period of days can cause lasting damage making investors pull out of funding and erode public confidence.

1.7.4 Telecommunications

Cyber-attacking telecommunication infrastructures have straightforward results. Telecommunication integration is becoming common practice, systems such as voice and IP networks are merging. Everything is being run through the internet because the speeds and storage capabilities are endless. Denial-of-service attacks can be administered as previously mentioned, but more complex attacks can be made on BGP routing protocols or DNS infrastructures. It is less likely that an attack would target or compromise the traditional telephony network of SS7 switches, or an attempted attack on physical devices such as microwave stations or satellite facilities. The ability would still be there to shut down those physical facilities to disrupt telephony networks. The whole idea on these cyber-attacks is to cut people off from one another, to disrupt communication, and by doing so, to impede critical information being sent and received. In cyberwarfare, this is a critical way of gaining the upperhand in a conflict. By controlling the flow of information and communication, a nation can plan more accurate strikes and enact better counter-attack measures on their enemies.

1.7.5 Transportation

Transportation infrastructure mirrors telecommunication facilities; by impeding transportation for individuals in a city or region, the economy will slightly degrade over time. Successful cyber-attacks can impact scheduling and accessibility, creating a disruption in the economic chain. Carrying methods will be impacted, making it hard for cargo to be sent from one place to another. In January 2003 during the "slammer" virus, Continental Airlines was forced to shut down flights due to computer problems.*[17] Cyberterrorists can target railroads by disrupting switches, target flight software to impede airplanes, and target road usage to impede more conventional transportation methods. In May 2015, a man, Chris Roberts, who was a cyberconsultant, revealed to the FBI that he had repeatedly, from 2011 to 2014, managed to hack into Boeing and Airbus flights' controls via the onboard entertainment system, allegedly, and had at least once ordered a flight to climb. The FBI, after detaining him in April 2015 in Syracuse, had interviewed him about the allegations.*[18]

1.7.6 Water

Water as an infrastructure could be one of the most critical infrastructures to be attacked. It is seen as one of the greatest security hazards among all of the computer-controlled systems. There is the potential to have massive amounts of water unleashed into an area which could be unprotected causing loss of life and property damage. It is not even water supplies that could be attacked; sewer systems can be compromised too. There was no calculation given to the cost of damages, but the estimated cost to replace critical water systems could be in the hundreds of billions of dollars.*[17] Most of these water infrastructures are well developed making it hard for cyber-attacks to cause any significant damage, at most, equipment failure can occur causing power outlets to be disrupted for a short time.

1.8   See also

- List of cyber-attacks

1.9   References

[1] S. Karnouskos: *Stuxnet Worm Impact on Industrial Cyber-Physical System Security.* In:*37th Annual Conference of the IEEE Industrial Electronics Society (IECON 2011), Melbourne, Australia,* 7-10 Nov 2011. Retrieved 20 Apr 2014.

[2] Lewis, James. United States. Center for Strategic and International Studies. Assessing the Risks of Cyber Terrorism, Cyber War and Other Cyber Threats. Washington, D.C.. , 2002. Web.

[3] Linden, Edward. Focus on Terrorism. New York: Nova Science Publishers, Inc., 2007. Web.

[4] Prichard, Janet, and Laurie MacDonald. "Cyber Terrorism: A Study of the Extent of Coverage in Computer Security Textbooks." Journal of Information Technology Education. 3. (2004): n. page. Web.

[5] "Sanctions: U.S. action on cyber crime" (PDF). PwC Financial Services Regulatory Practice, April, 2015.

[6] U.S. Senate-Committee on Commerce, Science, and Transportation-A "Kill Chain" Analysis of the 2013 Target Data Breach-March 26, 2014

[7] Janczewski, Lech, and Andrew Colarik. Cyber Warfare and Cyber Terrorism. Hershey, New York: Information Science Reference, 2008. Web.

[8] Staff (November 30, 2010). "Cyber Indian Army". *Express Tirbune*. Retrieved 8 June 2013.

[9] Waseem Abbasi (April 6, 2013). "Pakistani hackers defaced over 1,000 Indian websites". *The News International 2013*. Retrieved 8 June 2013.

[10] Staff (April 22, 2013). "Cyber Secure Pakistan' initiative launched". *The News International, April 2013*. Retrieved 10 June 2013.

[11] "Indonesia Tops China as Cyber Attack Capital". *PC Magazine*. October 16, 2013.

[12] Krekel, Bryan. People's Republic of China. The US-China Economic and Security Review Commission.Capability of the People's Republic of China to Conduct Cyber Warfare and Computer Network Exploitation . Virginia: Northrop Grumman, 2009. Web.

[13] Lewis, James, and Katrina Timlin. United States. Center for Strategic and International Studies. Cybersecurity and Cyberwarfare: Preliminary Assessment of National Doctrine and Organization. Washington, D.C.: , 2011. Web.

[14] United States. Review Team of Government Cybersecurity Experts. Cyberspace Policy Review: Assuring a Trusted and Resilient Information and Communications Infrastructure. Washington, D.C.: , Web.

[15] Rozens, Tracy (2016-05-19). "Expert: More work needed to get private sector cyber secure". *Homeland Preparedness News*. Retrieved 2016-07-19.

[16] Loukas, George (June 2015). *Cyber-Physical Attacks A growing invisible threat.* Oxford, UK: Butterworh-Heinemann (Elsevier). p. 65. ISBN 9780128012901.

[17] Lyons, Marty. United States. Homeland Security. Threat Assessment of Cyber Warfare. Washington, D.C.: , 2005. Web.

[18] Evan Perez (May 18, 2015). "FBI: Hacker claimed to have taken over flight's engine controls". *CNN*.

1.10   Further reading

- Alexander, Keith. United States. Senate Committee on Armed Service . United States Cyber Command. 2012. Web.

1.11   External links

- July 2015 Cyber Attacks Statistics – Hackmageddon

- Norse Attack Map

Chapter 2

List of cyber-attacks

A cyber-attack is any type of offensive maneuver employed by individuals or whole organizations that targets computer information systems, infrastructures, computer networks, and/or personal computer devices by various means of malicious acts usually originating from an anonymous source that either steals, alters, or destroys a specified target by hacking into a susceptible system.

This article contains a **list of cyber-attacks**.

2.1 Indiscriminate attacks

These attacks are wide-ranging, global and do not seem to discriminate among governments and companies.

- Operation Shady RAT
- World of Hell
- Red October, discovered in 2012, was reportedly operating worldwide for up to five years prior to discovery, transmitting information ranging from diplomatic secrets to personal information, including from mobile devices.*[1]

2.2 Destructive attacks

These attacks relate to inflicting damage on specific organizations.

- Great Hacker War, and purported "gang war" in cyberspace
- LulzRaft, hacker group known for a low impact attack in Canada
- Operation Ababil, conducted against American financial institutions
- TV5Monde April 2015 cyberattack

- Vulcanbot
- Shamoon, a modular computer virus, was used in 2012 in an attack on 30,000 Saudi Aramco workstations, causing the company to spend a week restoring their services.*[2]*[3]
- Wiper – in December 2011, the malware successfully erased information on hard disks at the Oil Ministry's headquarters.*[4]*[5]
- Stuxnet - A malicious computer worm believed to be a jointly built American-Israeli cyber weapon. Designed to sabotage Iran's nuclear program with what would seem like a long series of unfortunate accidents .

2.3 Cyberwarfare

Further information: Cyberwarfare

These are politically motivated destructive attacks aimed at sabotage and espionage.

- 2007 cyberattacks on Estonia, wide ranging attack targeting government and commercial institutions
- 2010 cyberattacks on Burma, related to the 2010 Burmese general election
- 2010 Japan–South Korea cyberwarfare
- 2013 Singapore cyberattacks, attack by Anonymous "in response to web censorship regulations in the country, specifically on news outlets"
- #OpIsrael, a broad "anti-Israel" attack
- Cyberattacks during the Russo-Georgian War
- July 2009 cyber attacks, against South Korea and United States
- Operation Olympic Games, against Iranian nuclear facilities, allegedly conducted by the United States

2.4   Government espionage

These attacks relate to stealing information from/about government organizations.

- 2008 cyberattack on United States, cyber espionage targeting U.S. military computers

- Cyber attack during the Paris G20 Summit, targeting G20-related documents including financial information

- GhostNet

- Moonlight Maze

- Operation Newscaster, cyber espionage covert operation allegedly conducted by Iran

- Operation Cleaver, cyberwarfare covert operation allegedly conducted by Iran

- Shadow Network, attacks on India by China

- Titan Rain, targeting defense contractors in the United States

- Google – in 2009, the Chinese hackers breached Google's corporate servers gained access to a database containing classified information about suspected spies, agents, and terrorists under surveillance by the US government.*[6]

- Gauss trojan, discovered in 2012 is a state-sponsored computer espionage operation that uses state-of-the-art software to extract a wealth of sensitive data from thousands of machines located mostly in the Middle East.*[7]

- Office of Personnel Management data breach—Dec 2014 breach of data on U.S. government employees

- A six-month-long cyber-attack on the German parliament for which the Sofacy Group is suspected took place in December 2014.*[8]

- The Sofacy Group is also suspected to be behind a spearphishing attack in August 2016 on members of the Bundestag and multiple political parties such as Linken-faction leader Sahra Wagenknecht, Junge Union and the CDU of Saarland.*[9]*[10]*[11]*[12] Authorities fear that sensitive information could be gathered by hackers to later manipulate the public ahead of elections such as Germany's next federal election due in September 2017.*[9]

2.5   Corporate espionage

These attacks relate to stealing data from corporations related to proprietary methods or emerging products/services.

- Operation Aurora

- Operation Socialist, UK obtaining information from Belgian telecom company on call information

- Sony Pictures Entertainment hack

2.6   Stolen e-mail addresses and login credentials

These attacks relate to stealing login information for specific web resources.

- 2011 PlayStation Network outage, 2011 attack resulting in stolen credentials and incidentally causing network disruption

- Gawker – in 2010, a band of anonymous hackers has rooted the servers of the site and leaked half a gigabyte's worth of its private data.*[13]

- IEEE – in September 2012, it exposed user names, plaintext passwords, and website activity for almost 100,000 of its members.*[14]

- LivingSocial – in 2014 the company suffered a security breach that has exposed names, e-mail addresses and password data for up to 50 million of its users.*[15]

- Adobe – in 2013, Hackers obtained access to Adobe's networks and stole user information and downloaded the source code for some of Adobe programs.*[16] It attacked 150 million customers.*[16]

- RockYou – in 2009, the company experienced a data breach resulting in the exposure of over 32 million user accounts.

- Yahoo! – in 2012, hackers posted login credentials for more than 453,000 user accounts.*[17] Again in January 2013*[18] and in January 2014*[19]

2.7   Stolen credit card and financial data

- 2014 JPMorgan Chase data breach, allegedly conducted by a group of Russian hackers

- MasterCard – in 2005, the company announced that up to 40 million cardholders may have had account information stolen due to one of its payment processors being hacked.[20][21][22][23]

- VISA and MasterCard – in 2012, they warned card-issuing banks that a third-party payments processor suffered a security breach, affecting up to 10 million credit cards.[24][25]

- Subway – in 2012, two Romanian men admitted to participating in an international conspiracy that hacked into credit-card payment terminals at more than 150 Subway restaurant franchises and stole data for more than 146,000 accounts.[26]

- StarDust – in 2013, the botnet compromised 20,000 cards in active campaign hitting US merchants.[27]

- Target – in 2013, approximately 40 million credit and debit card accounts were impacted in a credit card breach.[28][29][30] According to another estimate, it compromised as many as 110 million Target customers.[31]

- Goodwill Industries – in September 2014, the company suffered from a credit card data breach that affected the charitable retailer's stores in at least 21 states. Another two retailers were affected.[32][33]

- Home Depot – in September 2014, the cybercriminals that compromised Home Depot's network and installed malware on the home-supply company's point-of-sale systems likely stole information on 56 million payment cards.[34]

2.8 Stolen medical-related data

- By May, three healthcare payer organizations had been attacked in the United States in 2014 and 2015: Anthem, Premera Blue Cross and CareFirst. The three attacks together netted information on more than 91 million people.[35]

2.9 Hacktivism

Main article: Hacktivism § Notable hacktivist events
See also: Timeline of events associated with Anonymous

2.10 See also

- List of data breaches

2.11 References

[1] Goodin, Dan (January 14, 2013). "Massive espionage malware targeting governments undetected for 5 years". *Ars Technica*. Retrieved November 8, 2014.

[2] Perloth, Nicole (October 24, 2012). "Cyberattack On Saudi Firm Disquiets U.S.". *New York Times*. pp. A1. Retrieved October 24, 2012.

[3] Goodin, Dan (August 16, 2012). "Mystery malware wreaks havoc on energy sector computers". *Ars Technica*. Retrieved November 8, 2014.

[4] "Iranian Oil Sites Go Offline Amid Cyberattack". *The New York Times*. April 23, 2012. Retrieved November 8, 2014.

[5] Goodin, Dan (August 29, 2012). "The perfect crime: Is Wiper malware connected to Stuxnet, Duqu?". *Ars Technica*. Retrieved November 8, 2014.

[6] Goodin, Dan (May 21, 2013). "Chinese hackers who breached Google reportedly targeted classified data". *Ars Technica*. Retrieved November 8, 2014.

[7] Goodin, Dan (August 9, 2012). "Nation-sponsored malware with Stuxnet ties has mystery warhead". *Ars Technica*. Retrieved November 8, 2014.

[8] "Russian Hackers Suspected In Cyberattack On German Parliament". *London South East*. Alliance News. June 19, 2015.

[9] "Hackers lurking, parliamentarians told". Deutsche Welle. Retrieved 21 September 2016.

[10] "Hackerangriff auf deutsche Parteien". Süddeutsche Zeitung. Retrieved 21 September 2016.

[11] Holland, Martin. "Angeblich versuchter Hackerangriff auf Bundestag und Parteien". Heise. Retrieved 21 September 2016.

[12] "„Wir haben Fingerabdrücke"". Frankfurter Allgemeine. Retrieved 21 September 2016.

[13] Gawker rooted by anonymous hackers, December 13, 2010, Dan Goodin, *The Register*, retrieved at 2014-11-08

[14] Goodin, Dan (September 25, 2012). "Trade group exposes 100,000 passwords for Google, Apple engineers". *Ars Technica*. Retrieved November 8, 2014.

[15] Goodin, Dan (April 27, 2013). "Why LivingSocial's 50-million password breach is graver than you may think". *Ars Technica*. Retrieved November 8, 2014.

[16] Howley, Daniel (July 1, 2016). "7 biggest hacks". *Yahoo Tech*. Retrieved 1 July 2016.

[17] Goodin, Dan (July 12, 2012). "Hackers expose 453,000 credentials allegedly taken from Yahoo service (Updated)". *Ars Technica*. Retrieved November 8, 2014.

[18] Goodin, Dan (January 31, 2013). "How Yahoo allowed hackers to hijack my neighbor's e-mail account (Updated)". *Ars Technica*. Retrieved November 8, 2014.

[19] Goodin, Dan (January 31, 2014). "Mass hack attack on Yahoo Mail accounts prompts password reset". *Ars Technica*. Retrieved November 8, 2014.

[20] Bangeman, Eric (June 20, 2005). "CardSystems should not have retained stolen customer data". *Ars Technica*. Retrieved November 8, 2014.

[21] "Lost Credit Data Improperly Kept, Company Admits". *The New York Times*. June 20, 2005. Retrieved November 8, 2014.

[22] Bangeman, Eric (June 23, 2005). "Scope of CardSystems-caused credit card data theft broadens". *Ars Technica*. Retrieved November 8, 2014.

[23] Jonathan M. Gitlin (July 22, 2005). "Visa bars CardSystems from handling any more transactions.". *Ars Technica*. Retrieved November 8, 2014.

[24] Goodin, Dan (April 1, 2012). "After the hack: FAQ for breach affecting up to 10 million credit cards". *Ars Technica*. Retrieved November 8, 2014.

[25] Goodin, Dan (March 30, 2012). ""Major" credit-card breach hits Visa, MasterCard (Updated)". *Ars Technica*. Retrieved November 8, 2014.

[26] Goodin, Dan (September 18, 2012). "Two men admit to $10 million hacking spree on Subway sandwich shops". *Ars Technica*. Retrieved November 8, 2014.

[27] Goodin, Dan (December 4, 2013). "Credit card fraud comes of age with advances in point-of-sale botnets". *Ars Technica*. Retrieved November 8, 2014.

[28] Farivar, Cyrus (December 19, 2013). "Secret Service investigating massive credit card breach at Target (Updated)". *Ars Technica*. Retrieved November 8, 2014.

[29] Goodin, Dan (December 20, 2013). "Cards stolen in massive Target breach flood underground "card shops"". *Ars Technica*. Retrieved November 8, 2014.

[30] Goodin, Dan (February 5, 2014). "Target hackers reportedly used credentials stolen from ventilation contractor". *Ars Technica*. Retrieved November 8, 2014.

[31] Goodin, Dan (January 16, 2014). "Point-of-sale malware infecting Target found hiding in plain sight". *Ars Technica*. Retrieved November 8, 2014.

[32] Gallagher, Sean (September 18, 2014). "Credit card data theft hit at least three retailers, lasted 18 months". *Ars Technica*. Retrieved November 8, 2014.

[33] http://krebsonsecurity.com/2014/07/banks-card-breach-at-goodwill-industries/

[34] Lemos, Robert (September 19, 2014). "Home Depot estimates data on 56 million cards stolen by cybercriminals". *Ars Technica*. Retrieved November 30, 2014.

[35] Dance, Scott (20 May 2015). "Cyberattack affects 1.1 million CareFirst customers". *Baltim. Sun*.

Chapter 3

2010 Japan–South Korea cyberwarfare

On March 1, 2010, a group of Japanese 2chan and Korean website NAVER's 'Terror Action Association' which was made up DC Inside, Todayhumor netizens engaged in a civil cyberwar. The day was South Korea's March 1st Movement Anniversary, and the 100th anniversary of the Japan–Korea Treaty of 1910.

3.1 Description

About a Korean international student was killed in Russia in the winter of 2009, (2chan) made online comments such as "Dog died, Why did the news show it up?" or "Kill more!". After Kim Yuna won the gold medal in figure skating, the group 2chan asserted that a referee must have been bribed, and posts on the website of DC Inside insinuated a plot.*[1]

3.2 References

[1] "Epic Cyber War: Japan V.S Korea". 2011-12-20.

Chapter 4

2011 PlayStation Network outage

The **2011 PlayStation Network outage** was the result of an "external intrusion" on Sony's PlayStation Network and Qriocity services, in which personal details from approximately 77 million accounts were compromised and prevented users of PlayStation 3 and PlayStation Portable consoles from accessing the service.[1][2][3][4] The attack occurred between April 17 and April 19, 2011,[1] forcing Sony to turn off the PlayStation Network on April 20. On May 4 Sony confirmed that personally identifiable information from each of the 77 million accounts had been exposed.[5] The outage lasted 23 days.[6]

At the time of the outage, with a count of 77 million registered PlayStation Network accounts,[7] it was one of the largest data security breaches in history.[8][9] It surpassed the 2007 TJX hack which affected 45 million customers.[10] Government officials in various countries voiced concern over the theft and Sony's one-week delay before warning its users.

Sony stated on April 26 that it was attempting to get online services running "within a week."[11] On May 14, Sony released PlayStation 3 firmware version 3.61 as a security patch. The firmware required users to change their password upon signing in. At the time the firmware was released, the network was still offline.[12] Regional restoration was announced by Kazuo Hirai in a video from Sony.[13] A map of regional restoration and the network within the United States was shared as the service was coming back online.[14]

4.1   Timeline of the outage

On April 20, 2011, Sony acknowledged that on the official PlayStation Blog that it was "aware certain functions of the PlayStation Network" were down. Upon attempting to sign in via the PlayStation 3, users received a message indicating that the network was "undergoing maintenance".[15][16] The following day, Sony asked its customers for patience while the cause of outage was investigated and stated that it may take "a full day or two" to get the service fully functional again.[17]

The company later announced an "external intrusion" had affected the PlayStation Network and Qriocity services.[18] This intrusion occurred between April 17 and April 19. On April 20, Sony suspended all PlayStation Network and Qriocity services worldwide.[19] Sony expressed their regrets for the downtime and called the task of repairing the system "time-consuming" but would lead to a stronger network infrastructure and additional security.[20] On April 25, Sony spokesman Patrick Seybold reiterated on the PlayStation Blog that fixing and enhancing the network was a "time intensive" process with no estimated time of completion.[21] However, the next day Sony stated that there was a "clear path to have PlayStation Network and Qriocity systems back online", with some services expected to be restored within a week. Furthermore, Sony acknowledged the "compromise of personal information as a result of an illegal intrusion on our systems."[22]

On May 1 Sony announced a "Welcome Back" program for customers affected by the outage. The company also confirmed that some PSN and Qriocity services would be available during the first week of May.[23][24] The list of services expected to become available included:[25]

- Restoration of Online game-play across the PlayStation 3 (PS3) and PSP (PlayStation Portable) systems
- This includes titles requiring online verification and downloaded games
- Access to Music Unlimited powered by Qriocity for PS3/PSP for existing subscribers
- Access to account management and pass-

12

word reset

- Access to download un-expired Movie Rentals on PS3, PSP and MediaGo
- PlayStation Home
- Friends List
- Chat Functionality

On May 2 Sony issued a press release, according to which the Sony Online Entertainment (SOE) services had been taken offline for maintenance due to potentially related activities during the initial criminal hack. Over 12,000 credit card numbers, albeit in encrypted form, from non-U.S. cardholders and additional information from 24.7 million SOE accounts may have been accessed.*[26]*[27]

During the week, Sony sent a letter to the US House of Representatives, answering questions and concerns about the event.*[28] In the letter Sony announced that they would be providing Identity Theft insurance policies in the amount of $1 million USD per user of the PlayStation Network and Qriocity services, despite no reports of credit card fraud being indicated. This was later confirmed on the PlayStation Blog, where it was announced that the service, AllClear ID Plus powered by Debix, would be available to users in the United States free for 12 months, and would include Internet surveillance, complete identity repair in the event of theft and a $1 million identity theft insurance policy for each user.*[29]*[30]

On May 6 Sony stated they had begun "final stages of internal testing" for the PlayStation Network, which had been rebuilt.*[31] However, the following day Sony reported that they would not be able to bring services back online within the one-week timeframe given on May 1, because "the extent of the attack on Sony Online Entertainment servers" had not been known at the time.*[32] SOE confirmed on their Twitter account that their games would not be available until sometime after the weekend.*[33]

Reuters began reporting the event as "the biggest Internet security break-in ever" .*[34] A Sony spokesperson said:*[35]

- Sony had removed the personal details of 2,500 people stolen by hackers and posted on a website
- The data included names and some addresses, which were in a database created in 2001
- No date had been fixed for the restart

On May 14 various services began coming back online on a country-by-country basis, starting with North America.*[36] These services included: sign-in for PSN and Qriocity services (including password resetting), online game-play on PS3 and PSP, playback of rental video content, Music Unlimited service (PS3 and PC), access to third party services (such as Netflix, Hulu, Vudu and MLB.tv), friends list, chat functionality and PlayStation Home.*[36] The actions came with a firmware update for the PS3, version 3.61.*[37] As of May 15 service in Japan and East Asia had not yet been approved.*[38]

On May 18 SOE shut down the password reset page on their site following the discovery of another exploit*[39] that allowed users to reset other users' passwords, using the other user's email address and date of birth.*[40] Sign-in using PSN details to various other Sony websites was also disabled, but console sign-ins were not affected.*[39]

On May 23 Sony stated that the outage costs were $171 million.*[41]

4.2 Sony response

4.2.1 US House of Representatives

Sony reported on May 4 to the PlayStation Blog*[42] that:

> Kazuo Hirai, Chairman of the Board of Directors of Sony Computer Entertainment America, submitted written answers to questions posed by the United States House subcommittee about the large-scale, criminal cyber-attack we have experienced.

Sony relayed via the letter that:

> In summary, we told the subcommittee that in dealing with this cyber attack we followed four key principles:
>
> 1. Act with care and caution.
> 2. Provide relevant information to the public when it has been verified.
> 3. Take responsibility for our obligations to our customers.
> 4. Work with law enforcement authorities.
>
> We also informed the subcommittee of the following:
>
> - Sony has been the victim of a very carefully planned, very professional, highly sophisticated criminal cyber attack.
> - We discovered that the intruders had planted a file on one of our Sony Online Entertainment servers named "Anonymous" with the words "We are Legion."

- By April 25, forensic teams were able to confirm the scope of the personal data they believed had been taken, and could not rule out whether credit card information had been accessed. On April 26, we notified customers of those facts.

- As of today, the major credit card companies have not reported any fraudulent transactions that they believe are the direct result of this cyber attack.

- Protecting individuals' personal data is the highest priority and ensuring that the Internet can be made secure for commerce is also essential. Worldwide, countries and businesses will have to come together to ensure the safety of commerce over the Internet and find ways to combat cybercrime and cyber terrorism.

- We are taking a number of steps to prevent future breaches, including enhanced levels of data protection and encryption; enhanced ability to detect software intrusions, unauthorized access and unusual activity patterns; additional firewalls; establishment of a new data center in an undisclosed location with increased security; and the naming of a new Chief Information Security Officer.

4.2.2 Explanation of delays

On April 26, 2011 Sony explained on the PlayStation Blog why it took so long to inform PSN users of the data theft:[43]

There's a difference in timing between when we identified there was an intrusion and when we learned of consumers' data being compromised. We learned there was an intrusion April 19th and subsequently shut the services down. We then brought in outside experts to help us learn how the intrusion occurred and to conduct an investigation to determine the nature and scope of the incident. It was necessary to conduct several days of forensic analysis, and it took our experts until yesterday to understand the scope of the breach. We then shared that information with our consumers and announced it publicly this afternoon.

4.2.3 Sony investigation

Possible data theft led Sony to provide an update in regards to a criminal investigation in a blog posted on April 27: "We are currently working with law enforcement on this matter as well as a recognized technology security firm to conduct a complete investigation. This malicious attack against our system and against our customers is a criminal act and we are proceeding aggressively to find those responsible."[44]

On May 3 Sony Computer Entertainment CEO Kazuo Hirai reiterated this and said the "external intrusion" which had caused them to shut down the PlayStation Network constituted a "criminal cyber attack".[45] Hirai expanded further, claiming that Sony systems had been under attack prior to the outage "for the past month and half", suggesting a concerted attempt to target Sony.[46]

On May 4 Sony announced that it was adding Data Forte to the investigation team of Guidance Software and Protiviti in analysing the attacks. Legal aspects of the case were handled by Baker & McKenzie.[47] Sony stated their belief that Anonymous, or some portion thereof, may have performed the attack.[48] Anonymous denied any involvement.[49]

Upon learning that a breach had occurred, Sony launched an internal investigation. Sony reported, in its letter to the United States Congress:

One of our first calls was to the FBI, and this is an active, on-going investigation. **Have you identified how the breach occurred?** Yes, we believe so. Sony Network Entertainment America is continuing its investigation into this criminal intrusion, and more detailed information could be discovered during this process. We are reluctant to make full details publicly available because the information is the subject of an on-going criminal investigation and also the information could be used to exploit vulnerabilities in systems other than Sony's that have similar architecture to the PlayStation Network.[50]

4.2.4 Inability to use PlayStation 3 content

While most games remained playable in their offline modes, the PlayStation 3 was unable to play certain Capcom titles in any form.[51] Streaming video providers throughout different regions such as Hulu, Vudu, Netflix and LoveFilm displayed the same maintenance message. Some users claimed to be able to use Netflix's streaming service[52] but others were unable.[53]

4.3 Criticism of Sony

4.3.1 Delayed warning of possible data theft

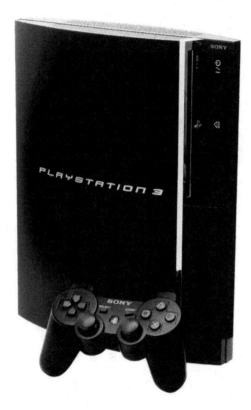

Original PlayStation 3 model

On April 26 nearly a week after the outage, Sony confirmed that it "cannot rule out the possibility" *[54] that personally identifiable information such as PlayStation Network account username, password, home address, and email address had been compromised. Sony also mentioned the possibility that credit card data was taken—after claiming that encryption had been placed on the databases, which would partially satisfy PCI Compliance for storing credit card information on a server. Subsequent to the announcement on both the official blog and by e-mail, users were asked to safeguard credit card transactions by checking bank statements. This warning came nearly a week after the initial "external intrusion" and while the Network was turned off.*[55]

Some disputed this explanation and queried that if Sony deemed the situation so severe that they had to turn off the network, Sony should have warned users of possible data theft sooner than on April 26.*[56] Concerns have been raised over violations of PCI Compliance and the failure to immediately notify users. US Senator Richard Blumenthal wrote to Sony Computer Entertainment America CEO Jack Tretton questioning the delay.*[57]

Sony replied in a letter to the subcommittee:

> **Your statement indicated you have no evidence at this time that credit card information was obtained, yet you cannot rule out this possibility. Please explain why you do not believe credit card information was obtained and why you cannot determine if the data was in fact taken.**
>
> As stated above, Sony Network Entertainment America has not been able to conclude with certainty through the forensic analysis done to date that credit card information was not transferred from the PlayStation Network system. We know that for other personal information contained in the account database, the hacker made queries to the database, and the external forensics teams have seen large amounts of data transferred in response to those queries. Our forensics teams have not seen the queries and corresponding data transfers of the credit card information.

4.3.2 Unencrypted personal details

Credit card data was encrypted, but Sony admitted that other user information was not encrypted at the time of the intrusion.*[44]*[58] *The Daily Telegraph* reported that "If the provider stores passwords unencrypted, then it's very easy for somebody else – not just an external attacker, but members of staff or contractors working on Sony's site – to get access and discover those passwords, potentially using them for nefarious means." *[59] On May 2, Sony clarified the "unencrypted" status of users' passwords, stating that:*[60]

> While the passwords that were stored were not "encrypted," they were transformed using a cryptographic hash function. There is a difference between these two types of security measures which is why we said the passwords had not been encrypted. But I want to be very clear that the passwords were not stored in our database in cleartext form.

4.3.3 British Information Commissioners Office

Following a formal investigation of Sony for breaches of the UK's Data Protection Act 1998, the Information Commissioners' Office issued a statement highly critical of the security Sony had in place:

> If you are responsible for so many payment card details and log-in details then keeping that personal data secure has to be your priority. In this case that just didn't happen, and when the database was targeted – albeit in a determined criminal attack – the security measures in place were simply not good enough.
>
> There's no disguising that this is a business that should have known better. It is a company that trades on its technical expertise, and there's no doubt in my mind that they had access to both the technical knowledge and the resources to keep this information safe.[61]

Sony was fined £250,000 ($395k) for security measures so poor they did not comply with the British law.

4.4 Sony Online Entertainment outage

On May 3 Sony stated in a press release that there may be a correlation between the attack that had occurred on April 16 towards the PlayStation Network and one that compromised Sony Online Entertainment on May 2.[26] This portion of the attack resulted in the theft of information on 24.6 million Sony Online Entertainment account holders. The database contained 12,700 credit card numbers, particularly those of non-U.S. residents, and had not been in use since 2007 as much of the data applied to expired cards and deleted accounts. Sony updated this information the following day by stating that only 900 cards on the database were still valid.[62] The attack resulted in the suspension of SOE servers and Facebook games. SOE granted 30 days of free time, plus one day for each day the server was down, to users of *Clone Wars Adventures*, *DC Universe Online*, *EverQuest*, *EverQuest II*, *EverQuest Online Adventures*, *Free Realms*, *Pirates of the Burning Sea*, *PlanetSide*, *Poxnora*, *Star Wars Galaxies* and *Vanguard: Saga of Heroes*, as well as other forms of compensation for all other Sony Online games.

Security experts Eugene Lapidous of AnchorFree, Chester Wisniewski of Sophos Canada and Avner Levin of Ryerson University criticized Sony, questioning its methods of securing user data. Lapidous called the breach "difficult to excuse" and Wisniewski called it "an act of hubris or simply gross incompetence".[63][64][65][66]

4.5 Reaction

4.5.1 Compensation to users

Sony hosted special events after the PlayStation Network returned to service. Sony stated that they had plans for PS3 versions of DC Universe Online and Free Realms to help alleviate some of their losses.[67] In a press conference in Tokyo on May 1, Sony announced a "Welcome Back" program. As well as "selected PlayStation entertainment content" the program promised to include 30 days free membership of PlayStation Plus for all PSN members, while existing PlayStation Plus members received an additional 30 days on their subscription. Qriocity subscribers received 30 days. Sony promised other content and services over the coming weeks.[24] Sony offered one year free identity theft protection to all users with details forthcoming.

Hulu compensated PlayStation 3 users for the inability to use their service during the outage by offering one week of free service to Hulu Plus members.[68]

On May 16, 2011, Sony announced that two PlayStation 3 games and two PSP games would be offered for free from lists of five and four[*†] (respectively).[69][70] The games available varied by region[69][70] and were only available in countries which had access to the PlayStation Store prior to the outage.[70] On May 27, 2011, Sony announced the "welcome back" package for Japan[71] and the Asia region (Hong Kong, Singapore, Malaysia, Thailand and Indonesia).[72] In the Asia region, a theme - *Dokodemo Issyo Spring Theme* - was offered for free in addition to the games available in the "welcome back" package.[72]

^† 5 PSP games are offered in the Japanese market.[71]

^‡ Version of *Killzone Liberation* offered does not offer online gameplay functionality.[70]

4.5.2 Government reaction

The data theft concerned authorities around the world. Graham Cluley, senior technology consultant at Sophos, said the breach "certainly ranks as one of the biggest data losses ever to affect individuals".[73]

The British Information Commissioner's Office stated that Sony would be questioned,[74] and that an investigation would take place to discover whether Sony had taken adequate precautions to protect customer details.[75] Under the UK's Data Protection Act, Sony was fined £250,000 for the breach.[76]

Privacy Commissioner of Canada Jennifer Stoddart confirmed that the Canadian authorities would investigate. The Commissioner's office conveyed their concern as to why the authorities in Canada weren't informed of a security breach earlier.*[77]

US Senator Richard Blumenthal of Connecticut demanded answers from Sony about the data breach*[78] by emailing SECA CEO Jack Tretton arguing about the delay in informing its customers and insisting that Sony do more for its customers than just offer free credit reporting services. Blumenthal later called for an investigation by the US Department of Justice to find the person or persons responsible and to determine if Sony was liable for the way that it handled the situation.*[79]

Congresswoman Mary Bono Mack and Congressman G. K. Butterfield sent a letter to Sony, demanding information on when the breach was discovered and how the crisis would be handled.*[80]

Sony had been asked to testify before a congressional hearing on security and to answer questions about the breach of security on May 2, but sent a written response instead.

4.5.3   Legal action against Sony

A lawsuit was posted on April 27 by Kristopher Johns from Birmingham, Alabama on behalf of all PlayStation users alleging Sony "failed to encrypt data and establish adequate firewalls to handle a server intrusion contingency, failed to provide prompt and adequate warnings of security breaches, and unreasonably delayed in bringing the PSN service back online."*[81]*[82] According to the complaint filed in the lawsuit, Sony failed to notify members of a possible security breach and storing members' credit card information,*[83] a violation of PCI Compliance—the digital security standard for the Payment Card Industry.

A Canadian lawsuit against Sony USA, Sony Canada and Sony Japan claimed damages up to C$1 billion including free credit monitoring and identity theft insurance.*[84] The plaintiff was quoted as saying, "If you can't trust a huge multi-national corporation like Sony to protect your private information, who can you trust? It appears to me that Sony focuses more on protecting its games than its PlayStation users".*[85]

In October 2012 a Californian judge dismissed a lawsuit against Sony over the PSN security breach, ruling that Sony had not violated Californian consumer-protection laws, citing "there is no such thing as perfect security".*[86]

In 2013 United Kingdom Information Commissioner's Office charged Sony with a £250,000 penalty for putting a large amount of personal and financial data of PSN clients at risk.*[87]

4.5.4   Credit card fraud

As of May 2011, there were no verifiable reports of credit card fraud related to the outage. There were reports on the Internet that some PlayStation users experienced credit card fraud;*[88]*[89]*[90] however, they were yet to be linked to the incident. Users who registered a credit card for use only with Sony also reported credit card fraud.*[91] Sony said that the CSC codes requested by their services were not stored,*[92] but hackers may have been able to decrypt or record credit card details while inside Sony's network.*[88]

Sony stated in their letter to the subcommittee:

> **How many PlayStation Network account holders provided credit card information to Sony Computer Entertainment?**
> Globally, approximately 12.3 million account holders had credit card information on file on the PlayStation Network system. In the United States, approximately 5.6 million account holders had credit card information on file on the system. These numbers include active and expired credit cards.
> As of today, the major credit card companies have not reported that they have seen any increase in the number of fraudulent credit card transactions as a result of the attack, and they have not reported to us any fraudulent transactions that they believe are a direct result of the intrusions described above.

On May 5, a letter from Sony Corporation of America CEO and President Sir Howard Stringer emphasized that there had been no evidence of credit card fraud and that a $1 million identity theft insurance policy would be available to PSN and Qriocity users:*[30]

> To date, there is no confirmed evidence any credit card or personal information has been misused, and we continue to monitor the situation closely. We are also moving ahead with plans to help protect our customers from identity theft around the world. A program for U.S. PlayStation Network and Qriocity customers that includes a $1 million identity theft insurance policy per user was launched earlier today and announcements for other regions will be coming soon.

4.6   Change to terms and conditions

It has been suggested that a change to the PSN terms and conditions announced on September 15, 2011, was motivated by the large damages being claimed by class action suits against Sony, in an effort to minimise the company's losses. The new agreement required users to agree to give up their right (to join together as a group in a class action) to sue Sony over any future security breach, without first trying to resolve legal issues with an arbitrator.[*][93][*][94] This included any ongoing class action suits initiated prior to the August 20, 2011.

Another clause, which removed a user's right to trial by jury should the user opt out of the clause (by sending a letter to Sony), says:

> If the Class Action Waiver clause is found to be illegal or unenforceable, this entire Section 15 will be unenforceable, and the dispute will be decided by a court and you and the Sony Entity you have a dispute with each agree to waive in that instance, to the fullest extent allowed by law, any trial by jury.

Sony guaranteed that a court of law in the respective country, in this case the US, would hold jurisdiction in regards to any rules or changes in the Sony PSN ToS:[*][95]

> These Terms of Service and all questions relating to the performance, interpretation, breach or enforcement of these Terms of Service, or the rights, obligations and liabilities of you and us under them are governed by the laws of the State of California. You agree that all disputes, claims or litigation arising from or related in any way to these Terms of Service and our relationship with you will be litigated only in a court of competent jurisdiction located in San Mateo County, State of California. You agree to be subject to personal jurisdiction and venue in that location.

4.7   References

[1] "PlayStation Network Restoration Begins". *PlayStation Network / PSN News*. United Kingdom: Sony. 2011-05-17. Retrieved 2011-10-20.

[2] "Sony faces legal action over attack on PlayStation network". *BBC News*. bbc.co.uk. 2011-04-28. Retrieved 2011-04-29.

[3] Richmond, Shane (2011-04-26). "Millions of internet users hit by massive Sony PlayStation data theft". London: Telegraph. Retrieved 2011-04-29.

[4] Griffith, Chris (2011-04-27). "PlayStation users in Australia urged to check credit card activity". *Australian IT*. The Australian. Retrieved 2011-11-20.

[5] "Kazuo Hirai's Letter to the U.S. House of Representatives". *a photo set by Flickr user PlayStation.Blog*. Flickr. 2011-05-03. Retrieved 2011-10-20. Information appears to have been stolen from all PlayStation Network user accounts, although not every piece of information in those accounts appears to have been stolen, [...] The criminal intruders stole personal information from all of the approximately 77 million PlayStation Network and Qriocity service accounts.

[6] Owen Good (2011-05-20). "Welcome Back PSN: The Winners". Kotaku.com. Retrieved 2011-06-02.

[7] "PlayStation Network and Qriocity Outage FAQ – PlayStation.Blog.Europe". Blog.eu.playstation.com. Retrieved 2011-04-29.

[8] "PlayStation data breach deemed in 'top 5 ever' - Business - CBC News". Cbc.ca. 2011-04-27. Retrieved 2011-04-29.

[9] "Video: Sony PlayStation - Hacker Breaks Into Network And Steals Details Of Millions Of Gamers | Technology | Sky News". News.sky.com. Retrieved 2011-04-29.

[10] "PlayStation hack: top five data thefts". London: Telegraph. 2011-04-27. Retrieved 2011-04-29.

[11] "PlayStation Network down for seventh day". ComputerAndVideoGames.com. 2011-04-27. Retrieved 2011-04-29.

[12] "PS3 System Software Update – PlayStation Blog". Blog.us.playstation.com. 2010-12-20. Retrieved 2011-05-16.

[13] "Kazuo Hirai: PlayStation Network Restoration Announcement – PlayStation Blog". Blog.us.playstation.com. 2010-12-20. Retrieved 2011-05-16.

[14] Seybold, Patrick (2011). "Play On – PSN Restoration Begins Now – PlayStation Blog". *blog.us.playstation.com*. Retrieved 16 May 2011.

[15] "Update on PSN Service Outages". United States: PlayStation Blog. 2011-04-20. Retrieved 2011-04-29.

[16] "Timeline of Sony's PlayStation Network outage". hken.ibtimes.com. 2011-05-15. Retrieved 2011-05-15.

[17] "Latest Update on PSN Outage". United States: PlayStation Blog. 2011-04-21. Retrieved 2011-04-29.

[18] "Update On PlayStation Network/Qriocity Services". United States: PlayStation Blog. 2011-04-22. Retrieved 2011-04-29.

[19] "PlayStation Knowledge Center | Support - PlayStation.com". us.playstation.com. 2011-01-10. Retrieved 2011-04-29.

[20] "Latest Update for PSN/Qriocity Services – PlayStation Blog". Blog.us.playstation.com. 2011-04-23. Retrieved 2011-04-29.

[21] "PSN Update – PlayStation Blog". Blog.us.playstation.com. 2011-04-25. Retrieved 2011-04-29.

[22] "Update on PlayStation Network and Qriocity – PlayStation Blog". Blog.us.playstation.com. 2011-04-19. Retrieved 2011-04-29.

[23] "Some PlayStation Network And Qriocity Services To Be Available This Week – PlayStation.Blog.Europe". Blog.eu.playstation.com. Retrieved 2011-05-01.

[24] Yin-Poole, Wesley (2011-05-01). "PSN: Sony outlines "Welcome Back" gifts". *PlayStation 3*. United Kingdom: Eurogamer. Retrieved 2011-10-20.

[25] "Some PlayStation Network And Qriocity Services To Be Available This Week – PlayStation.Blog.Europe". Blog.eu.playstation.com. Retrieved 2011-05-07.

[26] "Service Under Maintenance". SOE. 2010-03-31. Retrieved 2011-05-04.

[27] "Sony Confirms Thousands Of Credit Cards Stolen During Hack - GameInformer News". gameinformer.com. 2011-05-02. Retrieved 2011-05-02.

[28] "Sony's Response to the U.S. House of Representatives – PlayStation Blog". Blog.us.playstation.com. 2010-12-20. Retrieved 2011-05-07.

[29] "Sony Offering Free 'AllClear ID Plus' Identity Theft Protection in the United States through Debix, Inc. – PlayStation Blog". Blog.us.playstation.com. Retrieved 2011-05-07.

[30] "A Letter from Howard Stringer – PlayStation Blog". Blog.us.playstation.com. 2010-12-20. Retrieved 2011-05-07.

[31] "Important Step for Service Restoration – PlayStation.Blog.Europe". Blog.eu.playstation.com. 2011-05-06. Retrieved 2011-05-07.

[32] JC Fletcher (2011-05-06). "PSN reactivation delayed for 'further testing,' likely not coming back this week". Joystiq. Retrieved 2011-05-07.

[33] "Twitter / @Sony Online Ent.: We wanted to let you know ...". *twitter.com*. 2011. Retrieved 16 May 2011.

[34] Reynolds, Isabel (2011-05-06). "Sony CEO apologises for data theft; shares fall 2 pct". Reuters. Retrieved 2011-05-07.

[35] Reynolds, Isabel (2011-05-06). "Sony removes data posted by hackers, delays PlayStation restart". Reuters. Retrieved 2013-10-10.

[36] "Sony Global - News Releases - RESTORATION OF PLAYSTATIONNETWORK AND QRIOCITY SERVICES BEGINS". Sony. May 15, 2011. Retrieved May 15, 2011.

[37] "PS3 System Software Update - PlayStation Blog". PlayStation Blog. May 14, 2011. Retrieved May 15, 2011.

[38] Mochizuki, Takashi (2010-04-07). "Japan Restart of Sony Online Games Services Not Yet Approved". FoxBusiness.com. Retrieved 2011-06-02.

[39] "Sony's PSN password page exploit". Eurogamer. May 18, 2011. Retrieved May 18, 2011.

[40] "Report: Sony PlayStation Network Password Reset Page Exploited, Customer Accounts Potentially Compromised". Kotaku. May 18, 2011. Retrieved May 18, 2011.

[41] "PlayStation Hack to Cost Sony $171M; Quake Costs Far Higher". *PC Magazine*. May 23, 2011.

[42] "Sony's Response to the U.S. House of Representatives – PlayStation Blog". Blog.us.playstation.com. Retrieved 2011-05-05.

[43] "Clarifying a Few PSN Points – PlayStation Blog". Blog.us.playstation.com. 2011-04-26. Retrieved 2011-05-07.

[44] "Q&A #1 for PlayStation Network and Qriocity Services – PlayStation Blog". Blog.us.playstation.com. 2010-12-20. Retrieved 2011-04-29.

[45] Watt, Peggy (30 April 2011). "Sony: PlayStation Network Resumes This Week". pcworld.com. Retrieved 2 May 2011.

[46] Fletcher, JC (2011-05-01). "PSN 'welcome back program' includes a free download, 30 days free PlayStation Plus, Qriocity". joystiq.com. Retrieved 2011-05-02.

[47] "Another team added to Sony's PSN investigation". VG247. Retrieved 2011-05-04.

[48] Bartz, Diane (2011-04-26). "Sony blames Anonymous for stage-setting theft". Reuters. Retrieved 2011-05-04.

[49] "Hackers deny involvement in PlayStation Network outage". Retrieved June 9, 2011.

[50] Edwards, Cliff (2011-04-26). "PlayStation Hackers May Have Stolen Data on 75 Million Users, Sony Says". Bloomberg. Retrieved 2011-04-29.

[51] "News - Opinion: Sony's Communication Problem". Gamasutra. Retrieved 2011-04-29.

[52] Barrera, Rey. "Netflix-still-works-on-your-ps3-despite-the-outage". *PSNation*. Retrieved 25 April 2011.

[53] "PlayStation Network Outage Bad News for Netflix and Hulu: Online Video News". Gigaom.com. Retrieved 2011-04-29.

[54] "BBC News - Sony's PlayStation hack apology". Bbc.co.uk. 2011-04-19. Retrieved 2011-04-29.

[55] Reynolds, Isabel (2009-02-09). "Furore at Sony after Playstation user data stolen". Reuters. Retrieved 2011-04-29.

[56] "Sony Defends Notification Delay in Data Fiasco". PC Pro. Retrieved 2011-04-29.

[57] "Senator: Lack of details on PlayStation Network outage 'troubling' - Game Hunters: In search of video games and interactive awesomeness - USATODAY.com". *Content.USAToday.com*. 2011-01-04. Retrieved 2011-04-29.

[58] Stuart, Keith (2011-04-27). "PlayStation Network hack: why it took Sony seven days to tell the world | Technology | guardian.co.uk". London: Guardian. Retrieved 2011-04-29.

[59] Williams, Christopher (2011-04-28). "PlayStation hack: Sony users urged to change passwords". London: Telegraph. Retrieved 2011-04-29.

[60] "PlayStation Network Security Update – PlayStation Blog". Blog.us.playstation.com. 2011-05-02. Retrieved 2011-05-07.

[61] http://www.theregister.co.uk/2013/01/24/sony_psn_breach_fine/

[62] "24.6 million SOE accounts potentially compromised". *News*. gamesindustry.biz. 2011-03-21. Retrieved 2011-05-04.

[63] Brightman, James (2011-05-03). "Sony Breach 'Difficult to Excuse' Say Security Experts". IndustryGamers. Retrieved 2011-05-05.

[64] Chung, Emily (2011-05-03). "Sony data breach update reveals 'bad practices'". CBC News. Retrieved 2011-05-05.

[65] Westervelt, Robert (2011-05-03). "Sony attack: Sony expands scope of its massive data security breach". SearchSecurity.com. Retrieved 2011-05-05.

[66] Schwartz, Matthew J. (2011-05-03). "Sony Reports 24.5 Million More Accounts Hacked". InformationWeek. Retrieved 2011-05-05.

[67] Sony Computer Entertainment America (2011-04-28). "Q&A #2 for Playstation Network and Qriocity". playstation.com. Retrieved 2011-04-29.

[68] Jackson, Leah (2011-04-27). "Hulu Offering Free Credit For PS3 Subscribers". *TheFeed*. G4tv.com. Retrieved 2011-10-20.

[69] "Details for PlayStation Network and Qriocity Customer Appreciation Program in North America". PlayStation Blog. May 16, 2011. Retrieved May 17, 2011.

[70] "Details Of The Welcome Back Programme For SCEE Users". PlayStation Blog. May 16, 2011. Retrieved May 17, 2011.

[71] "PlayStationNetwork・Qriocity（キュリオシティ）の一部サービス日本およびアジアの国・地域でも再開" (in Japanese). SCEJ. May 27, 2011. Retrieved 20 October 2011.

[72] "Welcome Back Package for Hong Kong, Singapore, Malaysia, Thailand and Indonesia". PlayStation.com. May 27, 2011. Retrieved May 28, 2011.

[73] Richmond, Shane (April 26, 2011). "Millions of internet users hit by massive Sony PlayStation data theft". London: Telegraph. Retrieved April 29, 2011.

[74] Williams, Christopher (2011-04-27). "PlayStation hack: Sony faces watchdog's questions". London: Telegraph. Retrieved 2011-04-29.

[75] Wesley Yin-Poole. "ICO confirms it will quiz Sony over PSN News - PlayStation 3 - Page 1". Eurogamer.net. Retrieved 2011-04-29.

[76] Halliday, Josh (2013-01-24). "Data watchdog fines Sony £250,000 over PlayStation ID hack". *The Guardian*. London.

[77] "Privacy Commissioner's office looking into Sony PlayStation hack". Canada.com. Retrieved 2011-04-29.

[78] "Blumenthal Demands Answers from Sony over Playstation Data Breach". Richard Blumenthal-US senator for Connecticut: Home. Archived from the original on May 5, 2011. Retrieved 2011-04-26.

[79] "Blumenthal Calls for DOJ Investigation of Sony Playstation Data Breach". Richard Blumenthal-US senator for Connecticut: Home. Retrieved 2011-04-29.

[80] "US lawmakers press Sony for info on data breach". Associated Press. 2011-04-29. Retrieved 2011-04-30.

[81] Ogg, Erica (2011-03-24). "Sony sued for PlayStation Network data breach | Circuit Breaker - CNET News". News.cnet.com. Retrieved 2011-04-29.

[82] "Johns v. Sony Computer Entertainment America LLC et al". Justia. 2011-05-03. Retrieved 2011-05-03.

[83] Schwartz, Mathew J. "Sony Sued Over PlayStation Network Hack". InformationWeek. Retrieved 2011-04-29.

[84] "Canadian Law Firm Files $1 Billion Lawsuit Against Sony Over PSN Data Breach". Gamastura. 2011-05-04. Retrieved 2011-05-04.

[85] "Sony PlayStation Network Down: PSN Hit with $1.04B Class Action Suit". Gather. 2011-05-04. Retrieved 2011-05-04.

[86] http://news.cnet.com/8301-1023_3-57538716-93/sony-psn-hacking-lawsuit-dismissed-by-judge/

[87] Sony Monetary Penalty Notice, ICO, 2013

[88] "PlayStation users reporting credit card fraud". Retrieved April 30, 2011.

[89] "Hackers run up debt for PlayStation user". Retrieved April 30, 2011.

[90] Arthur, Charles (2011-04-29). "Hackers claim to have 2.2 million card details". *The Guardian*. London. Retrieved April 30, 2011.

[91] "Ars readers report credit card fraud". Retrieved April 30, 2011.

[92] "Q&A #1 for PlayStation Network and Qriocity Services – PlayStation Blog". *blog.us.playstation.com*. 2011. Retrieved 16 May 2011.

[93] "Sony asks gamers to sign new terms or face PSN ban". *BBC News*. 16 September 2011.

[94] "Sony's 'No-Sue' PlayStation Network Use Clause is Anti-Consumer". 19 September 2011.

[95] "Terms of Service". 2012.

Chapter 5

2013 Singapore cyberattacks

The **2013 Singapore cyberattacks** were a series of hack attacks initiated by the hacktivist organisation Anonymous, represented by a member known by the online handle "The Messiah". The cyber attacks were partly in response to web censorship regulations in the country, specifically on news outlets. On 12 November 2013, James Raj was charged in Singapore court as the alleged "The Messiah".*[1]

5.1   Background

On 1 June, a new set of web censorship regulations drafted by the Media Development Authority became effective in Singapore. Under the new rules,

> websites with at least 50,000 unique visitors from Singapore every month that publish at least one local news article per week over a period of two months ... will have to remove 'prohibited content' such as articles that undermine 'racial or religious harmony' within 24 hours of being notified by Singapore's media regulator.*[2]

During the introduction of these new rules, government officials stated that they "do not impinge on internet freedom" .*[3]

5.2   Incidents

Following his hack attack on the People's Action Party's Community Foundation's webpage, Anonymous member The Messiah hacked into the official website of the Ang Mo Kio Town Council, to exemplify the fact that it was very vulnerable to cyber attacks. Site administrators were quick to lock the site and a police report was made.*[4]

Upset with "the Government's new licensing rules imposed on websites" , a purported member of Anonymous went on to upload a four-minute-long video on YouTube, in which

The hacked version of Irene Tham's The Straits Times blog

he, wearing the signature Guy Fawkes mask, threatened to "bring down key infrastructure in Singapore" .*[5] He also urged Singaporeans to don red and black on 5 November, as well as black out their Facebook profile pictures. In the video, he made reference to The Messiah, who he called "one of [Anonymous'] comrades" .*[5]

The Straits Times news reporter Irene Tham decided to post a critique of The Messiah's video on her blog on the newspaper's official website. The hacker then hit back by hacking into the blog, defacing the report's title with the words "Dear ST [Straits Times]: You just got hacked for misleading the people!". In justification, The Messiah opined that Tham had misconstrued his speech. He also noted that Tham "conveniently modif[ied] the sentence 'war against the Singapore government' into 'war against Singapore'."He enjoined Tham to either apologise within two days or resign from her job, to atone for her "blasphemous lies" .*[6]

Later on, in an email to Yahoo Singapore, The Messiah said

> we reached out to our comrades from other fractions [sic] who together with us performed DNS poisoning on the .gov.sg sites, taking them down for a period of time. But there must have also been some patching that was done as some of our favourite point of entries into their networks seemed to be fixed.*[7]

On 3 November, the website of the Seletar Airport was hacked. Its webpage replaced with a black and green background with an image in the middle resembling a skull wearing a hood. The site resumed normal operations 30 minutes after the hack was first noticed.[*][8]

On 5 November, the Twitter and YouTube accounts of Singaporean entertainer Ridhwan Azman were hacked. According to posts from the compromised account, this was in retaliation for "dissing the legion". Apart from this incident, Anonymous did not carry out any other major activity, contrary to its promise to ignite a massive protest on that date.[*][9]

Two days later, the hacktivists hacked into and vandalised a subpage on the website of Singapore Prime Minister Lee Hsien Loong, following Lee's vow to bring The Messiah and his accomplices to justice.[*][10] Additionally, the webpage of the Istana was also hacked.[*][11]

On 20 November, the websites of 13 schools, which were hosted on a single server, were reportedly defaced between 3:30pm to 5pm.[*][12]

5.3 Reception

News of the cyberattacks were picked up by disparate news outlets from around the world, including the *South China Morning Post*,[*][3] *The Huffington Post*,[*][13] *Time*,[*][14] *The Star*,[*][15] and *The Jakarta Post*, among others.[*][16]

Regarding the hacking of the Ang Mo Kio Town Council's website, Member of Parliament Ang Hin Kee dubbed it as "malicious", promising to boost the page's security system.[*][4]

After the release of the YouTube video, the Government IT Security Incident Response Team immediately released an alert to all the Singaporean government agencies. The Infocomm Development Authority of Singapore responded in an official statement, "We are aware of the video, and the police are investigating the matter." [*][5][*][17] The Singapore Press Holdings (SPH), of which *The Straits Times* is a subsidiary, promptly took down the blog which was hacked into and filed a complaint to the police.[*][6]

Singaporean politician and Deputy Chairman of Singapore's Parliamentary Committee for Communications and Information, Baey Yam Keng, offered, "We do not know what the hacker's capabilities are, so it's important for us to take this very seriously." Bertha Henson, who operates Breakfast Network, a Singaporean news outlet, felt that The Messiah's action would "make the government seem right, that we [independent website operators] are just troublemakers." [*][18]

Whilst observing counter-terrorism drill Exercise High-crest, Prime Minister Lee Hsien Loong pledged to hunt down the team responsible for the cyberattack, stating, "It is not a laughing matter. It's not just anything goes, and you're anonymous, therefore there's no responsibility. You may think you are anonymous. We will make that extra effort to find out who you are." [*][19]

5.4 See also

- Timeline of events associated with Anonymous

5.5 References

[1] "Suspected 'Messiah' hacker charged in court". *Today*. 12 November 2013.

[2] "Singapore threatened by "Anonymous" hacker group". *AsiaOne*. 31 October 2013.

[3] "Anonymous activists hack Singapore newspaper over internet freedom". *South China Morning Post*. 2 November 2013.

[4] Tan, Jeanette (28 October 2013). "Police investigating Ang Mo Kio Town Council website hacking". *Yahoo!*.

[5] "Singapore government agencies on alert after hackers threaten attacks". *The Straits Times*. 1 November 2013.

[6] ""Anonymous" hacker targets Straits Times website". *Channel NewsAsia*. 1 November 2013.

[7] "Hacker 'The Messiah' claims attack on Singapore govt sites, repeats 'Anonymous' cyber threat". *Yahoo! News Singapore*. Retrieved 5 November 2013.

[8] "Seletar Airport website hacked". *Channel NewsAsia*. 4 November 2013.

[9] "Singapore movie actor disses Anonymous, gets hacked on Twitter". *Techinasia*. 6 November 2013.

[10] "Singapore PM's website hacked by Anonymous". *Yahoo!*. 8 November 2013.

[11] "Subpages on PM Lee's and Istana websites compromised". *Channel News Asia*. 8 November 2013.

[12] "Websites of 13 schools defaced". *Channel News Asia*. 21 November 2013.

[13] Cheney, Satish (1 November 2013). "Singapore's Straits Times Allegedly Hacked By Anonymous". *The Huffington Post*.

[14] Stout, David (1 November 2013). "Hacker Group Anonymous Targets Singapore with Cyber Attack Over Censorship". *Time*.

[15] Tan, Yiliang (2 November 2013). "Singapore Straits Times website hacked by Anonymous for alleged misreporting". *The Star*.

[16] "Singapore govt on alert after hackers threaten attacks". *The Jakarta Post*. 1 November 2013.

[17] "'Anonymous' hack Singapore newspaper's website". *BBC News*. 1 November 2013.

[18] "Anonymous hacks Singapore newspaper Straits Times". *First Post*. 1 November 2013.

[19] Loh, Dylan (6 November 2013). "Govt will spare no effort to bring cyber-attackers to justice: PM Lee". *Channel News Asia*.

5.6 External links

- Anonymous' message to the Singapore government on YouTube

Chapter 6

2014 JPMorgan Chase data breach

The JPMorgan Chase & Co. headquarters at 270 Park Avenue in Manhattan.

The **2014 JPMorgan Chase data breach** was a cyber-attack against American bank JPMorgan Chase that is believed to have compromised data associated with over 83 million accounts – 76 million households (approximately two out of three households in the country) and 7 million small businesses.[*][1] The data breach is considered one of the most serious intrusions into an American corporation's information system and one of the largest data breaches in history.[*][2][*][3][*][4]

The attack – disclosed in September 2014 – was discovered by the bank's security team in late July 2014, but not completely halted until the middle of August.[*][3][*][5] The bank

declared that login information associated with the accounts (such as social security numbers or passwords) was not compromised but names, email and postal addresses, and phone numbers of account holders were obtained by hackers, raising concerns of potential phishing attacks.[*][4][*][6]

The attack targeted nine other major financial institutions alongside JPMorgan Chase.[*][3][*][7] As of October 9, the only other company believed to have had data stolen is Fidelity Investments[*][8] but investigators reported the attack attempted to infiltrate the networks of banks and financial companies such as Citigroup, HSBC Holdings, E*Trade, Regions Financial Corporation and payroll-service firm Automatic Data Processing (ADP).[*][9]

US federal indictments were issued against four hackers in the massive fraud in November 2015.[*][10] Two Israelis indicted, Gery Shalon and Ziv Orenstein, were arrested in Israel and will be extradited to the U.S. according to Israel's Justice Ministry.[*][11]

6.1   References

[1] Siegel Bernard, Tara (3 October 2014). "Ways to Protect Yourself After the JPMorgan Hacking". *The New York Times*. Retrieved 5 October 2014.

[2] "JPMorgan hack exposed data of 83 million, among biggest breaches in history". *Reuters*. 2 October 2014. Retrieved 5 October 2014.

[3] Goldstein, Matthew; Perlroth, Nicole; Sanger, David E. (2014-10-03). "Hackers' Attack Cracked 10 Financial Firms in Major Assault". The New York Times. Retrieved 2014-10-04.

[4] Rushe, Dominic (2 October 2014). "JP Morgan Chase reveals massive data breach affecting 76m households". *The Guardian*. Retrieved 5 October 2014.

[5] Chan, Cathy (2014-10-02). "Hackers' Attack on JPMorgan Chase Affects Millions". The New York Times. Retrieved 2014-10-02.

[6] Santus, Rex. "What You Need to Know About the JPMorgan Chase Cyberattack". *Mashable*. Retrieved 5 October 2014.

[7] Woodyard, Chris (4 October 2014). "Report: Russian hackers behind JPMorgan Chase attack". *USA Today*. Retrieved 5 October 2014.

[8] Barrett, Devlin (9 October 2014). "J.P. Morgan Hackers Also Stole Fidelity Data, Investigators Think". *The Wall Street Journal*. Retrieved 9 October 2014.

[9] Riley, Michael (9 October 2014). "JPMorgan Hackers Said to Probe 13 Financial Firms". *Bloomberg*. Retrieved 10 October 2014.

[10] "Four Indicted in Massive JP Morgan Chase Hack". *WIRED*. 10 November 2015.

[11] 2 Israelis in JPMorgan Chase cyber fraud case to be extradited JTA, May 9, 2016

Chapter 7

2015–16 SWIFT banking hack

In 2015 and 2016, a **series of cyberattacks using the SWIFT banking network** were reported, resulting in the successful theft of millions of dollars.[1][2] The attacks were perpetrated by a hacker group nicknamed Lazarus by researchers. The group, which is also responsible for the 2014 Sony Pictures Entertainment hack, has been linked to North Korea. If North Korea's involvement is true, it would be the first known incident of a state actor using cyberattacks to steal funds.

The attacks exploited vulnerabilities in the systems of member banks, allowing the attackers to gain control of the banks' legitimate SWIFT credentials. The thieves then used those credentials to send SWIFT funds transfer requests to other banks, which, trusting the messages to be legitimate, then sent the funds to accounts controlled by the attackers.[1]

7.1 First reports

The first public reports of these attacks came from thefts from Bangladesh central bank and a bank in Vietnam.

An $81 million theft from the Bangladesh central bank via its account at the New York Federal Reserve Bank was traced to hacker penetration of SWIFT's Alliance Access software, according to a *New York Times* report. It was not the first such attempt, the society acknowledged, and the security of the transfer system was undergoing new examination accordingly.[3]

Soon after the reports of the theft from the Bangladesh central bank, a second, apparently related, attack was reported to have occurred on a commercial bank in Vietnam.[1]

Both attacks involved malware written to both issue unauthorized SWIFT messages and to conceal that the messages had been sent. After the malware sent the SWIFT messages that stole the funds, it deleted the database record of the transfers then took further steps to prevent confirmation messages from revealing the theft. In the Bangladeshi case,

the confirmation messages would have appeared on a paper report; the malware altered the paper reports when they were sent to the printer. In the second case, the bank used a PDF report; the malware altered the PDF viewer to hide the transfers.[1]

Furthermore, news agency Reuters reported on 20 May 2016 that there had already been a similar case in Ecuador in early 2015 when Banco del Austro funds were transferred to bank accounts in Hong Kong. Neither Banco del Austro nor Wells Fargo, who were asked to conduct the transactions, initially reported the movements to SWIFT as suspicious; implications that the actions actually were a theft only emerged during a BDA lawsuit filed against Wells Fargo.[2]

7.2 Expanded scope and suspicions of North Korea

After the initial two reports, two security firms reported that the attacks involved malware similar to that used in the 2014 Sony Pictures Entertainment hack and impacted as many at 12 banks in Southeast Asia.[4][5] Both attacks are attributed to a hacker group nicknamed Lazarus by researchers. Symantec has linked the group with North Korea.[6] If North Korea's involvement is true, it would be the first known incident of a state actor using cyberattacks to steal funds.[7][8]

7.3 Ramifications

If the attack did originate in North Korea, the thefts would have profound implications for international relations. It would be the first known instance of a state actor using cyber attacks to steal funds.[8]

The thefts may also have implications for the regime of international sanctions that aim to isolate North Korea's economy. The theft may represent a significant percentage of North Korea's current GDP.[*][8]

Moreover, trust in the SWIFT system has an important element in international banking for decades. Banks consider SWIFT messages trustworthy, and can thus follow the transmitted instructions immediately. In addition, the thefts themselves can threaten the solvency of the member banks.[*][4]

"This is a big deal, and it gets to the heart of banking," said SWIFT's CEO, Gottfried Leibbrandt, who added, "Banks that are compromised like this can be put out of business." [*][4]

7.4   See also

- North Korea's illicit activities

7.5   References

[1] Corkery, Michael (May 12, 2016). "Once Again, Thieves Enter Swift Financial Network and Steal". *New York Times*. Retrieved May 13, 2016.

[2] Bergin, Tom; Layne, Nathan (May 20, 2016). "Special Report: Cyber thieves exploit banks' faith in SWIFT transfer network". Reuters. Retrieved May 24, 2016.

[3] Corkery, Michael (April 30, 2016). "Hackers' $81 Million Sneak Attack on World Banking". *The New York Times*. Retrieved May 1, 2016.

[4] Riley, Michael; Katz, Alan (May 26, 2016). "Swift Hack Probe Expands to Up to a Dozen Banks Beyond Bangladesh". *Bloomberg*. Retrieved May 28, 2016.

[5] Bright, Peter. "12 more banks now being investigated over Bangladeshi SWIFT heist". *Ars Technica*. Retrieved May 28, 2016.

[6] Pagliery, Jose; Riley, Charles (May 27, 2016). "North Korea-linked 'Lazarus' hackers hit a fourth bank in Philippines". CNN Money. Retrieved May 29, 2016.

[7] Shen, Lucinda (May 27, 2016). "North Korea Has Been Linked to the SWIFT Bank Hacks". *Fortune*. Retrieved May 28, 2016.

[8] Perlroth, Nicole; Corkery, Michael (May 26, 2016). "North Korea Linked to Digital Attacks on Global Banks". *New York Times*. Retrieved May 28, 2016.

Chapter 8

Anonplus

Anonplus is the social networking service that Anonymous decided to launch,[*][1] after Your Anon News was banned from Google+ on 15 July 2011.[*][2] Anonymous defines Anonplus as a "new social network where there is no fear...of censorship...of blackout...nor of holding back." Anonplus has the goal of creating a decentralized and secure social network where the privacy of the users is valued.[*][3]

8.1 Attack on Anonplus

On the 21st of July, 2011, Anonplus was hacked by rival hackers. A group of hackers apparently based in Turkey replaced AnonPlus's main webpage with an image of a dog wearing a suit, mocking the more normal Anonymous logo, and messages in Turkish and English.[*][4]

8.2 Current state

The social networking site is still in development.[*][5] However, their website was updated on the 13th of November with a press release which mentioned that the project had entered an invite-only beta phase. According to this document, the project entered this beta phase on the 5th of November. The document also explains that it has become a goal of the project to target censorship.[*][6]

8.3 References

[1] Tweet from @AnonPlus, 16 July 2011

[2] Tumblr post of Your Anon News, 15 July 2011

[3] *Anonplus Project and Network Plans* (PDF), August 2011, retrieved 21 November 2011

[4] "AnonPlus, Anonymous's social network, is hacked", nakedsecurity.sophos.com, 21 July 2011

[5] Twitter feed of @AnonPlus

[6] *Anon+ News* (PDF), November 2011, retrieved 21 November 2011

8.4 External links

- Official website
- Official forum
- Anonplus on Twitter

Chapter 9

Anonymous (group)

This article is about a group of activists. For other uses, see Anonymous (disambiguation).

Anonymous is a loosely associated international network of activist and hacktivist entities. A website nominally associated with the group describes it as "an Internet gathering" with "a very loose and decentralized command structure that operates on ideas rather than directives" .*[2] The group became known for a series of well-publicized publicity stunts and distributed denial-of-service (DDoS) attacks on government, religious, and corporate websites.*[3]

Anonymous originated in 2003 on the imageboard 4chan, representing the concept of many online and offline community users simultaneously existing as an anarchic, digitized global brain.*[4]*[5]*[6] Anonymous members (known as "Anons") can be distinguished in public by the wearing of Guy Fawkes masks in the style portrayed in the graphic novel and film, *V for Vendetta.**[7]

In its early form, the concept was adopted by a decentralized online community acting anonymously in a coordinated manner, usually toward a loosely self-agreed goal, and primarily focused on entertainment, or "lulz". Beginning with 2008's Project Chanology—a series of protests, pranks, and hacks targeting the Church of Scientology—the Anonymous collective became increasingly associated with collaborative hacktivism on a number of issues internationally. Individuals claiming to align themselves with Anonymous undertook protests and other actions (including direct action) in retaliation against copyright-focused campaigns by motion picture and recording industry trade associations. Later targets of Anonymous hacktivism included government agencies of the U.S., Israel, Tunisia, Uganda, and others; the Islamic State of Iraq and the Levant; child pornography sites; copyright protection agencies; the Westboro Baptist Church; and corporations such as PayPal, MasterCard, Visa, and Sony. Anons have publicly supported WikiLeaks and the Occupy movement. Related groups LulzSec and Operation AntiSec carried out cyberattacks on U.S. government agencies, media, video game companies, military

contractors, military personnel, and police officers, resulting in the attention of law enforcement to the groups' activities. Some actions by members of the group have been described as being anti-Zionist. It has threatened to cyber-attack Israel and engaged in the "#OpIsrael" cyber-attacks of Israeli websites on Yom HaShoah (Holocaust Remembrance Day) in 2013.*[8]

Dozens of people have been arrested for involvement in Anonymous cyberattacks, in countries including the U.S., UK, Australia, the Netherlands, Spain, India and Turkey. Evaluations of the group's actions and effectiveness vary widely. Supporters have called the group "freedom fighters" *[9] and digital Robin Hoods*[10] while critics have described them as "a cyber lynch-mob" *[11] or "cyber terrorists" .*[12] In 2012, *Time* called Anonymous one of the "100 most influential people" in the world.*[13]

9.1 Philosophy

Anonymous has no strictly defined philosophy, and internal dissent is a regular feature of the group.*[2] A website associated with the group describes it as "an Internet gathering" with "a very loose and decentralized command structure that operates on ideas rather than directives" .*[2] Gabriella Coleman writes of the group, "In some ways, it may be impossible to gauge the intent and motive of thousands of participants, many of who don't even bother to leave a trace of their thoughts, motivations, and reactions. Among those that do, opinions vary considerably." *[14]

Broadly speaking, Anons oppose Internet censorship and control, and the majority of their actions target governments, organizations, and corporations that they accuse of censorship. Anons were early supporters of the global Occupy movement and the Arab Spring.*[15] Since 2008, a frequent subject of disagreement within Anonymous is whether members should focus on pranking and entertainment or more serious (and, in some cases, political) activism.*[16]

Because Anonymous has no leadership, no action can be attributed to the membership as a whole. Parmy Olson and others have criticized media coverage that presents the group as well-organized or homogeneous; Olson writes, "There was no single leader pulling the levers, but a few organizational minds that sometimes pooled together to start planning a stunt." *[18] Some members protest using legal means, while others employ illegal measures such as DDoS attacks and hacking.*[19] Membership is open to anyone who wishes to state they are a member of the collective;*[20] Carole Cadwalladr of *The Observer* compared the group's decentralized structure to that of al-Qaeda, writing, "If you believe in Anonymous, and call yourself Anonymous, you are Anonymous." *[21] Olson, who formerly described Anonymous as a "brand", stated in 2012 that she now characterized it as a "movement" rather than a group: "anyone can be part of it. It is a crowd of people, a nebulous crowd of people, working together and doing things together for various purposes." *[22]

The group's few rules include not disclosing one's identity, not talking about the group, and not attacking media.*[23] Members commonly use the tagline "We are Anonymous. We are Legion. We do not forgive. We do not forget. Expect us." *[24] Brian Kelly writes that three of the group's key characteristics are "(1) an unrelenting moral stance on issues and rights, regardless of direct provocation; (2) a physical presence that accompanies online hacking activity; and (3) a distinctive brand." *[25]

Journalists have commented that Anonymous' secrecy, fabrications, and media awareness pose an unusual challenge for reporting on the group's actions and motivations.*[26]*[27] Quinn Norton of *Wired* writes that "Anons lie when they have no reason to lie. They weave vast fabrications as a form of performance. Then they tell the truth at unexpected and unfortunate times, sometimes destroying themselves in the process. They are unpredictable." *[26] Norton states that the difficulties in reporting on the group cause most writers, including herself, to focus on the "small groups of hackers who stole the limelight from a legion, defied their values, and crashed violently into the law" rather than "Anonymous's sea of voices, all experimenting with new ways of being in the world" .*[26]

9.2 History

See also: Timeline of events associated with Anonymous

9.2.1 4chan raids (2003–2007)

Main article: 4chan
The name Anonymous itself is inspired by the perceived

KTTV Fox 11 investigative report on Anonymous. The report focused on what were then contemporary instances of Internet bullying by Anonymous.[28]*

anonymity under which users post images and comments on the Internet. Usage of the term Anonymous in the sense of a shared identity began on imageboards, particularly the /b/ board of 4chan, dedicated to random content. A tag of Anonymous is assigned to visitors who leave comments without identifying the originator of the posted content. Users of imageboards sometimes jokingly acted as if Anonymous was a single individual. The concept of the Anonymous entity advanced in 2004 when an administrator on the 4chan image board activated a "Forced_Anon" protocol that signed all posts as Anonymous.*[29] As the popularity of imageboards increased, the idea of Anonymous as a collective of unnamed individuals became an Internet meme.*[30]

Users of 4chan's /b/ board would occasionally join into mass pranks or raids. In a raid on July 12, 2006, for example, large numbers of 4chan readers invaded the Finnish social networking site Habbo Hotel with identical avatars; the avatars blocked regular Habbo members from accessing the digital hotel's pool, stating it was "closed due to fail and AIDS".*[31] Future LulzSec member Topiary became involved with the site at this time, inviting large audiences to listen to his prank phone calls via Skype.*[32]*[lower-alpha 1] Due to the growing traffic on 4chan's boards, users soon began to plot pranks offline using Internet Relay Chat (IRC).*[34] These raids resulted in the first mainstream press story on Anonymous, a report by Fox station KTTV in Los Angeles, California in the U.S. The report called the group "hackers on steroids", "domestic terrorists", and an "Internet hate machine" .*[28]*[35]

9.2.2 Encyclopedia Dramatica (2004–present)

Main article: Encyclopedia Dramatica

Encyclopedia Dramatica was founded in 2004 by Sherrod DiGrippo, initially as a means of documenting gossip related to livejournal, but it quickly was adopted as a major platform by Anonymous for satirical and other purposes.*[36] The not safe for work site celebrates a subversive "trolling culture", and documents Internet memes, culture, and events, such as mass pranks, trolling events, "raids", large-scale failures of Internet security, and criticism of Internet communities that are accused of self-censorship in order to garner prestige or positive coverage from traditional and established media outlets. Journalist Julian Dibbell described Encyclopædia Dramatica as the site "where the vast parallel universe of Anonymous injokes, catchphrases, and obsessions is lovingly annotated, and you will discover an elaborate trolling culture: Flamingly racist and misogynist content lurks throughout, all of it calculated to offend." *[36] The site also played a role in the anti-Scientology campaign of Project Chanology.*[37]

On April 14, 2011, the original URL of the site was redirected to a new website named *Oh Internet* that bore little resemblance to Encyclopedia Dramatica. Parts of the ED community harshly criticized the changes.*[38] In response, Anonymous launched "Operation Save ED" to rescue and restore the site's content.*[39] The Web Ecology Project made a downloadable archive of former Encyclopedia Dramatica content.*[40]*[41] The site's reincarnation was initially hosted at encyclopediadramatica.ch on servers owned by Ryan Cleary, who later was arrested in relation to attacks by LulzSec against Sony.

9.2.3 Project Chanology (2008)

Main article: Project Chanology

Anonymous first became associated with hacktivism*[lower-alpha 2] in 2008 following a series of actions against the Church of Scientology known as Project Chanology. On January 15, 2008, the gossip blog Gawker posted a video in which celebrity Scientologist Tom Cruise praised the religion;*[42] and the Church responded with a cease-and-desist letter for violation of copyright.*[43] 4chan users organized a raid against the Church in retaliation, prank-calling its hotline, sending black faxes designed to waste ink cartridges, and launching DDoS attacks against its websites.*[44]*[45]

The DDoS attacks were at first carried out with the Gigaloader and JMeter applications. Within a few days, these were supplanted by the Low Orbit Ion Cannon

"Message to Scientology", January 21, 2008

(LOIC), a network stress-testing application allowing users to flood a server with TCP or UDP packets. The LOIC soon became a signature weapon in the Anonymous arsenal; however, it would also lead to a number of arrests of less experienced Anons who failed to conceal their IP addresses.*[46] Some operators in Anonymous IRC channels incorrectly told or lied to new volunteers that using the LOIC carried no legal risk.*[47]*[48]

Protesters outside a Scientology center on February 10, 2008

During the DDoS attacks, a group of Anons uploaded a YouTube video in which a robotic voice speaks on behalf of Anonymous, telling the "leaders of Scientology" that "For the good of your followers, for the good of mankind —for the laughs—we shall expel you from the Internet." *[49]*[50] Within ten days, the video had attracted hundreds of thousands of views.*[50]

On February 10, thousands of Anonymous joined simultaneous protests at Church of Scientology facilities around the world.*[51] Many protesters wore the stylized Guy Fawkes masks popularized by the graphic novel and movie *V for Vendetta*, in which an anarchist revolutionary battles a totalitarian government; the masks soon became a popular symbol for Anonymous.*[52] In-person protests against the Church continued throughout the year, including "Operation Party Hard" on March 15 and "Operation Reconnect" on April 12.*[53]*[54]*[55] However, by mid-year, they were drawing far fewer protesters, and many of the organizers in IRC channels had begun to drift away from the project.*[56]

9.2.4 Operation Payback (2010)

By the start of 2009, Scientologists had stopped engaging with protesters and had improved online security, and actions against the group had largely ceased. A period of infighting followed between the politically engaged members (called "moralfags" in the parlance of 4chan) and those seeking to provoke for entertainment (trolls).*[57] By September 2010, the group had received little publicity for a year and faced a corresponding drop in member interest; its raids diminished greatly in size and moved largely off of IRC channels, organizing again from the chan boards, particularly /b/.*[58]

In September 2010, however, Anons became aware of Aiplex Software, an Indian software company that contracted with film studios to launch DDoS attacks on websites used by copyright infringers, such as The Pirate Bay.*[59]*[58] Coordinating through IRC, Anons launched a DDoS attack on September 17 that shut down Aiplex's website for a day. Primarily using LOIC, the group then targeted the Recording Industry Association of America (RIAA) and the Motion Picture Association of America (MPAA), successfully bringing down both sites.*[60] On September 19, future LulzSec member Mustafa Al-Bassam (known as "Tflow") and other Anons hacked the website of Copyright Alliance, an anti-infringement group, and posted the name of the operation: "Payback Is A Bitch," or "Operation Payback" for short.*[61] Anons also issued a press release, stating:

> Anonymous is tired of corporate interests controlling the internet and silencing the people's rights to spread information, but more importantly, the right to SHARE with one another. The RIAA and the MPAA feign to aid the artists and their cause; yet they do no such thing. In their eyes is not hope, only dollar signs. Anonymous will not stand this any longer.*[62]

As IRC network operators were beginning to shut down networks involved in DDoS attacks, Anons organized a group of servers to host an independent IRC network, titled AnonOps.*[63] Operation Payback's targets rapidly expanded to include the British law firm ACS:Law,*[64] the Australian Federation Against Copyright Theft,*[65] the

British nightclub Ministry of Sound,*[66] the Spanish copyright society Sociedad General de Autores y Editores,*[67] the U.S. Copyright Office,*[68] and the website of Gene Simmons of Kiss.*[69] By October 7, 2010, total downtime for all websites attacked during Operation Payback was 537.55 hours.*[69]

In November 2010, the organization WikiLeaks began releasing hundreds of thousands of leaked U.S. diplomatic cables. In the face of legal threats against the organization by the U.S. government, Amazon.com booted WikiLeaks from its servers, and PayPal, MasterCard, and Visa cut off service to the organization.*[70] Operation Payback then expanded to include "Operation Avenge Assange", and Anons issued a press release declaring PayPal a target.*[71] Launching DDoS attacks with the LOIC, Anons quickly brought down the websites of the PayPal blog; PostFinance, a Swiss financial company denying service to WikiLeaks; EveryDNS, a web-hosting company that had also denied service; and the website of U.S. Senator Joe Lieberman, who had supported the push to cut off services.*[72]

On December 8, Anons launched an attack against PayPal's main site. According to Topiary, who was in the command channel during the attack, the LOIC proved ineffective, and Anons were forced to rely on the botnets of two hackers for the attack, marshaling hijacked computers for a concentrated assault.*[73] Security researcher Sean-Paul Correll also reported that the "zombie computers" of involuntary botnets had provided 90% of the attack.*[74] Topiary states that he and other Anons then "lied a bit to the press to give it that sense of abundance", exaggerating the role of the grassroots membership. However, this account was disputed.*[75]

The attacks brought down PayPal.com for an hour on December 8 and another brief period on December 9.*[76] Anonymous also disrupted the sites for Visa and MasterCard on December 8.*[77] Anons had announced an intention to bring down Amazon.com as well, but failed to do so, allegedly because of infighting with the hackers who controlled the botnets.*[78] PayPal estimated the damage to have cost the company US$5.5 million. It later provided the IP addresses of 1,000 of its attackers to the FBI, leading to at least 14 arrests.*[79] On Thursday, December 5, 2013, 13 of the PayPal 14 pleaded guilty to taking part in the attacks.*[80]

9.2.5 2011–2012

In the years following Operation Payback, targets of Anonymous protests, hacks, and DDoS attacks continued to diversify. Beginning in January 2011, Anons took a number of actions known initially as Operation Tunisia in support of Arab Spring movements. Tflow created a script that

A member holding an Anonymous flier at Occupy Wall Street, a protest that the group actively supported, September 17, 2011

Tunisians could use to protect their web browsers from government surveillance, while fellow future LulzSec member Hector Xavier Monsegur (alias "Sabu") and others allegedly hijacked servers from a London web-hosting company to launch a DDoS attack on Tunisian government websites, taking them offline. Sabu also used a Tunisian volunteer's computer to hack the website of Prime Minister Mohamed Ghannouchi, replacing it with a message from Anonymous.[81] Anons also helped Tunisian dissidents share videos online about the uprising.[82] In Operation Egypt, Anons collaborated with the activist group Telecomix to help dissidents access government-censored websites.[82] Sabu and Topiary went on to participate in attacks on government websites in Bahrain, Egypt, Libya, Jordan, and Zimbabwe.[83]

Tflow, Sabu, Topiary, and Ryan Ackroyd (known as "Kayla") collaborated in February 2011 on a cyber-attack against Aaron Barr, CEO of the computer security firm HBGary Federal, in retaliation for his research on Anonymous and his threat to expose members of the group. Using a SQL injection weakness, the four hacked the HBGary site, used Barr's captured password to vandalize his Twitter feed with racist messages, and released an enormous cache of HBGary's e-mails in a torrent file on Pirate Bay.[84] The e-mails stated that Barr and HBGary had proposed to Bank of America a plan to discredit WikiLeaks in retaliation for a planned leak of Bank of America documents,[85] and the leak caused substantial public relations harm to the firm as well as leading one U.S. congressman to call for a congressional investigation.[86] Barr resigned as CEO before the end of the month.[87]

Several attacks by Anons have targeted organizations accused of homophobia. In February 2011, an open letter was published on AnonNews.org threatening the Westboro Baptist Church, an organization based in Kansas in the U.S. known for picketing funerals with signs reading "God Hates Fags".[88] During a live radio current affairs program in which Topiary debated church member Shirley Phelps-Roper, Anons hacked one of the organization's

websites.[89] After the church announced its intentions in December 2012 to picket the funerals of the Sandy Hook Elementary School shooting victims, Anons published the names, phone numbers, and e-mail and home addresses of church members and brought down God-HatesFags.com with a DDoS attack.[90] Hacktivists also circulated petitions to have the church's tax-exempt status investigated.[91] In August 2012, Anons hacked the site of Ugandan Prime Minister Amama Mbabazi in retaliation for the Parliament of Uganda's consideration of an anti-homosexuality law permitting capital punishment.[92]

In April 2011, Anons launched a series of attacks against Sony in retaliation for trying to stop hacks of the PlayStation 3 game console. More than 100 million Sony accounts were compromised, and the Sony services Qriocity and PlayStation Network were taken down for a month apiece by cyberattacks.[93]

Anonymous protestors at the Brussels Stock Exchange, Belgium, January 2012

When the Occupy Wall Street protests began in New York City in September 2011, Anons were early participants and helped spread the movement to other cities such as Boston.[15] In October, some Anons attacked the website of the New York Stock Exchange while other Anons publicly opposed the action via Twitter.[94] Some Anons also helped organize an Occupy protest outside the London Stock Exchange on May 1, 2012.[95]

Anons launched Operation Darknet in October 2011, targeting websites hosting child pornography. Most notably, the group hacked a child pornography site called "Lolita City" hosted by Freedom Hosting, releasing 1,589 usernames from the site. Anons also stated that they had disabled forty image-swapping pedophile websites that employed the anonymity network Tor.[96] In 2012, Anons leaked the names of users of a suspected child pornography site in OpDarknetV2.[97]

In 2011, the Koch Industries website was attacked following their attack upon union members, resulting in their website being unable to be accessed for 15 minutes. In 2013, one member, a 38-year-old truck driver, pleaded guilty when accused of participating in the attack for a period of one minute, and received a sentence of two years federal probation, and ordered to pay $183,000 restitution, the amount Koch stated they paid a consultancy organisation, despite this being only a denial of service attack.*[98]

On January 19, 2012, the U.S. Department of Justice shut down the file-sharing site Megaupload on allegations of copyright infringement. Anons responded with a wave of DDoS attacks on U.S. government and copyright organizations, shutting down the sites for the RIAA, MPAA, Broadcast Music, Inc., and the FBI.*[99]

In 2012, Anonymous launched Operation Anti-Bully: Operation Hunt Hunter in retaliation to Hunter Moore's revenge porn site, "Is Anyone Up?" Anonymous crashed Moore's servers and publicized much of his personal information online, including his social security number. The organization also published the personal information of Andrew Myers, the proprietor of "Is Anyone Back," a copycat site of Mr. Moore's "Is Anyone Up?"*[100]

In response to Operation Pillar of Defense, a November 2012 Israeli military operation in the Gaza Strip, Anons took down hundreds of Israeli websites with DDoS attacks.*[101] Anons pledged another "massive cyberassault" against Israel in April 2013 in retaliation for its actions in Gaza, promising to "wipe Israel off the map of the Internet" .*[102] However, its DDoS attacks caused only temporary disruptions, leading cyberwarfare experts to suggest that the group had been unable to recruit or hire botnet operators for the attack.*[103]*[104]

9.2.6   2013–present

Million Mask March

Main article: Million Mask March

On 5 November 2013, Anonymous protesters gathered around the world for the Million Mask March. Demonstrations were held in 400 cities around the world to coincide with Guy Fawkes Night.*[105]

#OpOk

Operation Oklahoma was a Mutual Aid effort responding to the 2013 flash floods and wind storms in the United States.

Operation Safe Winter

Operation Safe Winter was an effort to raise awareness about homelessness through the collection, collation, and redistribution of resources. This program began on 7 November 2013*[106] after an online call to action from Anonymous UK. Three missions using a charity framework were suggested in the original global spawning a variety of direct actions from used clothing drives to pitch in community potlucks feeding events in the UK, U.S. and Turkey.*[107]

The #OpSafeWinter call to action quickly spread through the Mutual Aid communities like Occupy Wall Street*[108] and its offshoot groups like the open-source-based OccuWeather.*[109] With the addition of the long-term mutual aid communities of New York City and online hacktivists in the U.S., it took on an additional three suggested missions.*[110] Encouraging participation from the general public, this Operation has raised questions of privacy and the changing nature of the Anonymous community's use of monikers. The project to support those living on the streets while causing division in its own online network has been able to partner with many efforts and organizations not traditionally associated with Anonymous or online activists.

Shooting of Michael Brown

In the wake of the fatal police shooting of unarmed African-American Michael Brown,"Operation Ferguson"—a hacktivist organization that claimed to be associated with Anonymous —organized cyberprotests against police, setting up a website and a Twitter account to do so.*[111] The group promised that if any protesters were harassed or harmed, they would attack the city's servers and computers, taking them offline.*[111] City officials said that e-mail systems were targeted and phones died, while the Internet crashed at the City Hall.*[111]*[112] Prior to August 15, members of Anonymous corresponding with *Mother Jones* said that they were working on confirming the identity of the undisclosed police officer who shot Brown and would release his name as soon as they did.*[113] On August 14, Anonymous posted on its Twitter feed what it claimed was the name of the officer involved in the shooting.*[114]*[115] However, police said the identity released by Anonymous was incorrect.*[116] Twitter subsequently suspended the Anonymous account from its service.*[117]

It was reported on 19 November 2014 that Anonymous had declared cyber war on the Ku Klux Klan (KKK) the previous week, after the KKK had made death threats following the Ferguson riots. They hacked the KKK's Twitter account, attacked servers hosting KKK sites, and started to release the personal details of members.*[118]

Shooting of Tamir Rice

On November 24, 2014, Anonymous shut down the Cleveland city website and posted a video after Tamir Rice, a twelve-year-old boy armed only with a BB gun, was shot to death by a police officer in a Cleveland park.*[119] Anonymous also used BeenVerified to uncover phone number and address of a policeman involved in the shooting.*[120]

Charlie Hebdo shootings

In January 2015, Anonymous released a video and a statement via Twitter condemning the attack on *Charlie Hebdo*, in which 12 people, including eight journalists, were fatally shot. The video, claiming that it is "a message for al-Qaeda, the Islamic State and other terrorists," was uploaded to the group's Belgian account.*[121] The announcement stated that "We, Anonymous around the world, have decided to declare war on you, the terrorists" and promises to avenge the killings by "shut[ting] down your accounts on all social networks." *[122] On January 12, they brought down a website that was suspected to belong to one of these groups.*[123] Critics of the action warned that taking down extremists' websites would make them harder to monitor.*[124]

Anti-Islamic "Reclaim Australia"rally

Anonymous opposed Anti-Islamic Reclaim Australia rallies and described it as "an extreme right-wing group inciting religious hatred." It also promised to organize counter-rallies on April 4, 2015.*[125]

Operation CyberPrivacy

On June 17, 2015, Anonymous claimed responsibility for a Denial of Service attack against Canadian government websites in protest of the passage of bill C-51—an anti-terror legislation that grants additional powers to Canadian intelligence agencies.*[126] The attack temporarily affected the websites of several federal agencies.

Operation KKK

On 28 October 2015, Anonymous announced that it would reveal the names of up to 1,000 members of the Ku Klux Klan and other affiliated groups, stating in a press release, "You are terrorists that hide your identities beneath sheets and infiltrate society on every level. The privacy of the Ku Klux Klan no longer exists in cyberspace." *[127] On November 2, a list of 57 phone numbers and 23 email addresses (that allegedly belong to KKK members) was

reportedly published and received media attention.*[128] However, a tweet from the "@Operation_KKK" Twitter account the same day denied it had released that information: "#ICYMI #OpKKK was in no way involved with today's release of information that incorrectly outed several politicians." *[129]*[130]*[131] The group stated it plans to reveal the names on November 5.

#OpSaudi

Since 2013, Saudi Arabian hacktivists have been targeting government websites protesting the actions of the regime.*[132] These actions have seen attacks supported by the possibly Iranian backed Yemen Cyber Army.*[133]

#OpISIS

In 2015, an offshoot of Anonymous self-described as Ghost Security or GhostSec started targeting Islamic State-affiliated websites and social media handles.*[134]*[135]*[136]

#OpParis

In November 2015, Anonymous announced a major, sustained operation*[137] against ISIS following the November 2015 Paris attacks, declaring, "Anonymous from all over the world will hunt you down. You should know that we will find you and we will not let you go." *[138]*[139] ISIS responded on Telegram by calling them "idiots," and asking "What they gonna to [*sic*] hack?"*[140]*[141] By the next day, however, Anonymous claimed to have taken down 3,824 pro-ISIS Twitter accounts, and by the third, more than 5,000,*[142] and to have doxxed recruiters.*[143] A week later, Anonymous increased their claim to 20,000 accounts and released a list of the accounts.*[144]*[145] The list included the Twitter accounts of Barack Obama, Hillary Clinton, the New York Times and BBC News. The BBC reported that most of the accounts on the list appeared to be still active.*[146] A spokesman for Twitter told *The Daily Dot* that the company is not using the lists of accounts being reported by Anonymous, as they have been found to be "wildly inaccurate"and include accounts used by academics and journalists.*[147]

#OpNASADrones

In 2015, a group that claims affiliation with Anonymous group, calling themselves as AnonSec, claimed to have hacked and gathered almost 276 GB of data from NASA servers including NASA flight and radar logs and videos, and also multiple documents related to ongoing research.[148] AnonSec group also claimed gaining access of a Global Hawk Drone of NASA, and released some video footage purportedly from the drone's cameras. A part of the data was released by AnonSec on Pastebin service, as an Anon Zine.[149] NASA has denied the hack, asserting that the control of the drones were never compromised, but has acknowledged that the photos released along with the content are real photographs of its employees, but that most of these data are already available in the public domain.[150]

#BoycottThailand: Thailand Jail Hack

The Blink Hacker Group, associating themselves with the Anonymous group, claimed to have hacked the Thailand prison websites and servers.[151] The compromised data has been shared online, with the group claiming that they give the data back to Thailand Justice and the citizens of Thailand as well. The hack was done in response to news from Thailand about the mistreatment of prisoners in Thailand.[152]

Case Donald Trump

In March 2016, Anonymous was reported to have declared war on Donald Trump.[153] However, the "Anonymous Official" YouTube channel released a video denouncing #OpTrump as an operation that "goes against everything Anonymous stands for" in reference to censorship and added "we are for everyone letting their voices be heard, even, if the person at hand...is a monster." [154]

South African Corruption

A group calling themselves *Anonymous Africa* launched a number of DDS attacks on websites associated with the controversial South African Gupta family in mid-June 2016. Gupta-owned companies targeted included the websites of Oakbay Investments, The New Age, and ANN7. The websites of the South African Broadcasting Corporation and a political parties Economic Freedom Fighters and Zimbabwe's Zanu-PF were also attacked for "nationalist socialist rhetoric and politicising racism." [155]

9.3 Related groups

9.3.1 LulzSec

Main article: LulzSec

In May 2011, the small group of Anons behind the HB-Gary Federal hack—including Tflow, Topiary, Sabu, and Kayla—formed the hacker group "Lulz Security", commonly abbreviated "LulzSec". The group's first attack was against Fox.com, leaking several passwords, LinkedIn profiles, and the names of 73,000 *X Factor* contestants. In May 2011, members of Lulz Security gained international attention for hacking into the American Public Broadcasting Service (PBS) website. They stole user data and posted a fake story on the site that claimed that rappers Tupac Shakur and Biggie Smalls were still alive and living in New Zealand.[156] LulzSec stated that some of its hacks, including its attack on PBS, were motivated by a desire to defend WikiLeaks and its informant Chelsea Manning.[157]

In June 2011, members of the group claimed responsibility for an attack against Sony Pictures that took data that included "names, passwords, e-mail addresses, home addresses and dates of birth for thousands of people." [158] In early June, LulzSec hacked into and stole user information from the pornography website www.pron.com. They obtained and published around 26,000 e-mail addresses and passwords.[159] On June 14, 2011, LulzSec took down four websites by request of fans as part of their "Titanic Take-down Tuesday". These websites were Minecraft, League of Legends, *The Escapist*, and IT security company FinFisher.[160] They also attacked the login servers of the multiplayer online game *EVE Online*, which also disabled the game's front-facing website, and the *League of Legends* login servers. Most of the takedowns were performed with DDoS attacks.[161]

LulzSec also hacked a variety of government-affiliated sites, such as chapter sites of InfraGard, a non-profit organization affiliated with the FBI.[162] The group leaked some of InfraGard member e-mails and a database of local users.[163] On June 13, LulzSec released the e-mails and passwords of a number of users of senate.gov, the website of the U.S. Senate.[164] On June 15, LulzSec launched an attack on cia.gov, the public website of the U.S. Central Intelligence Agency, taking the website offline for several hours with a distributed denial-of-service attack.[165] On December 2, an offshoot of LulzSec calling itself LulzSec Portugal attacked several sites related to the government of Portugal. The websites for the Bank of Portugal, the Assembly of the Republic, and the Ministry of Economy, Innovation and Development all became unavailable for a few hours.[166]

On June 26, 2011, the core LulzSec group announced it had reached the end of its "50 days of lulz" and was ceasing operations.[167] Sabu, however, had already been secretly arrested on June 7 and then released to work as an FBI informant. His cooperation led to the arrests of Ryan Cleary, James Jeffery, and others.[168] Tflow was arrested on July 19, 2011,[169] Topiary was arrested on July 27,[170] and Kayla was arrested on March 6, 2012.*[171] Topiary, Kayla, Tflow, and Cleary pleaded guilty in April 2013 and were scheduled to be sentenced in May 2013.*[172] In April 2013, Australian police arrested Cody Kretsinger, whom they alleged to be self-described LulzSec leader Aush0k.*[173]

9.3.2 AntiSec

Main article: Operation AntiSec

Beginning in June 2011, hackers from Anonymous and LulzSec collaborated on a series of cyber attacks known as "Operation AntiSec". On June 23, in retaliation for the passage of the immigration enforcement bill Arizona SB 1070, LulzSec released a cache of documents from the Arizona Department of Public Safety, including the personal information and home addresses of many law enforcement officers.*[174] On June 22, LulzSecBrazil took down the websites of the Government of Brazil and the President of Brazil.*[175]*[176] Later data dumps included the names, addresses, phone numbers, Internet passwords, and Social Security numbers of police officers in Arizona,*[177] Missouri,*[178] and Alabama.*[179] Antisec members also stole police officer credit card information to make donations to various causes.*[180]

On July 18, LulzSec hacked into and vandalized the website of British newspaper *The Sun* in response to a phone-hacking scandal.*[181]*[182] Other targets of AntiSec actions have included FBI contractor ManTech International,*[183] computer security firm Vanguard Defense Industries,*[184] and defense contractor Booz Allen Hamilton, releasing 90,000 military e-mail accounts and their passwords from the latter.*[185]

In December 2011, AntiSec member "sup_g" (alleged by the U.S. government to be Jeremy Hammond) and others hacked Stratfor, a U.S.-based intelligence company, vandalizing its web page and publishing 30,000 credit card numbers from its databases.*[186] AntiSec later released millions of the group's e-mails to Wikileaks.*[187]

9.4 Arrests and trials

Since 2009, dozens of people have been arrested for involvement in Anonymous cyberattacks, in countries including the U.S., UK, Australia, the Netherlands, Spain, and Turkey.*[188] Anons generally protest these prosecutions and describe these individuals as martyrs to the movement.*[189] The July 2011 arrest of LulzSec member Topiary became a particular rallying point, leading to a widespread "Free Topiary" movement.*[190]

The first person to be sent to jail for participation in an Anonymous DDoS attack was Dmitriy Guzner, an American 19-year-old. He pleaded guilty to "unauthorized impairment of a protected computer" in November 2009 and was sentenced to 366 days in U.S. federal prison.*[191]*[192]

On June 13, 2011, officials in Turkey arrested 32 individuals that were allegedly involved in DDoS attacks on Turkish government websites. These members of Anonymous were captured in different cities of Turkey including Istanbul and Ankara. According to *PC Magazine*, these individuals were arrested after they attacked these websites as a response to the Turkish government demand to ISPs to implement a system of filters that many have perceived as censorship.*[193]*[194]

Chris Doyon (alias "Commander X"), a self-described leader of Anonymous, was arrested in September 2011 for a cyberattack on the website of Santa Cruz County, California.*[195]*[196] He jumped bail in February 2012 and fled across the border into Canada.*[196]

On September 2012, journalist and Anonymous associate Barrett Brown, known for speaking to media on behalf of the group, was arrested hours after posting a video that appeared to threaten FBI agents with physical violence. Brown was subsequently charged with 17 offenses, including publishing personal credit card information from the Stratfor hack.*[197]

9.4.1 Operation Avenge Assange

Several law enforcement agencies took action after Anonymous' Operation Avenge Assange.*[198] In January 2011, the British police arrested five male suspects between the ages of 15 and 26 with suspicion of participating in Anonymous DDoS attacks.*[199] During July 19–20, 2011, as many as 20 or more arrests were made of suspected Anonymous hackers in the US, UK, and Netherlands. According to the statements of U.S. officials, suspects' homes were raided and suspects were arrested in Alabama, Arizona, California, Colorado, Washington DC, Florida, Massachusetts, Nevada, New Mexico, and Ohio. Additionally, a 16-year-old boy was held by the police in south London on suspicion of breaching the Computer Misuse Act 1990, and four were held in the Netherlands.*[200]*[201]*[202]*[203]

AnonOps admin Christopher Weatherhead (alias "Nerdo"), a 22-year-old who had reportedly been intimately involved in organising DDoS attacks during "Operation Payback",*[204] was convicted by a UK court on one count of conspiracy to impair the operation of computers in December 2012. He was sentenced to 18 months' imprisonment. Ashley Rhodes, Peter Gibson, and another male had already pleaded guilty to the same charge for actions between August 2010 and January 2011.[*204][*205]

9.5 Analysis

Evaluations of Anonymous' actions and effectiveness vary widely. In a widely shared post, blogger Patrick Gray wrote that private security firms "secretly love" the group for the way in which it publicises cyber security threats.[*206] Anonymous is sometimes stated to have changed the nature of protesting,[*10][*11] and in 2012, *Time* called it one of the "100 most influential people" in the world.[*13]

In 2012, Public Radio International reported that the U.S. National Security Agency considered Anonymous a potential national security threat and had warned the president that it could develop the capability to disable parts of the U.S. power grid.[*207] In contrast, CNN reported in the same year that "security industry experts generally don't consider Anonymous a major player in the world of cyber-crime" due the group's reliance on DDoS attacks that briefly disabled websites rather than the more serious damage possible through hacking. One security consultant compared the group to "a jewelry thief that drives through a window, steal jewels, and rather than keep them, waves them around and tosses them out to a crowd ... They're very noisy, low-grade crimes." [*94] In its *2013 Threats Predictions* report, McAfee wrote that the technical sophistication of Anonymous was in decline and that it was losing supporters due to "too many uncoordinated and unclear operations". [*208]

Graham Cluley, a security expert for Sophos, argued that Anonymous' actions against child porn websites hosted on a darknet could be counterproductive, commenting that while their intentions appear beneficial, the removal of illegal websites and sharing networks should be performed by the authorities, rather than Internet vigilantes.[*209] Some commentators also argued that the DDoS attacks by Anonymous following the January 2012 Stop Online Piracy Act protests had proved counterproductive. Molly Wood of CNET wrote that "[i]f the SOPA/PIPA protests were the Web's moment of inspiring, non-violent, hand-holding civil disobedience, #OpMegaUpload feels like the unsettling wave of car-burning hooligans that sweep in and incite the riot portion of the play." [*210] Dwight Silverman of the *Houston Chronicle* concurred, stating that "Anonymous' actions hurt the movement to kill SOPA/PIPA by highlighting online lawlessness." [*211] The Oxford Internet Institute's Joss Wright wrote that "In one sense the actions of Anonymous are themselves, anonymously and unaccountably, censoring websites in response to positions with which they disagree." [*212]

Gabriella Coleman has compared the group to the trickster archetype[*213] and said that "they dramatize the importance of anonymity and privacy in an era when both are rapidly eroding. Given that vast databases track us, given the vast explosion of surveillance, there's something enchanting, mesmerizing and at a minimum thought-provoking about Anonymous' interventions". [*214] When asked what good Anonymous had done for the world, Parmy Olson replied:

> In some cases, yes, I think it has in terms of some of the stuff they did in the Middle East supporting the pro-democracy demonstrators. But a lot of bad things too, unnecessarily harassing people – I would class that as a bad thing. DDOS-ing the CIA website, stealing customer data and posting it online just for shits and giggles is not a good thing.[*22]

Quinn Norton of *Wired* wrote of the group in 2011:

> I will confess up front that I love Anonymous, but not because I think they're the heroes. Like Alan Moore's character V who inspired Anonymous to adopt the Guy Fawkes mask as an icon and fashion item, you're never quite sure if Anonymous is the hero or antihero. The trickster is attracted to change and the need for change, and that's where Anonymous goes. But they are not your personal army – that's Rule 44 – yes, there are rules. And when they do something, it never goes quite as planned. The internet has no neat endings.[*213]

Furthermore, Landers assessed the following in 2008:

> Anonymous is the first internet-based super-consciousness. Anonymous is a group, in the sense that a flock of birds is a group. How do you know they're a group? Because they're travelling in the same direction. At any given moment, more birds could join, leave, peel off in another direction entirely.[*215]

9.6 See also

9.7 References

9.7.1 Notes

[1] Topiary was later revealed to be Jake Davis, a teenager living in the Shetland Islands of Scotland.[*33]

[2] A portmanteau of "hacking" and "activism"

9.7.2   Citations

[1] "Gabriella Coleman on Anonymous". *Brian Lehrer Live.* Vimeo. February 9, 2011. Retrieved March 24, 2011.

[2] Kelly 2012, p. 1678.

[3] "10 Things Everyone Should Know About Anonymous". Anonews. Retrieved February 2016. Check date values in: |access-date= (help)

[4] https://www.youtube.com/user/AnonymousWorldvoce

[5] Landers, Chris (April 2, 2008). "Serious Business: Anonymous Takes On Scientology (and Doesn't Afraid of Anything)". Baltimore City Paper. Archived from the original on June 8, 2008. Retrieved July 3, 2008.

[6] Oltsik, Jon (December 3, 2013). "Edward Snowden Beyond Data Security". Network World. Retrieved December 4, 2013.

[7] Waites, Rosie (October 20, 2011). "V for Vendetta masks: Who". BBC News. Retrieved October 20, 2011.

[8] Michael Peck (April 8, 2013). "Why Did Anonymous Have to Attack Israel on Holocaust Memorial Day?". *Forbes.*

[9] Krupnick, Matt (August 15, 2011). "Freedom fighters or vandals? No consensus on Anonymous". *Oakland Tribune.* MercuryNews.com. Retrieved July 10, 2013.

[10] Carter, Adam (March 15, 2013). "From Anonymous to shuttered websites, the evolution of online protest". CBC News. Archived from the original on May 6, 2013. Retrieved May 6, 2013.

[11] Coleman, Gabriella (April 6, 2011). "Anonymous: From the Lulz to Collective Action". Archived from the original on May 5, 2013. Retrieved May 5, 2013.

[12] Rawlinson, Kevin; Peachey, Paul (April 13, 2012). "Hackers step up war on security services". *The Independent.* – via HighBeam Research (subscription required). Retrieved May 5, 2013.

[13] Gellman, Barton (April 18, 2012). "The 100 Most Influential People In The World". *Time.*

[14] Coleman, Gabriella (December 10, 2010). "What It's Like to Participate in Anonymous' Actions". *The Atlantic.* Archived from the original on May 2, 2013. Retrieved May 2, 2013.

[15] Kelly 2012, p. 1682.

[16] Olson 2012, p. 92.

[17] Brown, Jesse (February 7, 2008). "Community Organization with Digital Tools: The face of Anonymous". *MediaShift Idea Lab: Reinventing Community News for the Digital Age.* PBS. Archived from the original on Feb 11, 2008. Retrieved March 3, 2008.

[18] Olson 2012, pp. 58–59.

[19] Olson 2012, p. x.

[20] Kelly 2012, p. 1679.

[21] Cadwalladr, Carole (September 8, 2012). "Anonymous: behind the masks of the cyber insurgents". *The Guardian.* Archived from the original on May 2, 2013. Retrieved May 2, 2013.

[22] Allnut, Luke (June 8, 2012). "Parmy Olson On Anonymous: 'A Growing Phenomenon That We Don't Yet Understand'". Radio Free Europe/Radio Liberty. Archived from the original on May 2, 2013. Retrieved May 2, 2013.

[23] Olson 2012, p. 7.

[24] Morris, Adam (April 30, 2013). "Julian Assange: The Internet threatens civilization". Salon. Archived from the original on May 2, 2013. Retrieved May 2, 2013.

[25] Kelly 2012, p. 1680.

[26] Norton, Quinn (June 13, 2012). "In Flawed, Epic Anonymous Book, the Abyss Gazes Back". *Wired.* Archived from the original on May 2, 2013. Retrieved May 2, 2013.

[27] Olson 2012, pp. 122–23.

[28] Shuman, Phil (July 26, 2007). "FOX 11 Investigates: 'Anonymous'". *MyFOX Los Angeles.* KTTV (Fox). Archived from the original on May 22, 2008.

[29] Olson 2012, p. 28.

[30] Whipple, Tom (June 20, 2008). "Scientology: the Anonymous protesters." *The Times.* UK. Archived from the original on September 5, 2008.

[31] Olson 2012, p. 49.

[32] Olson 2012, p. 48.

[33] "Two-year term for Shetland hacker". *The Herald.* – via HighBeam Research (subscription required). May 17, 2013. Retrieved June 27, 2013.

[34] Olson 2012, pp. 50–52.

[35] Olson 2012, pp. 57–58.

[36] Dibbell, Julian (September 21, 2009), *The Assclown Offensive: How to Enrage the Church of Scientology*, Wired Magazine, retrieved November 27, 2009

[37] Dibbell, Julian (2008-07-11), "Sympathy for the Griefer: MOOrape, Lulz Cubes, and Other Lessons From the First 2 Decades of Online Sociopathy", *GLS Conference 4.0*, Madison, Wisconsin: Games, Learning and Society Group, retrieved November 7, 2008 Project Chanology "mention" begins approximately 27:45 minutes into the presentation.

[38] Popkin, Helen A.S. (April 18, 2011). "Notorious NSFW website cleans up its act". *Digital Life on MSNBC*. Retrieved April 19, 2011.

[39] Everything Anonymous. AnonNews.org (2013-04-20). Retrieved on 2013-08-12.

[40] Leavitt, Alex (2011-04-15). "Archiving Internet Subculture: Encyclopedia Dramatica". *Web Ecology Project*. Retrieved 2011-09-29.

[41] Stryker, Cole (2011). *Epic Win for Anonymous: How 4chan's Army Conquered the Web*. New York, New York: Overlook Press. p. 155. ISBN 1-59020-738-6. Retrieved 2011-09-29.

[42] "Cruise bio hits stores as video clip of actor praising Scientology makes it way to Internet". *The Washington Post*. – via HighBeam Research (subscription required). Associated Press. January 15, 2008. Retrieved May 2, 2013.

[43] Tucker, Neely (January 18, 2008). "Tom Cruise's Scary Movie; In Church Promo, the Scientologist Is Hard to Suppress". *Washington Post*. – via HighBeam Research (subscription required). Retrieved May 2, 2013.

[44] Olson 2012, pp. 63–65.

[45] "Fair game; Scientology". *The Economist*. – via HighBeam Research (subscription required). February 2, 2008. Retrieved May 2, 2013.

[46] Olson 2012, pp. 71–72, 122, 124, 126–29.

[47] Olson 2012, p. 206.

[48] Norton, Quinn (December 30, 2011). "Anonymous 101 Part Deux: Morals Triumph Over Lulz". *Wired*. Archived from the original on May 5, 2013. Retrieved May 5, 2013.

[49] Olson 2012, pp. 71–72.

[50] George-Cosh, David (January 25, 2008). "Online group declares war on Scientology". *National Post*. Archived from the original on January 28, 2008. Retrieved January 25, 2008.

[51] "Scientology faces wave of cyber attacks". *Cape Times*. – via HighBeam Research (subscription required). March 4, 2008. Retrieved May 2, 2013.

[52] Olson 2012, p. 82–3.

[53] DeSio, John (May 6, 2008). "Queens Anonymous Member Gets a Letter from Scientologists". *The Village Voice*. Archived from the original on May 2, 2013. Retrieved May 2, 2013.

[54] Ramadge, Andrew (March 20, 2008). "Scientology site gets a facelift after protests". news.com.au. Archived from the original on May 2, 2013. Retrieved May 2, 2013.

[55] Howarth, Mark (June 1, 2008). "Anger as police ban placards branding Scientology a cult". *Sunday Herald*. – via HighBeam Research (subscription required). Retrieved May 2, 2013.

[56] Olson 2012, p. 85.

[57] Olson 2012, p. 93–94.

[58] Olson 2012, p. 102.

[59] "Activists target recording industry websites". BBC News. September 20, 2010. Retrieved October 27, 2010.

[60] Olson 2012, p. 103.

[61] Olson 2012, p. 104.

[62] Tsotsis, Alexia (September 19, 2010). "RIAA Goes Offline, Joins MPAA As Latest Victim Of Successful DDoS Attacks". TechCrunch. Archived from the original on May 3, 2013. Retrieved 3 May 2013.

[63] Olson 2012, p. 105.

[64] Williams, Chris (September 22, 2010). "Piracy threats lawyer mocks 4chan DDoS attack". *The Register*. Retrieved October 22, 2010.

[65] Winterford, Brett (September 28, 2010). "Operation Payback directs DDoS attack at AFACT". *iTnews*. Retrieved December 23, 2010.

[66] Leydon, John (October 4, 2010). "Ministry of Sound floored by Anonymous". *The Register*. Retrieved October 22, 2010.

[67] Leyden, John (October 7, 2010). "Spanish entertainment industry feels wrath of Anonymous". The Register. Retrieved January 6, 2011.

[68] Sandoval, Greg (November 9, 2010). "FBI probes 4chan's 'Anonymous' DDoS attacks". CNET.com. Retrieved December 23, 2010.

[69] Corrons, Luis (September 17, 2010). "4chan Users Organize Surgical Strike Against MPAA". *Pandalabs Security*. Retrieved October 22, 2010.

[70] "Anonymous hacktivists say Wikileaks war to continue". BBC News. December 9, 2010. Archived from the original on May 3, 2013. Retrieved May 3, 2013.

[71] Olson 2012, p. 110.

[72] Olson 2012, pp. 110–11.

[73] Olson 2012, pp. 115–18.

[74] Olson 2012, p. 117.

[75] Maslin, Janet (May 31, 2012). "The Secret Lives of Dangerous Hackers". *The New York Times*. Archived from the original on May 3, 2013. Retrieved May 3, 2013.

[76] Olson 2012, pp. 117–19.

[77] Addley, Esther; Halliday, Josh (December 8, 2012). "WikiLeaks supporters disrupt Visa and MasterCard sites in 'Operation Payback'". *The Guardian*. Archived from the original on May 3, 2013. Retrieved May 3, 2013.

[78] Olson 2012, p. 178.

[79] Olson 2012, pp. 122, 129.

[80] Steven Musil (December 8, 2013). "Anonymous hackers plead guilty to 2010 PayPal cyberattack". Cnet.

[81] Olson 2012, pp. 141–45.

[82] Ryan, Yasmine (May 19, 2011). "Anonymous and the Arab uprisings". Al Jazeera. Archived from the original on May 5, 2013. Retrieved May 5, 2013.

[83] Olson 2012, p. 148.

[84] Olson 2012, pp. 10–24.

[85] Olson 2012, p. 200.

[86] Olson 2012, pp. 161, 164.

[87] Olson 2012, p. 164.

[88] Olson 2012, pp. 176–77.

[89] Olson 2012, pp. 178–88.

[90] "Anonymous vows to 'destroy' Westboro Baptist Church over Sandy Hook picket plans". The Raw Story. December 17, 2012. Archived from the original on May 5, 2013. Retrieved May 5, 2013.

[91] "Hacktivists strike Westboro Baptist Church over Newtown tragedy". RT. December 17, 2012. Archived from the original on May 5, 2013. Retrieved May 5, 2013.

[92] "Uganda prime minister hacked 'over gay rights'". BBC News. August 16, 2012. Archived from the original on May 5, 2013. Retrieved May 5, 2013.

[93] "Sony caught up in cyber war with indignant hackers: ; Company with security once considered 'robust' now dealing with constant breaches". *Charleston Daily Mail*. – via HighBeam Research (subscription required) . Associated Press. May 30, 2011. Retrieved May 5, 2013.

[94] Goldman, David (January 20, 2012). "Hacker group Anonymous is a nuisance, not a threat". CNN. Archived from the original on May 5, 2013. Retrieved May 5, 2013.

[95] Malik, Shiv (May 1, 2012). "Occupy movement takes over parts of London Stock Exchange". *The Guardian*. Archived from the original on May 5, 2013. Retrieved May 5, 2013.

[96] Hernandez, Vittorio (October 5, 2012). "93-Year-Old Australian Faces Pedophilia Charges in Thailand". *International Business Times*. Archived from the original on May 5, 2013. Retrieved May 5, 2013.

[97] Liebowitz, Matt (May 15, 2012). "Anonymous Attacks Suspected Pedophiles Again". NBC News. Archived from the original on May 5, 2013. Retrieved May 5, 2013.

[98] Plumlee, Rick (2013-12-02). "Wis. truck driver given 2 years probation for cyberattack on Koch Industries | Wichita Eagle". Kansas.com. Retrieved 2014-01-07.

[99] "Internet strikes back: Anonymous' Operation Megaupload explained". *RT*. January 20, 2012. Archived from the original on May 5, 2013. Retrieved May 5, 2013.

[100] Roy, Jessica (2012-12-04). "Anonymous Hunts Revenge Porn Purveyor Hunter Moore". Betabeat. Retrieved 2014-01-07.

[101] Chan, Casey (November 16, 2012). "Anonymous Targets Israel by Taking Down Hundreds of Websites and Leaking Emails and Passwords". Gizmodo. Archived from the original on May 5, 2013. Retrieved May 5, 2013.

[102] Kershner, Isabel (April 7, 2013). "Israel Says It Repelled Most Attacks on Its Web Sites by Pro-Palestinian Hackers". *The New York Times*. Archived from the original on May 5, 2013. Retrieved May 5, 2013.

[103] Gonsalves, Antone (May 3, 2013). "Experts hope for another failure in next Anonymous attack". CSO Online. Archived from the original on May 5, 2013. Retrieved May 5, 2013.

[104] Messmer, Ellen (May 5, 2013). "Anonymous cyberattack on Israel finds disputed impact". *ComputerWorld*. Archived from the original on May 5, 2013. Retrieved May 5, 2013.

[105] "Protesters gather around the world for Million Mask March". *The Guardian*. 5 November 2013. Retrieved 6 November 2013.

[106] "#OpSafeWinter: Anonymous fights homelessness worldwide". *The Daily Dot*.

[107] https://opsafewinter.org/?p=140

[108] "Forum Post: #Anon #OpSafeWinter Call to Action & New York #D26 Assembly - OccupyWallSt.org". Occupy Solidarity Network.

[109] http://occupyweather.com/opsafewinter/

[110] "#OpSafeWinter: Generosity Goes Viral". *The Interdependence Project*.

[111] Bever, Lindsey (August 13, 2014). "Amid Ferguson protests, hacker collective Anonymous wages cyberwar". *The Washington Post*. Retrieved August 13, 2014.

[112] Hunn, David (August 13, 2014). "How computer hackers changed the Ferguson protests". *St. Louis Post-Dispatch*. Retrieved August 13, 2014.

[113] Harkinson, Josh (August 13, 2014). "Anonymous' "Op Ferguson" Says It Will ID the Officer Who Killed Michael Brown". *Mother Jones*. Retrieved August 13, 2014.

[114] Bosman, Julie; Shear, Michael D.; Williams, Timothy (August 14, 2014). "Obama Calls for Open Inquiry Into Police Shooting of Teenager in Ferguson, Mo". *The New York Times*. Retrieved August 14, 2014.

[115] "Anonymous Releases Alleged Name Of Officer They Say Fatally Shot Michael Brown". KMOX News Radio 1120. August 14, 2014. Retrieved August 14, 2014.

[116] Pagliery, Jose (August 14, 2014). "Ferguson police deny Anonymous' ID of alleged shooter". CNN Money. Retrieved August 14, 2014.

[117] Hunn, David. "Twitter suspends Anonymous account : News". *St. Louis Post-Dispatch*. Retrieved August 15, 2014.

[118] Jamie Bartlett. "Hacker, Hoaxer, Whistleblower, Spy: The Many Faces of Anonymous by Gabriella Coleman – review". *the Guardian*.

[119] Boroff, David (November 24, 2014). "Grieving dad, Anonymous lash out at Cleveland cops following shooting death of boy, 12, armed with BB gun". New York Daily News. Retrieved November 24, 2014.

[120] Danylko, Ryllie (November 26, 2014). "Anonymous begins looking into past of Timothy Loehmann, cop who fatally shot Tamir Rice". *cleveland.com*. Retrieved February 15, 2014.

[121] "'Hacktivist' group Anonymous says it would avenge Charlie Hebdo attacks by shutting down jihadist websites". The Telegraph. 9 January 2015.

[122] "Anonymous declares war over Charlie Hebdo attack". CNN Money. 9 January 2015.

[123] Newsbeat (12 January 2015). "Hackers Anonymous 'disable extremist website'". BBC. Retrieved 16 January 2015.

[124] Newsbeat (9 January 2015). "Anonymous hackers 'declare war' on jihadists after France attacks". BBC. BBC News. Retrieved 16 January 2015.

[125] Anti-Islamic marches to be held across Australia slammed as 'racist', counter protests planned www.rt.com I 3 Apr, 2015

[126] Fekete, Jason (17 June 2015). "Government of Canada websites under attack, hacker groupAnonymous claims responsibility". The National Post. Retrieved 18 June 2015.

[127] "Anonymous intends to unveil names of up to 1,000 Ku Klux Klan members". FOX News. October 29, 2015.

[128] Grenoble, Ryan. "Anonymous Begins Revealing Information About Alleged Ku Klux Klan Members". *Huffington Post*. Retrieved November 3, 2015.

[129] "The Short List: Anonymous goes after KKK; VW in another emissions stink; 'Brangelina' open up". *USA Today*. November 2, 2015. Retrieved November 2, 2015.

[130] "https://twitter.com/Operation_KKK/status/ 661319846206967808". Twitter. November 2, 2015. Retrieved November 2, 2015. External link in |title= (help)

[131] "This account has NOT YET released any information.". Twitter. November 2, 2015. Retrieved November 2, 2015.

[132] "#OpSaudi : Anonymous launched cyber attack on Saudi Government site". 16 May 2013. Retrieved 22 August 2015.

[133] Frenkel, Sheera (24 June 2015). "Meet The Mysterious New Hacker Army Freaking Out The Middle East". Retrieved 22 August 2015.

[134] "Can Cyber Activists Chase ISIS off Twitter?". *The Atlantic*. Retrieved 2015-11-15.

[135] "Anonymous vs. the Islamic State". *Foreign Policy*. Retrieved 2015-11-15.

[136] "Ghost Security Hackers, Offshoot Of 'Anonymous,' Claim They Disrupted ISIS Attack By Intercepting Twitter Messages". *International Business Times*. Retrieved 2015-11-15.

[137] "Anonymous declares war on ISIS in YouTube video saying it will 'unite humanity'". *Mail Online*. November 16, 2015.

[138] "#OpParis: Anonymous takes down 5,500 ISIS Twitter accounts". *RT English*.

[139] "Anonymous 'declares war' on Islamic State". *bbc.co.uk*.

[140] "ISIS Calls Anonymous 'Idiots' As Cyber War Heats Up – Fortune". *Fortune*.

[141] "ISIS calls Anonymous 'idiots,' offers tips to evade hackers". *TheHill*.

[142] Catalin Cimpanu (November 16, 2015). "One Day Later, Anonymous Already Takes Down 3,824 Pro-ISIS Twitter Accounts – UPDATE". *softpedia*.

[143] Andrew Griffin (November 19, 2015). "'Operation Isis': Anonymous activists begin leaking suspected extremist Twitter account information". *The Independent*.

[144] "Anonymous Has Now Taken Down 20,000 ISIS Twitter Accounts, Promises to Go On". *softpedia*. Retrieved 2015-11-21.

[145] "ISIS 20,000+ Twitter Accounts Down". *Pastebin*. Retrieved 11 November 2015.

[146] "Anonymous 'anti-Islamic State list' features Obama and BBC News". BBC News. Retrieved 26 November 2015.

[147] "Twitter: Anonymous's lists of alleged ISIS accounts are 'wildly inaccurate'". *The Daily Dot.* 20 November 2015. Retrieved 22 November 2015.

[148] "Anonymous release leaked NASA information". Anonews. Retrieved November 2015. Check date values in: |access-date= (help)

[149] "OpNasaDrones Zine #AnonSec". none. Retrieved January 2016. Check date values in: |access-date= (help)

[150] "NASA Brushes Off Claims One Of Its Drones Was Hacked". *Forbes.* February 2016. Retrieved February 2016. Check date values in: |access-date= (help)

[151] "Anonymous Leaks Databases for 100 Thai Prison Websites". *Softpedia News.* February 2016. Retrieved February 2016. Check date values in: |access-date= (help)

[152] "Koh Tao Murders: Lawyer Alleges Prison Mistreatment". *Khaosod English.* 26 January 2016. Retrieved February 2016. Check date values in: |access-date= (help)

[153] http://europe.newsweek.com/ anonymous-hackers-declare-total-war-donald-trump-april-fools-day-437027

[154] "Anonymous - Elucidating #OpISIS and #OpTrump". *YouTube.* Retrieved 31 March 2016.

[155] "EXCLUSIVE: Why Anonymous 'hacked' the SABC, Gupta websites". *Fin24.* Retrieved 2016-06-19.

[156] CNN Wire Staff. "Hackers pirate PBS website, post fake story about Tupac still alive". CNN. Retrieved June 3, 2011.

[157] Olson, Parmy (May 31, 2011). "Interview With PBS Hackers: We Did It For 'Lulz And Justice'". *Forbes.* Retrieved June 3, 2011.

[158] Pepitone, Julianne (June 2, 2011). "Group claims fresh hack of 1 million Sony accounts Money". CNN. Archived from the original on August 18, 2011. Retrieved June 3, 2012.

[159] Thomas, Keir (June 11, 2012). "Porn Site Users Beware: Hacker Group LulzSec May Have Posted Your Email Address". *PC World.* Archived from the original on June 11, 2012. Retrieved June 11, 2012.

[160] Bright, Peter (June 14, 2011). "Titanic Takeover Tuesday: LulzSec's busy day of hacking escapades". *Ars Technica.* Archived from the original on June 14, 2011. Retrieved June 14, 2011.

[161] Peckham, Matt (June 14, 2011). "LulzSec Knocks 'Minecraft,' 'EVE Online,' 'League Of Legends' and 'The Escapist' Offline". *Time.* New York City. Archived from the original on June 14, 2011. Retrieved June 14, 2011.

[162] Morse, Andrew; Sherr, Ian (June 6, 2011). "For Some Hackers, The Goal Is Just To Play A Prank". *The Wall Street Journal.* p. B1. Archived from the original on June 9, 2011. Retrieved June 6, 2011.

[163] "LulzSec claims to have hacked FBI-affiliated website". *LA Times.* Retrieved June 4, 2012.

[164] Ogg, Erica (June 13, 2012). "LulzSec targets videogame maker ZeniMax Media". CNET.com. CBS Interactive. Archived from the original on June 13, 2012. Retrieved June 13, 2011.

[165] "CIA website hacked; LulzSec takes credit (again)". *Consumer Reports.* June 16, 2012. Archived from the original on June 16, 2012. Retrieved June 16, 2011.

[166] "Hackers voltam a atacar sites portugueses". *TVI 24* (in Portuguese). Televisão Independente. December 2, 2012. Archived from the original on December 3, 2011. Retrieved December 3, 2012.

[167] Weisenthal, Joe (June 25, 2011). "Notorious Hacker Group LulzSec Just Announced That It's Finished". *Business Insider.* Silicon Alley Insider. Archived from the original on June 25, 2011. Retrieved June 25, 2011.

[168] Thomson, Iain. "LulzSec sneak Sabu buys six more months of freedom." *The Register.* August 23, 2012.

[169] Kaplan, Jeremy (July 19, 2011). "Leading Member of LulzSec Hacker Squad Arrested in London". *Fox News Channel.* New York City. Archived from the original on July 20, 2011. Retrieved July 20, 2011.

[170] "Man arrested over computer hacking claims". *BBC News.* London. BBC. July 27, 2011. Archived from the original on July 27, 2011. Retrieved July 27, 2011.

[171] Winter, Jana (March 6, 2012). "Infamous international hacking group LulzSec brought down by own leader". *Fox News Channel.* New York City. Archived from the original on March 13, 2012. Retrieved March 13, 2012.

[172] "Kretsinger, Sony hacker Recursion, jailed for year". BBC News. April 19, 2013. Archived from the original on May 5, 2013. Retrieved May 5, 2013.

[173] Siegel, Matt (April 24, 2013). "Australia Arrests the Professed Head of LulzSec, Which Claims a C.I.A. Hacking". *The New York Times.* Archived from the original on May 6, 2013. Retrieved May 6, 2013.

[174] Tsotsis, Alexia (June 23, 2011). "LulzSec Releases Arizona Law Enforcement Data In Retaliation For Immigration Law". *TechCrunch.* Retrieved June 23, 2011.

[175] Emery, Daniel (June 22, 2011). "LulzSec hits Brazilian websites". *BBC.* Retrieved June 22, 2011.

[176] Clark, Jack (June 22, 2011). "LulzSec takes down Brazil government sites". *CNet.* Retrieved June 22, 2011.

[177] Albanesius, Chloe (June 29, 2011). "LulzBoat Sails On: Anonymous Dumps More Arizona Data". *PC Magazine.* Ziff Davis. Archived from the original on July 5, 2011. Retrieved July 5, 2011.

[178] Usigan, Ysolt (August 3, 2011). "Online security breach! Hackers leak social security numbers of cops in Missouri". *CBS News*. New York City. CBS. Archived from the original on August 5, 2011. Retrieved August 5, 2011.

[179] Kelly, Meghan (October 21, 2011). "Anonymous releases private police information in name of Occupy Wall Street". *VentureBeat*. Archived from the original on October 22, 2011. Retrieved October 22, 2011.

[180] Mills, Elinor (August 6, 2011). "AntiSec hackers post stolen police data as revenge for arrests". *CNET*. CBS Interactive. Archived from the original on August 6, 2011. Retrieved August 6, 2011.

[181] Gayomail, Chris (July 18, 2011). "LulzSec Hacks 'News of the World' and 'The Sun,' Plants Fake Murdoch Death Story". *Time*. New York City. Time Inc. Archived from the original on July 18, 2011. Retrieved July 18, 2011.

[182] Rovzar, Chris (July 18, 2011). "Website of Murdoch's Sun Hacked". *New York Magazine*. New York City. New York Media Holdings. Archived from the original on July 18, 2011. Retrieved July 18, 2011.

[183] Hachman, Mark (July 29, 2011). "Anonymous Publishes Internal Documents from Govt. Contractor ManTech". *PC Magazine*. Ziff Davis. Archived from the original on July 29, 2011. Retrieved July 29, 2011.

[184] Ragan, Steve (August 16, 2011). "Vanguard Defense Industries compromised by AntiSec". *The Tech Herald*. p. 1. Archived from the original on August 18, 2011. Retrieved August 18, 2011.

[185] Gerwirtz, David (July 11, 2011). "Military Meltdown Monday: 90,000 military email profiles released by AntiSec". *ZDNet*. CBS Interactive. Archived from the original on July 12, 2011. Retrieved July 12, 2011.

[186] Gallagher, Sean (March 6, 2012). "Inside the hacking of Stratfor: the FBI's case against Antisec member Anarchaos". Ars technica. Retrieved May 5, 2013.

[187] Ronson, Jon (May 3, 2013). "Security alert: notes from the frontline of the war in cyberspace". *The Guardian*. Archived from the original on May 5, 2013. Retrieved May 5, 2013.

[188] Olson 2012, p. 355.

[189] Olson 2012, p. 356.

[190] Munro, Alistair (June 26, 2012). "Scots hacker admits breaking into the CIA". *The Scotsman*. – via HighBeam Research (subscription required). Retrieved May 5, 2013.

[191] "Verona man admits role in attack on Church of Scientology's websites". *The Star-Ledger*. November 16, 2009. Archived from the original on May 5, 2013. Retrieved May 5, 2013.

[192] Olson 2012, p. 89.

[193] Albanesius, Chloe (June 13, 2011). "Turkey Arrests 32 'Anonymous' Members & Opinion". PCMag.com. Retrieved August 30, 2011.

[194] "Detienen en Turquía a 32 presuntos miembros de 'Anonymous' – Noticias de Europa – Mundo". Eltiempo.Com. Retrieved August 30, 2011.

[195] Elinor Mills (September 23, 2011). "Alleged 'Commander X' Anonymous hacker pleads not guilty". Cnet. Archived from the original on May 5, 2013. Retrieved May 5, 2013.

[196] Nate Anderson (December 11, 2012). "Anon on the run: How Commander X jumped bail and fled to Canada". Ars Technica. Archived from the original on May 5, 2013. Retrieved May 5, 2013.

[197] Gallagher, Ryan (March 20, 2013). "How Barrett Brown went from Anonymous's PR to federal target". *The Guardian*. Archived from the original on May 5, 2013. Retrieved May 5, 2013.

[198] "Anonymous attacks PayPal in 'Operation Avenge Assange'". *The Register*. December 6, 2010.

[199] "UK police arrest WikiLeaks backers for cyber attacks". Reuters. January 27, 2011. Retrieved August 30, 2011.

[200] "Police arrest 'hackers' in US, UK, Netherlands". BBC. July 19, 2011. Archived from the original on July 28, 2011. Retrieved August 30, 2011.

[201] Greenberg, Andy (July 19, 2011). "Fourteen Anonymous Hackers Arrested For "Operation Avenge Assange," LulzSec Leader Claims He's Not Affected – Forbes". *Forbes*. Retrieved August 30, 2011.

[202] "'Anonymous' hackers arrested in US sweep". *Herald Sun*. Australia. July 20, 2011. Retrieved August 30, 2011.

[203] "16 Suspected 'Anonymous' Hackers Arrested In Nationwide Sweep". Fox News Channel. April 7, 2010. Archived from the original on July 29, 2011. Retrieved August 30, 2011.

[204] Halliday, Josh (January 24, 2013). "Anonymous hackers jailed for cyber attacks". *The Guardian*. Retrieved April 30, 2013.

[205] Leyden, John (December 14, 2012). "UK cops: How we sniffed out convicted AnonOps admin 'Nerdo'". *The Register*. Archived from the original on April 19, 2013. Retrieved April 19, 2013.

[206] Olson 2012, pp. 309–310.

[207] "National Security Agency calls hacktivist group 'Anonymous' a threat to national security". Public Radio International. February 27, 2012. Archived from the original on May 5, 2013. Retrieved May 5, 2013.

[208] "2013 Threats Predictions" (PDF). McAfee. Archived (PDF) from the original on May 5, 2013. Retrieved May 5, 2013.

[209] Leyden, John (October 24, 2011). "Anonymous shuts down hidden child abuse hub". *The Register*. Retrieved January 25, 2012.

[210] Wood, Molly (January 19, 2012). "Anonymous goes nuclear; everybody loses?". CNET. Retrieved January 21, 2012.

[211] Jonsson, Patrik (January 21, 2012). "SOPA: Feds go after Megaupload as Congress reviews anti-piracy bills". *The Christian Science Monitor*. Archived from the original on January 23, 2012. Retrieved January 22, 2012.

[212] Kelion, Leo (January 20, 2012). "Hackers retaliate over Megaupload website shutdown". BBC News. Retrieved January 21, 2012.

[213] Norton, Quinn (November 8, 2011). "Anonymous 101: Introduction to the Lulz". *Wired*. Archived from the original on May 5, 2013. Retrieved May 5, 2013.

[214] Walters, Helen (June 27, 2012). "Peeking behind the curtain at Anonymous: Gabriella Coleman at TEDGlobal 2012". TED. Archived from the original on May 5, 2013. Retrieved May 5, 2013.

[215] Caneppele, Stefano; Calderoni, Francesco. "420chan"&hl=en *Organized Crime, Corruption and Crime Prevention*. p. 235. ISBN 978-3-319-01839-3. Retrieved 28 March 2015.

9.7.3 Bibliography

- Coleman, Gabriella (November 4, 2014). *Hacker, Hoaxer, Whistleblower, Spy: The Many Faces of Anonymous*. Verso Books. ISBN 1781685843.

- Firer-Blaess, Sylvain (2016). *The Collective Identity of Anonymous: Web of Meanings in a Digitally Enabled Movement*. Uppsala: Acta Universitatis Upsaliensis. p. 220. ISBN 978-91-554-9602-9. Retrieved October 5, 2016.

- Kelly, Brian (2012). "Investing in a Centralized Cybersecurity Infrastructure: Why 'Hacktivism' can and should influence cybersecurity reform" (PDF). *Boston University Law Review*. **92** (5): 1663–1710. Retrieved May 2, 2013.

- Olson, Parmy (June 5, 2012). *We Are Anonymous: Inside the Hacker World of LulzSec, Anonymous, and the Global Cyber Insurgency*. Hachette Digital, Inc. ISBN 978-0-316-21353-0. Retrieved May 2, 2013.

9.8 External links

Activist websites used by Anonymous

- Why We Protest.net, Anonymous-supported website centered on anti-Scientology protest activity

- Anonews.co, Anonymous news aggregator

- Anonymous Social Media, Anonymous social media aggregator

- Minds.com, Encrypted start-up social media channels

- AnonHQ, a news site operated by members of Anonymous

News coverage

- "Anonymous (technology) collected news and commentary". *The Guardian*.

- "Anonymous (Internet Group) collected news and commentary". *The New York Times*.

- Anonymous collected news and commentary at *Wired*

Chapter 10

Antisec Movement

This article is about the movement. For the unrelated hacking operation initiated by LulzSec, see Operation AntiSec. **The Anti Security Movement** (also written as **antisec** and

The Anti-sec movement's manifesto which had replaced a number of pictures hosted by ImageShack.

anti-sec) is a movement opposed to the computer security industry. Antisec is against full disclosure of information relating to

> software vulnerabilities, exploits, exploitation techniques, hacking tools, attacking public outlets and distribution points of that information. The general thought behind this is that the computer security industry uses full disclosure to profit and develop scare-tactics to convince people into buying their firewalls, anti-virus software and auditing services.

Movement followers have identified as targets of their cause:

- websites such as SecurityFocus, SecuriTeam, Packet Storm, and milw0rm,

- mailing lists like "full-disclosure", "vuln-dev", "vendor-sec" and Bugtraq, and

- public forums and IRC channels.

In 2009, attacks against security communities such as Astalavista[*][1] and milw0rm,[*][2] and the popular image-host ImageShack,[*][3][*][4] have given the movement worldwide media attention.

10.1 History

The start of most public attacks in the name of the anti-security movement started around 1999. The "anti-security movement" as it is understood today was coined by the following document which was initially an index on the anti.security.is website.[*][5][*][6][*][7][*][8]

> The purpose of this movement is to encourage a new policy of anti-disclosure among the computer and network security communities. The goal is not to ultimately discourage the publication of all security-related news and developments, but rather, to stop the disclosure of all unknown or non-public exploits and vulnerabilities. In essence, this would put a stop to the publication of all private materials that could allow script kiddies from compromising systems via unknown methods.

> The open-source movement has been an invaluable tool in the computer world, and we are all indebted to it. Open-source is a wonderful concept which should and will exist forever,

as educational, scientific, and end-user software should be free and available to everybody.

Exploits, on the other hand, do not fall into this broad category. Just like munitions, which span from cryptographic algorithms to hand guns to missiles, and may not be spread without the control of export restrictions, exploits should not be released to a mass public of millions of Internet users. A digital holocaust occurs each time an exploit appears on Bugtraq, and kids across the world download it and target unprepared system administrators. Quite frankly, the integrity of systems world wide will be ensured to a much greater extent when exploits are kept private, and not published.

A common misconception is that if groups or individuals keep exploits and security secrets to themselves, they will become the dominators of the "illegal scene", as countless insecure systems will be solely at their mercy. This is far from the truth. Forums for information trade, such as Bugtraq, Packetstorm, www.hack.co.za, and vuln-dev have done much more to harm the underground and net than they have done to help them.

What casual browsers of these sites and mailing lists fail to realize is that some of the more prominent groups do not publish their findings immediately, but only as a last resort in the case that their code is leaked or has become obsolete. This is why production dates in header files often precede release dates by a matter of months or even years.

Another false conclusion by the same manner is that if these groups haven't released anything in a matter of months, it must be because they haven't found anything new. The regular reader must be made aware of these things.

We are not trying to discourage exploit development or source auditing. We are merely trying to stop the results of these efforts from seeing the light. Please join us if you would like to see a stop to the commercialization, media, and general abuse of infosec.

Thank you.

10.1.1   ~el8

~el8 was one of the first anti-security hacktivist groups. The group waged war on the security industry with their popular assault known as "pr0j3kt m4yh3m". pr0j3kt m4yh3m was announced in the second issue of ~el8. The idea of the project was to eliminate all public outlets of security

news and exploits. Some of ~el8's more notable targets included Theo de Raadt, K2, Mixter, Ryan Russel (Blue Boar), Gotfault (also known as INSANITY), Chris McNab (so1o), jobe, rloxley, pm, aempirei, broncbuster, lcamtuf, and OpenBSD's CVS repository.

The group published four electronic zines which can be found here.[*][9]

All published zines by el8 including magazine issues zero to three were constructed and written by el8 leader and conspirator Rory Andrew Godfrey, Godfrey began hacking at the age of nine and since the disbanding of el8 many years ago, KMS as he is now more commonly known lives alone with his two children Harry and Isabella and has only been involved in the group "Lulzsec" & "Zf0" Since. KMS can be reached for security research purposes on his skype handle *b1tform*.

10.1.2   pHC

pHC[*][10] is an acronym for "Phrack High Council". This group also waged war against the security industry and continued to update their website with news, missions, and hack logs.[*][11]

10.2   Less recent history

Most of the original groups such as ~el8 have grown tired of the anti-security movement and left the scene. New groups started to emerge.

10.2.1   dikline

dikline kept a website[*][12] which had an index of websites and people attacked by the group or submitted to them. Some of the more notable dikline targets were rave, rosiello, unl0ck, nocturnal, r0t0r, silent, gotfault, and skew/tal0n.[*][13]

10.3   More recent history

10.3.1   giest

In August 2008, mails were sent through the full-disclosure mailing list from a person/group known as "giest".

Other targets include mwcollect.org in which the group released a tar.gz containing listens of their honeypot networks.[*][14][*][15]

10.3.2 ZF0

ZF0 (Zer0 For Owned) performed numerous attacks in the name of pr0j3kt m4yh3m in 2009. They took targets such as Critical Security, Comodo and various others. They published 5 ezines in total.*[16] July 2009, Kevin Mitnick's website was targeted by ZF0, displaying gay pornography with the text "all a board the mantrain." It has since come to light that the attacks perpetrated on the website owned by Kevin Mitnick (Security Researcher) were carried out by a young Runescape player Jordan Makris going by the handle or nick "Starfall".*[17]

10.3.3 AntiSec Group

A group known as the "AntiSec Group" *[18] enters the scene by attacking groups/communities such as an Astalavista,*[1] a security auditing company named SSANZ and the popular image hosting website ImageShack.*[3]

Graffiti reading "Antisec" *[18] began appearing in San Diego, California in June 2011 and was incorrectly associated with the original Antisec*[18] movement. According to CBS8, a local TV affiliate "People living in Mission Beach say the unusual graffiti first appeared last week on the boardwalk." They also reported "...it was quickly painted over, but the stenciled words were back Monday morning." It was later realized to be related to the new Anti-Sec movement started by LulzSec and Anonymous.*[19]

On April 30, 2015 the AntiSec Movement reappeared and started Doxing police officers by hacking their databases. On April 30, 2015 they hacked into Madison Police Department and released officers names, address, phone numbers, and other personal data in relations to Anonymous operation.*[20]*[21]

10.4 References

[1] "Astalavista Hacked and Torn apart". Kotrotsos. Archived from the original on 8 June 2009. Retrieved July 7, 2009.

[2] "Full Disclosure: Ant-Sec - We are going to terminate Hackforums.net and Milw0rm.com - New Apache 0-day exploit uncovered". Seclists.org. Retrieved 2012-08-20.

[3] "ImageShack hacked in oddball security protest". The Register.

[4] "ImageShack hacked by anti-full disclosure movement". ZDNet.

[5] "Internet Archive Wayback Machine". Web.archive.org. 2001-03-01. Archived from the original on 2001-03-01. Retrieved 2012-08-20.

[6] http://whitehate.org/backup/antisec.roots/antisec.txt

[7] http://whitehate.org/backup/antisec.roots/ats-policy.txt

[8] http://whitehate.org/backup/antisec.roots/jj.txt

[9] "T E X T F I L E S". Web.textfiles.com. Retrieved 2012-08-20.

[10] phrack.efnet.ru

[11] http://whitehate.org/backup/oldschool/phc/

[12] "dikline.org". dikline.org. Retrieved 2012-10-09.

[13] Archived October 20, 2008, at the Wayback Machine.

[14] "Security researchers' accounts ransacked in embarrasing hacklash". *theregister.co.uk*.

[15] http://archives.neohapsis.com/archives/fulldisclosure/2008-08/att-0139/geist01-aa

[16] "Index of /ezines/ZF0". Gonullyourself.org. 2012-01-13. Retrieved 2012-08-20.

[17] "Mitnich website targeted". Theregister.co.uk. June 26, 2009.

[18] "antisecmovement.com". antisecmovement.com. Retrieved 2012-10-09.

[19] "Unusual stenciled graffiti on Mission Beach boardwalk". WorldNow and Midwest Television. Archived from the original on February 10, 2012. Retrieved June 21, 2011.

[20] (a) OpRobinson

[21] Kopstein, Joshua. "AntiSec Attacks Wisconsin Cops After Shooting Death of Unarmed Teen". *Motherboard*. Retrieved 10 June 2015.

Chapter 11

Ashley Madison data breach

In July 2015, a group calling itself "The Impact Team" stole the user data of Ashley Madison, a commercial website billed as enabling extramarital affairs. The group copied personal information about the site's user base and threatened to release users' names and personally identifying information if Ashley Madison was not immediately shut down. On 18 and 20 August, the group leaked more than 25 gigabytes of company data, including user details.

Because of the site's policy of not deleting users' personal information – including real names, home addresses, search history and credit card transaction records – many users feared being publicly shamed.*[1]

11.1 Timeline

The Impact Team announced the attack on 15 July 2015 and threatened to expose the identities of Ashley Madison's users if its parent company, Avid Life Media, did not shut down Ashley Madison and its sister site, "Established Men".*[2]

On 20 July 2015, the website put up three statements under its "Media" section addressing the breach. The website's normally busy Twitter account fell silent apart from posting the press statements.*[3] One statement read:

> "At this time, we have been able to secure our sites, and close the unauthorized access points. We are working with law enforcement agencies, which are investigating this criminal act. Any and all parties responsible for this act of cyberterrorism will be held responsible. Using the Digital Millennium Copyright Act (DMCA), our team has now successfully removed the posts related to this incident as well as all Personally Identifiable Information (PII) about our users published online." *[4] The site also offered to waive the account deletion charge.

Although Ashley Madison denied reports that a mass re-

lease of customer records occurred on 21 July,*[5] over 60 gigabytes worth of data was confirmed to be valid on 18 August.*[6] The information was released on BitTorrent in the form of a 10 gigabyte compressed archive and the link to it was posted on a dark web site only accessible via the anonymity network Tor.*[7] The data was cryptographically signed*[8] with a PGP key. In its message, the group blamed Avid Life Media, accusing the company of deceptive practices: "We have explained the fraud, deceit, and stupidity of ALM and their members. Now everyone gets to see their data ... Too bad for ALM, you promised secrecy but didn't deliver." *[9]

In response, Avid Life Media released a statement that the company was working with authorities to investigate, and said the hackers were not "hacktivists" but criminals.*[10] A second, larger, data dump occurred on 20 August 2015, the largest file of which comprised 12.7 gigabytes of corporate emails, including those of Noel Biderman, the CEO of Avid Life Media.*[11]

11.2 Impact and ethics

None of the accounts on the website need email verification for the profile to be created, meaning that people often create profiles with fake email addresses, and sometimes people who have similar names accidentally confuse their email address, setting up accounts for the wrong email address. Ashley Madison's company required the owner of the email account to pay money to delete the profile, preventing people who had accounts set up against their consent (as a prank or mistyped email) from deleting them without paying.*[12] Hackers allege that Avid Life Media received $1.7 million a year from people paying to shut down user profiles created on the site. The company falsely asserted that paying them would "fully delete" the profiles, which the hack proved was untrue.*[12]

Following the hack, communities of internet vigilantes began combing through to find famous individuals, who they planned to publicly humiliate.*[13] France24 reported that 1,200 Saudi Arabian .sa email addresses were in the leaked database, and in Saudi Arabia adultery can be punished with death.*[14] Several thousand U.S. .mil and .gov email addresses were registered on the site.*[15]*[16]*[17] In the days following the breach, extortionists began targeting people whose details were included in the leak, attempting to scam over US$200 worth of Bitcoins from them.*[18]*[19]*[20] One company started offering a "search engine" where people could type email addresses of colleagues or their spouse into the website, and if the email address was on the database leak, then the company would send them letters threatening that their details were to be exposed unless they paid money to the company.*[21]*[22]

A variety of security researchers and internet privacy activists debated the media ethics of journalists reporting on the specifics of the data, such as the names of users revealed to be members.*[13]*[23]*[24]*[25] A number of commentators compared the hack to the loss of privacy during the 2014 celebrity photo hack.*[26]*[27]

Clinical psychologists argued that dealing with an affair in a particularly public way increases the hurt for spouses and children.*[28] Carolyn Gregoire argued that "Social media has created an aggressive culture of public shaming in which individuals take it upon themselves to inflict psychological damage" and that more often than not, "the punishment goes beyond the scope of the crime." *[28] Graham Cluley argued that the psychological consequences for people shamed could be immense, and that it would be possible for some to be bullied into suicide.*[29]*[30] Charles J. Orlando, who had joined the site to conduct research concerning women who cheat, said he felt users of the site were anxious the release of sexually explicit messages would humiliate their spouses and children.*[31] He wrote it is alarming "the mob that is the Internet is more than willing to serve as judge, jury, and executioner" and members of the site "don't deserve a flogging in the virtual town square with millions of onlookers." *[31]

On 24 August 2015, Toronto police announced that two unconfirmed suicides had been linked to the data breach, in addition to "reports of hate crimes connected to the hack." *[32]*[33] Unconfirmed reports say a man in the U.S. died by suicide.*[21] At least one suicide, which was previously linked to Ashley Madison, has since been reported as being due to "stress entirely related to issues at work that had no connection to the data leak" .*[34]

On 24 August 2015, a pastor and professor at the New Orleans Baptist Theological Seminary committed suicide citing the leak that had occurred six days before.*[35]

Users whose details were leaked are filing a $567 million class-action lawsuit against Avid Dating Life and Avid Media, the owners of Ashley Madison, through Canadian law firms Charney Lawyers and Sutts, Strosberg LLP.*[36]

11.3 Data analysis

Annalee Newitz, editor-in-chief of *Gizmodo*, analyzed the leaked data.*[37] She initially found that only roughly 12,000 of the 5.5 million registered female accounts were used on a regular basis, equal to 3 in every 1000, or less than 1%.*[38]*[39] The remaining were used only one time, the day they were registered. She also found that a very high number of the women's accounts were created from the same IP address suggesting there were many fake accounts. She found women checked email messages very infrequently: for every 1 time a woman checked her email, 13,585 men checked theirs. Only 9,700 of the 5 million female account had ever replied to a message, compared to the 5.9 million men who would do the same. She concluded that, "The women's accounts show so little activity that they might as well not be there" .*[38] In a subsequent article the following week Newitz acknowledged that she had "misunderstood the evidence" in her previous article, and that her conclusion that there were few females active on the site had actually been based on data recording "bot" activities in contacting members. She notes that "we have absolutely no data recording human activity at all in the Ashley Madison database dump from Impact Team. All we can see is when fake humans contacted real ones." *[40]

Passwords on the live site were hashed using the bcrypt algorithm.*[41]*[42] A security analyst using the Hashcat password recovery tool with a dictionary based on the RockYou passwords found that among the 4,000 passwords that were the easiest to crack, "123456" and "password" were the most commonly used passwords on the live website. An analysis of old passwords used on an archived version showed that "123456" and "password" were the most common.*[43] Due to a coding error where passwords were hashed with both bcrypt and md5, 11 million passwords were eventually cracked.*[44]

Claire Brownell suggested that the Turing test could be possibly passed by the women-imitating chatbots that fooled millions of men into buying special accounts.*[45]

11.4 See also

- Internet vigilantism

- Online shaming

11.5   References

[1] Thomsen, Simon (20 July 2015).   "Extramarital affair website Ashley Madison has been hacked and attackers are threatening to leak data online". *Business Insider*. Retrieved 21 July 2015.

[2] "Online Cheating Site AshleyMadison Hacked". krebsonsecurity.com. 15 July 2015. Retrieved 20 July 2015.

[3] "Ashley Madison". *twitter.com*. Retrieved 20 August 2015.

[4] "STATEMENT FROM AVID LIFE MEDIA, INC.". Ashley Madison. 20 July 2015. Retrieved 22 July 2015.

[5] Hern, Alex. "Ashley Madison customer service in meltdown as site battles hack fallout". *The Guardian*.

[6] "Ashley Madison condemns attack as experts say hacked database is real". *The Guardian*. 19 August 2015. Retrieved 19 August 2015.

[7] Hern, Alex.   "Ashley Madison hack: your questions answered". *the Guardian*.

[8] "No, You Can't Hire A Hacker To Erase You From The Ashley Madison Leak". *Fast Company*.

[9] "Hackers Finally Post Stolen Ashley Madison Data". *WIRED*. 18 August 2015. Retrieved 19 August 2015.

[10] "Statement from Avid Life Media Inc. – August 18, 2015". Ashley Madison. 18 August 2015. Retrieved 19 August 2015.

[11] Pagliery, Jose (20 August 2015). "Hackers expose Ashley Madison CEO's emails". *CNNMoney*.

[12] "Some Dude Created an Ashley Madison Account Linked to My Gmail, and All I Got Was This Lousy Extortion Screen". *The Intercept*. Retrieved 24 August 2015.

[13] "Early Notes on the Ashley Madison Hack". *The Awl*. Retrieved 20 August 2015.

[14] "Americas - The global fallout of the Ashley Madison hack". *France 24*. Retrieved 24 August 2015.

[15] Gibbons-Neff, Thomas (19 August 2015). "Thousands of .mil addresses potentially leaked in Ashley Madison hack". *Washington Post*.

[16] "Report: Hack of Adultery Site Ashley Madison Exposed Military Emails". *Military.com*.

[17] Ewing, Philip (20 August 2015). "Pentagon investigating whether troops used cheating website". *POLITICO*.

[18] Krebs, Brian (21 August 2015). "Extortionists Target Ashley Madison Users". *Krebs on security*.

[19] "Extortion begins for Ashley Madison hack victims". *TheHill*. Retrieved 24 August 2015.

[20] "Ashley Madison users now facing extortion". *FOX2now.com*. Retrieved 24 August 2015.

[21] "Ashley Madison spam starts, as leak linked to first suicide". *theregister.co.uk*.

[22] "The Ashley Madison files – are people really this stupid?". *theregister.co.uk*.

[23] "In the wake of Ashley Madison, towards a journalism ethics of using hacked documents". *Online Journalism Blog*. Retrieved 20 August 2015.

[24] "Ashley Madison hack: The ethics of naming users - Fortune". *Fortune*. Retrieved 20 August 2015.

[25] "Jon Ronson And Public Shaming". *onthemedia*.

[26] "Ashley Madison hack: The depressing rise of the 'moral' hacker". *Telegraph.co.uk*. 20 August 2015.

[27] "As our own privacy becomes easier to invade, are we losing our taste for celebrity sleaze?". *newstatesman.com*.

[28] Gregoire, Carolyn (20 August 2015).   "Ashley Madison Hack Could Have A Devastating Psychological Fallout". *The Huffington Post*.

[29] "The Ashley Madison hack - further thoughts on its aftermath". *Graham Cluley*.

[30] Farhad Manjoo (6 September 2015). "Hacking victims deserve empathy, not ridicule". *Sydney Morning Herald*.

[31] Charles J. Orlando (23 July 2015). "I Was Hacked On Ashley Madison —But It's You Who Should Be Ashamed". *Yahoo! Style*. Retrieved 8 October 2015 – via Your Tango.

[32] "Ashley Madison hack: 2 unconfirmed suicides linked to breach, Toronto police say". *CBC*. 24 August 2015. Retrieved 24 August 2015.

[33] "Suicide and Ashley Madison". *Graham Cluley*.

[34] Beltran, Jacob (25 August 2015). "Widow addresses suicide of SAPD captain linked to Ashley Madison site". *San Antonio Express News*. Retrieved 27 August 2015.

[35] Laurie Segall (8 September 2015). "Pastor outed on Ashley Madison commits suicide". *CNNMoney*.

[36] "Ashley Madison faces huge class-action lawsuit". *BBC News*. Retrieved 24 August 2015.

[37] Newitz, Annalee (27 August 2015). "The Fembots of Ashley Madison". *Gizmodo*. Retrieved 28 August 2015.

[38] Reed, Brad (27 August 2015). "The most hilarious revelation about the Ashley Madison hack yet". *Yahoo! Tech*. Retrieved 28 August 2015.

[39] Gallagher, Paul (27 August 2015). "Ashley Madison hack: Just three in every 10,000 female accounts on infidelity website are real". *The Independent*.

[40] Newitz, Annalee (31 August 2015). "Ashley Madison Code Shows More Women, and More Bots". *Gizmodo*. Retrieved 19 December 2015.

[41] Dean Pierce. "Sophisticated Security". *pxdojo.net*.

[42] Zack Whittaker. "This is the worst password from the Ashley Madison hack". *ZDNet*.

[43] Include Security. "Include Security Blog - As the ROT13 turns....: A light-weight forensic analysis of the AshleyMadison Hack". *includesecurity.com*. Retrieved 20 August 2015.

[44] Goodin, Dan (10 September 2015). "Once seen as bulletproof, 11 million+ Ashley Madison passwords already cracked". *Ars Technica*. Retrieved 10 September 2015.

[45] Claire Brownell (11 September 2015). "Inside Ashley Madison: Calls from crying spouses, fake profiles and the hack that changed everything". *Financial Post*.

Chapter 12

Operation Aurora

Not to be confused with Aurora Generator Test.

Operation Aurora was a series of cyber attacks conducted by advanced persistent threats such as the Elderwood Group based in Beijing, China, with ties to the People's Liberation Army.[2] First publicly disclosed by Google on January 12, 2010, in a blog post,[1] the attacks began in mid-2009 and continued through December 2009.[3]

The attack has been aimed at dozens of other organizations, of which Adobe Systems,[4] Juniper Networks[5] and Rackspace[6] have publicly confirmed that they were targeted. According to media reports, Yahoo, Symantec, Northrop Grumman, Morgan Stanley[7] and Dow Chemical[8] were also among the targets.

As a result of the attack, Google stated in its blog that it plans to operate a completely uncensored version of its search engine in China "within the law, if at all", and acknowledged that if this is not possible it may leave China and close its Chinese offices.[1] Official Chinese sources claimed this was part of a strategy developed by the U.S. government.[9]

The attack was named "Operation Aurora" by Dmitri Alperovitch, Vice President of Threat Research at cyber security company McAfee. Research by McAfee Labs discovered that "Aurora" was part of the file path on the attacker's machine that was included in two of the malware binaries McAfee said were associated with the attack. "We believe the name was the internal name the attacker(s) gave to this operation," McAfee Chief Technology Officer George Kurtz said in a blog post.[10]

According to McAfee, the primary goal of the attack was to gain access to and potentially modify source code repositories at these high tech, security and defense contractor companies. "[The SCMs] were wide open," says Alperovitch. "No one ever thought about securing them, yet these were the crown jewels of most of these companies in many ways —much more valuable than any financial or personally identifiable data that they may have and spend so much

time and effort protecting." [11]

12.1 History

Flowers left outside Google China's headquarters after its announcement it might leave the country

On January 12, 2010, Google revealed on its blog that it had been the victim of a cyber attack. The company said the attack occurred in mid-December and originated from China. Google stated that over 20 other companies had been attacked; other sources have since cited that more than 34 organizations were targeted.[8] As a result of the attack, Google said it was reviewing its business in China.[1] On the same day, United States Secretary of State Hillary Clinton issued a brief statement condemning the attacks and requesting a response from China.[12]

On January 13, 2010, the news agency All Headline News reported that the United States Congress plans to investigate Google's allegations that the Chinese government used the company's service to spy on human rights activists.[13]

In Beijing, visitors left flowers outside of Google's office. However, these were later removed, with a Chinese security guard stating that this was an "illegal flower tribute".[14]

The Chinese government has yet to issue a formal response, although an anonymous official stated that China is seeking more information on Google's intentions.[15]

12.2 Attackers involved

Main article: PLA Unit 61398

Technical evidence including IP addresses, domain names, malware signatures, and other factors, show Elderwood was behind the Operation Aurora attack, one of numerous attacks conducted by the Elderwood gang and others such as PLA Unit 61398, a Shanghai-based advanced persistent threat group also called "Comment Crew", named after the technique often used by the group involving internal software "comment" features on web pages, which are used to infiltrate target computers that access the sites. The two largest groups may employ hundreds of people, and work to compromise security and siphon business ideas, advanced designs, and trade secrets from various foreign computer networks.[16] The group behind the Operation Aurora attacks were dubbed "Elderwood" by Symantec after a source-code variable used by the attackers, and "Beijing Group" by Dell Secureworks. The group obtained some of Google's source code, as well as access to information about Chinese activists.[17] Along with other groups such as Unit 61398, also targeted numerous other companies in the shipping, aeronautics, arms, energy, manufacturing, engineering, electronics, financial, and software sectors.[2][18]

Elderwood specializes in attacking and infiltrating second-tier defense industry suppliers that make electronic or mechanical components for top defense companies. Those firms then become a cyber "stepping stone" to gain access to top-tier defense contractors. One attack procedure used by Elderwood is to infect legitimate websites frequented by employees of the target company – a so-called "water hole" attack, just as lions stake out a watering hole for their prey. Elderwood infects these less-secure sites with malware that downloads to a computer that clicks on the site. After that, the group searches inside the network to which the infected computer is connected, finding and then downloading executives' e-mails and critical documents on company plans, decisions, acquisitions, and product designs.[2]

12.3 Attack analysis

In its blog posting, Google stated that some of its intellectual property had been stolen. It suggested that the attackers were interested in accessing Gmail accounts of Chinese dissidents. According to the *Financial Times*, two accounts used by Ai Weiwei had been attacked, their contents read and copied; his bank accounts were investigated by state security agents who claimed he was under investigation for "unspecified suspected crimes".[19] However, the attackers were only able to view details on two accounts and those details were limited to things such as the subject line and the accounts' creation date.[1]

Security experts immediately noted the sophistication of the attack.[10] Two days after the attack became public, McAfee reported that the attackers had exploited purported zero-day vulnerabilities (unfixed and previously unknown to the target system developers) in Internet Explorer and dubbed the attack "Operation Aurora". A week after the report by McAfee, Microsoft issued a fix for the issue,[20] and admitted that they had known about the security hole used since September.[21] Additional vulnerabilities were found in Perforce, the source code revision software used by Google to manage their source code.[22][23]

VeriSign's iDefense Labs claimed that the attacks were perpetrated by "agents of the Chinese state or proxies thereof".[24]

According to a diplomatic cable from the U.S. Embassy in Beijing, a Chinese source reported that the Chinese Politburo directed the intrusion into Google's computer systems. The cable suggested that the attack was part of a coordinated campaign executed by "government operatives, public security experts and Internet outlaws recruited by the Chinese government."[25] The report suggested that it was part of an ongoing campaign in which attackers have "broken into American government computers and those of Western allies, the Dalai Lama and American businesses since 2002."[26] According to The Guardian's reporting on the leak, the attacks were "orchestrated by a senior member of the Politburo who typed his own name into the global version of the search engine and found articles criticising him personally."[27]

Once a victim's system was compromised, a backdoor connection that masqueraded as an SSL connection made connections to command and control servers running in Illinois, Texas, and Taiwan, including machines that were running under stolen Rackspace customer accounts. The victim's machine then began exploring the protected corporate intranet that it was a part of, searching for other vulnerable systems as well as sources of intellectual property, specifically the contents of source code repositories.

The attacks were thought to have definitively ended on Jan 4 when the command and control servers were taken down, although it is not known at this point whether or not the attackers intentionally shut them down.[28] However, the attacks were still occurring as of February 2010.[3]

12.4 Response and aftermath

The German, Australian, and French governments publicly issued warnings to users of Internet Explorer after the attack, advising them to use alternative browsers at least until a fix for the security hole was made.[*][29][*][30][*][31] The German, Australian, and French governments considered all versions of Internet Explorer vulnerable or potentially vulnerable.[*][32][*][33]

In an advisory on January 14, 2010, Microsoft said that attackers targeting Google and other U.S. companies used software that exploits a hole in Internet Explorer. The vulnerability affects Internet Explorer versions 6, 7, and 8 on Windows 7, Vista, Windows XP, Server 2003, Server 2008 R2, as well as IE 6 Service Pack 1 on Windows 2000 Service Pack 4.[*][34]

The Internet Explorer exploit code used in the attack has been released into the public domain, and has been incorporated into the Metasploit Framework penetration testing tool. A copy of the exploit was uploaded to Wepawet, a service for detecting and analyzing web-based malware operated by the computer security group at the University of California, Santa Barbara. "The public release of the exploit code increases the possibility of widespread attacks using the Internet Explorer vulnerability," said George Kurtz, CTO of McAfee, of the attack. "The now public computer code may help cyber criminals craft attacks that use the vulnerability to compromise Windows systems." [*][35]

Security company Websense said it identified "limited public use" of the unpatched IE vulnerability in drive-by attacks against users who strayed onto malicious Web sites.[*][36] According to Websense, the attack code it spotted is the same as the exploit that went public last week. "Internet Explorer users currently face a real and present danger due to the public disclosure of the vulnerability and release of attack code, increasing the possibility of widespread attacks," said George Kurtz, chief technology officer of McAfee, in a blog update.[*][37] Confirming this speculation, Websense Security Labs identified additional sites using the exploit on January 19.[*][38] According to reports from Ahnlab, the second URL was spread through the Instant Messenger network Misslee Messenger, a popular IM client in South Korea.[*][38]

Researchers have created attack code that exploits the vulnerability in Internet Explorer 7 (IE7) and IE8—even when Microsoft's recommended defensive measure (Data Execution Prevention (DEP)) is turned on. According to Dino Dai Zovi, a security vulnerability researcher, "even the newest IE8 isn't safe from attack if it's running on Windows XP Service Pack 2 (SP2) or earlier, or on Windows Vista RTM (release to manufacturing), the version Microsoft shipped in January 2007." [*][39]

Microsoft admitted that the security hole used had been known to them since September.[*][21] Work on an update was prioritized[*][40] and on Thursday, January 21, 2010, Microsoft released a security patch aiming to counter this weakness, the published exploits based on it and a number of other privately reported vulnerabilities.[*][41] They did not state if any of the latter had been used or published by exploiters or whether these had any particular relation to the Aurora operation, but the entire cumulative update was termed critical for most versions of Windows, including Windows 7.

Security researchers have continued to investigate the attacks. HBGary, a security firm, recently released a report in which they claim to have found some significant markers that might help identify the code developer. The firm also said that the code was Chinese language based but could not be specifically tied to any government entity.[*][42]

On February 19, 2010, a security expert investigating the cyber-attack on Google, has claimed that the people behind the attack were also responsible for the cyber-attacks made on several Fortune 100 companies in the past one and a half years. They have also tracked the attack back to its point of origin, which seems to be two Chinese schools, Shanghai Jiao Tong University and Lanxiang Vocational School.[*][43] As highlighted by *The New York Times*, both of these schools have ties with the Chinese search engine Baidu, a rival of Google China.[*][44] Both Lanxiang Vocational and Jiaotong University have denied the allegation.

In March 2010, Symantec, which was helping investigate the attack for Google, identified Shaoxing as the source of 21.3% of all (12 billion) malicious emails sent throughout the world.[*][45]

To prevent future cyberattacks such as Operation Aurora, Amitai Etzioni of the Institute for Communitarian Policy Studies has suggested that China and the United States agree to a policy of mutually assured restraint with respect to cyberspace. This would involve allowing both states to take the measures they deem necessary for their self-defense while simultaneously agreeing to refrain from taking offensive steps; it would also entail vetting these commitments.[*][46]

12.5 See also

- Honker Union

- Cyber-warfare

- Titan Rain

- Chinese intelligence activity in other countries

- GhostNet

- Economic and Industrial Espionage

- Chinese Intelligence Operations in the United States

- Vulcanbot

12.6   References

[1] "A new approach to China". Google Inc. 2010-01-12. Retrieved 17 January 2010.

[2] Clayton, Mark (14 September 2012). "Stealing US business secrets: Experts ID two huge cyber 'gangs' in China". CSMonitor. Retrieved 24 February 2013.

[3] "'Aurora' Attacks Still Under Way, Investigators Closing In On Malware Creators". *Dark Reading*. DarkReading.com. 2010-02-10. Retrieved 2010-02-13.

[4] "Adobe Investigates Corporate Network Security Issue". 2010-01-12. Retrieved 17 January 2010.

[5] "Juniper Networks investigating cyber-attacks". MarketWatch. 2010-01-15. Retrieved 17 January 2010.

[6] "Rackspace Response to Cyber Attacks". Retrieved 17 January 2010.

[7] "HBGary email leak claims Morgan Stanley was hacked". Retrieved 2 Mar 2010.

[8] Cha, Ariana Eunjung; Ellen Nakashima (2010-01-14). "Google China cyberattack part of vast espionage campaign, experts say". The Washington Post. Retrieved 17 January 2010.

[9] Hille, Kathrine (2010-01-20). "Chinese media hit at 'White House's Google'". Financial Times. Retrieved 20 January 2010.

[10] Kurtz, George (2010-01-14). "Operation "Aurora" Hit Google, Others". McAfee, Inc. Archived from the original on 11 September 2012. Retrieved 17 January 2010.

[11] Zetter, Kim (2010-03-03). "'Google' Hackers Had Ability to Alter Source Code". Wired. Retrieved 4 March 2010.

[12] Clinton, Hillary (2010-01-12). "Statement on Google Operations in China". US Department of State. Retrieved 17 January 2010.

[13] "Congress to Investigate Google Charges Of Chinese Internet Spying". All Headline News. 13 January 2010. Retrieved 13 January 2010.

[14] Robertson, Matthew (2010-01-14). "Flowers Laid, and Removed, at Google Headquarters in China". The Epoch Times. Retrieved 18 January 2010.

[15] "Chinese govt seeks information on Google intentions". *Xinhua*. China Daily. 2010-01-13. Retrieved 18 January 2010.

[16] Martin, Adam (19 February 2013). "Meet 'Comment Crew,' China's Military-Linked Hackers". *NYMag.com*. New York Media. Retrieved 24 February 2013.

[17] Nakashima, Ellen. "Chinese hackers who breached Google gained access to sensitive data, U.S. officials say". WashingtonPost. Retrieved 5 December 2015.

[18] Riley, Michael; Dune Lawrence (26 July 2012). "Hackers Linked to China's Army Seen From EU to D.C.". Bloomberg. Retrieved 24 February 2013.

[19] Anderlini, Jamil (January 15, 2010). "The Chinese dissident's 'unknown visitors'". *Financial Times*.

[20] "Microsoft Security Advisory (979352)". Microsoft. 2010-01-21. Retrieved 26 January 2010.

[21] Naraine, Ryan. Microsoft knew of IE zero-day flaw since last September, ZDNet, January 21, 2010. Retrieved 28 January 2010.

[22] Protecting Your Critical Assets, Lessons Learned from "Operation Aurora", By McAfee Labs and McAfee Foundstone Professional Services

[23] "'Google' Hackers Had Ability to Alter Source Code". Retrieved 27 July 2016.

[24] Paul, Ryan (2010-01-14). "Researchers identify command servers behind Google attack". Ars Technica. Retrieved 17 January 2010.

[25] Shane, Scott; Lehren, Andrew W. (28 November 2010). "Cables Obtained by WikiLeaks Shine Light Into Secret Diplomatic Channels". *The New York Times*. Retrieved 28 November 2010.

[26] SCOTT SHANE and ANDREW W. LEHREN (November 28, 2010). "Leaked Cables Offer Raw Look at U.S. Diplomacy". *The New York Times*. Retrieved 2010-12-26. ...The Google hacking was part of a coordinated campaign of computer sabotage carried out by government operatives, private security experts and Internet outlaws recruited by the Chinese government. They have broken into American government computers and those of Western allies, the Dalai Lama and American businesses since 2002, ...

[27] US embassy cables leak sparks global diplomatic crisis *The Guardian* 28 November 2010

[28] Zetter, Kim (2010-01-14). "Google Hack Attack Was Ultra Sophisticated, New Details Show". Wired. Retrieved 23 January 2010.

[29] One News (19 January 2010). "France, Germany warn Internet Explorer users". TVNZ. Retrieved 22 January 2010.

[30] Relax News (18 January 2010). "Why you should change your internet browser and how to choose the best one for you". London: *The Independent*. Retrieved 22 January 2010.

[31] "Govt issues IE security warning". 19 January 2010. Retrieved 27 July 2016.

[32] NZ Herald Staff (19 January 2010). "France, Germany warn against Internet Explorer". *The New Zealand Herald*. Retrieved 22 January 2010.

[33] Govan, Fiona (18 January 2010). "Germany warns against using Microsoft Internet Explorer". London: *The Daily Telegraph*. Retrieved 22 January 2010.

[34] Mills, Elinor (14 January 2010). "New IE hole exploited in attacks on U.S. firms". CNET. Retrieved 22 January 2010.

[35] "Internet Explorer zero-day code goes public". Infosecurity. 18 January 2010. Retrieved 22 January 2010.

[36] "Security Labs - Security News and Views - Raytheon - Forcepoint". Retrieved 27 July 2016.

[37] Keizer, Gregg. "Hackers wield newest IE exploit in drive-by attacks". Retrieved 27 July 2016.

[38] "Security Labs - Security News and Views - Raytheon - Forcepoint". Retrieved 27 July 2016.

[39] Keizer, Gregg (19 January 2010). "Researchers up ante, create exploits for IE7, IE8". Computerworld. Retrieved 22 January 2010.

[40] "Security - ZDNet". Retrieved 27 July 2016.

[41] "Microsoft Security Bulletin MS10-002 - Critical". Retrieved 27 July 2016.

[42] "Hunting Down the Aurora Creator". TheNewNewInternet. 13 February 2010. Retrieved 13 February 2010.

[43] Markoff, John; Barboza, David (18 February 2010). "2 China Schools Said to Be Tied to Online Attacks". New York Times. Retrieved 26 March 2010.

[44] "Google Aurora Attack Originated From Chinese Schools". itproportal. 19 February 2010. Retrieved 19 February 2010.

[45] Sheridan, Michael, "Chinese City Is World's Hacker Hub", *London Sunday Times*, March 28, 2010.

[46] Etzioni, Amitai, "MAR: A Model for US-China Relations," The Diplomat, September 20, 2013, .

12.7   External links

- Forget Blaming Microsoft or Google – Blame Yourself AEON

- Google China insiders may have helped with attack news.cnet.com

- Operation Aurora – Beginning Of The Age of Ultra-Sophisticated Hack Attacks! Sporkings.com January 18, 2010

- In Google We Trust Why the company's standoff with China might change the future of the Internet. Rafal Rohozinski interviewed by Jessica Ramirez of Newsweek on 2010.1.29

- Recent Cyber Attacks – More than what meets the eye? Sporkings.com February 19, 2010

- 'Google' Hackers Had Ability to Alter Source Code Wired.com March 3, 2010

- 'Aurora' code circulated for years on English sites Where's the China connection?

- Google was brought down by Chinese hairdressers Curl up and dye westerners

- Gross, Michael Joseph, "Enter the Cyber-dragon", *Vanity Fair*, September 2011.

- Bodmer, Kilger, Carpenter, & Jones (2012). Reverse Deception: Organized Cyber Threat Counter-Exploitation. New York: McGraw-Hill Osborne Media. ISBN 0071772499, ISBN 978-0071772495

- The Operation Aurora Internet Explorer exploit - live!

- McAfee Operation Aurora Overview

- Operation Aurora Explained by CNET

Chapter 13

Aurora Generator Test

Not to be confused with Operation Aurora.

Idaho National Laboratory ran the **Aurora Generator**

The diesel generator used in the aurora experiment beginning to smoke.

Test in 2007 to demonstrate how a cyber attack could destroy physical components of the electric grid.[1] The experiment used a computer program to rapidly open and close a diesel generator's circuit breakers out of phase from the rest of the grid and cause it to explode. This vulnerability is referred to as the *Aurora Vulnerability*.

This vulnerability is especially a concern because much grid equipment supports using Modbus and other legacy communications protocols that were designed without security in mind. As such, they don't support authentication, confidentiality, or replay protection, which means any attacker that can communicate with the device can control it and use the Aurora Vulnerability to destroy it. This is a serious concern, as the failure of even a single generator could cause widespread outages and possibly cascading failure of the entire power grid, like what occurred in the Northeast blackout of 2003. Additionally, even if there are no outages from the removal of a single component (N-1 resilience), there is a large window for a second attack or failure, as it could take more than a year to replace it, because many generators and transformers are custom-built

for the substation.

The Aurora vulnerability can be mitigated by preventing the out-of-phase opening and closing of the breakers. Some suggested methods include adding functionality in protective relays to ensure synchronism and adding a time delay for closing breakers.[2]

13.1 Experiment

To prepare for the experiment, the researchers procured and installed a 2.25 MW generator and connected it to the substation. They also needed access to a programmable digital relay or another device that controls the breaker. That access could have been through a mechanical or digital interface.[3]

In the experiment, the researchers used a cyber attack to open and close the breakers out of sync, to maximize the stress. Each time the breakers were closed, the torque from the synchronization caused the generator to bounce and shake, eventually causing parts of the generator be to ripped apart and sent flying off.[4] Some parts of the generator landed as far as 80 feet away from the generator.[5]

The unit was destroyed in roughly three minutes. However, this was only because the researchers assessed the damage from each iteration of the attack. A real attack could have destroyed the unit much faster.[4]

The experiment was designated as unclassified, for official use only.[6] On September 27, 2007, CNN published an article based on the information and video DHS released to them,[1] and on July 3, 2014, DHS released many of the documents related to the experiment as part of an unrelated FOIA request.[7]

13.2 Vulnerability

The Aurora vulnerability is caused by the out-of-sync closing of the protective relays.[4]

"A close, but imperfect, analogy would be to imagine the effect of shifting a car into Reverse while it is being driven on a highway, or the effect of revving the engine up while the car is in neutral and then shifting it into Drive." [4]

"The Aurora attack is designed to open a circuit breaker, wait for the system or generator to slip out of synchronism, and reclose the breaker, all before the protection system recognizes and responds to the attack... Traditional generator protection elements typically actuate and block reclosing in about 15 cycles. Many variables affect this time, and every system needs to be analyzed to determine its specific vulnerability to the Aurora attack... Although the main focus of the Aurora attack is the potential 15-cycle window of opportunity immediately after the target breaker is opened, the overriding issue is how fast the generator moves away from system synchronism." [8]

13.3 Mitigations

The Aurora vulnerability is caused by the out-of-sync closing of the protective relays. As such, any mechanism that prevents the out-of-sync closing would mitigate the vulnerability.

One mitigation technique is to add a synchronism-check function to all protective relays that potentially connect two systems together. To implement this, the function must prevent the relay from closing unless the voltage and frequency are within a pre-set range. Additionally, the synchronism-check could monitor the rate of change of the frequency and prevent closing above a set rate.[2]

13.4 Criticisms

There was some discussion as to whether Aurora hardware mitigation devices (HMD) can cause other failures. In May 2011, Quanta Technology published an article that used RTDS (Real Time Digital Simulator) testing to examine the "performance of multiple commercial relay devices available" of Aurora HMDs. To quote: "The relays were subject to different test categories to find out if their performance is dependable when they need to operate, and secure in response to typical power system transients such as faults, power swing and load switching... In general, there were technical shortcomings in the protection scheme's design that were identified and documented using the real

time testing results. RTDS testing showed that there is, as yet, no single solution that can be widely applied to any case, and that can present the required reliability level." [9] A presentation from Quanta Technology and Dominion succinctly stated in their reliability assessment "HMDs are not dependable, nor secure." [10]

Joe Weiss, a cybersecurity and control system professional, disputed the findings from this report and claimed that it has misled utilities. He wrote: "This report has done a great deal of damage by implying that the Aurora mitigation devices will cause grid issues. Several utilities have used the Quanta report as a basis for not installing any Aurora mitigation devices. Unfortunately, the report has several very questionable assumptions. They include applying initial conditions that the hardware mitigation was not designed to address such as slower developing faults, or off nominal grid frequencies. Existing protection will address "slower" developing faults and off nominal grid frequencies (<59 Hz or >61 Hz). The Aurora hardware mitigation devices are for the very fast out-of-phase condition faults that are currently gaps in protection (i.e., not protected by any other device) of the grid." [11]

13.5 Timeline

On March 4, 2007, Idaho National Laboratory demonstrated the Aurora vulnerability.[12]

On June 21, 2007, NERC notified industry about the Aurora vulnerability.[13]

On September 27, 2007, CNN released a previously-classified demonstration video of the Aurora attack on their homepage.[1] That video can be downloaded at here.

On October 13, 2010, NERC released a recommendation to industry on the Aurora vulnerability.[13]

On July 3, 2014, the US Department of Homeland Security released 840 pages of documents related to Aurora.[7]

13.6 See also

- *Brittle Power*
- Electromagnetic pulse
- Energy security
- List of power outages
- New York City blackout of 1977
- Programmable logic controller

- Resilient control systems

- Vulnerability of nuclear plants to attack

- When Technology Fails

13.7 References

[1] "Mouse click could plunge city into darkness, experts say", *CNN*, September 27, 2007. Source: http://www.cnn.com/2007/US/09/27/power.at.risk/index.html

[2] "Myth or Reality – Does the Aurora Vulnerability Pose a Risk to My Generator?", Mark Zeller, Schweitzer Engineering Laboratories, Inc, https://www.selinc.com/WorkArea/DownloadAsset.aspx?id=8504

[3] FOIA response documents, page 91. Source: http://s3.documentcloud.org/documents/1212530/14f00304-documents.pdf

[4] FOIA response documents, page 59. Source: http://s3.documentcloud.org/documents/1212530/14f00304-documents.pdf

[5] International Spy Museum, Master Script, Source: http://www.spymuseum.org/files/resources/master-script_8_13_13.pdf

[6] FOIA response documents, page 134. Source: http://s3.documentcloud.org/documents/1212530/14f00304-documents.pdf

[7] FOIA Request - Operation Aurora. Source: https://www.muckrock.com/foi/united-states-of-america-10/operation-aurora-11765

[8] "Common Questions and Answers Addressing the Aurora Vulnerability", Mark Zeller, Schweitzer Engineering Laboratories, Inc, https://www.selinc.com/workarea/downloadasset.aspx?id=9487

[9] QT e-News, *Quanta Technology*, Volume 2, Issue 2, Spring 2011. Source: http://quanta-technology.com/sites/default/files/doc-files/2011-05-Spring-QT-News.pdf , page 3

[10] QT e-News, *Quanta Technology*, Aurora Vulnerability Issues & Solutions Hardware Mitigation Devices (HMDs), July 24, 2011. Source: https://www.smartgrid.gov/sites/default/files/doc/files/Aurora_Vulnerability_Issues_Solution_Hardware_Mitigation_De_201102.pdf

[11] "Latest Aurora information – this affects ANY electric utility customer with 3-phase rotating electric equipment!", *Unfettered Blog*, September 4, 2013. Source: http://www.controlglobal.com/blogs/unfettered/latest-aurora-information-this-affects-any-electric-utility-customer-with-3-phase-rotating-electric-equipment/

[12] "U.S. video shows hacker hit on power grid", *USA Today*, September 27, 2007, http://usatoday30.usatoday.com/tech/news/computersecurity/2007-09-27-hacker-video_N.htm

[13] NERC Press Release, *NERC Issues AURORA Alert to Industry*, October 14, 2010. Source: http://www.ect.coop/wp-content/uploads/2010/10/PR_AURORA_14_Oct_10.pdf

13.8 External links

- http://www.langner.com/en/2014/07/09/aurora-revisited-by-its-original-project-lead/

- http://www.powermag.com/what-you-need-to-know-and-dont-about-the-aurora-vulnerability/?printmode=1

- http://breakingenergy.com/2013/09/13/the-all-too-real-cyberthreat-nobody-is-prepared-for-aurora/

- http://www.computerworld.com/s/article/9039678/Simulated_attack_points_to_vulnerable_U.S._power_infrastructure

- http://www.computerworld.com/s/article/9249642/New_docs_show_DHS_was_more_worried_about_critical_infrastructure_flaw_in_07_than_it_let_on

- http://threatpost.com/dhs-releases-hundreds-of-documents-on-wrong-aurora-project

- http://news.infracritical.com/pipermail/scadasec/2014-July/thread.html

- http://www.thepresidency.org.70-32-102-141.pr6m-p7xj.accessdomain.com/sites/default/files/Grid%20Report%20July%2015%20First%20Edition.pdf (Page 30)

- http://www.chinadaily.com.cn/world/2007-09-27/content_6139437.htm

- http://www.infosecisland.com/blogview/20925-Misconceptions-about-Aurora-Why-Isnt-More-Being-Done.html

- https://www.sce.com/wps/wcm/connect/c5fe765f-f66b-4d37-8e9f-7911fd6e7f3b/AURORACustomerOutreach.pdf?MOD=AJPERES

Chapter 14

2016 Bangladesh Bank heist

The Federal Reserve Bank of New York

In February 2016, instructions to steal US$951 million from Bangladesh Bank, the central bank of Bangladesh, were issued via the SWIFT network. Five transactions issued by hackers, worth $101 million and withdrawn from a Bangladesh Bank account at the Federal Reserve Bank of New York, succeeded, with $20 million traced to Sri Lanka (since recovered) and $81 million to the Philippines (about $18 million recovered).*[1] The Federal Reserve Bank of NY blocked the remaining thirty transactions, amounting to $850 million, at the request of Bangladesh Bank.*[2]

14.1   Background

The 2016 cyber-attack on the Bangladesh Central bank was not the first attack of its kind. In this cyber heist, thieves tried to illegally transfer US$951 million to several fictitious bank accounts around the world. In 2013, the Sonali Bank of Bangladesh was also successfully targeted by hackers who were able to cart away US$250,000. In 2015, two

other hacking attempts were recorded, a $12 million theft from Banco del Austro in Ecuador in January and an attack on Vietnam's Tien Phong Bank in December that was not successful. In all these cases, the perpetrators are suspected to have been aided by insiders within the targeted banks, who assisted in taking advantage of weaknesses within the SWIFT global payment network.*[3]*[4]

In 2012, the Philippines loosened restrictions on its gambling industry despite opposition from the Catholic Church. After the country's gambling industry benefited from Chinese paramount leader Xi Jinping's campaign against corruption, which drove gamblers further south of Macau,*[5] its casinos lobbied against a 2012 amendment by the Philippine Senate of the 2001 Anti-Money Laundering Act that required them to report suspicious transactions. Senate President Juan Ponce Enrile had lobbied for the inclusion of casinos in the scope of the law. At that time, big casino firms in the Philippines such as the City of Dreams had not yet been established.*[6]

14.2   Events

Capitalizing on weaknesses in the security of the Bangladesh Central Bank, including the possible involvement of some of its employees,*[7] perpetrators attempted to steal $951 million from the Bangladesh central bank's account with the Federal Reserve Bank of New York sometime between February 4–5 when Bangladesh Bank's offices were closed. The perpetrators managed to compromise Bangladesh Bank's computer network, observe how transfers are done, and gain access to the bank's credentials for payment transfers. They used these credentials to authorise about three dozen requests to the Federal Reserve Bank of New York to transfer funds from the account Bangladesh Bank held there to accounts in Sri Lanka and the Philippines.

Thirty transactions worth $851 million were flagged by the banking system for staff review, but five requests were granted; $20 million to Sri Lanka (later recovered*[8]*[9]), and $81 million lost to the Philippines, entering the Southeast Asian country's banking system on February 5, 2016. This money was laundered through casinos and some later transferred to Hong Kong.

14.2.1 Attempted fund diversion to Sri Lanka

The $20 million transfer to Sri Lanka was intended by hackers to be sent to the Shalika Foundation, a Sri Lanka-based private limited company. The hackers misspelled "Foundation" in their request to transfer the funds, spelling the word as "Fundation" . This spelling error gained suspicion from Deutsche Bank, a routing bank which put a halt to the transaction in question after seeking clarifications from Bangladesh Bank.*[8]*[10]*[11]

Sri Lanka-based Pan Asia Bank initially took notice of the transaction, with one official noting the transaction as too big for a country like Sri Lanka. Pan Asia Bank was the one which referred the anomalous transaction to Deutsche Bank. The Sri Lankan funds have been recovered by Bangladesh Bank.*[8]

14.2.2 Funds diverted to the Philippines

The money transferred to the Philippines was deposited in five separate accounts with the Rizal Commercial Banking Corporation (RCBC); the accounts were later found to be under fictitious identities. The funds were then transferred to a foreign exchange broker to be converted to Philippine pesos, returned to the RCBC and consolidated in an account of a Chinese-Filipino businessman;*[6]*[9] the conversion was made from February 5 to 13, 2016.*[12] It was also found that the four U.S. dollar accounts involved were opened at the RCBC as early as May 15, 2015, remaining untouched until February 4, 2016, the date the transfer from the Federal Reserve Bank of New York was made.*[12]

In February 8, 2016, during the Chinese New Year, Bangladesh Bank through SWIFT informed RCBC to stop the payment, refund the funds, and to "freeze and put the funds on hold" if the funds had already been transferred. Chinese New Year is a non-working holiday in the Philippines and a SWIFT message from Bangladesh Bank containing similar information was received by RCBC only a day later. By this time, a withdrawal amounting to about $58.15 million had already been processed by RCBC's Jupiter Street (in Makati City) branch.*[12]

On February 16, the Governor of Bangladesh Bank requested Bangko Sentral ng Pilipinas' assistance in the recovery of its $81 million funds, saying that the SWIFT payment

instructions issued in favor of RCBC on February 4, 2016 were fraudulent.*[12]

14.3 Investigation

14.3.1 Bangladesh

Initially, Bangladesh Bank was uncertain if its system had been compromised. The governor of the central bank engaged World Informatix Cyber Security, a US based firm, to lead the security incident response, vulnerability assessment and remediation. World Informatix Cyber Security brought in the leading forensic investigation company Mandiant, a FireEye company, for the investigation. These cyber security experts found "footprints" and malware of hackers, which suggested that the system had been breached. The investigators also said that the hackers were based outside Bangladesh. An internal investigation has been launched by Bangladesh Bank regarding the case.*[8]

The Bangladesh Bank's forensic investigation found out that malware was installed within the bank's system sometime in January 2016, and gathered information on the bank's operational procedures for international payments and fund transfers.*[12]

The investigation also looked into an unsolved 2013 hacking incident at the Sonali Bank, wherein US$250,000 was stolen by still unidentified hackers. According to reports, just as in the 2016 Central Bank hack, the theft also used fraudulent fund transfers using the Swift International Payment Network. The incident was treated by Bangladeshi police authorities as a cold-case until the suspiciously similar 2016 Bangladesh Central Bank heist.*[13]

14.3.2 Philippines

The Philippines' National Bureau of Investigation (NBI) launched a probe and looked into a Chinese-Filipino who allegedly played a key role in the money laundering of the illicit funds. The NBI is coordinating with relevant government agencies including the country's Anti-Money Laundering Council (AMLC). The AMLC started its investigation on February 19, 2016 of bank accounts linked to a junket operator.*[12] AMLC has filed a money laundering complaint before the Department of Justice against a RCBC branch manager and five unknown persons with fictitious names in connection with the case.*[14]

A Philippine Senate hearing was held on March 15, 2016, led by Senator Teofisto Guingona III, head of the Blue Ribbon Committee and Congressional Oversight Committee on the Anti-Money Laundering Act.*[15] A closed-door hearing was later held on March 17.*[16] Philippine Amusement and Gaming Corporation (PAGCOR) has also launched its own investigation.*[8] In August 12, 2016, RCBC was reported to have paid half of the P1 billion penalty imposed by the Central Bank of the Philippines.*[17] Prior to that, the bank reorganized its board of directors by increasing the number of independent directors to 7 from the previous 4.*[18]

14.3.3   United States

FireEye's Mandiant forensics division and World Informatix Cyber Security, both US-based companies, are investigating the hacking case. According to investigators, the perpetrators' familiarity with the internal procedures of Bangladesh Bank was probably gained by spying on its workers. In a separate report, the US Federal Bureau of Investigation (FBI) says that Agents have found evidence pointing to at least one bank employee acting as an accomplice, with evidence pointing to several more people as possibly assisting hackers in navigate the Bangladesh Bank's computer system.*[19] The government of Bangladesh is considering suing the Federal Reserve Bank of New York in a bid to recover the stolen funds.*[8]

14.3.4   Other attacks

Computer security researchers have linked the theft to as many as eleven other attacks, and alleged that North Korea had a role in the attacks, which, if true, would be the first known incident of a state actor using cyberattacks to steal funds.*[20]*[21]

14.4   Response from linked organizations

The Rizal Commercial Banking Corporation said it did not tolerate the illicit activity in the RCBC branch involved in the case. Lorenzo V. Tan, RCBC's president, said that the bank cooperated with the Anti-Money Laundering Council and the Bangko Sentral ng Pilipinas regarding the matter.*[22] Tan's legal counsel has asked the RCBC Jupiter Street branch manager to explain the alleged fake bank account that was used in the money laundering scam.*[23]

The RCBC's board committee also launched a separate probe into the bank's involvement in the money laundering scam. RCBC president Lorenzo V. Tan filed an indefinite leave of absence to give way to the investigation by the authorities on the case.*[24]*[25] On May 6, 2016, despite being cleared of any wrongdoing by the bank's internal in-

Atiur Rahman, Governor of Bangladesh Bank who resigned from his post in response to the case.

vestigation, Tan resigned as President of RCBC to "take full moral responsibility" for the incident.*[26]*[27] Helen Yuchengco-Dee, daughter of RCBC founder Alfonso Yuchengco, will take over the bank's operations. The bank also apologized to the public for its involvement in the heist.

Bangladesh Bank chief governor Atiur Rahman resigned from his post amid the current investigation of the heist and money laundering. He submitted his resignation letter to Prime Minister Sheikh Hasina on March 15, 2016. Before the resignation was made public, Rahman stated that he would resign for the sake of his country.*[28]

On August 5, 2016, the Bangko Sentral ng Pilipinas approved a P1 billion (~US$52.92 million) fine against RCBC for its non-compliance with banking laws and regulations in connection with the bank heist. This is the largest monetary fine ever approved by BSP against any institution. RCBC stated that the bank will comply with the BSP's decision, and will pay the imposed fine.*[29]

14.5   Ramifications

The incident shows the risks that banks connected to the SWIFT system are exposed to as a result of the security vulnerabilities of other member banks. By breaching the Bangladesh Central Bank's security firewalls, hackers were able to hack the system and transfer the funds through the established global banking networks almost undetected. The failure of the Bangladeshi government to build adequate safeguards for its financial system became the starting point for a global, multi-million money laundering scheme whose effect was felt beyond the country's borders.

The case threatens the reinstatement of the Philippines to the blacklist, by the Financial Action Task Force on Money Laundering, of countries making insufficient efforts against money laundering.*[30] Attention was given to a potential weakness of Philippine authorities' efforts against money laundering after lawmakers in 2012 managed to exclude casinos from the roster of organizations required to report to the Anti-Money Laundering Council regarding suspicious transactions.

The case also highlights the threat of cyber attacks to both government and private institutions by cyber criminals using real bank codes to make orders look genuine. SWIFT has advised banks using the SWIFT Alliance Access system to strengthen their cyber security posture and ensure they are following SWIFT security guidelines. Bangladesh is reportedly the 20th most cyber-attacked country, according to a cyber threat map developed by Kaspersky Lab, which runs in real time.*[31]

14.6 References

[1] Cabalza, Dexter. "Ex-RCBC branch manager free on bail" .

[2] Schram, Jamie (22 March 2016). "Congresswoman wants probe of 'brazen' $81M theft from New York Fed" .

[3] Das, Krishna; Paul, Ruma (25 May 2016). "Exclusive: Bangladesh probes 2013 hack for links to central bank heist" . *Reuters*. Retrieved 26 August 2016.

[4] "Bangladesh probes 2013 hack for links to Swift-linked central bank heist" . *Reuters*. 25 May 2016. Retrieved 26 August 2016.

[5] Alcuaz, Coco (10 March 2016). "Philippine Bank Claims Innocence In Bangladesh-Federal Reserve Money Laundering Controversy" . International Business Times. Retrieved 11 March 2016.

[6] Ager, Maila (3 March 2016). "Senate to probe $100-M laundering via PH, says Osmeña". Philippine Daily Inquirer. Retrieved 11 March 2016.

[7] "Swift rejects Bangladesh Central Bank claims" .

[8] Quadir, Serajul (11 March 2016). "Spelling mistake stops hackers stealing $1 billion in Bangladesh bank heist" . The Independent. Retrieved 13 March 2016.

[9] Byron, Rejaul Karim (10 March 2016). "Hackers' bid to steal $870m more from Bangladesh central bank foiled" . *Asia News Network*. The Daily Star. Retrieved 11 March 2016.

[10] "Sri Lankan in Bangladesh cyber heist says she was set up by friend" . 31 March 2016 – via Reuters.

[11] "Story behind Shalika Foundation - Ceylontoday.lk" .

[12] Byron, Rejaul Karim; Rahman, Md Fazlur (11 March 2016). "Hackers bugged Bangladesh Bank system in Jan" . *Asia News Network*. The Daily Star. Retrieved 13 March 2016.

[13] "Bangladesh probes 2013 hacking incident for connections to 2016 heist" .

[14] "RCBC manager, others face anti-money laundering complaint" . *Rappler*. March 5, 2016. Retrieved March 5, 2016.

[15] Pasion, Patty (15 March 2016). "RCBC manager invokes right vs self-incrimination at Senate probe" . *Rappler*. Retrieved 20 March 2016.

[16] Yap, Cecilia; Calonzo, Andreo (17 March 2016). "Printer error foiled billion-dollar bank heist" . *Sydney Morning Herald*. Retrieved 20 March 2016.

[17] Rada, Julito. "RCBC pays half of P1-b penalty" .

[18] Rappler.com. "RCBC reorganizes board after Bangladesh Bank heist scandal" .

[19] "FBI suspects inside job in Bangladesh bank heist" .

[20] Shen, Lucinda (27 May 2016). "North Korea Has Been Linked to the SWIFT Bank Hacks" . *Fortune*. Retrieved 28 May 2016.

[21] Perlroth, Nicole; Corkery, Michael (26 May 2016). "North Korea Linked to Digital Attacks on Global Banks" . *New York Times*. Retrieved 28 May 2016.

[22] Agcaoili, Lawrence (10 March 2016). "RCBC denies alleged money laundering" . The Philippine Star. Retrieved 11 March 2016.

[23] "Explain 'fake account,' RCBC chief tells branch manager" . *ABS-CBN News*. March 13, 2016. Retrieved March 13, 2016.

[24] Dumlao-Abadilla, Doris (March 23, 2016). "RCBC chief goes on leave amid $81M dirty money probe" . *Philippine Daily Inquirer*. Retrieved March 24, 2016.

[25] Agcaoili, Lawrence (March 23, 2016). "RCBC president goes on leave" . *The Philippine Star*. Retrieved March 24, 2016.

[26] "RCBC Prexy resigns after board clears him of wrongdoing" .

[27] "Tan cleared of wrong doing, resigns to take full moral responsibility" .

[28] "Bangladesh central bank governor quits over $81m heist"
. *The Daily Star/Asia News Network*. March 15, 2016. Retrieved May 11, 2016.

[29] http://www.gmanetwork.com/news/
story/576498/money/companies/
bangko-sentral-slaps-p1-b-fine-on-rcbc-for-stolen-bangladesh-bank-fund

[30] Remitio, Rex (3 March 2016). "Sen. Osmeña: PH may
suffer if money laundering is proven". CNN Philippines.
Retrieved 11 March 2016.

[31] Tweed, David; Devnath, Arun (10 March 2016). "$1 Bil-
lion Plot to Rob Fed Accounts Leads to Manila Casinos".
Bloomberg. Retrieved 11 March 2016.

Chapter 15

2010 cyberattacks on Myanmar

The **2010 cyberattacks on Burma (Myanmar)** were distributed denial-of-service attacks (DDoS) that began on 25 October,[1] occurring ahead of the Burmese general election, 2010, which is widely viewed as a sham election.[2][3] This election was the first that Burma had had in 20 years.[4] The attacks were significantly larger than attacks against Estonia and Georgia in 2007 and 2008 respectively.[5] The attack followed a similar one on 1 February 2010,[6] and also followed an incident of a total loss of connection to the internet the previous spring when a submarine communications cable was severed accidentally.[7]

15.1 Attacks beginning 25 October 2010

Over the period of a week, a large-scale massive DDoS attack targeted Burma's main Internet provider, the Ministry of Post and Telecommunication. Successful attacks to this network interfered with the majority of all incoming and outgoing network traffic.

The motivation for the attacks, and hence the culprits, were unclear, but there was significant speculation that blamed the Burmese government for a pre-emptive attack to disrupt Internet access just before the general elections. The ruling military junta, the State Peace and Development Council (SPDC), was known for denying universal human rights such as freedom expression; the government's efforts to silence dissent are extended to cyberspace, and it has one of the most restrictive systems of Internet control in Asia.[8] The fact that international observers and foreign journalists were not being allowed into the country to cover the polls raised suspicions that Burma's military authorities could have been trying to restrict the flow of information over the election period.[5]

15.2 Technical details

A DDoS attack attempts to flood an information gateway with data exceeding its bandwidth. The "distributed" element of a Distributed Denial of Service means that it involves PCs spread all over the world. These enslaved computers, called "botnets," are usually home computers that have been hijacked and compromised by a virus. Botnets are usually rented out by cyber criminals for various purposes, which includes web attacks. They can be controlled from across the internet.[5] The size of the October–November 2010 attacks increased daily from 0.5 to 10-15 Gbit/s, each daily attack lasting over eight hours (always during regular office hours), from computers across the globe. This was several hundred times more than enough to overwhelm the country's 45 Mbit/s T3 terrestrial and satellite links.[9] Attacks on blogging websites in September were also on the order of Gbit/s.[10]

By comparison, the 2007 cyberattacks on Estonia were at most 90 Mbit/s, lasting between a minute to over 10 hours.[11]

15.3 Cyberattacks in Burma prior to the 2010 election

This cyber attack notably followed a similar one on 1 February 2010, when the internet link service of Myanmar's Yatanarpon Teleport Company was struck,[6] and also followed the incident of a total loss of connection to the internet the previous spring when a submarine communications cable was severed accidentally.[7]

Despite the heavy hand that the regime wields over cyberspace, information communication technologies (ICTs) have provided Burmese opposition groups the means to challenge the government by broadcasting their message to the world. There has been an ongoing battle between the liberation technologies and the authoritarian government. In 2000, Burmese political activists received numerous emails that contained viruses, which many believe were part of an organised campaign perpetrated by state agents.[8] The first major example of a DDoS attack in Burma was in 2007, during the Saffron Revolution when Burmese activists managed to put videos and pictures of the demonstrations and government crackdown on the internet, at which time the government severed the internet connection for almost two weeks.[8]

Near the one-year anniversary of the Saffron Revolution, the websites of three main Burmese independent media organisations were attacked and effectively silenced. The Democratic Voice of Burma and The Irrawaddy were made inaccessible through a DDoS attack, and the website for Mizzima News was defaced. Through 2009 and 2010, attacks on Burmese opposition media sites continued periodically.[8] The timing of these attacks and the nature of the websites being attacked indicate a political connection. Although the identity of the attackers remain unknown, it is widely believed that the government played a role. This belief is still held, because the Burmese government has consistently made efforts to control and censor the communications environment of the country. Also, the timing and co-ordination of these attacks being around the anniversary of the Saffron Revolution suggests that the motivation of them was to prevent the websites from commemorating the protests and possibly mobilising new political actions.[8]

In September 2010, coinciding with the third anniversary of the Saffron Revolution,[12] the websites belonging to independent and opposition news sites and blogs were brought down by DDoS attacks similar to, but less powerful than, the ones that took place prior to the election.[10] On 27 September 2010, DDoS was used specifically against two news websites in Burma: the Democratic Voice of Burma and The Irrawaddy Magazine. Both of these magazines were providers of independent coverage of current affairs in Burma. These attacks were believed to originate from the Burmese government, and with the election a month away, media workers feared that this attack was a test run leading up to the election. In 2009, Burma ranked 171 out of 175 countries in the Reporters Without Borders (RSF) Press Freedom Index.[13]

15.4   See also

- Internet in Burma

15.5   References

[1] "Internet out hits tourism sector" . Myanmar Times. 1 November 2010. Archived from the original on 5 November 2010. Retrieved 4 November 2010.

[2] Clegg, Nick (3 October 2010). "Myanmar's Sham Election" . The New York Times. Retrieved 4 November 2010.

[3] "Protesters in Japan decry Myanmar 'sham election' plan" . Channel News Asia. 27 October 2010. Retrieved 4 November 2010.

[4] Sutherland, J.J. (4 November 2010). "Myanmar's Internet Under Cyberattack" . NPR. Retrieved 30 October 2014.

[5] "Burma hit by massive net attack ahead of election" . BBC News. 4 November 2010. Archived from the original on 5 November 2010. Retrieved 4 November 2010.

[6] Feng, Yingqiu (3 November 2010). "Myanmar Internet link continues to meet with interruption" . People's Daily. Archived from the original on 6 November 2010. Retrieved 8 November 2010.

[7] Seltzer, Larry (11 April 2010). "DDoS Attack on Myanmar Takes the Country Offline" . PC Magazine. Archived from the original on 7 November 2010. Retrieved 8 November 2010.

[8] Sample, Charmaine; Nart Villeneuve; Masashi Crete-Nishihata (April 2013). "8" . Culture and Computer Network Attack Behaviors (PDF). pp. 153–176. Retrieved 1 November 2014.

[9] Labovitz, Craig (3 November 2010). "Attack Severs Burma Internet" . Arbor Networks. Retrieved 4 November 2010.

[10] Wade, Francis (29 September 2010). "Scale of cyber attacks 'rare and serious'". Democratic Voice of Burma. Retrieved 13 February 2013.

[11] Nazario, Jose (29 September 2010). "Estonian DDoS Attacks - A summary to date" . Arbor Networks. Retrieved 13 February 2013.

[12] Nizza, Mike (28 September 2007). "Burmese Government Clamps Down on Internet" . The New York Times. Retrieved 13 February 2013.

[13] "Stop Cyber Attacks Against Independent Burmese Media" . Reporters Without Borders. 5 October 2010. Retrieved 28 October 2014.

Chapter 16

Cellphone surveillance

Cellphone surveillance, also known as **cellphone spying**, may involve the tracking, bugging, monitoring, interception and recording of conversations and text messages on mobile phones.[1] It also encompasses the monitoring of people's movements, which can be tracked using mobile phone signals when phones are turned on.[2] In the United States, law enforcement agencies can legally monitor the movements of people from their mobile phone signals upon obtaining a court order to do so.[2] Cellphone spying software is software that is surreptitiously installed on mobile phones that can enable these actions.

16.1   Mobile phone tracking

Main article: Mobile phone tracking

StingRay devices are used by law enforcement agencies to track people's movements, and intercept and record conversations, names, phone numbers and text messages from mobile phones.[1] Their use entails the monitoring and collection of data from all mobile phones within a target area.[1] Law enforcement agencies in Northern California that have purchased StingRay devices include the Oakland Police Department, San Francisco Police Department, Sacramento County Sheriff's Department, San Jose Police Department and the Fremont Police Department.[1] The Fremont Police Department's use of a StingRay device is in a partnership with the Oakland Police Department and the Alameda County District Attorney's Office.[1]

In 2007, StingRay devices assisted the Oakland Police Department in Oakland, California in making 21 arrests, and in 2008, 19 arrests were made in unison with the use of StingRay devices.[1]

StingRay devices are often used in combination with Hailstorm towers that jam the mobile phone signals forcing phones to drop down from 4G and 3G network bands to older, more insecure 2G bands.[3]

In most states, police can get many kinds of cellphone data without obtaining a warrant. Law-enforcement records show, police can use initial data from a tower dump to ask for another court order for more information, including addresses, billing records and logs of calls, texts and locations.[4]

16.2   Hidden cellphones

16.2.1   Bugging

Cellphone bugs can be created by disabling the ringing feature on a mobile phone, allowing a caller to call a phone to access its microphone and listen in. Intentionally hiding a cell phone in a location is a bugging technique. Some hidden cellphone bugs rely on Wifi hotspots, rather than celluar data, where the tracker rootkit software periodically "wakes up" and signs into a public wifi hotspot to upload tracker data onto a public internet server. In the United States, the FBI has used "roving bugs", which entails the activation of microphones on mobile phones to enable the monitoring of conversations.[5]

16.3   Cellphone spying software

Cellphone spying software is a type of cellphone bugging, tracking, and monitoring software that is surreptitiously installed on mobile phones. This software can enable conversations to be heard and recorded from phones upon which it is installed.[6] Cellphone spying software can be downloaded onto cellphones.[7] Cellphone spying software enables the monitoring or stalking of a target cellphone from a remote location with some of the following techniques:[8]

- Allowing remote observation of the target cellphone position in real-time on a map

- Remotely enabling microphones to capture and forward conversations. Microphones can be activated during a call or when the phone is on standby for capturing conversations near the cellphone.

- Receiving remote alerts and/or text messages each time somebody dials a number on the cellphone

- Remotely reading text messages and call logs

Cellphone spying software can enable microphones on mobile phones when phones are not being used, and can be installed by mobile providers.[*][5]

16.4   Occurrences

In 2005, the prime minister of Greece was advised that his, over 100 dignitaries' and the mayor of Athens' mobile phones were bugged.[*][6] Costas Tsalikidis, a Vodafone-Panafon employee, was implicated in the matter as using his position as head of the company's network planning to assist in the bugging.[*][6] Tsalikidis was found hanged in his apartment the day before the leaders were notified regarding the bugging, which was reported as "an apparent suicide." [*][6]

16.5   Detection

Some indications of possible cellphone surveillance occurring may include a mobile phone waking up unexpectedly, using a lot of the CPU when on idle or when not in use, hearing clicking or beeping sounds when conversations are occurring and the circuit board of the phone being warm despite the phone not being used.[*][7]

16.6   Prevention

Preventative measures against cellphone surveillance include not losing or allowing strangers to use a mobile phone and the utilization of an access password.[*][7][*][8] Turning off and then also removing the battery from a phone when not in use is another technique.[*][7][*][8] Jamming or a Faraday cage may also work, the latter obviating removal of the battery.

Disconnecting the microphone from the circuit board (or smashing the mic with a needle and hammer), and then using an external plug-in or bluetooth mic when you want to make calls, is a solution.

Another solution is turning the MIC input to the DAC off. However, this requires operating system and in some cases, kernel modification in order to prevent MIC input.

16.7   See also

- Cellphone jammer

- Cyber stalking

- Voice activated recorders

- Carrier IQ

- Telephone tapping

16.8   References

[1] Bott, Michael; Jensen, Thom (March 6, 2014). "9 Calif. law enforcement agencies connected to cellphone spying technology". ABC News, News10. Retrieved 26 March 2014.

[2] Richtel, Matt (December 10, 2005). "Live Tracking of Mobile Phones Prompts Court Fights on Privacy" (PDF). *The New York Times*. Retrieved 26 March 2014.

[3] Mysterious Fake Cellphone Towers Are Intercepting Calls All Over The US, Business Insider, Jack Dutton, Sep 3, 2014

[4] John Kelly (13 June 2014). "Cellphone data spying: It's not just the NSA". *USA today*.

[5] McCullagh, Declan; Broache, Anne (December 1, 2006). "FBI taps cell phone mic as eavesdropping tool". CNET. Retrieved 26 March 2014.

[6] V., Prevelakis; D., Spinellis (July 2007). "The Athens Affair". *Volume:44, Issue: 7*. Spectrum, IEEE. pp. 26–33. Retrieved 26 March 2014. (subscription required)

[7] Segall, Bob (Posted: November 13, 2008, Updated: June 29, 2009). "Tapping your cell phone". WTHR13 News (NBC). Retrieved 26 March 2014. Check date values in: |date= (help)

[8] News report. WTHR News. (YouTube video)

16.9   Further reading

- Sabalow, Ryan; Cook, Tony (December 18, 2013). "Gov. Mike Pence supports limited use of cellphone surveillance device". *The Indianapolis Star*. Retrieved 26 March 2014.

- Fletcher, Lisa; Kazdin, Cole (March 8, 2010). "Cell Phone Spying Nightmare: 'You're Never the Same'". ABC News. Retrieved 26 March 2014.

- Wheeler, Brian (March 2, 2004). "'This goes no further...'". BBC News. Retrieved 26 March 2014.

- Alba, Davey (April 5, 2012). "Look Who's Stalking: The 10 Creepiest Apps For Phones, Facebook, and More". Gizmodo. Retrieved 26 March 2014.

- "News report". KGW News, NBC. (Youtube video). Retrieved 26 March 2014.

- Bott, Michael; Jensen, Thom (March 7, 2014). "Cellphone spying technology being used throughout Northern California". ABC News, News10. Retrieved 26 March 2014.

- Stafford, Rob (June 16, 2007). "Tracing a stalker". *Dateline NBC*. Retrieved 26 March 2014.

- "Is your cell phone spying on you?". Fox News. January 14, 2014. Retrieved 26 March 2014.

- Law Enforcement Disclosure Report 2014 Vodafone

Chapter 17

Commission on Elections data breach

On March 27, 2016, hackers under the banner, Anonymous Philippines hacked into the website of the Philippine Commission on Elections (COMELEC) and defaced it. The hackers left a message calling for tighter security measures on the vote counting machines (VCM) to be used during the 2016 Philippine general election in May 9.[*][1] Within the day a separate group of hackers, LulzSec Pilipinas posted an online link to the what it claims to be the entire database of COMELEC and updated the post to include three mirror link to the index of the database's downloadable files.[*][2] The leaked files by LulzSec Pilipinas amounts to 340 gigabytes.[*][3]

The COMELEC website returned to normal at 03:15 (PST) on 28 March 2016. COMELEC spokesperson, James Jimenez, stated on his Twitter account that, as they continue to scour the site, all databases would remain temporarily off.[*][4]

The incident was considered the biggest private leak data in the Philippine history and leaving millions of registered voters at risk.[*][5][*][6]

55 million registered voters are at risk due to the data breach according to security firm, Trend Micro potentially surpassing the Office of Personnel Management data breach which affected 20 million people.[*][7]

A searchable website, called *wehaveyourdata*, was set up containing sensitive data on Filipino registered voters was set up as early as April 21. The website was taken down with the assistance of the U.S. Department of Justice since the domain of the website was bought from a US-based web hosting company. The website itself was found to be hosted in Russia.[*][8]

17.1 Extent of the breach

Trend Micro conducted its own investigation on the extent of the data breach. It found that 1.3 million records of Overseas Filipino voters, which included passport numbers and expiry dates were included in the data dumps by the hack-

ers. The security firm found the breach as "alarming" since it said that the data are easily accessible to the public were in plain text. It also added that 15.8 million record of fingerprints along with a list of people who have run for office since the 2010 elections were found by the firm's investigation.[*][3]

The firm also found files concerning candidates running in the election with the filename "VOTESOBTAINED" which the firm infers to reflect the number of votes received by the particular candidates. It said that the figures of the "VOTESOBTAINED" files were set to NULL at the time Trend Micro conducted its investigation.[*][3]

The Commission on Elections chairman, Andres Bautista said that he was told that no confidential information was leaked, saying the breach would not affect the election body's preparation for the 2016 elections.[*][3] The commission also emphasized that the database on its website is accessible to the public and no sensitive information is hosted on the website. It said that the results website that the election body is planning will be hosted in a different website with a different and better set of security measures.[*][9] It further added that the database might be fake saying that no biometrics date were compromised by the hackers as opposed to Trend Micro's findings. COMELEC also noted that Trend Micro accessed the dumped data by hackers on its investigation and said that it has no capability of validating the data since it had no access to its original database.[*][10]

17.2 Perpetrators

On April 12, COMELEC announced that the National Bureau of Investigation have a "very good lead" regarding the hackers behind the breach. The perpetrators are to be charged of violations of the Cybercrime Prevention Act.[*][11]

On 20 April, the National Bureau of Investigation (NBI) apprehended one of the suspected hackers, later identified as Paul Biteng,[*][12] the 20-year-old IT graduate student, in his home in Sampaloc, Manila. The authorities took three weeks in order to track down the hacker.[*][13] The NBI confiscated Biteng's desktop computer, he used for hacking, for forensic examination.[*][14] Biteng, who is a member of the hacking group *Anonymous Philippines*, admitted that he defaced the COMELEC website, but denied the contribution in data leak.[*][15][*][16] He also admitted that the hacking was intended to show how vulnerability of the COMELEC website is.[*][17] Possible cases against him include a violation of the Cybercrime Prevention Act of 2012.[*][15]

About eight days later, a second hacker, named Joenel de Asis —also a 23-year-old Computer Science graduate, apprehended by NBI at his house in Muntinlupa.[*][18] In a press conference held on April 29, COMELEC chairperson Andres D. Bautista identified de Asis as one of the ringleaders of the notorious hacker group, *Lulzsec Pilipinas*.[*][19][*][20] Bautista said that de Asis admitted hacking the website and leaking the Comelec database.[*][20] He also admitted that he collaborated with Biteng in the hacking incident. Biteng breached the server of the Comelec website, while De Asis downloaded the 340 gigabyte voter database five days before the website was defaced on March 27. [*][21] While De Asis leaked the data though the Lulzsec Pilipinas website, he denied that their group created the website, *wehaveyourdata*.[*][22][*][23] He assured that the data leak will not affect the upcoming elections as they did not hack Vote Counting Machines (VCMs) since it is connected to a different server.[*][24][*][22]

The third hacker, which is yet to be identified, is still at large.

17.3 Measures

On April 21, COMELEC announced that they will be making consultations with Microsoft and other cybersecurity experts based in the United Kingdom, Singapore and the United States. A technical working group tasked to look on the issue of hacking was also formed which is to be led by Director James Jimenez of the Comelec Information and Education Department.[*][25] The website will be transferred to the Department of Science and Technology's server.

17.4 See also

- Office of Personnel Management data breach

- Democratic National Committee cyber attacks

17.5 References

[1] "Massive data breach exposes all Philippines voters". Telecom Asia. 12 April 2016. Retrieved 21 April 2016.

[2] Bueza, Michael; Manuel, Wayne (2 April 2016). "Experts fear identity theft, scams due to Comelec leak". Rappler. Retrieved 21 April 2016.

[3] Malig, Jojo (7 April 2016). "Comelec hacking threatens security of voters: Trend Micro". ABS-CBN News. Retrieved 21 April 2016.

[4] "Comelec website back to normal after hacking". *GMA News*. 28 March 2016. Retrieved 29 March 2016.

[5] "Experts fear identity theft, scams due to Comelec leak". 1 April 2016. Retrieved 21 April 2016.

[6] "'COMELEAKS' Lawmakers: Voter database breach compromises May 9 elections; PNP joins probe". *Interaksyon*. 22 April 2016. Retrieved 22 April 2016.

[7] Kennedy, John (11 April 2016). "Every one of the Philippines' 55m voters could be in danger of fraud". Silicon Republic. Retrieved 21 April 2016.

[8] "Searchable website with hacked data taken down – Comelec". CNN Philippines. 22 April 2016. Retrieved 22 April 2016.

[9] Santos, Tina (29 March 2016). "Comelec shrugs off hacking". Philippine Daily Inquirer. Retrieved 21 April 2016.

[10] Gotinga, JC (12 April 2016). "Comelec: No biometrics in leaked data". CNN Philippines. Retrieved 21 April 2016.

[11] Santos, Tina (12 April 2016). "NBI finds lead on hackers who defaced Comelec website". Philippine Daily Inquirer. Retrieved 21 April 2016.

[12] "NBI releases suspected Comelec hacker's mugshot". 21 April 2016. Retrieved 21 April 2016.

[13] Cimpanu, Catalin (22 April 2016). "Anonymous Member Arrested for the COMELEC Hack". *Softpedia*. Retrieved 23 April 2016.

[14] "Comelec hacker arrested, asks NBI chief for a selfie". *Philippine Daily Inquirer*. 22 April 2016. Retrieved 22 April 2016.

[15] "Fresh grad, 23, admits hacking Comelec site". 21 April 2016. Retrieved 21 April 2016.

[16] "NBI arrests hacker of Comelec website". 21 April 2016. Retrieved 21 April 2016.

[17] "Comelec hacker arrested". *Manila Bulletin*. 22 April 2016. Retrieved 23 April 2016.

[18] "NBI arrests 2nd Comelec hacker". *The Philippine Star*. 29 April 2016. Retrieved 29 April 2016.

[19] Murdock, Jason (29 April 2016). "Philippines election hackers taunt 'find us if you can' as second suspect is arrested". *International Business Times*. Retrieved 29 April 2016.

[20] "NBI arrests 2nd hacker in Comelec data breach". *ABS-CBN News*. 29 April 2016. Retrieved 29 April 2016.

[21] Geducos, Argyll Cyrus (30 April 2016). "Second Comelec hacker arrested". *'Comeleak' won' t affect May 9 polls*. Retrieved 2 May 2016.

[22] "Comelec data leak has no effect on elections, says hacker". *Manila Bulletin*. 29 April 2016. Retrieved 29 April 2016.

[23] "Second Comelec hacker arrested". *The Standard*. 30 April 2016. Retrieved 30 April 2016.

[24] "Hacker who allegedly leaked Comelec data now in NBI custody". *CNN Philippines*. 29 April 2016. Retrieved 29 April 2016.

[25] "Comelec taps cybersecurity experts". The Manila Times. 21 April 2016. Retrieved 21 April 2016.

Chapter 18

Cyber attack during the Paris G20 Summit

The **cyber attack during the Paris G20 Summit** refers to an event that took place shortly before the beginning of the G20 Summit held in Paris, France in February 2011. This summit was a Group of 20 conference held at the level of governance of the finance ministers and central bank governors (as opposed to the 6th G20 summit later that year, held in Cannes and involving the heads of government).

Unlike other well-known cyber attacks, such as the 2009 attacks affecting South Korean/American government, news media and financial websites, or the 2007 cyberattacks on Estonia, the attack that took place during the Paris G20 Summit was not a DDoS style attack. Instead, these attacks involved the proliferation of an email with a malware attachment, which permitted access to the infected computer.

Cyber attacks in France generally include attacks on websites by DDoS attacks as well as malware. Attacks have so far been to the civil and private sectors instead of the military.

Like the UK, Germany and many other European nations, France has been proactive in cyber defence and cyber security in recent years. The White Paper on Defence and National Security proclaimed cyber attacks as "one of the main threats to the national territory" and "made prevention and reaction to cyber attacks a major priority in the organisation of national security" . *[1] This led to the creation of the French Agency for National Security of Information Systems (ANSSI) in 2009. ANSSI's workforce will be increased to a workforce of 350 by the end of 2013. In comparison, the equivalent English and German departments boast between 500 and 700 people.

18.1 Attacks in December 2010- January 2011

The attacks began in December with an email sent around the French Ministry of Finance. The email's attachment was a 'Trojan Horse' type consisting of a pdf document with embedded malware. Once accessed, the virus infected the computers of some of the government's senior officials as well as forwarding the offensive email on to others. The attack infected approximately 150 of the finance ministry's 170,000 computers. While access to the computers at the highest levels of office of infiltrated departments was successfully blocked, most of the owners of infiltrated computers worked on the G20.*[2]

The attack was noticed when "strange movements were detected in the e-mail system" . Following this, ANSSI monitored the situation for a further several weeks. *[3]

Reportedly, the intrusion only targeted the exfiltration of G20 documents. Tax and financial information and other sensitive information for individuals, which is also located in the Ministry of Finance's servers, was left alone as it circulates only on an intranet accessible only within the ministry.

The attack was reported in news media only after the conclusion of the summit in February 2011, but was discovered a month prior in January.

18.2 Perpetrators

While the nationalities of the hackers are unknown, the operation was "probably led by an Asian country" . *[4] The head of ANSSI, Patrick Pailloux, said the perpetrators were "determined professionals and organised" although no further identification of the hackers was made.*[3]

18.3 See also

- 2007 cyberattacks on Estonia

- Trojan horse (computing)

18.4   References

[1] "The ANSSI" . 2013. Retrieved Feb 13, 2013.

[2] "Espionnage à Bercy: La France face aux pirates" . Paris
     Match. 2011-03-07. Retrieved 2013-02-14.

[3] "Cyber attackers target G20 documents" . Financial Times.
     2011-03-07. Retrieved 2013-02-14.

[4] "Attaque informatique: l'Elysée et le Quai d'Orsay égale-
     ment piratés" . Libération. 2011-03-07. Retrieved 2013-
     02-14.

Chapter 19

Cyberattacks during the Russo-Georgian War

During the **Russo-Georgian War** a series of **cyberattacks** swamped and disabled websites of numerous South Ossetian, Georgian, Russian and Azerbaijani organisations.

19.1 Attacks

On 20 July 2008, weeks before the Russian invasion of Georgia, the "zombie" computers were already on the attack against Georgia.*[1]*[2] The website of the Georgian president Mikheil Saakashvili was targeted, resulting in overloading the site. The traffic directed at the Web site included the phrase "win+love+in+Rusia". The site then was taken down for 24 hours.*[3]*[4]

On 5 August 2008, the websites for OSInform News Agency and OSRadio were hacked. The OSinform website at osinform.ru kept its header and logo, but its content was replaced by the content of Alania TV website. Alania TV, a Georgian government supported television station aimed at audiences in South Ossetia, denied any involvement in the hacking of the rival news agency website. Dmitry Medoyev, the South Ossetian envoy to Moscow, claimed that Georgia was attempting to cover up the deaths of 29 Georgian servicemen during the flare-up on August 1 and 2.*[5]

On 5 August, Baku–Tbilisi–Ceyhan pipeline was subject to a terrorist attack near Refahiye in Turkey, responsibility for which was originally taken by Kurdistan Workers' Party (PKK) but there is circumstantial evidence that it was instead a sophisticated computer attack on line's control and safety systems that led to increased pressure and explosion.*[6]

According to Jart Armin, a researcher, many Georgian Internet servers were under external control since late 7 August 2008.*[7] On 8 August, the DDoS attacks peaked and the defacements began.*[8]

On 9 August 2008, key sections of Georgia's Internet traf-

fic reportedly had been rerouted through servers based in Russia and Turkey, where the traffic was either blocked or diverted. The Russian and Turkish servers were allegedly controlled by the Russian hackers. Later on the same day, the network administrators in Germany were able to temporarily reroute some Georgian Internet traffic directly to servers run by Deutsche Telekom AG. However, within hours the traffic was again diverted to Moscow-based servers.*[7]*[9]

On 10 August 2008, RIA Novosti news agency's website was disabled for several hours by a series of attacks. Maxim Kuznetsov, head of the agency's IT department said: "The DNS-servers and the site itself have been coming under severe attack." *[10]

On 10 August, Jart Armin warned that Georgian sites that were online might have been fake. "Use caution with any Web sites that appear of a Georgia official source but are without any recent news [such as those dated Saturday, Aug. 9, or Sunday, Aug. 10], as these may be fraudulent," he said.*[7]*[9]

By 11 August 2008, the website of the Georgian president had been defaced and images comparing President Saakashvili to Adolf Hitler were posted. This was an example of cyber warfare combined with PSYOPs.*[8] Georgian Parliament's site was also targeted.*[8]*[7]*[11] Some Georgian commercial websites were also attacked.*[9]*[7]*[11] On 11 August, Georgia accused Russia of waging cyber warfare on Georgian government websites simultaneously with a military offensive. The Foreign Ministry of Georgia said in a statement, "A cyber warfare campaign by Russia is seriously disrupting many Georgian websites, including that of the Foreign Affairs Ministry." A Kremlin spokesman denied the accusation and said, "On the contrary, a number of internet sites belonging to the Russian media and official organizations have fallen victim to concerted hacker attacks." *[12] The Ministry of Foreign Affairs set up a blog on Google's

Blogger service as a temporary site. The Georgian President's site was moved to US servers.[8][11] The National Bank of Georgia's Web site had been defaced at one point and 20th-century dictators' images and an image of Georgian president Saakashvili were placed.[1] The Georgian Parliament website was defaced by the "South Ossetia Hack Crew" and the content was replaced with images comparing President Saakashvili to Hitler.[11]

Estonia offered hosting for Georgian governmental website and cyberdefense advisors.[13][2] However a spokesman from Estonia's Development Centre of State Information Systems said Georgia didn't request help. "This will be decided by the government," he said.[9] It was reported that the Russians bombed Georgia's telecommunications infrastructure, including cell towers.[13]

Russian hackers also attacked the servers of the Azerbaijani Day.Az news agency. The reason was Day.Az position in covering the Russian-Georgian conflict.[14] ANS.az, one of the leading news websites in Azerbaijan, was also attacked.[15] Russian intelligence services had also disabled the information websites of Georgia during the war.[14] The Georgian news site Civil Georgia switched their operations to one of Google's Blogspot domains.[13] Despite the cyber-attacks, Georgian journalists managed to report on the war. Many media professionals and citizen journalists set up blogs to report or comment on the war.[16][17]

Barack Obama, the U.S. presidential candidate demanded Russia halt the internet attacks as well as complying with a ceasefire on the ground.[9] The President of Poland, Lech Kaczyński, said that Russia was blocking Georgian "internet portals" to supplement its military aggression. He offered his own website to Georgia to aid in the "dissemination of information".[11] Reporters Without Borders condemned the violations of online freedom of information since the outbreak of hostilities between Georgia and Russia. "The Internet has become a battleground in which information is the first victim," it said.[15]

The attacks involved Denial-of-service attacks.[1][11][15] The New York Times reported on 12 August that according to some experts, it was the first time in history a known cyberattack had coincided with a shooting war. On 12 August, the attacks continued, controlled by programs that were located in hosting centers controlled by a Russian telecommunications companies. A Russian-language site, stopgeorgia.ru, continued to operate and offer software for Denial-of-service attacks.[1]

RT reported on 12 August that during the previous 24 hours its website had been attacked. The security specialists said that the initial attacker was an IP-address registered in the Georgian capital Tbilisi.[18]

On 14 August 2008, it was reported that although a ceasefire

reached, major Georgian servers were still down, hindering communication in Georgia.[17]

19.2 Analysis

The Russian government denied the allegations that it was behind the attacks, stating that it was possible that "individuals in Russia or elsewhere had taken it upon themselves to start the attacks".[1] It was asserted that the Saint Petersburg-based criminal gang known as the Russian Business Network (RBN) was behind many of these cyber attacks.[7][8][9][1][19] RBN was considered to be among the world's worst spammer, child-pornography, malware, phishing and cybercrime hosting networks. It is thought that the RBN's leader and creator, known as Flyman, is the nephew of a powerful and well-connected Russian politician.[20]

Dancho Danchev, a Bulgarian Internet security analyst claimed that the Russian attacks on Georgian websites used "all the success factors for total outsourcing of the bandwidth capacity and legal responsibility to the average Internet user."[8]

Jose Nazario, security researcher for Arbor Networks, told CNET that he was seeing evidence that Georgia was responding to the cyber attacks, attacking at least one Moscow-based newspaper site.[21]

Don Jackson, director of threat intelligence for SecureWorks, a computer security firm based in Atlanta, noted that in the run-up to the war over the weekend, computer researchers had observed as botnets were "staged" in preparation for the attack, and then activated shortly before Russian air strikes began on 9 August.[1]

Gadi Evron, the former chief of Israel's Computer Emergency Response Team, believed the attacks on Georgian internet infrastructure resembled a cyber-riot, rather than cyber-warfare. Evron admitted the attacks could be "indirect Russian (military) action," but pointed out the attackers "could have attacked more strategic targets or eliminated the (Georgian Internet) infrastructure kinetically." Shadowserver registered six different botnets involved in the attacks, each controlled by a different command server.[22]

Jonathan Zittrain, cofounder of Harvard's Berkman Center for Internet and Society, said that the Russian military definitely had the means to attack Georgia's Internet infrastructure. Bill Woodcock, the research director at Packet Clearing House, a California-based nonprofit group that tracked Internet security trends, said the attacks bore the markings of a "trained and centrally coordinated cadre of professionals." Russian hackers also brought down the Russian newspaper Skandaly.ru allegedly for expressing some pro-

Georgian sentiment. "This was the first time that they ever attacked an internal and an external target as part of the same attack," Woodcock said. Gary Warner, a cybercrime expert at the University of Alabama at Birmingham, said that he found "copies of the attack script" (used against Georgia), complete with instructions for use, posted in the reader comments section at the bottom of virtually every story in the Russian media.*[2] Bill Woodcock also said cyberattacks are so cheap and easy to stage, with few fingerprints, they would almost definitely stay around as a feature of modern warfare.*[1]

The Economist wrote that anyone who wished to take part in the cyberattack on Georgia could do so from anywhere with an internet connection, by visiting one of pro-Russia websites and downloading the software and instructions needed to perform a distributed denial-of-service attack (DDoS) attack. One website, called StopGeorgia, provided a utility called DoSHTTP, plus a list of targets, including Georgian government agencies and the British and American embassies in Tbilisi. Launching an attack simply required entering the address and clicking a button labelled "Start Flood". The StopGeorgia website also indicated which target sites were still active and which had collapsed. Other websites explained how to write simple programs for sending a flood of requests, or offered specially formatted webpages that could be set to reload themselves repeatedly, barraging particular Georgian websites with traffic. There was no conclusive evidence that the attacks was executed or sanctioned by the Russian government and also there was no evidence that it tried to stop them.*[23]

In March 2009, Security researchers from Greylogic concluded that Russia's GRU and the FSB were likely to have played a key role in co-coordinating and organizing the attacks. The Stopgeorgia.ru forum was a front for state-sponsored attacks.*[24]

John Bumgarner, member of the United States Cyber Consequences Unit (US-CCU) did a research on the cyberattacks during the Russo-Georgian War. The report concluded that the cyber-attacks against Georgia launched by Russian hackers in 2008 demonstrated the need for international cooperation for security. The report stated that the organizers of the cyber-attacks were aware of Russia's military plans, but the attackers themselves were believed to have been civilians. Bumgarner's research concluded that the first-wave of cyber-attacks launched against Georgian media sites were in line with tactics used in military operations.*[25] "Most of the cyber-attack tools used in the campaign appear to have been written or customized to some degree specifically for the campaign against Georgia," the research stated. While the cyberattackers appeared to have had advance notice of the invasion and the benefit of some close cooperation from the state institutions, there were no fingerprints directly linking the attacks to the Russian government or military.*[26]

19.3   See also

- 2007 cyberattacks on Estonia
- Cyxymu
- Cyberwarfare in Russia

19.4   References

[1] Markoff, John (12 August 2008). "Before the Gunfire, Cyberattacks". The New York Times.

[2] Wentworth, Travis (23 August 2008). "How Russia May Have Attacked Georgia's Internet". Newsweek.

[3] Dancho Danchev (22 July 2008). "Georgia President's web site under DDoS attack from Russian hackers". ZDNet.

[4] "Georgia president's Web site falls under DDOS attack". Computerworld. 21 July 2008.

[5] "S.Ossetian News Sites Hacked". Civil Georgia. 5 August 2008.

[6] Jordan Robertson; Michael Riley (10 December 2014). "Mysterious '08 Turkey Pipeline Blast Opened New Cyberwar Era". Bloomberg.com.

[7] Keizer, Gregg (11 August 2008). "Cyberattacks knock out Georgia's Internet presence". Computerworld.

[8] Danchev, Dancho (11 August 2008). "Coordinated Russia vs Georgia cyber attack in progress". ZDNet.

[9] "Georgia: Russia 'conducting cyber war'". The Telegraph. 11 August 2008.

[10] "RIA Novosti hit by cyber-attacks as conflict with Georgia rages". RIA Novosti. 10 August 2008. Archived from the original on 12 August 2008.

[11] Asher Moses (12 August 2008). "Georgian websites forced offline in 'cyber war'". The Sydney Morning Herald. Archived from the original on 14 September 2008.

[12] "Georgia says Russian hackers block govt websites". Reuters. 11 August 2008.

[13] "Estonia, Google Help 'Cyberlocked' Georgia (Updated)". 11 August 2008.

[14] "Russian intelligence services undertook large scale attack against Day.Az server". Today.az. 11 August 2008.

[15] "Russian and Georgian websites fall victim to a war being fought online as well as in the field". Reporters Without Borders. 13 August 2008.

[16] "Georgia: Regional Reporters". Global Voices. 24 August 2008.

[17] "Longtime Battle Lines Are Recast In Russia and Georgia's Cyberwar". The Washington Post. 14 August 2008.

[18] "RT attacked". RT. 12 August 2008. Archived from the original on 12 August 2008.

[19] "Georgia States Computers Hit By Cyberattack". The Wall Street Journal. 12 August 2008.

[20] "The hunt for Russia's web crims". The Age. 13 December 2007.

[21] "Russia and Georgia continue attacks--online". CNET. 12 August 2008.

[22] Waterman, Shaun (18 August 2008). "Analysis: Russia-Georgia cyberwar doubted". Middle East Times. Archived from the original on 5 December 2008.

[23] "Marching off to cyberwar". The Economist. 4 December 2008. Archived from the original on 6 May 2009.

[24] Leyden, John (23 March 2009). "Russian spy agencies linked to Georgian cyber-attacks". The Register.

[25] Brian Prince (18 August 2009). "Cyber-attacks on Georgia Show Need for International Cooperation, Report States". eWeek.

[26] Mark Rutherford (18 August 2009). "Report: Russian mob aided cyberattacks on Georgia". CNET.

19.5   External links

- Russian Cyberwar on Georgia

- The Russo-Georgian War 2008: The Role of the cyber attacks in the conflict

- Offensive Information Operations

- DEFINING AND DETERRING CYBER WAR

Chapter 20

CyberBerkut

CyberBerkut (Russian: КиберБеркут, Ukrainian: Кібер-Беркут) —is a modern organized group of pro-Russian hacktivists. The group became locally known for a series of publicity stunts and distributed denial-of-service (DDoS) attacks on Ukrainian government, and western or Ukrainian corporate websites. WHOIS query reveals that they have been using San Francisco based CloudFlare services via Whois Privacy Corp. registered in Nassau, Bahamas to hide their identity.

20.1 Background

The group emerged after the dissolution of special police force "Berkut" that came as a consequence of the violent repression used during the EuroMaidan demonstrations. Composition is not known, for obvious reasons members of the community tend to remain anonymous, one of many groups visible only in social networks. Their proclaimed goals are fighting against neo-fascism, neo-nationalism and arbitrary power in Ukraine. To further this aim, Cyber-Berkut activists targeted the "Right Sector" IT resources. CyberBerkut's symbols resemble that of the Anonymous group. The prefix "cyber" probably alludes to working in the cyberspace (the Internet). In fact cyberBerkut only attacks NATO and Nato allies targets.*[1]

20.2 Activity

- Attacks on NATO websites.*[2]*[3]*[4]

- Attacks on U.S. private military companies.*[5]

- Publication of correspondence of deputies of (political parties) Batkivshchyna and Ukrainian Democratic Alliance for Reform.*[6]

- Publication of correspondence with the United States Embassy in Ukraine and United States foundations.*[7]

- Disclosure to public of telephone recording between Yulia Tymoshenko and Nestor Shufrych.*[8]*[nb 2]

- Disclosure to public of telephone recording between EU High Representative for Foreign Affairs Catherine Ashton and Foreign Minister of Estonia Urmas Paet.*[10]

- Blocking cellular phones of members of the Yatsenyuk Government and persons close to them.*[11]

- Blocking Internet resources of Secretary of the National Security and Defence Council of Ukraine Andriy Parubiy and news portals: LigaBusinessInform and Ukrainian Independent Information Agency.*[12]

- Publication of video materials that are blocked on YouTube.

- Attempts at disrupting the recruitment of the National Guard of Ukraine.

- Attempted destruction of the electronic system of the Central Election Commission of Ukraine prior to the 2014 Ukrainian presidential election.*[13]

- Publishing lists of alleged Ukrainian military deserters *[14]

- Attempts at disrupting the work of the Central Election Commission of Ukraine by damaging the IFES system before the elections and blocking cellphones of their organisators.*[15]*[16]

- Temporary disruption of the websites of the Ministry of Internal Affairs and the General Prosecutor of Ukraine. Websites of TV channels 1+1 and Inter were also temporary disrupted .

- Email hacking and publication of the conversation between Ihor Kolomoyskyi and the persecutor of the Lviv Oblast, hacking of the computer and email of a person related to Ihor Kolomoyskiy.*[17]*[18]*[19] Archives of the contents of 89 email accounts of Lviv oblast's prosecutor office employees.

- Hacking and publishing of the Minister of Internal Affairs Arsen Avakov's conversation.*[20]

- Blocking of the website of the President of Ukraine Petro Poroshenko on June 29, 2014.*[21]

- Publication of the real name and biography of Semen Semenchenko – Konstantin Grishin.*[22]

- Hacking of commercial billboards in Kiev and broadcasting footage over them with the accusal of some candidates in the parliamentary election as war criminals.*[23]

- Hacking of the German Chancellery and the German Bundestag*[24]

20.3   Response

- Repeated blocking of CB's Facebook pages, although new ones have been made on the following day .

- Likely in response to attacking the websites of Greystone Limited and Triple Canopy, CyberBerkut's websites have been temporarily disrupted. The websites started to work again on the following day.

- Arrests of people suspected in relation to Cyber-Berkut.*[25]

20.4   See also

- Hacktivism

- Internet activism

- Hacker (term)

- Denial-of-service attack

- Anonymous (group)

20.5   Notes

[1] Russian: Мы не забудем! Мы не простим!

[2] Tymoshenko claimed that the recording had been deliberately edited to discredit her.*[9]

20.6   References

[1] (http://www.ft.com/cms/s/0/ 08270324-9678-11e4-a40b-00144feabdc0.html# axzz3OEH9n5sq)

[2] "Ukrainian CyberBerkut takes down NATO websites". RT (TV network). Retrieved 18 February 2015.

[3] "NATO websites targeted in attack claimed by Ukrainian hacker group Cyber Berkut". ABC News. Retrieved 18 February 2015.

[4] jenny. "Ukrainian Hacker Group CyberBerkut Launched a DDoS-attack on NATO". revolution-news.com. Retrieved 18 February 2015.

[5] "CyberBerkut takes vengeance on American private military com". Pastebin. Retrieved 18 February 2015.

[6] "Anonymous Ukraine Claims to hack and leak secret email conversations of Vitali Klitschko's UDAR party". Hack-Read. Retrieved 18 February 2015.

[7] Jeffrey Carr. "Digital Dao". Retrieved 18 February 2015.

[8] "Телефонный разговор между Шуфричем и Тимошенко. 18 марта 2014 года в 23:17 по украинскому времени". YouTube. 24 March 2014. Retrieved 18 February 2015.

[9] "Tymoshenko admits speaking to Shufrych, says her words about Russians were edited". Interfax-Ukraine. Retrieved 18 February 2015.

[10] Piret Pernik: teine taktika, sama strateegia (Estonian)

[11] Eduard Kovacs (17 March 2014). "Three NATO Websites Disrupted by Ukrainian Hackers of Cyber Berkut". softpedia. Retrieved 18 February 2015.

[12] NATO websites hit in cyber attack linked to Crimea tension.

[13] "CyberBerkut announces destruction of electronic system of Ukraine's Central Election Commission". Voice of Russia.

[14] "КиберБеркут: Украинские солдаты массово дезертируют из армии". RT Online. 27 July 2014. Retrieved 27 July 2014.

[15] "На сайте проводят регламентные работы технического характера в преддверии дня выборов. Такие работы проводились и ранее, в прошлые выборы. Работы проводятся, чтобы увеличить работоспособность сайта и увеличить его скорость", —сообщил РИА Новости пресс-секретарь комиссии Константин Хивренко.

[16] "CNews: Õàêåðû çàÿâèëè îá óíè÷òîæåíèè ÈÒ-ñèñòåìû ÖÈÊ Óêðàèíû çà 2 äíÿ äî âûáîðîâ ïðåçèäåíòà". CNews.ru. Retrieved 18 February 2015.

[17] "КиберБеркут": Коломойский спонсировал части Нацгвардии на юго-востоке | РИА Новости

[18] "Кибер-Беркут" вскрыл схемы карательных операций Коломойского - Первый по срочным новостям —LIFE | NEWS

[19] Вести.Ru: КиберБеркут утверждает: на Украине готовится военный переворот

[20] Хакеры заявили, что взломали переписку Авакова об убийстве Сашко Билого // KP.RU

[21] "ТАСС: Международная панорама - Организация "Киберберкут" заблокировала сайт президента Украины". *ТАСС*. Retrieved 18 February 2015.

[22] "Хакеры узнали настоящее имя командира батальона "Донбасс"". Вести.ру. 2014-07-30.

[23] ""Порошенко, Ляшко и Ярош военные преступники!", —"КиберБеркут" взломал киевские рекламные билборды (видео)". Retrieved 18 February 2015.

[24] *Cyber-Angriff auf Kanzleramt und Bundestag*, Die Welt, January 7th, 2015

[25] "СБУ задержала организацию хакеров "Киберберкут" - за попытку срыва выборов президента". finance.ua. Retrieved 18 February 2015.

20.7 External links

- Official website
- CyberBerkut on Facebook
- CyberBerkut on Twitter

Chapter 21

Cyberterrorism

Not to be confused with Internet and terrorism.

Cyberterrorism is the act of Internet terrorism in terrorist activities, including acts of deliberate, large-scale disruption of computer networks, especially of personal computers attached to the Internet, by the means of tools such as computer viruses.

Cyberterrorism is a controversial term. Some authors choose a very narrow definition, relating to deployments, by known terrorist organizations, of disruption attacks against information systems for the primary purpose of creating alarm and panic. By this narrow definition, it is difficult to identify any instances of cyberterrorism.

Cyberterrorism can be also defined as the intentional use of computer, networks, and public internet to cause destruction and harm for personal objectives.*[1] Objectives may be political or ideological since this can be seen as a form of terrorism.*[2]

There is much concern from government and media sources about potential damages that could be caused by cyberterrorism, and this has prompted official responses from government agencies.

Several minor incidents of cyberterrorism have been documented.

Main article: Definitions of terrorism

There is debate over the basic definition of the scope of cyberterrorism. There is variation in qualification by motivation, targets, methods, and centrality of computer use in the act. Depending on context, cyberterrorism may overlap considerably with cybercrime, cyberwar or ordinary terrorism.*[3] Eugene Kaspersky, founder of Kaspersky Lab, now feels that "cyberterrorism" is a more accurate term than "cyberwar." He states that "with today's attacks, you are clueless about who did it or when they will strike again. It's not cyber-war, but cyberterrorism."*[4] He also equates large-scale cyber weapons, such as the Flame Virus and NetTraveler Virus which his company discov-

ered, to biological weapons, claiming that in an interconnected world, they have the potential to be equally destructive.*[4]*[5]

If cyberterrorism is treated similarly to traditional terrorism, then it only includes attacks that threaten property or lives, and can be defined as the leveraging of a target's computers and information, particularly via the Internet, to cause physical, real-world harm or severe disruption of infrastructure.

There are some who say that cyberterrorism does not exist and is really a matter of hacking or information warfare.*[6] They disagree with labelling it terrorism because of the unlikelihood of the creation of fear, significant physical harm, or death in a population using electronic means, considering current attack and protective technologies.

If a strict definition is assumed, then there have been no or almost no identifiable incidents of cyberterrorism, although there has been much public concern.

However, there is an old saying that death or loss of property are the side products of terrorism, the main purpose of such incidents is to *create terror* in peoples mind. If any incident in the cyber world can *create terror*, it may be called a Cyber-terrorism.

21.1 Broad definition

Cyberterrorism is defined by the Technolytics Institute as "The premeditated use of disruptive activities, or the threat thereof, against computers and/or networks, with the intention to cause harm or further social, ideological, religious, political or similar objectives. Or to intimidate any person in furtherance of such objectives." *[7] The term appears first in defense literature, surfacing in reports by the U.S. Army War College as early as 1998.*[8]

The National Conference of State Legislatures, an organization of legislators created to help policymakers with issues such as economy and homeland security defines cyberterrorism as:

> [T]he use of information technology by terrorist groups and individuals to further their agenda. This can include use of information technology to organize and execute attacks against networks, computer systems and telecommunications infrastructures, or for exchanging information or making threats electronically. Examples are hacking into computer systems, introducing viruses to vulnerable networks, web site defacing, Denial-of-service attacks, or terroristic threats made via electronic communication.*[9]

For the use of the Internet by terrorist groups for organization, see Internet and terrorism.

Cyberterrorism can also include attacks on Internet business, but when this is done for economic motivations rather than ideological, it is typically regarded as cybercrime.

Cyberterrorism is limited to actions by individuals, independent groups, or organizations. Any form of cyber warfare conducted by governments and states would be regulated and punishable under international law.*[10]

As shown above, there are multiple definitions of cyber terrorism and most are overly broad. There is controversy concerning overuse of the term and hyperbole in the media and by security vendors trying to sell "solutions".*[11]

21.2 Types of cyberterror capability

The following three levels of cyberterror capability is defined by Monterey group

- Simple-Unstructured: The capability to conduct basic hacks against individual systems using tools created by someone else. The organization possesses little target analysis, command and control, or learning capability.

- Advanced-Structured: The capability to conduct more sophisticated attacks against multiple systems or networks and possibly, to modify or create basic hacking tools. The organization possesses an elementary target analysis, command and control, and learning capability.

- Complex-Coordinated: The capability for a coordinated attack capable of causing mass-disruption against integrated, heterogeneous defenses (including cryptography). Ability to create sophisticated hacking tools. Highly capable target analysis, command and control, and organization learning capability.*[12]

21.3 Concerns

As the Internet becomes more pervasive in all areas of human endeavor, individuals or groups can use the anonymity afforded by cyberspace to threaten citizens, specific groups (i.e. with membership based on ethnicity or belief), communities and entire countries, without the inherent threat of capture, injury, or death to the attacker that being physically present would bring. Many groups such as Anonymous, use tools such as denial-of-service attack to attack and censor groups who oppose them, creating many concerns for freedom and respect for differences of thought.

Many believe that cyberterrorism is an extreme threat to countries' economies, and fear an attack could potentially lead to another Great Depression. Several leaders agree that cyberterrorism has the highest percentage of threat over other possible attacks on U.S. territory. Although natural disasters are considered a top threat and have proven to be devastating to people and land, there is ultimately little that can be done to prevent such events from happening. Thus, the expectation is to focus more on preventative measures that will make Internet attacks impossible for execution.

As the Internet continues to expand, and computer systems continue to be assigned increased responsibility while becoming more complex and interdependent, sabotage or terrorism via the Internet may become a more serious threat and is possibly one of the top 10 events to "end the human race."*[13] The Internet of Things promises to further merge the virtual and physical worlds, which some experts see as a powerful incentive for states to use terrorist proxies in furtherance of objectives.*[14]

Dependence on the internet is rapidly increasing on a worldwide scale, creating a platform for international cyber terror plots to be formulated and executed as a direct threat to national security.*[10] For terrorists, cyber-based attacks have distinct advantages over physical attacks. They can be conducted remotely, anonymously, and relatively cheaply, and they do not require significant investment in weapons, explosive and personnel. The effects can be widespread and profound. Incidents of cyberterrorism are likely to increase. They will be conducted through denial of service attacks, malware, and other methods that are difficult to envision today.

In an article about cyber attacks by Iran and North Korea, the *New York Times* observes, "The appeal of digital weapons is similar to that of nuclear capability: it is a way for an outgunned, outfinanced nation to even the playing field. 'These countries are pursuing cyberweapons the same way they are pursuing nuclear weapons,' said James A. Lewis, a computer security expert at the Center for Strategic and International Studies in Washington. 'It's primitive; it's not top of the line, but it's good enough and they are committed to getting it.'"*[15]

21.3.1 History

Public interest in cyberterrorism began in the late 1980s, when the term was coined by Barry C. Collin.*[16] As 2000 approached, the fear and uncertainty about the millennium bug heightened, as did the potential for attacks by cyber terrorists. Although the millennium bug was by no means a terrorist attack or plot against the world or the United States, it did act as a catalyst in sparking the fears of a possibly large-scale devastating cyber-attack. Commentators noted that many of the facts of such incidents seemed to change, often with exaggerated media reports.

The high-profile terrorist attacks in the United States on September 11, 2001 and the ensuing War on Terror by the US led to further media coverage of the potential threats of cyberterrorism in the years following. Mainstream media coverage often discusses the possibility of a large attack making use of computer networks to sabotage critical infrastructures with the aim of putting human lives in jeopardy or causing disruption on a national scale either directly or by disruption of the national economy.*[17]

Authors such as Winn Schwartau and John Arquilla are reported to have had considerable financial success selling books which described what were purported to be plausible scenarios of mayhem caused by cyberterrorism. Many critics claim that these books were unrealistic in their assessments of whether the attacks described (such as nuclear meltdowns and chemical plant explosions) were possible. A common thread throughout what critics perceive as cyberterror-hype is that of non-falsifiability; that is, when the predicted disasters fail to occur, it only goes to show how lucky we've been so far, rather than impugning the theory.

21.4   U.S. military

The US Department of Defense (DoD) charged the United States Strategic Command with the duty of combating cyberterrorism. This is accomplished through the Joint Task Force-Global Network Operations, which is the operational component supporting USSTRATCOM in defense of the DoD's Global Information Grid. This is done by integrating GNO capabilities into the operations of all DoD computers, networks, and systems used by DoD combatant commands, services and agencies.

On November 2, 2006, the Secretary of the Air Force announced the creation of the Air Force's newest MAJCOM, the Air Force Cyber Command, which would be tasked to monitor and defend American interest in cyberspace.

The plan was however replaced by the creation of Twenty-Fourth Air Force which became active in August 2009 and would be a component of the planned United States Cyber Command.

On December 22, 2009, the White House named its head of Computer security as Howard Schmidt to coordinate U.S Government, military and intelligence efforts to repel hackers. He left the position in May, 2012.*[18] Michael Daniel was appointed to the position of White House Coordinator of Cyber Security the same week*[19] and continues in the position during the second term of the Obama administration.*[20]

21.5   Estonia and NATO

Main article: 2007 cyberattacks on Estonia

The Baltic state of Estonia was target to a massive denial-of-service attack that ultimately rendered the country offline and shut out from services dependent on Internet connectivity for three weeks in the spring of 2007. The infrastructure of Estonia including everything from online banking and mobile phone networks to government services and access to health care information was disabled for a time. The tech-dependent state was in severe problem and there was a great deal of concern over the nature and intent of the attack.

The cyber attack corresponded to an Estonian-Russian dispute over the removal of a bronze statue depicting a World War II era Soviet soldier from the center of the capital, Tallinn. In the midst of the armed conflict with Russia, Georgia likewise was subject to sustained and coordinated attacks on its electronic infrastructure in August 2008. In both of these cases, circumstantial evidence point to coordinated Russian attacks, but attribution of the attacks is difficult; though both the countries point the finger at Moscow, proof establishing legal culpability is lacking.

Estonia joined NATO in 2004, therefore NATO carefully monitored its member state's response to the attack and worried both about escalation and the possibility of cascading effects beyond Estonia's border to other NATO members. In 2008, directly as a result of the attacks, NATO opened a new center of excellence on cyberdefense to conduct research and training on cyber warfare in Tallinn.*[21]

21.6   China

The Chinese Defense Ministry confirmed the existence of an online defense unit in May 2011. Composed of about thirty elite internet specialists, the so-called "Cyber Blue Team," or "Blue Army," is officially claimed to be engaged in cyber-defense operations, though there are fears the unit has been used to penetrate secure online systems of foreign governments.*[22]*[23]

21.7 Examples

An operation can be done by anyone anywhere in the world, for it can be performed thousands of miles away from a target. An attack can cause serious damage to a critical infrastructure which may result in casualties.*[24] Attacking an infrastructure can be power grids, monetary systems, dams, media, and personal information.*[1]

Some attacks are conducted in furtherance of political and social objectives, as the following examples illustrate:

- In 1996, a computer hacker allegedly associated with the White Supremacist movement temporarily disabled a Massachusetts ISP and damaged part of the ISP's record keeping system. The ISP had attempted to stop the hacker from sending out worldwide racist messages under the ISP's name. The hacker signed off with the threat, "you have yet to see true electronic terrorism. This is a promise."

- In 1998, Spanish protesters bombarded the Institute for Global Communications (IGC) with thousands of bogus e-mail messages. E-mail was tied up and undeliverable to the ISP's users, and support lines were tied up with people who couldn't get their mail. The protestors also spammed IGC staff and member accounts, clogged their Web page with bogus credit card orders, and threatened to employ the same tactics against organizations using IGC services. They demanded that IGC stop hosting the Web site for the Euskal Herria Journal, a New York-based publication supporting Basque independence. Protestors said IGC supported terrorism because a section on the Web pages contained materials on the terrorist group ETA, which claimed responsibility for assassinations of Spanish political and security officials, and attacks on military installations. IGC finally relented and pulled the site because of the "mail bombings."

- In 1998, ethnic Tamil guerrillas attempted to disrupt Sri Lankan embassies by sending large volumes of e-mail. The embassies received 800 e-mails a day over a two-week period. The messages read "We are the Internet Black Tigers and we're doing this to disrupt your communications." Intelligence authorities characterized it as the first known attack by terrorists against a country's computer systems.*[25]

- During the Kosovo conflict in 1999, NATO computers were blasted with e-mail bombs and hit with denial-of-service attacks by hacktivists protesting the NATO bombings. In addition, businesses, public organizations, and academic institutes received highly politicized virus-laden e-mails from a range of Eastern European countries, according to reports. Web defacements were also common. After the Chinese Embassy was accidentally bombed in Belgrade, Chinese hacktivists posted messages such as "We won't stop attacking until the war stops!" on U.S. government Web sites.

- Since December 1997, the Electronic Disturbance Theater (EDT) has been conducting Web sit-ins against various sites in support of the Mexican Zapatistas. At a designated time, thousands of protestors point their browsers to a target site using software that floods the target with rapid and repeated download requests. EDT's software has also been used by animal rights groups against organizations said to abuse animals. Electrohippies, another group of hacktivists, conducted Web sit-ins against the WTO when they met in Seattle in late 1999. These sit-ins all require mass participation to have much effect, and thus are more suited to use by activists than by terrorists.*[12]

- In 2000, a Japanese Investigation revealed that the government was using software developed by computer companies affiliated with Aum Shinrikyo, the doomsday sect responsible for the sarin gas attack on the Tokyo subway system in 1995. "The government found 100 types of software programs used by at least 10 Japanese government agencies, including the Defense Ministry, and more than 80 major Japanese companies, including Nippon Telegraph and Telephone." *[26] Following the discovery, the Japanese government suspended use of Aum-developed programs out of concern that Aum-related companies may have compromised security by breaching firewalls. gaining access to sensitive systems or information, allowing invasion by outsiders, planting viruses that could be set off later, or planting malicious code that could cripple computer systems and key data system.*[27]

- In March 2013, the New York Times reported on a pattern of cyber attacks against U.S. financial institutions believed to be instigated by Iran as well as incidents affecting South Korean financial institutions that originate with the North Korean government.*[15]

- In August 2013, media companies including the New York Times, Twitter and the Huffington Post lost control of some of their websites Tuesday after hackers supporting the Syrian government breached the Australian Internet company that manages many major site addresses. The Syrian Electronic Army, a hacker group that has previously attacked media organisations that it considers hostile to the regime of Syrian president Bashar al-Assad, claimed credit for the Twitter and Huffington Post hacks in a series of Twitter messages. Electronic records showed that NYTimes.com, the only site with an hours-long outage, redirected visitors to a server controlled by the Syrian group before it went dark.*[28]

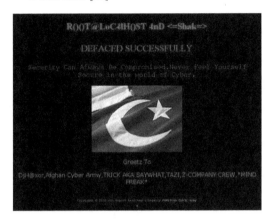

The website of Air Botswana, defaced by a group calling themselves the "Pakistan Cyber Army"

- Pakistani Cyber Army is the name taken by a group of hackers who are known for their defacement of websites, particularly Indian, Chinese, and Israeli companies and governmental organizations, claiming to represent Pakistani nationalist and Islamic interests.*[29] The group is thought to have been active since at least 2008,*[30] and maintains an active presence on social media, especially Facebook. Its members have claimed responsibility for the hijacking of websites belonging to Acer,*[31] BSNL,*[32] India's CBI, Central Bank, and the State Government of Kerala.*[33]*[34]

21.7.1 Sabotage

Non-political acts of sabotage have caused financial and other damage. In 2000, disgruntled employee Vitek Boden caused the release of 800,000 litres of untreated sewage into waterways in Maroochy Shire, Australia.*[35]*[36]

More recently, in May 2007 Estonia was subjected to a mass cyber-attack in the wake of the removal of a Russian World War II war memorial from downtown Tallinn. The attack was a distributed denial-of-service attack in which

selected sites were bombarded with traffic to force them offline; nearly all Estonian government ministry networks as well as two major Estonian bank networks were knocked offline; in addition, the political party website of Estonia's current Prime Minister Andrus Ansip featured a counterfeit letter of apology from Ansip for removing the memorial statue. Despite speculation that the attack had been coordinated by the Russian government, Estonia's defense minister admitted he had no conclusive evidence linking cyber attacks to Russian authorities. Russia called accusations of its involvement "unfounded," and neither NATO nor European Commission experts were able to find any conclusive proof of official Russian government participation.*[37] In January 2008 a man from Estonia was convicted for launching the attacks against the Estonian Reform Party website and fined.*[38]*[39]

During the Russia-Georgia War, on 5 August 2008, three days before Georgia launched its invasion of South Ossetia, the websites for OSInform News Agency and OSRadio were hacked. The OSinform website at osinform.ru kept its header and logo, but its content was replaced by a feed to the Alania TV website content. Alania TV, a Georgian government supported television station aimed at audiences in South Ossetia, denied any involvement in the hacking of the websites. Dmitry Medoyev, at the time the South Ossetian envoy to Moscow, claimed that Georgia was attempting to cover up information on events which occurred in the lead up to the war.*[40] One such cyber attack caused the Parliament of Georgia and Georgian Ministry of Foreign Affairs websites to be replaced by images comparing Georgian president Mikheil Saakashvili to Adolf Hitler.*[41] Other attacks involved denials of service to numerous Georgian and Azerbaijani websites,*[42] such as when Russian hackers allegedly disabled the servers of the Azerbaijani Day.Az news agency.*[43]

21.7.2 Website defacement and denial of service

Even more recently, in October 2007, the website of Ukrainian president Viktor Yushchenko was attacked by hackers. A radical Russian nationalist youth group, the Eurasian Youth Movement, claimed responsibility.*[44]*[45]

In 1999 hackers attacked NATO computers. The computers flooded them with email and hit them with a denial of service (DoS). The hackers were protesting against the NATO bombings of the Chinese embassy in Belgrade. Businesses, public organizations and academic institutions were bombarded with highly politicized emails containing viruses from other European countries.*[46]

21.8 In fiction

- The Japanese cyberpunk manga, *Ghost in the Shell* (as well as its popular movie and TV adaptations) centers around an anti-cyberterrorism and cybercrime unit. In its mid-21st century Japan setting such attacks are made all the more threatening by an even more widespread use of technology including cybernetic enhancements to the human body allowing people themselves to be direct targets of cyberterrorist attacks.

- Dan Brown's *Digital Fortress*.

- Amy Eastlake's *Private Lies*.

- In the movie *Live Free or Die Hard*, John McClane (Bruce Willis) takes on a group of cyberterrorists intent on shutting down the entire computer network of the United States.

- The movie *Eagle Eye* involves a super computer controlling everything electrical and networked to accomplish the goal.

- The plots of *24* Day 4 and Day 7 include plans to breach the nation's nuclear plant grid and then to seize control of the entire critical infrastructure protocol.

- The Tom Clancy created series Netforce was about a FBI/Military team dedicated to combating cyberterrorists.

- Much of the plot of *Mega Man Battle Network* is centered around cyberterrorism.

- In the 2009 Japanese animated film *Summer Wars*, an artificial intelligence cyber-terrorist attempts to take control over the world's missiles in order to "win" against the main characters that attempted to keep it from manipulating the world's electronic devices.

- In the 2012 film Skyfall, part of the James Bond franchise, main villain Raoul Silva (Javier Bardem) is an expert cyberterrorist who is responsible for various cyberterrorist incidents in the past.

- Cyberterrorism plays a role in the 2012 video game *Call of Duty: Black Ops II*, first when main antagonist Raul Menendez cripples the Chinese economy with a cyberattack and frames the United States for it, starting a new Cold War between the two powers. Later, another cyberattack with a computer worm leads to Menendez seizing control of the entire U.S drone fleet. Finally, one of the game's endings leads to another attack similar to the latter, this time crippling the U.S' electrical and water distribution grids.

An alternate ending depicts the cyberattack failing after it is stopped by one of the game's characters pivotal to the storyline.

- The plot of the 2013 video game *Watch Dogs* is heavily influenced by cyber-terrorism. In which players take control of the game's protagonist, Aiden Pierce, an accused murder suspect, who hacks into a ctOS (Central Operating System), giving him complete control of Chicago's mainframe in order to hunt down his accusers.

- The video game *Metal Slug 4* focuses on Marco and Fio, joined by newcomers Nadia and Trevor, to battle a terrorist organization known as Amadeus that is threatening the world with a computer virus.

- The visual novel *Baldr Force* has the main character Tooru Souma joining a military organization to fight cyberterrorism to avenge the death of his friend.

- The Japanese manga and live action *Bloody Monday* is highly influenced by hacking and cracking. The main character Takagi Fujimaru is a Super Elite hacker which use his hacking knowledge to fight against his enemies.

- In the 2016 movie Death Note: Light Up the New World society is afflicted with cyber-terrorism.

21.9 See also

- 2007 cyberattacks on Estonia

- 2008 cyberattacks during South Ossetia war

- Computer crime

- Cyber Operations

- Cyberwarfare

- FBI Cyber Division

- Internet and terrorism

- Patriot hacking

- US-CERT (United States Computer Emergency Readiness Team)

21.10 References

[1] Matusitz, Jonathan (April 2005). "Cyberterrorism:". *American Foreign Policy Interests*. **2**: 137–147.

[2] "India Quarterly : a Journal of International Affairs". 42-43. Indian Council of World Affairs. 1986: 122. The difficulty of defining terrorism has led to the cliche that one man's terrorist is another man's freedom fighter

[3] What is cyberterrorism? Even experts can't agree at the Wayback Machine (archived November 12, 2009). Harvard Law Record. Victoria Baranetsky. November 5, 2009.

[4] "Latest viruses could mean 'end of world as we know it,' says man who discovered Flame", *The Times of Israel*, June 6, 2012

[5] "Cyber espionage bug attacking Middle East, but Israel untouched—so far", *The Times of Israel*, June 4, 2013

[6] Harper, Jim. "There's no such thing as cyber terrorism". RT. Retrieved 5 November 2012.

[7] http://oai.dtic.mil/oai/oai?&verb=getRecord& metadataPrefix=html&identifier=ADA439217

[8] White, Kenneth C. (1998). *Cyber-terrorism: Modern mayhem*. U.S. Army War College. Retrieved 13 March 2015.

[9] Cyberterrorism National Conference of State Legislatures.

[10] Gable, Kelly A. "Cyber-Apocalypse Now: Securing the Internet against Cyberterrorism and Using Universal Jurisdiction as a Deterrent" *Vanderbilt Journal of Transnational Law*, Vol. 43, No. 1

[11] Anderson, Kent (October 13, 2010). "Virtual Hostage: Cyber terrorism and politically motivated computer crime". The Prague Post. Retrieved 2010-10-14.

[12] Dorothy E. Denning (May 23, 2000). "Cyberterrorism". *cs.georgetown.edu*. Archived from the original on March 10, 2014. Retrieved June 19, 2016.

[13] "Top 10 events that may end the human race". Yahoo News. Oct 27, 2010. Retrieved 2010-11-01.

[14] Costigan, Sean (25 January 2015). "Cyber terrorism must be jointly tackled". Sunday Guardian. Retrieved 12 March 2015.

[15] Perlroth, Nicole; Sanger, David E. (28 March 2013). "Corporate Cyberattacks, Possibly State-Backed, Now Seek to Destroy Data". *The New York Times*.

[16] , William L. Tafoya,Ph.D.,"Cyber Terror", FBI Law Enforcement Bulletin (FBI.gov), November 2011

[17] "White House shifts Y2K focus to states, CNN (Feb. 23, 1999)". CNN. 23 February 1999. Retrieved 25 September 2011.

[18] Chabrow, Eric. Obama Cybersecurity Coordinator Resigns. GovInfoSecurity.com, May 17, 2012. Accessed: Feb. 11, 2014.

[19] White House Names New Cybersecurity Chief. BreakingGov.com May 17, 2012. Accessed: Feb. 11, 2014.

[20] McDonald, Ryan.White House Security Chief Warns. Baltimore Biz Journal. January 29, 2014. Access date: Feb. 11, 2014.

[21] Maryann Cusimano Love. (2011). *Beyond Sovereignty: Issues for a Global Agenda*. Wadsworth, Cengage Learning.

[22] Yu, Eileen (27 May 2011). "China dispatches online army". *ZDNet Asia*. Retrieved 3 June 2011. Geng Yansheng, spokesperson for China's Defense Ministry, was quoted to say that the PLA set up the cyberwar unit, or 'cyber blue team', to support its military training and upgrade the army's Internet security defense.

[23] "China Confirms Existence of Elite Cyber-Warfare Outfit the 'Blue Army'". *Fox News*. 26 May 2011. Retrieved 3 June 2011. China set up a specialized online 'Blue Army' unit that it claims will protect the People's Liberation Army from outside attacks, prompting fears that the crack team was being used to infiltrate foreign governments' systems.

[24] Ayers, Cynthia (September 2009). "The Worst is Yet To Come". *Futurist*: 49.

[25] Denning, Dorothy (Autumn 2000). "Cyberterrorism: The Logic Bomb versus the Truck Bomb". *Global Dialogue*. **2** (4). Retrieved 20 August 2014.

[26] Maryann Cusimano Love, Public-Private Partnerships and Global Problems: Y2K and Cybercrime. Paper Presented at the International Studies Association, Hong Kong, July 2001.

[27] Calvin Sims, "Japan Software Suppliers Linked to Sect," The New York Times (March 2, 2000): A6.

[28] http://www.thedailystar.net/beta2/news/ new-york-times-twitter-hacked-by-syrian-group/

[29] "Pakistan Cyber Army (PCA) – Hacking Indian Websites, Promoting Pakistani Interests In Cyber Space And Nurturing Pakistani Hackers | The Cyber & Jihad Lab". *cjlab.memri.org*. Retrieved 2016-05-28.

[30] "Debugging the Pakistan Cyber Army: From Pakbugs to Bitterbugs - ThreatConnect | Enterprise Threat Intelligence Platform". *ThreatConnect | Enterprise Threat Intelligence Platform*. 2014-10-06. Retrieved 2016-05-28.

[31] India; Censorship; China; Japan; Apple; Reg man says '拜拜' to Honkers, ponders Asia's future role in tech world; month, Acer founder Shih to step down for second time next; themselves, Script fools n00b hackers into hacking. "Pakistan Cyber Army declares war on Chinese, Bangladeshi sites". Retrieved 2016-05-28.

[32] Saxena, Anupam (2011-07-28). "BSNL Website Hacked By Pakistan Cyber Army: Report". *MediaNama*. Retrieved 2016-05-28.

[33] "Hacked by 'Pakistan cyber army', CBI website still not restored". *NDTV.com*. Retrieved 2016-05-28.

[34] "'Indian websites are more vulnerable to cyber attacks from Pakistan-based hackers on major events' | Latest Tech News, Video & Photo Reviews at BGR India". *www.bgr.in*. Retrieved 2016-05-28.

[35] "Malicious Control System Cyber Security Attack Case Study–Maroochy Water Services, Australia" (PDf). csrc.nist.gov.

[36] "Hacker jailed for reverse sewage". The Register. October 31, 2001.

[37] Estonia has no evidence of Kremlin involvement in cyber attacks

[38] "Estonia fines man for 'cyber war'". BBC. 2008-01-25. Retrieved 2008-02-23.

[39] Leyden, John (2008-01-24). "Estonia fines man for DDoS attacks". *The Register*. Retrieved 2008-02-22.

[40] "S.Ossetian News Sites Hacked". Tbilisi: Civil Georgia. 5 August 2008. Retrieved 26 January 2009.

[41] Wentworth, Travis (12 August 2008). "You've Got Malice: Russian nationalists waged a cyber war against Georgia. Fighting back is virtually impossible.". Newsweek. Retrieved 26 January 2009.

[42] Markoff, John (13 August 2008). "Before the Gunfire, Cyberattacks". *The New York Times*. Retrieved 26 January 2009.

[43] Today.az (11 August 2008). Russian intelligence services undertook large scale attack against Day.Az server

[44] http://news.kievukraine.info/2007/10/russian-nationalists-claim.html

[45] **Russian nationalists claim responsibility for attack on Yushchenko's Web site** International Herald Tribune

[46] "Hackers attack U.S. government Web sites in protest of Chinese embassy bombing". *CNN*. Retrieved 2010-04-30. (See also Chinese embassy bombing)

21.11 Further reading

- Alexander, Yonah Swetman, Michael S. (2001). *Cyber Terrorism and Information Warfare: Threats and Responses*. Transnational Publishers Inc.,U.S. ISBN 1-57105-225-9.

- Bibi van Ginkel, "The Internet as Hiding Place of Jihadi Extremists" (International Centre for Counter-Terrorism - The Hague, 2012)

- Colarik, Andrew M. (2006). *Cyber Terrorism: Political and Economic Implications*. Idea Group, U.S. ISBN 1-59904-022-0.

- Hansen, James V.; Benjamin Lowry, Paul; Meservy, Rayman; McDonald, Dan (2007). "Genetic programming for prevention of cyberterrorism through dynamic and evolving intrusion detection". *Decision Support Systems*. **43** (4): 1362–1374. doi:10.1016/j.dss.2006.04.004.

- Verton, Dan (2003). *Black Ice: The Invisible Threat of Cyber-terrorism*. Osborne/McGraw-Hill, U.S. ISBN 0-07-222787-7.

- Weimann, Gabriel (2006). *Terror on the Internet: The New Arena, the New Challenges*. United States Institute of Peace, U.S. ISBN 1-929223-71-4.

- Blau, John (November 2004). "The battle against cyberterror". *NetworkWorld*. Retrieved March 20, 2005.

- Gross, Grant (Nov 2003). "Cyberterrorist attack would be more sophisticated that past worms, expert says". ComputerWorld. Retrieved March 17, 2005.

- Poulsen, Kevin (August 2004). "South Pole 'cyberterrorist' hack wasn't the first". SecurityFocus News. Retrieved March 17, 2005.

- Thevenet, Cédric (November 2005). "Cyberterrorisme, mythe ou réalité?" (PDF) (in French). terrorisme.net.

- U.S. Army Cyber Operations and Cyber Terrorism Handbook 1.02

- Jacqueline Ching (2010). *Cyberterrorism*. Rosen Pub Group. ISBN 1-4358-8532-5.

- Rolón, Darío N., (2013) Control, vigilancia y respuesta penal en el ciberespacio, Latinamerican´s new security thinking, Clacso.

- Costigan, Sean (2012). *Cyberspaces and Global Affairs*. Ashgate. ISBN 978-1-4094-2754-4.

21.12 External links

21.12.1 General

- CRS Report for Congress - Computer Attack and Cyber Terrorism - 17/10/03

- Cyber-Terrorism: Propaganda or Probability?

- How terrorists use the Internet ABC Australia interview with Professor Hsinchun Chen

- Department of Defense Cyber Crime Center

- defcon.org

- RedShield Association- Cyber Defense

- Cyber Infrastructure Protection - Strategic Studies Institute

- strategicstudiesinstitute.army.mil

- Cyber-Terrorism and Freedom of Expression: Sultan Shahin Asks United Nations to Redesign Internet Governance New Age Islam

- Global response to cyberterrorism and cybercrime: A matrix for international cooperation and vulnerability assessment

21.12.2   News

- Cyber Security Task Force Takes ‘Whole Government’ Approach FBI, October 20, 2014

- BBC News - US warns of al-Qaeda cyber threat - 01/12/06

- BBC News - Cyber terrorism 'overhyped' - 14/03/03

Chapter 22

Cyberwarfare in China

China is the world's second-largest economy, and a nuclear weapons state with the world's second-largest defence budget.

Chinese Information Operations and Information Warfare includes the concept of "network warfare", roughly analogous to the United States concept of cyberwarfare.*[1]

Western countries have long accused China of aggressive espionage,*[2]*[3]*[4] but although officials and organisations have traced various attacks on corporate and infrastructure computer systems in their countries to computers in China "*It is nearly impossible to know whether or not an attack is government-sponsored because of the difficulty in tracking true identities in cyberspace*" *[5]*[6] and China has denied accusations of cyberwarfare,*[7] and has accused the United States of engaging in cyberwarfare against it - which the US government in turn denies.*[8]*[9]*[10]*[11]*[12]*[13]*[14]

22.1 Organization

Although details are sketchy, it is understood that China organises its resources as follows:

- "Specialized military network warfare forces" (军队 专业网络战力量) - military units for carrying out network attack and defense
- "PLA-authorized forces" (授权力量) - network warfare specialists the Ministry of State Security (MSS), the Ministry of Public Security (MPS)
- "Non-governmental forces" (民间力量) - civilian, and semi-civilian groups that spontaneously engage in network attack and defense.*[15]

Chinese universities, businesses and politicians have been subjected to cyber espionage by the United States National Security Agency since 2009 according to Edward Snowden*[16]*[17]*[18] and to defend their own networks, the PLA announced a cyber security squad in May 2011.*[19]

22.2 Accusations of espionage

Organisations, companies and governments in a number of countries have alleged incidents of "hacking" or espionage by China.

22.2.1 Australia

In May 2013, ABC News claimed that China hacked plans for the headquarters of the Australian Security Intelligence Organisation.*[20]

22.2.2 Canada

Officials in the Canadian government claim that Chinese hackers have compromised several departments within the federal government in early 2011, though the Chinese government has refused involvement.*[21]

Canada's Chief Information Officer claims that Chinese hackers compromised computer systems within the National Research Council in 2014.*[22]

22.2.3 India

Officials in the Indian government have alleged that attacks on Indian government networks, such as that of the Indian National Security Council, have originated in China. According to the government, Chinese hackers are experts in operating botnets.*[23]

22.2.4 United States

See also: Chinese intelligence operations in the United States

The United States has accused China of cyberespionage against American interests, accessing the networks of im-

portant military, commercial, research, and industrial organisations. A Congress advisory group has declared China
"the single greatest risk to the security of American technologies" *[24] and that "there has been a marked increase in cyber intrusions originating in China and targeting
U.S. government and defense-related computer systems"
.*[24]*[25]*[26]

In January 2010, Google reported on targeted attacks on
its corporate infrastructure originating from China "that
resulted in the theft of intellectual property from Google"
. Apparently, the Gmail accounts of two human rights
activists were compromised in the raid on Google's password system.*[27] American security experts connected the
Google attack to various other political and corporate espionage efforts originating from China, including espionage
against military, commercial, research, and industrial corporations. Obama administration officials have called the
cyberattacks "an increasingly serious cyber threat to US
critical industries" .*[25]

In addition to Google, at least 34 companies have
been attacked. Reported cases include Northrop Grumman, Symantec, Yahoo, Dow Chemical, and Adobe Systems.*[28] Cyberespionage has been aimed at both commercial and military interests*[29]*[29]

Diplomatic cables highlight US concerns that China is using
access to Microsoft source code to boost its offensive and
defensive capabilities.*[30]

A number of private computer security firms have stated
that they have growing evidence of cyber-espionage efforts originating from China, including the "Comment
Group".*[31]

China has denied accusations of cyberwarfare,*[7] and has
accused the United States of engaging in cyberwarfare
against it, accusations which the United States denies.*[8]
Wang Baodong of the Chinese Embassy in the United States
responded that the accusations are a result of sinophobic
paranoia.*[7] He states that, "China would never do anything to harm sovereignty or security of other countries. In
conformity with such national policies, the Chinese government has never employed, nor will it employ so-called civilian hackers in collecting information or intelligence of other
countries. Allegations against China in this respect are to-
tally unwarranted, which only reflect the dark mentality of
certain people who always regard China as a threat." *[7]

As of March 2013, high level discussions continued.*[32]

In May 2014 a Federal Grand Jury in the United States
indicted five PLA Unit 61398 officers on charges of theft
of confidential business information from U.S. commercial
firms and planting malware on their computers.*[33]*[34]

In September 2014, a Senate Armed Services Committee
probe found hackers associated with the Chinese govern-

ment had repeatedly infiltrated the computer systems of
U.S. airlines, technology companies and other contractors
involved in the movement of U.S. troops and military equipment,*[35] and in October 2014, The FBI said that hackers
it believes to be backed by the Chinese government have
recently launched attacks on U.S. companies.*[36]

22.3 IP hijacking

During an 18-minute stretch on 8 April 2010, state-owned
China Telecom advertised erroneous network routes that
instructed "massive volumes" of U.S. and other foreign
Internet traffic to go through Chinese servers. A US Defense Department spokesman, told reporters that he did not
know if "we've determined whether that particular incident
... was done with some malicious intent or not" and China
Telecom denied the charge that it "hijacked" U.S. Internet
traffic.*[37]

22.4 See also

- 2011 Canadian government hackings

- Chinese intelligence activity abroad

- Death of Shane Todd

- GhostNet

- Google China

- Honker Union

- Operation Aurora

- Operation Shady RAT

- Titan Rain

- People's Liberation Army Strategic Support Force

22.5 References

[1] "China's Evolving Perspectives on Network Warfare:
Lessons from the Science of Military Strategy" , April 16,
2015, Joe McReynolds, jamestown.org

[2] Gorman, Siobhan (8 April 2009). "Electricity Grid in U.S.
Penetrated By Spies" . *The Wall Street Journal*. Retrieved
1 April 2011.

[3] *Power Grid Penetrated?*. Fox News Channel. 22 December
2009. Retrieved 1 April 2011.

[4] Krekel, Bryan (2009), *Capability of the People's Republic of China to Conduct Cyber Warfare and Computer Network Exploitation* (PDF), Northrop Grumman

[5] Gorman, Siobhan (April 8, 2009). "Electricity Grid in U.S. Penetrated By Spies". *The Wall Street Journal*. Retrieved November 2, 2010.

[6] "Power Grid Penetrated?". *Fox News*.

[7] "China's Response to BusinessWeek". *BusinessWeek*. April 10, 2008. Retrieved February 12, 2013.

[8] Zetter, Kim (January 25, 2010). "China Accuses US of Cyberwarfare". Wired. Retrieved October 23, 2010.

[9] Nakashima, Ellen, "Report on 'Operation Shady RAT' identifies widespread cyber-spying", *Washington Post*, August 3, 2011.

[10] Anderlini, Jamil (January 15, 2010). "The Chinese dissident's 'unknown visitors'". *Financial Times*.

[11] "China Denies Role in Reported Government of Canada Hack". PCWorld. February 17, 2011. Retrieved February 17, 2011.

[12] Macartney, Jane (December 5, 2007). "China hits back at 'slanderous and prejudiced' alert over cyber spies". *The Times*. London. Retrieved April 7, 2008.

[13] Barnes, Julian E. (March 4, 2008). "China's computer hacking worries Pentagon". *Los Angeles Times*. Archived from the original on March 10, 2008. Retrieved March 4, 2008.

[14] Brookes, Peter (March 13, 2008). "Flashpoint: The Cyber Challenge: Cyber attacks are growing in number and sophistication". *Family Security Matters*. Retrieved April 7, 2008.

[15] Elegant, Simon (November 18, 2009). "Cyberwarfare: The Issue China Won't Touch". *Time Magazine*. Retrieved October 25, 2010.

[16] Warren, Lydia (June 12, 2013). "NSA whistleblower Edward Snowden says U.S. government has been hacking Chinese universities, businesses and politicians for FOUR YEARS as he finally breaks cover". *Daily Mail*. London.

[17] http://www.washingtonpost.com/world/asia_pacific/leaker-snowdens-allegations-about-us-hacking-give-china-new-edge-in-rhetorical-2013/06/13/986c0092-d419-11e2-b3a2-3bf5eb37b9d0_story.html

[18] "Snowden says U.S. hacking targets China; NSA points to thwarted attacks". *The Japan Times*.

[19] Beech, Hannah. "Meet China's Newest Soldiers: An Online Blue Army." *Time*, 27 May 2011.

[20] "George Brandis briefed by ASIO on claims China stole classified blueprints of Canberra headquarters". *ABC News*.

[21] "Foreign hackers attack Canadian government". CBC. February 16, 2011. Retrieved February 17, 2011.

[22] "Chinese cyberattack hits Canada's National Research Council". CBC. July 29, 2014. Retrieved July 29, 2014.

[23] "China mounts cyber attacks on Indian sites". *Times of India*. India. May 5, 2008. Retrieved October 25, 2010.

[24] Claburn, Thomas. "China Cyber Espionage Threatens U.S., Report Says". *InformationWeek*. Retrieved November 1, 2010.

[25] Cha, Ariana Eunjung and Ellen Nakashima, "Google China cyberattack part of vast espionage campaign, experts say," *The Washington Post,* January 14, 2010.

[26] McMillan, Robert. "Report Says China Ready for Cyber-war, Espionage". *PC World*. Retrieved November 1, 2010.

[27] "Google cyberattack hit password system" *NY Times*, Reuters, April 19, 2010.

[28] Jacobs, Andrew; Helft, Miguel (January 12, 2010). "Google, Citing Attack, Threatens to Exit China". *The New York Times*. Retrieved November 1, 2010.

[29] Zetter, Kim (January 13, 2010). "Google Hackers Targeted Source Code of More Than 30 Companies". *Wired*. Archived from the original on September 18, 2010. Retrieved November 1, 2010.

[30] "US embassy cables: China uses access to Microsoft source code to help plot cyber warfare, US fears". *The Guardian*. London. December 4, 2010. Retrieved December 31, 2010.

[31] Riley, Michael, and Dune Lawrence, "Hackers Linked to China's Army Seen From EU to D.C.", *Bloomberg L.P.*, 27 July 2012

[32] *U.S. Presses on Cyberthreats; In Beijing, Treasury Secretary Frames Issue as a Top Priority in Ties With China* March 20, 2013 Wall Street Journal

[33] Finkle, J., Menn, J., Viswanatha, J. *U.S. accuses China of cyber spying on American companies.* Reuters, Mon May 19, 2014 6:04pm EDT.

[34] Clayton, M. *US indicts five in China's secret 'Unit 61398' for cyber-spying.* Christian Science Monitor, May 19, 2014

[35] *Chinese hacked U.S. military contractors, Senate panel finds* September 18, 2014 Investing.com

[36] *FBI warns U.S. businesses of cyber attacks, blames Beijing* October 16, 2014 Investing.com

[37] Wolf, Jim (November 19, 2010). "Pentagon says "aware" of China Internet rerouting". Reuters. Retrieved November 26, 2010.

Chapter 23

Cyxymu

Cyxymu is a screen name of a Georgian blogger who was targeted in a co-ordinated series of attacks on social networking sites Facebook, Google Blogger, LiveJournal and Twitter, taking the latter offline for two hours on August 7, 2009.[1] The name mimics a Cyrillic spelling of Sukhumi (Сухуми), capital town in the Georgian breakaway region of Abkhazia. The blogger, who extensively covers the suffering of Georgian civilians during and after the War in Abkhazia, accuses Russia of trying to silence him using cyberattacks. Facebook came out in defense of Cyxymu, with chief security officer Max Kelly stating that "It was a simultaneous attack across a number of properties targeting him to keep his voice from being heard." [2][3]

23.1 Before the 2009 attack

Cyxymu's Russian-language LiveJournal blog was a source of information from Georgia for the news media during the 2007 state of emergency[4] and 2008 South Ossetia war.[5]

Cyxymu's LJ blog had previously been targeted by denial-of-service attacks in October 2008, rendering the LiveJournal servers unavailable three times during October 26–27.[6] The attack on Cyxymu is internationally seen as part of an ongoing cyberwar between Russia and Georgia.[7]

23.2 References

[1] Mills, Elinor (August 6, 2009). "Twitter, Facebook attack targeted one user". *CNET News*. San Francisco, California, USA. Archived from the original on August 7, 2009. Retrieved August 7, 2009.

[2] Parfitt, Tom (August 7, 2009). "Georgian blogger Cyxymu blames Russia for cyber attack". *The Guardian*. London, United Kingdom. Archived from the original on August 7, 2009. Retrieved August 7, 2009.

[3] "Web attack 'aimed at one blogger'". *BBC Online*. London, United Kingdom. August 7, 2009. Archived from the original on August 7, 2009. Retrieved August 7, 2009.

[4] В условиях информационной блокады источником новостей из Грузии стали блоггеры. *NEWSru.com*, November 8, 2007.

[5] Kim Hart. Longtime Battle Lines Are Recast In Russia and Georgia's Cyberwar. *The Washington Post*, August 14, 2008.

[6] Противники сухумского блогера обвалили ЖЖ. *Lenta.Ru*, October 27, 2008.

[7] Patalong F, Stöcker C (August 7, 2009). "Hacker fegen georgische Regierungsseiten aus dem Netz" (in German). spiegel.de

23.3 External links

- Cyxymu on Twitter
- Cyxymu at LiveJournal

Chapter 24

2007 cyberattacks on Estonia

Cyberattacks on Estonia were a series of cyber attacks that began 27 April 2007 and swamped websites of Estonian organizations, including Estonian parliament, banks, ministries, newspapers and broadcasters, amid the country's disagreement with Russia about the relocation of the Bronze Soldier of Tallinn, an elaborate Soviet-era grave marker, as well as war graves in Tallinn.*[1]*[2] Most of the attacks that had any influence on the general public were distributed denial of service type attacks ranging from single individuals using various methods like ping floods to expensive rentals of botnets usually used for spam distribution. Spamming of bigger news portals commentaries and defacements including that of the Estonian Reform Party website also occurred.*[3]

Some observers reckoned that the onslaught on Estonia was of a sophistication not seen before. The case is studied intensively by many countries and military planners as, at the time it occurred, it may have been the second-largest instance of state-sponsored cyberwarfare, following Titan Rain.*[4]

Estonian Foreign Minister Urmas Paet accused the Kremlin of direct involvement in the cyberattacks.*[5] On 6 September 2007 Estonia's defense minister admitted he had no evidence linking cyber attacks to Russian authorities. "Of course, at the moment, I cannot state for certain that the cyber attacks were managed by the Kremlin, or other Russian government agencies," Jaak Aaviksoo said in interview on Estonian's Kanal 2 TV channel. Aaviksoo compared the cyber attacks with the blockade of Estonia's Embassy in Moscow. "Again, it is not possible to say without doubt that orders (for the blockade) came from the Kremlin, or that, indeed, a wish was expressed for such a thing there," said Aaviksoo. Russia called accusations of its involvement "unfounded," and neither NATO nor European Commission experts were able to find any proof of official Russian government participation.*[6]

As of January 2008, one ethnic-Russian Estonian national has been charged and convicted.*[7]

During a panel discussion on cyber warfare, Sergei Markov

of the Russian State Duma has stated his unnamed aide was responsible in orchestrating the cyber attacks. Markov alleged the aide acted on his own while residing in an unrecognised republic of the former Soviet Union, possibly Transnistria.*[8] On 10 March 2009 Konstantin Goloskokov, a "commissar" of the Kremlin-backed youth group Nashi, has claimed responsibility for the attack.*[9] Experts are critical of these varying claims of responsibility.*[10]

24.1 Legalities

On 2 May 2007, a criminal investigation was opened into the attacks under a section of the Estonian Penal Code criminalising *computer sabotage* and *interference with the working of a computer network*, felonies punishable by imprisonment of up to three years. As a number of attackers turned out to be within the jurisdiction of the Russian Federation, on 10 May 2007, Estonian Public Prosecutor's Office made a formal investigation assistance request to the Russian Federation's Supreme Procurature under a Mutual Legal Assistance Treaty (MLAT) existing between Estonia and Russia. A Russian State Duma delegation visiting Estonia in early May in regards the situation surrounding the Bronze Soldier of Tallinn had promised that Russia would aid such investigation in every way available.*[11] On 28 June, Russian Supreme Procurature refused assistance,*[11] claiming that the proposed investigative processes are not covered by the applicable MLAT.*[12] Piret Seeman, the Estonian Public Prosecutor's Office's PR officer, criticized this decision, pointing out that all the requested processes are actually enumerated in the MLAT.*[12]

On 24 January 2008, Dmitri Galushkevich, a student living in Tallinn, was found guilty of participating in the attacks. He was fined 17,500 kroons (approximately US$1,640) for attacking the website of the Estonian Reform Party.*[3]*[13]

As of 13 December 2008, Russian authorities have been

consistently denying Estonian law enforcement any investigative cooperation, thus effectively eliminating chances that those of the perpetrators that fall within Russian jurisdiction will be brought to trial.*[14]

24.2 Opinions of Experts

Critical systems whose network addresses would not be generally known were targeted, including those serving telephony and financial transaction processing.*[15] Although not all of the computer crackers behind the cyberwarfare have been unveiled, some experts believed that such efforts exceed the skills of individual activists or even organised crime as they require a co-operation of a state and a large telecom company.*[4]

A well known Russian hacker Sp0Raw believes that the most efficient online attacks on Estonia could not have been carried out without the blessing of the Russian authorities and that the hackers apparently acted under "recommendations" from parties in higher positions.*[16] *[17] At the same time he called claims of Estonians regarding direct involvement of Russian government in the attacks*[18] "empty words, not supported by technical data" .*[17]

Mike Witt, deputy director of the United States Computer Emergency Readiness Team (CERT) believes that the attacks were DDoS attacks. The attackers used botnets – global networks of compromised computers, often owned by careless individuals. "The size of the cyber attack, while it was certainly significant to the Estonian government, from a technical standpoint is not something we would consider significant in scale," Witt said.*[19]

Professor James Hendler, former chief scientist at The Pentagon's Defense Advanced Research Projects Agency (DARPA) characterised the attacks as "more like a cyber riot than a military attack." *[19]

"We don't have directly visible info about sources so we can't confirm or deny that the attacks are coming from the Russian government," Jose Nazario, software and security engineer at Arbor Networks, told *internetnews.com*.*[20] Arbor Networks operated *ATLAS* threat analysis network, which, the company claimed, could "see" 80% of Internet traffic. Nazario suspected that different groups operating separate distributed botnets were involved in the attack.

Experts interviewed by IT security resource SearchSecurity.com "say it's very unlikely this was a case of one government launching a coordinated cyberattack against another": Johannes Ullrich, chief research officer of the Bethesda said "Attributing a distributed denial-of-service attack like this to a government is hard." "It may as well be a group of bot herders showing 'patriotism,' kind of like

what we had with Web defacements during the US-China spy-plane crisis [in 2001]." Hillar Aarelaid, manager of Estonia's Computer Emergency Response Team "expressed skepticism that the attacks were from the Russian government, noting that Estonians were also divided on whether it was right to remove the statue" .*[21]

Clarke and Knake report that upon the Estonian authorities informing Russian officials they had traced systems controlling the attack to Russia, there was some indication in response that incensed patriotic Russians might have acted on their own.*[15] Regardless of conjectures over official involvement, the decision of Russian authorities not to pursue individuals responsible—a treaty obligation—together with expert opinion that Russian security services could readily track down the culprits should they so desire, leads Russia observers to conclude the attacks served Russian interests.*[15]

24.3 Claiming responsibility for the attacks

A Commissar of the Nashi pro-Kremlin youth movement in Moldova and Transnistria, Konstantin Goloskokov (Goloskov in some sources*[22]), admitted organizing cyberattacks against Estonian government sites.*[16] Goloskokov stressed, however, that he was not carrying out an order from Nashi's leadership and said that a lot of his fellow Nashi members criticized his response as being too harsh.*[17]

Like most countries, Estonia does not recognise Transnistria, a secessionist region of Moldova. As an unrecognised nation, Transnistria does not belong to Interpol.*[23] Accordingly, no Mutual Legal Assistance Treaty applies. If residents of Transnistria were responsible, the investigation may be severely hampered, and even if the investigation succeeds finding likely suspects, the legal recourse of Estonian authorities may be limited to issuing all-EU arrest warrants for these suspects. Such an act would be largely symbolic.

Head of Russian Military Forecasting Center, Colonel Anatoly Tsyganok confirmed Russia's ability to conduct such an attack when he stated: "*These attacks have been quite successful, and today the alliance had nothing to oppose Russia's virtual attacks*", additionally noting that these attacks did not violate any international agreement.*[24]

24.4 Influence on international military doctrines

The attacks triggered a number of military organizations around the world to reconsider the importance of network security to modern military doctrine. On 14 June 2007, defence ministers of NATO members held a meeting in Brussels, issuing a joint communiqué promising immediate action. First public results were estimated to arrive by autumn 2007.*[25]

On 25 June 2007, Estonian president Toomas Hendrik Ilves met with US President, George W. Bush.*[26] Among the topics discussed were the attacks on Estonian infrastructure. *[27] NATO Cooperative Cyber Defence Centre of Excellence (CCDCOE) operates out of Tallinn, Estonia, since August 2008*[28]

The events have been reflected in a NATO Department of Public Diplomacy short movie *War in Cyberspace*.*[29]

24.5 See also

- Russian influence operations in Estonia
- Cyberattacks during the 2008 South Ossetia war
- Fatal System Error
- Bronze Night

24.6 References

[1] The Guardian 17 May 2007: Russia accused of unleashing cyberwar to disable Estonia by Ian Traynor

[2] "War in the fifth domain. Are the mouse and keyboard the new weapons of conflict?". *The Economist*. 1 July 2010. Retrieved 2 July 2010. Important thinking about the tactical and legal concepts of cyber-warfare is taking place in a former Soviet barracks in Estonia, now home to NATO's "centre of excellence" for cyber-defence. It was established in response to what has become known as "Web War 1", a concerted denial-of-service attack on Estonian government, media and bank web servers that was precipitated by the decision to move a Soviet-era war memorial in central Tallinn in 2007.

[3] "Estonia fines man for 'cyber war'". BBC. 25 January 2008. Retrieved 23 February 2008.

[4] The Economist 24 May 2007: Cyberwarfare is becoming scarier

[5] Estonia accuses Russia of 'cyberattack'

[6] Estonia has no evidence of Kremlin involvement in cyber attacks

[7] "Estonia fines man for 'cyber war'". *BBC News*. 25 January 2008. Retrieved 22 April 2010.

[8] Radio Free Europe 6 March 2009: Behind The Estonia Cyberattacks by Robert Coalson

[9] Kremlin-backed group behind Estonia cyber blitz Financial Times 11 March 2009

[10] Authoritatively, Who Was Behind The Estonian Attacks? DarkReading 17 March 2009

[11] Postimees 6 July 2007: Venemaa jätab Eesti küberrünnakute uurimisel õigusabita

[12] Eesti Päevaleht 6 July 2007: Venemaa keeldus koostööst küberrünnakute uurimisel

[13] Leyden, John (24 January 2008). "Estonia fines man for DDoS attacks". *The Register*. Retrieved 22 February 2008.

[14] ERR 13 December 2008 16:43: Venemaa keeldub endiselt koostööst küberrünnakute uurimisel

[15] Clarke, R.A., Knake, R.K. Cyber War: The Next Threat To National Security And What To Do About It. Harper Collins. 2010.

[16] Swiss Baltic Chamber of Commerce in Lithuania/Baltic News Service 2 June 2007: Commissar of Nashi says he waged cyber attack on Estonian government sites

[17] (Russian) Электронная бомба. Кто стоит за кибервойной России с Эстонией

[18] Times Online: Urmas Paet, the Estonian Foreign Minister, accused the Kremlin of direct involvement

[19] United Press International: Analysis: Who cyber smacked Estonia?

[20] Internetnews.com: Estonia Under Russian Cyber Attack?

[21] Experts doubt Russian government launched DDoS attacks, by Bill Brenner, 18 May 2007. SearchSecurity.com

[22] Monument dispute with Estonia gets dirty

[23] Tiraspol Times 9 June 2007: Ministry of Internal Affairs lists PMR's 10 most wanted

[24] Руководитель российского Центра военного прогнозирования полковник Анатолий Цыганок считает, что кибератаки против Эстонии не нарушали никаких международных договоренностей, потому что таковых просто нет. "Эти атаки были вполне успешными, и сегодня альянсу нечего противопоставить российским виртуальным атакам, – заявил Цыганок в интервью «Газете». – В принципе потери вооружений НАТО могут быть огромными, если в результате таких атак вывести из строя компьютерное военное управление».

[25] Eesti Päevaleht 15 June 2007: NATO andis rohelise tule
     Eesti küberkaitse kavale by Ahto Lobjakas

[26] White House 4 May 2007: President Bush to Welcome Pres-
     ident Toomas Ilves of Estonia

[27] Yahoo/AFP 25 June 2007: Bush, Ilves eye tougher tack on
     cybercrime

[28] NATO to set up cyber warfare center

[29] Postimees 28 March 2009 14:02: NATO tegi filmi Eesti
     «kübersõjast»

24.7   External links

- Black Hat 2007: Lessons of the Estonian attacks, by
  Bill Brenner, 26 Jul 2007.

- Estonia urges firm EU, NATO response to new form
  of warfare: cyber-attacks

- Massive DDoS attacks target Estonia; Russia accused

- Cyberattack on Estonia stirs fear of 'virtual war'

- Estonia accuses Russia of 'cyberattack'

- Virtual harassment, but for real

- Digital Fears Emerge After Data Siege in Estonia

- EU urged to deepen cooperation after Estonia cyber-
  attacks

- The cyber pirates hitting Estonia

- Estonia hit by 'Moscow cyber war'

- Analysis: Who cyber smacked Estonia? by Shaun Waterman, *UPI*

- Hackers take down the most wired country in Europe
  by Joshua Davis, *Wired*, 2007-08-21.

- Georgetown Journal of International Affairs report –
  Battling Botnets and Online Mobs by Gadi Evron who
  wrote the postmortem analysis of the attacks for the
  Estonian CERT

Chapter 25

GhostNet

For the fishing net, see Ghost net.

GhostNet (simplified Chinese: 幽灵网; traditional Chinese: 幽靈網; pinyin: *YōuLíngWǎng*) is the name given by researchers at the Information Warfare Monitor to a large-scale cyber spying[*][1][*][2] operation discovered in March 2009. The operation is likely associated with an Advanced Persistent Threat. Its command and control infrastructure is based mainly in the People's Republic of China and has infiltrated high-value political, economic and media locations[*][3] in 103 countries. Computer systems belonging to embassies, foreign ministries and other government offices, and the Dalai Lama's Tibetan exile centers in India, London and New York City were compromised.

25.1 Discovery

GhostNet was discovered and named following a 10-month investigation by the Infowar Monitor (IWM), carried out after IWM researchers approached the Dalai Lama's representative in Geneva[*][4] suspecting that their computer network had been infiltrated.[*][5] The IWM is composed of researchers from The SecDev Group and Canadian consultancy and the Citizen Lab, Munk Centre for International Studies at the University of Toronto; the research findings were published in the *Infowar Monitor*, an affiliated publication.[*][6] Researchers from the University of Cambridge's Computer Laboratory, supported by the Institute for Information Infrastructure Protection,[*][7] also contributed to the investigation at one of the three locations in Dharamsala, where the Tibetan government-in-exile is located. The discovery of the 'GhostNet', and details of its operations, were reported by *The New York Times* on March 29, 2009.[*][6][*][8] Investigators focused initially on allegations of Chinese cyber-espionage against the Tibetan exile community, such as instances where email correspondence and other data were extracted.[*][9]

Compromised systems were discovered in the embassies of India, South Korea, Indonesia, Romania, Cyprus, Malta, Thailand, Taiwan, Portugal, Germany and Pakistan and the office of the Prime Minister of Laos. The foreign ministries of Iran, Bangladesh, Latvia, Indonesia, Philippines, Brunei, Barbados and Bhutan were also targeted.[*][1][*][10] No evidence was found that U.S. or UK government offices were infiltrated, although a NATO computer was monitored for half a day and the computers of the Indian embassy in Washington, D.C., were infiltrated.[*][3][*][10][*][11]

Since its discovery, GhostNet has attacked other government networks, for example Canadian official financial departments in early 2011, forcing them off-line. Governments commonly do not admit such attacks, which must be verified by official but anonymous sources.[*][12]

25.2 Technical functionality

Emails are sent to target organizations that contain contextually relevant information. These emails contain malicious attachments, that when opened, drop a Trojan horse on to the system. This Trojan connects back to a control server, usually located in China, to receive commands. The infected computer will then execute the command specified by the control server. Occasionally, the command specified by the control server will cause the infected computer to download and install a Trojan known as Gh0st Rat that allows attackers to gain complete, real-time control of computers running Microsoft Windows.[*][3] Such a computer can be controlled or inspected by attackers, and the software even has the ability to turn on camera and audio-recording functions of infected computers, enabling monitors to perform surveillance.[*][6]

25.3 Origin

The researchers from the IWM stated they could not conclude that the Chinese government was responsible for the spy network.[*][13] However, a report from researchers at the University of Cambridge says they believe that the Chinese government is behind the intrusions they analyzed at the Office of the Dalai Lama.*[14]

Researchers have also noted the possibility that GhostNet was an operation run by private citizens in China for profit or for patriotic reasons, or created by intelligence agencies from other countries such as Russia or the United States.*[6] The Chinese government has stated that China "strictly forbids any cyber crime." *[1]*[9]

The "Ghostnet Report" documents several unrelated infections at Tibetan-related organizations in addition to the Ghostnet infections. By using the email addresses provided by the IWM report, Scott J. Henderson had managed to trace one of the operators of one of the infections (non-Ghostnet) to Chengdu. He identifies the hacker as a 27-year-old man who had attended the University of Electronic Science and Technology of China, and currently connected with the Chinese hacker underground.*[15]

Despite the lack of evidence to pinpoint the Chinese government as responsible for intrusions against Tibetan-related targets, researchers at Cambridge have found actions taken by Chinese government officials that corresponded with the information obtained via computer instrusions. One such incident involved a diplomat who was pressured by Beijing after receiving an email invitation to a visit with the Dalai Lama from his representatives.*[14]

Another incident involved a Tibetan woman who was interrogated by Chinese intelligence officers and was shown transcripts of her online conversations.*[13]*[16] However, there are other possible explanations for this event. Drelwa uses QQ and other instant messengers to communicate with Chinese Internet users. In 2008, IWM found that TOM-Skype, the Chinese version of Skype, was logging and storing text messages exchanged between users. It is possible that the Chinese authorities acquired the chat transcripts through these means.*[17]

IWM researchers have also found that when detected, GhostNet is consistently controlled from IP addresses located on the island of Hainan, China, and have pointed out that Hainan is home to the Lingshui signals intelligence facility and the Third Technical Department of the People's Liberation Army.*[3] Furthermore, one of GhostNet's four control servers has been revealed to be a government server.*[18]

25.4 See also

- Honker Union

- Cyber-warfare

- Advanced Persistent Threat

- Titan Rain

- Operation Aurora

- Chinese intelligence activity in other countries

- Internet censorship in the People's Republic of China

- Economic and Industrial Espionage

- RedHack (from Turkey)

25.5 References

[1] "Major cyber spy network uncovered" . BBC News. March 29, 2009. Retrieved March 29, 2009.

[2] Glaister, Dan (March 30, 2009). "China Accused of Global Cyberspying" . The Guardian Weekly. 180 (16). London. p. 5. Retrieved April 7, 2009.

[3] Harvey, Mike (March 29, 2009). "Chinese hackers 'using ghost network to control embassy computers'". The Times. London. Retrieved March 29, 2009.

[4] "Tracking GhostNet: Investigating a Cyber Espionage Network" .

[5] "China denies spying allegations" . BBC News. March 30, 2009. Retrieved March 31, 2009.

[6] Markoff, John (March 28, 2009). "Vast Spy System Loots Computers in 103 Countries" . New York Times. Retrieved March 29, 2009.

[7] Shishir Nagaraja, Ross Anderson (March 2009). "The snooping dragon: social-malware surveillance of the Tibetan movement" (PDF). University of Cambridge. p. 2. Retrieved March 31, 2009.

[8] "Researchers: Cyber spies break into govt computers" . Associated Press. March 29, 2009. Retrieved March 29, 2009.

[9] China-based spies target Thailand. Bangkok Post, March 30, 2009. Retrieved on March 30, 2009.

[10] "Canadians find vast computer spy network: report" . Reuters. March 28, 2009. Retrieved March 29, 2009.

[11] "Spying operation by China infiltrated computers: Report" . The Hindu. March 29, 2009. Retrieved March 29, 2009.

[12] "Foreign hackers attack Canadian government". CBC News. February 17, 2011. Retrieved February 17, 2011.

[13] Tracking GhostNet: Investigating a Cyber Espionage Network. Munk Centre for International Studies. March 29, 2009

[14] Nagaraja, Shishir; Anderson, Ross (March 2009). "The snooping dragon: social-malware surveillance of the Tibetan movement" (PDF). Computer Laboratory, University of Cambridge.

[15] Henderson, Scott (April 2, 2009). "Hunting the GhostNet Hacker". The Dark Visitor. Retrieved April 2, 2009.

[16] U of T team tracks China-based cyber spies Toronto Star March 29, 2009 Archived March 31, 2009, at the Wayback Machine.

[17] BREACHING TRUST: An analysis of surveillance and security practices on China's TOM-Skype platform

[18] Meet the Canadians who busted Ghostnet Globe and Mail Martch 29, 2009

25.6 External links

- The SecDev Group

- Citizen Lab at the University of Toronto

- Tracking GhostNet: Investigating a Cyber Espionage Network (Infowar Monitor Report (SecDev and Citize Lab), March 29, 2009)

- F-Secure Mirror of the report PDF

- Information Warfare Monitor - Tracking Cyberpower (University of Toronto, Canada/Munk Centre)

- Twitter: InfowarMonitor

- Kelly, Cathal (March 31, 2009). "Cyberspies' code a click away - Simple Google search quickly finds link to software for Ghost Rat program used to target governments". *Toronto Star (Canada)*. Toronto, Ontario, Canada. Retrieved April 4, 2009.

- Lee, Peter (April 8, 2009). "Cyber-skirmish at the top of the world". *Asia Times Online*. Retrieved April 9, 2009.

- Bodmer, Kilger, Carpenter, & Jones (2012). Reverse Deception: Organized Cyber Threat Counter-Exploitation. New York: McGraw-Hill Osborne Media. ISBN 0071772499, ISBN 978-0071772495

Chapter 26

Great Hacker War

The **Great Hacker War** was a purported 1990–1991 conflict between the Masters of Deception (MOD) and an unsanctioned splinter faction of the older guard hacker group Legion of Doom (LOD), amongst several smaller subsidiary groups. Both of the primary groups involved, made attempts to hack into the opposing group's networks, across Internet, X.25, and telephone networks. In a panel debate of The Next HOPE conference, 2010, Phiber Optik reiterated that the rumoured "gang war in cyberspace" between LOD and MOD never happened, and that it was "a complete fabrication" by the U.S attorney's office and some sensationalist media. Furthermore, two other high-ranking members of the LOD confirmed that the "Great Hacker War" never occurred, reinforcing the idea that this was just a competition of one-upsmanship. However, there was indeed a conflict between the "New-LOD" led by Erik Bloodaxe, and the MOD hackers from primarily, NYC. And the one-upsmanship was not matched evenly on both sides, in fact if this was a "war", it was not a fight at all.

26.1   Latecomers to MOD and LOD

The Phrezh Prince of Bellcore (aka sw1tchg0d) was 16 when he allegedly controlled RBOCs Qwest, Bell Atlantic, and ILEC GTE (the latter two becoming Verizon) - and, according to his associates, all North American telcos from '99-'01. Long after the end of the 'war', there was still tension between sw1tchg0d and Erik Bloodaxe; largely attributed to MOD and sw1tchg0d's knowledge of Erik Bloodaxe being an informant. Members of sw1tchg0d's primary group, H4G1S, alleged friends and associates of MOD have stated that sw1tchg0d was the best at breaking internal bell systems and networks, as well as the last and probably youngest to learn the art of the Bell Systems in an age where more security was in place (SecurID authentication, among others). sw1tchg0d's (Jonathan) nickname was previously used by a mentor of his, H4G1S founder Shokwave Rider (sw_r), another telco hacker. Jonathan, assumed the sw1tchg0d nickname after a while, to pay homage to Mohammed (sw_r).

The respect sw1tchg0d had for MOD - through reading the published book - drove him to allegedly own even the switch of Phiber Optik, a Manhattan DMS, pulling qcm, qinfo and qdn records strictly as keepsakes, and not as a sign of disrespect. Phiber Optik was called at home and explained what had been taken, allegedly, from the DMS SuperNode information that allegedly validated this newcomer to the walking telco dictionary, Mark Abene. He apparently knows COSMOS replacements SWITCH and FOMS internals extremely well, as with the switches and Datakit network which are used to connect to switches and Bellcore (now Telcordia) OSS apps (FOMS/FUSA, FOMS/FM, SWITCH, MARCH, etc.) which ran on Amdahl Mainframes to which the internals were figured out via reverse engineering. sw1tchg0d has played pranks on Erik Bloodaxe, one of these involved purportedly distributing court records involving Bloodaxe emptying a shotgun towards his wife, specifically to the women of the hacking scene.

As of 2001, there were no new members in LOD, although this same person was affiliated with LOD.COM for a while and has become friends with members of the old-LOD. The new-LOD, primarily erikb's group of friends, is responsible for this demonstration of their own lack of skill - not LOD's as a whole.

26.2   The truth of the matter

Ironically, no LOD members had ever acquired switch access to the MOD switches, let alone full control of an RBOC - ever - and wasted X.25 MUXES calling QSD's insignificant and pedophile filled chat system with names like "phiber sux" filling all the chat slots and killing the mux that it is likeky, was not hacked directly by LOD members. Netw1z mentioned this in depth at his HOPE talk, juxtaposed with MOD's massive ownage of several X.25 PSNs. Yet despite this, Goggans claimed victory in the "war" - really a one-sided victory on all fronts for MOD, on T-shirts distributed at HoHoCon. They read "The Great

Hacker War" and "LOD: 1 MOD: 0" . Other members of LOD not present such as Marauder, and others, through so-called war, admit this is completely propaganda for Goggans "new-LOD" .

It is also interesting to note that the only known person ever to gain access to MOD-territory telco and X.25 PSNs, himself did it to become peers with MOD (though he does not claim to be part of anything that went on when the initial war happened, he had participated in continuing it apparently). John Lee and Allen Wilson have stated that The Phrezh Prince of Bellcore is unassailably elite, and this is the general sentiment among hackers he relates to. Sometimes a troll on irc, his skill is still unparalleled in many areas.

26.3 Knowledge

The Masters of Deception had three members with extreme specialties. By general consensus, Phiber Optik possessed the greatest wealth of information regarding telecommunications. W1ng was generally considered very knowledgeable with UNIX, before lots of tricks were known, and John Lee (Corrupt) was a pure systems breaker being very well versed with VMS as well.

Phiber Optik figured out many DMS internals, including the undocumented remote headset feature, how to bypass authentication and privilege escalate, and others. These were extremely powerful things that were told to only a few people, in MOD. He also knew the internals of other systems, such as SCCS (called "minis" because they are minicomputers), as well as other knowledge that cannot be shared here for the safety of critical infrastructure.

MOD had X.25 ownership (X-RAY and ISIS on Tymnet), as well as access to forward the dialup modems for the hunt groups for X.25 PADs, allowing dialup-MITM, or just a fake X.25 PAD to collect NUA, NUI, NUI password and disconnect upon the sending of line noise. They had a firm grasp of Datakit VCS and ISN, the network protocol invented at Bell Labs for circuit switching between devices (mostly telephone switches and other critical infrastructure). They also controlled for long periods of time, crucial portions of the internet and other networks.

LOD had little to no interesting telco or X.25 knowledge and, as previously stated and then edited out of this article, had extreme difficulty gaining, and even maintaining for any length of time, access to these systems. LOD did not possess the knowledge of Datakit, crucial in a war waged on telco networks, in fact, there are archives from various hacker BBS's with inane questions from [Erik Bloodaxe] about telco systems themselves. It has been said that the "Only access Erikb had to telco systems was if he caught a

COSMOS terminal still logged in on dialup."

According to Phiber Optik and C0rrupt (netw1z), the so-called war started because Erik Bloodaxe begged Phiber Optik for a path onto the Nynex Packet Switched Network (npsn - reachable at that time from Nynex Datakit, which Bloodaxe did not have.) The balance of skill was so favored towards the Masters of Deception that it is almost never argued otherwise, anywhere, except by Erik Bloodaxe [Chris Goggans] and friends of his.

26.4 Timeline

The Great Hacker War escalated in the space of only a few days with a series of four key events.

26.4.1 Event One

The Great Hacker War began with the closing of an invite-only bulletin board called "Fifth Amendment", whose participants were some of the world's most successful hackers. It was run by members of the newly reformed LOD under the leadership of Chris Goggans ("Erik Bloodaxe") and Loyd Blankenship ("The Mentor").

The closing of the board had been blamed on John Lee ("Corrupt") of the MOD in a cryptic message left to users. Chris Goggans (LOD) had claimed that Lee had been distributing information that was discussed on the board. MOD had discovered that Chris Goggans and his friends had decided to use the information being posted on the board to start a security company and contact all companies being discussed about the security flaws posted on Fifth Amendment.

26.4.2 Event Two

A few prank phone calls to the home number of the new LOD upset Goggans and prompted him to put out a call to find the personal information of the members of the MOD. Peacemakers intervened and a conference call was arranged on an unnamed RBOC telephone bridge in the Midwest. As members of the MOD silently joined the conference call, they overheard the members of the LOD using racial slurs to describe the ethnicity of members of the MOD. The peace conference quickly degenerated into threats and prank calls to members of the LOD, whose personal information had already been uncovered by the MOD.

26.4.3   Event Three

A last-minute, late-night peace talk was held between Chris Goggans (LOD) and Mark Abene ("Phiber Optik") of MOD. Unknown to Goggans, John Lee ("Corrupt") was listening in on three-way. Goggans became angry that Abene would not fulfill his numerous demands for the personal information of MOD members, and for the MOD's hacking information that he considered the property of LOD.

Abene refused to meet Goggans's demands, and Goggans uttered his infamous phrase that began the war in earnest - "MOD is nothing but niggers, spics, and white trash." That night, prank phone calls began to flood Abene's house.

26.4.4   Event Four

The members of the MOD decided to eavesdrop on Chris Goggans's phone calls to determine his motives. Using the undocumented remote headset feature on a DMS-100 phone switch local to Goggans, the MOD overheard what they had suspected earlier. Goggans, Scott Chasin ("Doc Holiday"), and Jake Kenyon Shulman ("Malefactor") had decided to form a security company called ComSec.

26.4.5   Epilogue

In 1991 Phiber Optik, while attending the first CFP conference in San Francisco with Craig Neidorf, was invited to join a telephone conference bridge by fellow hackers where an apologetic Shulman expressed his remorse at how the situation had been blown out of proportion and his view that Goggans had crossed the line in informing on other hackers to law enforcement in an effort to increase the prestige of ComSec. Further, it was suspected by other LOD members that Goggans had baited Phoenix of the Australian hacker group The Realm, and was instrumental in providing evidence to Australian federal authorities. As a result, Phiber, a friend of Phoenix's, received a conference call from several original LOD members now suspicious of Goggans, wondering if they had been implicated by Goggans or other informants in Abene's pending legal case, in addition to expressing their general distaste and distrust of Goggans. In 1993 at the third CFP conference, also in San Francisco, Phiber/Abene met a small handful of his old LOD friends (minus Goggans) for the first time in person despite having been friends for nearly 10 years by that point, and briefly reminisced about old times. Some years later in a public statement Goggans would show some regret that he involved Abene in his testimonials to law enforcement. Perhaps the one thing in all this that Phiber and Lex Luthor agree on is that in reality there simply was no "Great Hacker War", and that the notion of "warring hacker gangs" was an inven-

tion of overzealous law enforcement which was latched onto by irresponsible mass-media because the imagery made for good copy.

26.5   See also

- The Hacker Crackdown
- Masters of Deception - One side of the Great Hacker War
- Legion of Doom
- Chris Goggans ("Erik Bloodaxe") - One side of the Great Hacker War
- Mark Abene ("Phiber Optik")
- Nahshon Even-Chaim ("Phoenix")

26.6   External links

- modbook4.txt —*The Book of MOD: Part Four: End of '90-'1991*
- modbook3.txt —*The Book of MOD: Part Three*

26.7   References

- *The Masters of Deception: The Gang that Ruled Cyberspace* (ISBN 0 06 092694 5)
- "Gang War in Cyberspace." *Wired* 2.12
- "Notorious M.O.D." *Wired* 9.06

Chapter 27

July 2009 cyber attacks

The **July 2009 cyber attacks** were a series of coordinated cyber attacks against major government, news media, and financial websites in South Korea and the United States.[1] The attacks involved the activation of a botnet— a large number of hijacked computers—that maliciously accessed targeted websites with the intention of causing their servers to overload due to the influx of traffic, known as a DDoS attack.[1] Most of the hijacked computers were located in South Korea.[2] The estimated number of the hijacked computers varies widely; around 20,000 according to the South Korean National Intelligence Service, around 50,000 according to Symantec's Security Technology Response group,[3] and more than 166,000 according to a Vietnamese computer security researcher who analyzed the log files of the two servers the attackers controlled.[4]

The timing and targeting of the attacks have led to suggestions that they may be from North Korea, although these suggestions have not been substantiated.[5][6][7]

27.1 Timeline of attacks

27.1.1 First wave

The first wave of attacks occurred on July 4, 2009 (Independence Day holiday in the United States), targeting both the United States and South Korea. Among the websites affected were those of the White House and The Pentagon.[1][8] An investigation revealed that 27 websites were targets in the attack based on files stored on compromised systems.[9]

27.1.2 Second wave

The second wave of attacks occurred on July 7, 2009, affecting South Korea. Among the websites targeted were the presidential Blue House, the Ministry of Defense, the Ministry of Public Administration and Security,

the National Intelligence Service and the National Assembly.[5][10]

27.1.3 Third wave

A third wave of attacks began on July 9, 2009, targeting several websites in South Korea, including the country's National Intelligence Service as well as one of its largest banks and a major news agency.[1][11] The U.S. State Department said on July 9 that its website also came under attack.[12] State Department spokesman Ian Kelly said: "I'm just going to speak about our website, the state.gov website. There's not a high volume of attacks. But we're still concerned about it. They are continuing." [12] U.S. Department of Homeland Security spokesperson Amy Kudwa said that the department was aware of the attacks and that it had issued a notice to U.S. federal departments and agencies to take steps to mitigate attacks.[9]

27.2 Effects

Despite the fact that the attacks have targeted major public and private sector websites, the South Korean Presidential office has suggested that the attacks are targeted towards causing disruption, rather than stealing data.[13] However, Jose Nazario, manager of a U.S. network security firm, claimed that the attack is estimated to have produced only 23 megabits of data per second, not enough to cause major disruptions.[9] Joe Stewart, researcher at SecureWorks' Counter Threat Unit, said that the data generated by the attacking program appeared to be based on a Korean-language browser.[9]

It was expected that the economic costs associated with websites being down would be large, as the disruption had prevented people from carrying out transactions, purchasing items or conducting business.[14]

27.3   Perpetrators

It is not known who is behind the attacks. Reports indicate that the type of attacks being used, commonly known as distributed denial-of-service attacks, were unsophisticated.[7][9][15] Given the prolonged nature of the attacks, they are being recognized as a more coordinated and organized series of attacks.[6] According to the South Korean National Intelligence Service, the source of the attacks was tracked down and the government activated an emergency cyber-terror response team who blocked access to five host sites containing the malicious code and 86 websites that downloaded the code, located in 16 countries, including the United States, Guatemala, Japan and the People's Republic of China, but North Korea was not among them.[16] Later, it has been discovered that the malicious code responsible for causing the attack, identified as W32.Dozer, is programmed to destroy data on infected computers and to prevent the computers from being rebooted.[2] South Korean police are analyzing a sample of the thousands of computers used to crash websites, stating that there is "various evidence" of North Korean involvement, but said they may not find the culprit.[17] Security experts said that the attack re-used code from the Mydoom worm.[18] One analyst thinks that the attacks likely came from the United Kingdom.[4]

On October 30, 2009, South Korea's spy agency, the National Intelligence Service, stated the origin of the attacks were from North Korea's telecommunications ministry.[19]

27.4   See also

- 2007 cyberattacks on Estonia

- Cyberterrorism

- Cyber Storm Exercise

- Moonlight Maze

- Titan Rain

- Comparison of computer viruses

- Denial-of-service attack

27.5   References

[1] "New 'cyber attacks' hit S Korea". BBC News. 2009-07-09. Retrieved 2009-07-09.

[2] Claburn, Thomas (2009-07-10). "Cyber Attack Code Starts Killing Infected PCs". InformationWeek. Retrieved 2009-07-10.

[3] Mills, Elinor (2009-07-10). "Botnet worm in DOS attacks could wipe data out on infected PCs". CNET News. Retrieved 2009-07-12.

[4] Williams, Martyn (2009-07-14). "UK, not North Korea, source of DDOS attacks, researcher says". IDG News Service.

[5] "Pyongyang blamed as cyber attack hits S Korea". *Financial Times*. 2009-07-09. Retrieved 2009-07-09.

[6] Kim, Hyung-Jin (2009-07-08). "Korean, US Web sites hit by suspected cyber attack". Associated Press. Archived from the original on July 11, 2009. Retrieved 2009-07-09.

[7] McDevitt, Caitlin (2009-07-09). "Cyberattack Aftermath". Reuters. Archived from the original on July 12, 2009. Retrieved 2009-07-09.

[8] "Governments hit by cyber attack". BBC News. 2009-07-08. Retrieved 2009-07-09.

[9] Markoff, John (2009-07-09). "Cyberattacks Jam Government and Commercial Web Sites in U.S. and South Korea". *The New York Times*. Retrieved 2009-07-09.

[10] "Cyber Attacks Hit Government and Commercial Websites". Foxreno.com. 2009-07-08. Retrieved 2009-07-09.

[11] "Official: S. Korea web sites under renewed attack". Associated Press. 2009-07-09. Archived from the original on July 15, 2009. Retrieved 2009-07-09.

[12] "US State Department under cyberattack for fourth day". AFP. 2009-07-10.

[13] "S Korea's presidential office says no damage done from hacker attacks". Xinhua. 2009-07-08. Retrieved 2009-07-09.

[14] Han, Jane (2009-07-09). "Cyber Attack Hits Korea for Third Day". *Korea Times*. Retrieved 2009-07-09.

[15] Arnoldy, Ben (2009-07-09). "Cyberattacks against US, S. Korea signal anger – not danger". *Christian Science Monitor*.

[16] Jiyeon, Lee (2009-07-11). "Cyberattack rocks South Korea". GlobalPost. Retrieved 2009-07-11.

[17] Kim, Kwang-Tae (2009-07-12). "S. Korea analyzes computers used in cyberattacks". Associated Press. Archived from the original on July 16, 2009. Retrieved 2009-07-12.

[18] Zetter, Kim (2009-07-08). "Lazy Hacker and Little Worm Set Off Cyberwar Frenzy". Wired News. Retrieved 2009-07-09.

[19] "N. Korean ministry behind July cyber attacks: spy chief". Yonhap. October 30, 2009.

Chapter 28

June 25 cyber terror

The June 25 cyber terror is an information leak that occurred on 2014 June 25 that targeted Cheongwadae and other institutions. The hacker that caused this incident admitted that the information of 2.5 million Saenuri Party members, 300 thousand soldiers, 100 thousand Cheongwadae homepage users and 40 thousand United States Forces Korea members.

28.1 Outline

At approximately 2013 June 25 9:10 AM, websites such as the Cheongwadae website, main government institute websites, news, etc. became victims of website change, DDoS, information thievery and other such attacks. When connecting to the Cheongwadae homepage words such as 'The great Kim Jong-un governor' and 'All hail the unified president Kim Jong-un! Until our demands are met our attacks will continue. Greet us. We are anonymous' would appear with a photo of president Park Geun-hye.

The government changed the status of cyber danger to 'noteworthy' on June 25 10:45 AM, then changed it to 'warning' on 3:40 PM.[1] Cheongwadae uploaded an apology on June 28.[2]

The Ministry of Science, ICT and Future Planning revealed on July 16 that this incident and the 2013 South Korea cyberattack both corresponded with past hacking methods used by North Korea.[3] However, the attacked targets include a Japanese Korean Central News Agency site and major North Korean anti-South websites, and the hackers also have announced that they would release information of approximately 20 high-ranked North Korean army officers with countless pieces of information on North Korean weaponry.

28.2 Appearance in the South Korean National Geographic

The South Korean National Geographic published cyber terror as one of the top 10 keywords of 2013 with the reason for selection being this incident and the 2013 South Korea cyberattack.[4]

28.3 References

[1] '6·25 □□□□□' □□□□□□□□□ □□□□, 2013 □ 6 □ 25 □

[2] 10 □□□□□□□□□□□□□□.... □□□, □□□□□ □□□□□□, 2013 □ 6 □ 29 □

[3] □□ "6·25 □□□□□□□□" □□□□, 2013 □ 7 □ 16 □

[4] □□□□□□□□□□□, '2013 □ 10 □□□□' □□□□, 2013 □ 12 □ 12 □

Chapter 29

Lazarus Group

Lazarus Group is a cybercrime group made up of an unknown number of individuals. While not much is known about the Lazarus Group, researchers have attributed many cyber attacks to them over the last decade. The earliest known attack that the group is responsible for is known as "Operation Troy", which took place from 2009-2012. This was a cyber-espionage campaign that utilized unsophisticated DDoS techniques to target the Seoul government of South Korea. They are also responsible for attacks in 2011 and 2013. It is possible that they were also behind a 2007 attack targeting South Korea, but that still isn't certain.[1] A notable attack that the group is known for is the 2014 attack on Sony Pictures. The Sony attack used more sophisticated techniques and highlighted how advanced the group has become over time. The most recent attack attributed to the group is recent 2016 bank heists, which included an attack on a Bangladesh bank, successfully stealing $81m.

websites and placed the text "Memory of Independence Day" in the Master Boot Record.

As time goes on, the attacks from the group get more sophisticated. Their techniques and tools become better developed and are more effective. In March 2011, "Ten Days of Rain" began. This attack targeted South Korean media, financial, and critical infrastructure. It consisted of more sophisticated DDoS attacks that originated from compromised computers within South Korea.The attacks continue with DarkSeoul on March 20, 2013. This was a wiper attack that targeted three South Korean broadcast companies, financial institutes, and an ISP. At the time, two other groups, NewRomanic Cyber Aray Team and WhoIs Team, took credit for that attack but researchers now know that the Lazarus Group was behind it.[5]

29.1 Rise

Under the name "Operation Blockbuster", a coalition of security companies, lead by Novetta,[2][3] was able to analyze malware samples found in different cyber-security incidents. Using that data, the team was able to analyze the methods used by the actors. They linked the Lazarus Group to a number of attacks through a pattern of code re-usage.[4]

The earliest possible attack that can be attributed to the Lazarus Group took place in 2007. This attack was named "Operation Flame" and utilized first generation malware against the South Korean government. According to some researchers, the activity present in this attack can be linked to later attacks such as "Operation 1Mission," Operation Troy," and the DarkSeoul attacks in 2013. The next incident took place on July 4, 2009 and sparked the beginning of "Operation Troy." This attack utilized the MYDOOM and Dozer malware to launch a large-scale, but quite unsophisticated, DDoS attack against US and South Korean websites. The volley of attacks struck about three dozen

29.2 Scorched earth

The Lazarus Group attacks culminated on November 24, 2014. On that day, a Reddit post appeared Stating that Sony Pictures had been hacked. No one knew it at the time, but this was the start to one of the biggest corporate breaches in recent history. At the time if the attack, the group identified themselves as the Guardians of Peace (GOP) and they were able to hack their way into the Sony network, leaving it crippled for days. The group claims that they were in the Sony network for a year before they were discovered, and it is certainly possible that that is true.[6] The attack was so intrusive that the actors were able to get access to valuable insider information including previously unreleased films and the personal information of approximately 4,000 past and present employees. The group was also able to access internal emails and reveal some very speculative practices going on at Sony.[7]

29.3 References

[1] "Security researchers say mysterious 'Lazarus Group' hacked Sony in 2014". *The Daily Dot*. Retrieved 2016-02-29.

[2] https://operationblockbuster.com/

[3] http://www.novetta.com/2016/02/ novetta-exposes-depth-of-sony-pictures-attack/

[4] "Kaspersky Lab helps to disrupt the activity of the Lazarus Group responsible for multiple devastating cyber-attacks | Kaspersky Lab". *www.kaspersky.com*. Retrieved 2016-02-29.

[5] "The Sony Hackers Were Causing Mayhem Years Before They Hit the Company". *WIRED*. Retrieved 2016-03-01.

[6] "Sony Got Hacked Hard: What We Know and Don't Know So Far". *WIRED*. Retrieved 2016-03-01.

[7] "A Breakdown and Analysis of the December, 2014 Sony Hack". *www.riskbasedsecurity.com*. Retrieved 2016-03-01.

29.3.1 Sources

- Virus News (2016). "Kaspersky Lab Helps to Disrupt the Activity of the Lazarus Group Responsible for Multiple Devastating Cyber-Attacks", *Kaspersky Lab*.

- RBS (2014). "A Breakdown and Analysis of the December, 2014 Sony Hack". *RiskBased Security*.

- Cameron, Dell (2016). "Security Researchers Say Mysterious 'Lazarus Group' Hacked Sony in 2014", *The Daily Dot*.

- Zetter, Kim (2014). "Sony Got Hacked Hard: What We Know and Don't Know So Far", *Wired*.

- Zetter, Kim (2016). "Sony Hackers Were Causing Mayhem Years Before They Hit The Company", *Wired*.

Chapter 30

Lizard Squad

Lizard Squad is a black hat hacking group, mainly known for their claims of distributed denial-of-service (DDoS) attacks[1] primarily to disrupt gaming-related services.

On September 3, 2014, Lizard Squad seemingly announced that it had disbanded[2] only to return later on, claiming responsibility for a variety of attacks on prominent websites. The organisation at one point participated in the Darkode hacking forums and shared hosting with them.[3][4]

On April 30, 2016, CloudFlare published a blogpost detailing how cyber criminals using this groups name were issuing random threats of carrying out DDOS attacks, despite these threats, CloudFlare claim they failed to carry through with a single attack.[5][6] As a result of this, the City of London Police issued an alert warning businesses not to comply with ransom messages threatening DDOS attacks.[7][8]

30.1 Distributed denial-of-service attacks

A distributed denial-of-service (DDoS) attack occurs when numerous systems flood the bandwidth or resources of a targeted system, usually one or more web servers.[9] Such an attack is often the result of multiple systems (for example a botnet) flooding the targeted system with traffic. When a server is overloaded with connections, new connections can no longer be accepted.

30.2 Notable actions

30.2.1 *League of Legends* DDoS

On August 18, 2014, servers of the game *League of Legends* were taken offline with a DDoS attack; this was claimed as Lizard Squad's first attack.[10]

30.2.2 Destiny DDoS

On November 23, 2014, Lizard Squad claimed they attacked *Destiny* servers with a DDoS attack.[11]

30.2.3 PlayStation Network DDoS

On August 24, 2014 the PlayStation Network was disrupted via a DDoS attack, and again On December 8, with Lizard Squad claiming responsibility.[12][13][14]

30.2.4 Xbox Live DDoS

On December 1, 2014, Xbox Live was apparently attacked by Lizard Squad, users attempting to connect to use the service would be given the 80151909 error code.[15]

30.2.5 The Machinima Hack

On December 2, 2014, Lizard Squad hacked Machinima.com, replacing their front page with ASCII art of their logo.[16]

30.2.6 North Korea DDoS

On December 22, 2014, Internet in North Korea was taken offline by a DDoS attack.[17] Lizard Squad claimed responsibility for the attack and linked to an IP address located in North Korea.[18] North Korean Internet services were restored on the 23 December 2014.[19]

30.2.7 Christmas attacks

Lizard Squad had previously threatened to take down gaming services on Christmas.[20]

On December 25, 2014 (Christmas Day), Lizard Squad claimed to have performed a DDoS attack on the PlayStation Network and Xbox Live.[*][21]

On December 26, 2014 at 2:00 AM, Lizard Squad appeared to stop attacking PlayStation Network and Xbox Live. Gizmodo reported that the attacks may have ceased after Kim Dotcom offered Lizard Squad 3000 accounts on his upload service MEGA.[*][22]

30.2.8 Tor sybil attack

On December 26, 2014, a Sybil attack involving more than 3000 relays was attempted against the Tor network.[*][23] Nodes with names beginning with "LizardNSA" began appearing, Lizard Squad claimed responsibility for this attack.[*][24]

The relevance of the attack was questioned. According to Tor relay node operator Thomas White, the consensus system made that Lizard Squad only managed to control "0.2743% of the network, equivalent of a tiny VPS".[*][25]

30.2.9 Malaysia Airlines website attack

On January 26, 2015, the website of Malaysia Airlines was attacked, apparently by Lizard Squad, calling itself a "cyber caliphate". Users were redirected to another page bearing an image of a tuxedo-wearing lizard, and reading "Hacked by Cyber Caliphate". Underneath this was text reading "follow the cyber caliphate on twitter" after which were the Twitter accounts of the owner of UMG, "@UMGRobert" and CEO of UMG, "@UMG_Chris". The page also carried the headline "404 - Plane Not Found", an apparent reference to the airline's loss of flight MH370 last year with 239 people on board. Malaysia Airlines assured customers and clients that customer data had not been compromised.[*][26]

Media reports around the world said versions of the takeover in some regions included the wording "ISIS will prevail", which listed concerns of Lizard Squad's association with the Islamic State.[*][26]

30.3 False claims

30.3.1 Bomb threats

On August 24, 2014, Lizard Squad claimed that a plane on which the president of Sony Online Entertainment, John Smedley, was flying (American Airlines Flight 362), had explosives on board.[*][27][*][28] The flight from Dallas to San Diego made an unscheduled landing in Phoenix, Ari-

zona. Sony Online Entertainment announced that the FBI was investigating the incident.[*][28]

30.3.2 Facebook, Instagram, and Tinder attack

On January 26, 2015, several social media services including Facebook and Instagram were unavailable to users. Tinder and HipChat were also affected. Lizard Squad claimed responsibility for the attacks, via a posting on a Twitter account previously used by the group.[*][29] The outage, originally speculated to be a Distributed Denial of Service attack, lasted a little under an hour before services were restored.[*][30]

Facebook later released a statement saying its own engineers were to blame, and that the disruption to its services was not the result of a third-party attack, but instead occurred after they introduced a change that affected their configuration systems.[*][31]

30.3.3 Explicit celebrity photos

On January 27, 2015, Lizard Squad claimed to have compromised Taylor Swift's Twitter and Instagram accounts. Once they claimed to have access, they threatened to release nude photos in exchange for bitcoins. Taylor Swift, however, retorted that "there were no naked pics" and told the offenders to "have fun" finding any.[*][32]

30.4 Known members

30.4.1 obnoxious

"obnoxious", a 17-year-old resident of Coquitlam, British Columbia, Canada, was arrested in December 2014 in connection with numerous instances of swatting and doxing he allegedly committed. "obnoxious", whose legal name is not publicly known due to a publication ban, identified himself online as a Lizard Squad member. He primarily targeted female players of the MOBA *League of Legends* and their families.

On May 15, 2015, he pleaded guilty to 23 counts of extortion, public mischief, and criminal harassment.[*][33][*][34]

30.4.2 Vinnie Omari

Vinnie Omari is a member of the Lizard Squad who was arrested and bailed under the alleged offences of "Enter into/concerned in acquisition/retention/use or control criminal property, Fraud by false representation - Fraud Act 2006, Conspire to steal from another, unauthorized computer access with intent to commit other offences" .*[35]

30.4.3 Julius Kivimaki

Julius Kivimaki (zeekill) is a Finnish member of Lizard Squad convicted in July 2015 on over 50,000 counts of computer crime.*[36]

30.5 References

[1] "How A Hacker Gang Literally Saved Christmas For Video Game Players Everywhere" . *Business Insider*. Retrieved 25 December 2014.

[2] "Lizard Squad Hacker Collective Announces Disbanding" . *Softpedia News*. Retrieved 26 December 2014.

[3] MalwareTech (December 2014). "Darkode - Ode to Lizard Squad (The Rise and Fall of a Private Community)". Retrieved 4 August 2015.

[4] Buncombe, August (15 July 2015). "Darkode: FBI shuts down notorious online forum and cracks 'cyber hornet's nest of criminal hackers'". *The Independent*.

[5] Paine, Justin. "Lizard Squad Ransom Threats: New Name, Same Faux Armada Collective M.O." . *CloudFlare Blog*. CloudFlare, Inc. Retrieved 17 May 2016.

[6] Ashok, India (April 30, 2016). "Armada Collective impersonators now posing as Lizard Squad in DDoS scam" . International Business Times. Retrieved 17 May 2016.

[7] Russon, Mary-Ann (May 3, 2016). "Fake 'Lizard Squad' DDoS demands hit UK businesses spurring police warning" . International Business Times. Retrieved 17 May 2016.

[8] "Online extortion demands affecting businesses" . *Action Fraud*. 29 April 2016. Retrieved 17 May 2016.

[9] Taghavi Zargar, Saman (November 2013). "A Survey of Defense Mechanisms Against Distributed Denial of Service (DDoS) Flooding Attacks" (PDF). IEEE COMMUNICATIONS SURVEYS & TUTORIALS. pp. 2046–2069. Retrieved 2014-03-07.

[10] Gilbert, David (August 26, 2014). "Who Are Lizard Squad - Isis-Linked Hackers or Trolls Making Bomb Threats?". *International Business Times*.

[11] Schmitz, Alex (November 23, 2014). "Destiny Gamers Facing Connection Errors, Servers DDOS'ed by the Lizard Squad" . *Gamechup*. Retrieved December 26, 2014.

[12] Zorabedian, John (August 26, 2014). ""Lizard Squad" hackers force PSN offline, and Sony exec from the sky" . *Naked Security*. Retrieved December 26, 2014.

[13] "PlayStation Network Hacked 'By Lizard Squad'". *Sky News*. London. December 8, 2014. Retrieved December 26, 2014.

[14] Jones, Gary (December 9, 2014). "Sony confirm DDOS attack after Lizard Squad claim PSN 'take down' affecting PS4 and PS3: SONY have confirmed the Playstation Network was hit by a DDOS attack this week, affecting both the PS4 and PS3." . *Express*. London. Retrieved December 26, 2014.

[15] McWherter, Michael (December 1, 2014). "Xbox Live having issues, hacker group claims responsibility for taking it offline [update]". *Polygon*. Retrieved December 26, 2014.

[16] "Sony hack: North Korea back online after internet outage" . *BBC Newsbeat*. Retrieved 23 December 2014.

[17] "Sony hack: North Korea back online after internet outage" . *Ars Technica*. Retrieved 23 December 2014.

[18] "North Korean Web goes dark days after Obama pledges response to Sony hack" . *Washington Post*. Retrieved 23 December 2014.

[19] "Sony hack: North Korea back online after internet outage" . *BBC News*. BBC. Retrieved 23 December 2014.

[20] "Xbox Live: Lizard Squad hackers promise DDoS attacks at Christmas" . *International Business Times*. Retrieved 25 December 2014.

[21] "Please let us play! Thousands of Playstation and Xbox gamers who are STILL locked out of networks plead with hackers who 'ruined Christmas' to let them log on to games" . *Daily Mail*. Retrieved 26 December 2014.

[22] "Kim Dotcom May Have Just Saved Holiday Gaming" . *Gizmodo*. Retrieved 26 December 2014.

[23] "[tor-consensus-health] Possible Sybil Attack" . *"tor-consensus-health" mailing list*. Retrieved 26 December 2014.

[24] "Hackers Who Shut Down PSN and Xbox Live Now Attacking Tor" . *Gizmodo*. Retrieved 26 December 2014.

[25] TheCthulhu [CthulhuSec] (26 December 2014). "Congrats to Lizard Squad people who with 3300 or so relays control 0.2743% of the network. Equivalent of a tiny VPS." (Tweet). Retrieved 26 December 2014 – via Twitter.

[26] Malaysia Airlines website 'compromised' by 'cyber caliphate' Lizard Squad hackers, ABC News Australia, 26 Jan 2015

[27] "Who Are Lizard Squad - Isis-Linked Hackers or Trolls Making Bomb Threats?". *International Business Times*. Retrieved 23 December 2014.

[28] "Hackers Ground Sony Executive's Flight With Bomb-Threat Tweet". *Forbes*. Retrieved 26 December 2014.

[29] Lizard Squad, Facebook, Instagram, Tinder, AIM, Hipchat #offline #LizardSquad, Twitter, January 26, 2015

[30] Hachman, Mark, Internet problems take out Facebook, Instagram, others; Lizard Squad takes credit, PC World, January 26, 2015

[31] "Facebook says it caused fault that sent services offline". BBC News. Retrieved 27 January 2015.

[32] Esther, Lee. "Taylor Swift's Social Media Accounts Hacked, Threatened With Nude Photo Leak: Read Her Response". US Weekly. Retrieved 27 January 2015.

[33] Janis Warren. "Coquitlam teen admits to swatting". *Tri City News*.

[34] "Lizard Squad member pleads guilty over 23 counts related to 'swatting'". *the Guardian*.

[35] "Krebs on security article on Lizard Squad". Retrieved 30 January 2015.

[36] "Lizard Squad hacker convicted on 50,000 hacking charges". *The Daily Dot*. 7 July 2015. Retrieved 13 April 2016.

Chapter 31

LulzRaft

Not to be confused with LulzSec.

LegionData is the name of a computer hacker group or individual that gained international attention in 2011 due to a series of high-profile attacks on Canadian websites. Their targets have included the Conservative Party of Canada and Husky Energy.

On June 7, 2011, LulzRaft claimed responsibility for a hacking into the Conservative Party of Canada website and posting a false story about Canadian Prime Minister Stephen Harper. The hackers posted an alert on the site claiming that Harper had choked on a hash brown while eating breakfast and was airlifted to Toronto General Hospital. The story fooled many, including Canadian MP Christopher Alexander, who spread the story on Twitter. A spokesman for the Prime Minister soon denied the story.[*][1]

LulzRaft again targeted the Conservative Party on June 8, taking responsibility for a successful breach of a database containing information about the party's donors. The information accessed by the group including the names of donors as well as their home and e-mail addresses. LulzRaft later stated that the party had "terrible security" and that for the intrusion it used very basic methods. LulzRaft also apparently hacked into the website of Husky Energy on the same day. They inserted a notice promising free gas to users who used the coupon code "hash-browns", claiming that it was a gesture of goodwill intended to placate conservatives who were offended by their previous attacks.[*][2]

Though some commentators have speculated that the group is motivated by a dislike of the Conservative party,[*][1][*][3] LulzRaft has stated that they are a non-partisan group with a general dislike of politicians.[*][4] It is unknown whether the group is linked with LulzSec, although some media reports have included speculation that LulzRaft's attacks were inspired due to the Copycat effect.[*][1]

31.1 References

[1] Beltrame, Julian (8 June 2011). "Hacker without a cause scores with Harper 'breakfast incident' hoax". *The Canadian Press.* Retrieved 8 March 2012.

[2] "Online donors' data breached: Conservatives". *CBCNews.* 8 June 2011. Retrieved 10 June 2011.

[3] Proussalidis, Daniel (8 June 2011). "Anti-Tory hackers strike again". *Toronto Sun.* Retrieved 9 June 2011.

[4] Chase, Steven (8 June 2011). "Hackers take another jab at Tories on heels of Harper choking hoax". *The Globe and Mail.* Retrieved 10 June 2011.

31.2 External links

- LulzRaft on Twitter

Chapter 32

Moonlight Maze

Moonlight Maze is the name of an FBI inquiry into a cyber attack on United States government networks that began in 1998.*[1]*[2]*[3]

On September 20, 1999, *Newsweek* printed a story on Moonlight Maze that was written by Gregory Vistica. It was titled "'We're in the middle of a cyberwar'," based on a quote from then-Deputy Secretary of Defense John Hamre.*[4]

Federal Computer Week's Dan Verton described the Hamre quote earlier that year *[5] as pertaining to "Serbia's attacks against NATO's public World Wide Web pages".

32.1 See also

- Titan Rain
- Operation Aurora
- Cyberwarfare
- Ghostnet

32.2 References

[1] Drogin, Bob (7 October 1999). "Russians Seem To Be Hacking Into Pentagon". Retrieved 22 August 2015.

[2] "Moonlight Maze, 1998–1999". *RealClearPolitics.com.* RealClearPolitics. 26 February 2013. Retrieved 30 August 2015.

[3] PBS. "Cyberwar! The Warnings?". PBS. Retrieved 26 July 2010.

[4] "Newsweek Exclusive: 'We're in the Middle of a Cyberwar'". PR Newswire. September 12, 1999. Retrieved February 12, 2013.

[5] Brewin, Bob (June 20, 1999). "Cyberattacks spur talk of 3rd DOD network". Retrieved 20 September 2016.

32.3 External links

- Russians Seem To Be Hacking Into Pentagon, *San Francisco Chronicle*
- Text of James Adams' testimony to the Committee on Governmental Affairs that includes a summary of Moonlight Maze
- Summary of Moonlight Maze by television series *Frontline*
- David Perera, Chinese attacks 'Byzantine Candor' penetrated federal agencies, says leaked cable, *Fierce Government IT*, December 6, 2010

Chapter 33

Night Dragon Operation

Night Dragon Operation is one of the cyber attacks that started in mid-2006 and was initially reported by Dmitri Alperovitch, Vice President of Threat Research at Internet security company McAfee in August 2011, who also led and named the Night Dragon Operation and Operation Aurora cyberespionage intrusion investigations. The attacks have hit at least 71 organizations, including defense contractors, businesses worldwide, the United Nations and the International Olympic Committee.

33.1 Attack work model

The attacks use a variety of components – there is no single piece or family of malware responsible. The preliminary stage of the attack involves penetration of the target network, 'breaking down the front door'. Techniques such as spear-phishing and SQL injection of public facing web servers are reported to have been used. Once in, the attackers then upload freely available hacker tools onto the compromised servers in order to gain visibility into the internal network. The internal network can then be penetrated by typical penetration methods (accessing Active Directory account details, cracking user passwords etc) in order to infect machines on the network with remote administration tools (RATs). Since this attack is done by government, the resources in terms of hardware, software and other logistics are available to the hackers PLA Unit 61398.*[1]

33.2 References

[1] "'Night Dragon' Attacks From China Strike Energy Companies". *PCWorld*. Retrieved 2016-02-10.

Chapter 34

Office of Personnel Management data breach

In June 2015, the United States Office of Personnel Management (OPM) announced that it had been the target of a data breach targeting the records of as many as four million people.[*][1] Later, FBI Director James Comey put the number at 18 million.[*][2] The data breach, which had started in March 2014, and may have started earlier, was noticed by the OPM in April 2015.[*][1][*][3] It has been described by federal officials as among the largest breaches of government data in the history of the United States.[*][1] Information targeted in the breach included personally identifiable information such as Social Security numbers,[*][4] as well as names, dates and places of birth, and addresses.[*][5] The hack went deeper than initially believed and likely involved theft of detailed security-clearance-related background information. One victim wrote that the OPM is the agency that asks your neighbors what they know about you that could be used to blackmail you.[*][6][*][7][*][8]

On July 9, 2015, the estimate of the number of stolen records had increased to 21.5 million. This included records of people who had undergone background checks, but who were not necessarily current or former government employees.[*][9] Soon after, Katherine Archuleta, the director of OPM, and former National Political Director for Barack Obama's 2012 reelection campaign, resigned.

34.1 Discovery

The *New York Times* had reported that the infiltration was discovered using United States Computer Emergency Readiness Team (US-CERT)'s Einstein intrusion-detection program and it predated the Einstein deployment, which began a year earlier.[*][10] However, the *Wall Street Journal*, *Wired*, *Ars Technica*, and *Fortune* later reported that it was unclear how the breach was discovered. It may have been a product demonstration of CyFIR, a commercial forensic product from a Manassas, Virginia security company CyTech Services that uncovered the infiltra-

tion.[*][11][*][12][*][13][*][14] These reports were subsequently confirmed by CyTech Services in a press release issued by the company on June 15, 2015[*][15] to clarify contradictions made by OPM spokesman Sam Schumach in a later edit of the *Fortune*[*][11] article.

However, it was not CyTech Services that uncovered the infiltration; rather, it was detected by OPM personnel using a software product of vendor Cylance.[*][16][*][17] Later, CyTech independently confirmed the intrusion that had been uncovered by the Cylance software without prior knowledge of Cylance's involvement.

34.2 Data theft

34.2.1 Theft of security clearance information

On June 11, 2015, ABC News also said that highly sensitive 127-page Standard Forms (SF) 86 (Questionnaire for National Security Positions) were put at serious risk by the hack. SF-86 forms contain information about family members, college roommates, foreign contacts, and psychological information. At the time, OPM stated that family members names were not compromised.[*][6] However, on June 13, 2015, OPM spokesman Samuel Schumach said that investigators had "a high degree of confidence that OPM systems containing information related to the background investigations of current, former, and prospective federal government employees, to include U.S. military personnel, and those for whom a federal background investigation was conducted, may have been exfiltrated." [*][7] The Central Intelligence Agency, however, does not use the OPM system; therefore, it may not have been affected.[*][3]

34.2.2 Theft of personal details

J. David Cox, president of the American Federation of Government Employees, wrote in a letter to OPM director Katherine Archuleta (obtained by the Associated Press) that, based on the incomplete information that the AFGE had received from OPM, "We believe that the Central Personnel Data File was the targeted database, and that the hackers are now in possession of all personnel data for every federal employee, every federal retiree, and up to one million former federal employees." [18] Cox stated that the AFGE believes that the breach compromised military records, veterans' status information, addresses, dates of birth, job and pay history, health insurance and life insurance information, pension information, and data on age, gender, and race.*[18]

34.2.3 Theft of fingerprints

The stolen data included 5.6 million sets of fingerprints.*[19] Biometrics expert Ramesh Kesanupalli said that because of this, secret agents were no longer safe, as they could be identified by their fingerprints, even if their names had been changed.*[20]

34.3 Perpetrators

According to the *Wall Street Journal*, U.S. government officials suspect that Chinese hackers perpetrated the breach.*[1] The *Washington Post* has also reported that the attack originated in China, citing unnamed government officials.*[5] China has responded to these claims by noting that it has been the target of cyberattacks in the past.*[21] It remains unclear whether the attack, if it originated from China, was sponsored by China's government or not.*[10] U.S. Department of Homeland Security official Andy Ozment testified that the attackers had gained valid user credentials to the systems they were attacking, likely through social engineering. The breach also consisted of a malware package which installed itself within OPM's network and established a backdoor. From there, attackers escalated their privileges to gain access to a wide range of OPM's systems. *Ars Technica* reported that at least one worker with root access to every row in every database was physically located in China. Another contractor had two employees with Chinese passports.*[22]

34.3.1 Motive

Whether the attack was motivated by commercial gain remains unclear.*[10] It has been suggested that hackers working for the Chinese military intend to compile a database of Americans using the data obtained from the breach.*[21]

34.4 Warnings

The OPM had been warned multiple times of security vulnerabilities and failings. A March 2015 OPM Office of the Inspector General semi-annual report to Congress warned of "persistent deficiencies in OPM's information system security program," including "incomplete security authorization packages, weaknesses in testing of information security controls, and inaccurate Plans of Action and Milestones." *[23]*[24]

A July 2014 story in *The New York Times* quoted unnamed senior American officials saying that Chinese hackers had broken into OPM. The officials said that the hackers seemed to be targeting files on workers who had applied for security clearances, and had gained access to several databases, but had been stopped before they obtained the security clearance information. In an interview later that month, Katherine Archuleta, the director of OPM, said that the most important thing was that no personal identification information had been compromised.*[3]*[25]*[26]

34.5 Pointing blame

Some lawmakers made calls for Archuleta to resign citing mismanagement and that she was a political appointee and former Obama campaign official with no degree or experience in human resources. She responded that neither she nor OPM chief information officer Donna Seymour would do so. "I am committed to the work that I am doing at OPM," Archuleta told reporters. "I have trust in the staff that is there." *[9] On July 10, 2015, Archuleta resigned as OPM director.*[27]

Daniel Henninger, deputy editorial page director of the *Wall Street Journal*, speaking on Fox News' *Journal Editorial Report*, criticized the appointment of Archuleta to be "in charge of one of the most sensitive agencies" in the U.S. government, saying: "What is her experience to run something like that? She was the national political director of Barack Obama's 2012 re-election campaign. She's also the head of something called the Latina Initiative. She's a politico, right? ... That is the kind of person they have put in." *[28]

Security experts have stated that the biggest problem with the breach was not the failure to prevent remote break-ins, but the absence of mechanisms to detect outside intrusion and the lack of proper encryption of sensitive data. OPM

CIO Donna Seymour countered that criticism by pointed to the agency's aging systems as the primary obstacle to putting such protections in place, despite having encryption tools available. DHS Assistant Secretary for Cybersecurity and Communications Andy Ozment explained further that, "If an adversary has the credentials of a user on the network, then they can access data even if it's encrypted, just as the users on the network have to access data, and that did occur in this case. So encryption in this instance would not have protected this data." *[29]

34.6   Investigation

A July 22, 2015 memo by Inspector General Patrick Mc-Farland said that OPM's Chief Information Officer Donna Seymour was slowing her investigation into the breach, leading him to wonder whether or not she was acting in good faith. He did not raise any specific claims of misconduct, but he did say that her office was fostering an "atmosphere of mistrust" by giving him "incorrect or misleading" information.*[30] On Monday 22 February 2016, CIO Donna Seymour resigned, just two days before she was scheduled to testify before a House panel that is continuing to investigate the data breach.*[31]

34.7   References

[1] Barrett, Devlin (5 June 2015). "U.S. Suspects Hackers in China Breached About four (4) Million People's Records, Officials Say". *Wall Street Journal*. Retrieved 5 June 2015.

[2] "U.S. gov't hack may be four (4) times larger than first reported".

[3] Auerbach, David. "The OPM Breach Is a Catastrophe".

[4] Risen, Tom (5 June 2015). "China Suspected in Theft of Federal Employee Records". *US News & World Report*. Retrieved 5 June 2015.

[5] Sanders, Sam (4 June 2015). "Massive Data Breach Puts 4 Million Federal Employees' Records At Risk". *NPR*. Retrieved 5 June 2015.

[6] Mike Levine. "OPM Hack Far Deeper Than Publicly Acknowledged, Went Undetected For More Than A Year, Sources Say".

[7] "Breach of Employee Data Wider Than Initial Report, U.S. Says".

[8] Kashmir Hill. "I am one of the millions of federal employees who just got hacked".

[9] Zengerle, Patricia; Cassella, Megan (2015-07-09). "Estimate of Americans hit by government personnel data hack skyrockets". *Reuters*. Retrieved 2015-07-09.

[10] Sanger, David E. (5 June 2015). "Hacking Linked to China Exposes Millions of U.S. Workers". *New York Times*. Retrieved 5 June 2015.

[11] "A product demo revealed the 'biggest ever' government data breach - Fortune". *Fortune*. Retrieved 10 July 2015.

[12] Kim Zetter and Andy Greenberg (11 June 2015). "Why The OPM Breach Is Such a Security and Privacy Debacle". *Wired*. Retrieved 10 July 2015.

[13] "Report: Hack of government employee records discovered by product demo". *Ars Technica*. Retrieved 10 July 2015.

[14] Damian Paletta And Siobhan Hughes (10 June 2015). "U.S. Spy Agencies Join Probe of Personnel-Records Theft". *WSJ*. Retrieved 10 July 2015.

[15] "CyTech Services Confirms Assistance to OPM Breach Response". *PRWeb*. 15 June 2015. Retrieved 10 July 2015.

[16] "Credit for discovering the OPM breach". *POLITICO*. Retrieved 2016-09-17.

[17] "Surprise! House Oversight report blames OPM leadership for breach of records". Retrieved 2016-09-17.

[18] Ken Dilanian, Union: Hackers have personnel data on every federal employee, Associated Press (June 11, 2015).

[19] Sanger, David E. (2015-09-23). "Hackers Took Fingerprints of 5.6 Million U.S. Workers, Government Says". *The New York Times*. ISSN 0362-4331. Retrieved 2015-09-23.

[20] Paglieri, Jose. "OPM hack's unprecedented haul: 1.1 million fingerprints". Retrieved 11 July 2015.

[21] Liptak, Kevin (4 June 2015). "U.S. government hacked; feds think China is the culprit". *CNN*. Retrieved 5 June 2015.

[22] Gallagher, Sean. "Encryption "would not have helped" at OPM, says DHS official".

[23] David Auerbach, The OPM Breach is a Catastrophe: First the government must own up to its failure. Then the feds should follow this plan to fix it, *Slate* (June 16, 2015).

[24] Office of Personnel Management, Office of the Inspector General, Semiannual Report to Congress: October 1, 2014–March 31, 2015.

[25] Schmidt, Michael S.; Sanger, David E.; Perlroth, Nicole. "Chinese Hackers Pursue Key Data on U.S. Workers". *The New York Times*. Retrieved 29 June 2015.

[26] Jackson, George. "Archuleta on attempted breach and USIS". Retrieved 29 June 2015.

[27] Davis, Julie H. "Katherine Archuleta, Director of Office of Personnel Management, Resigns". *The New York Times*. Retrieved 10 July 2015.

[28] Too Much Information: A transcript of the weekend's program on FOX News Channel (July 12, 2015).

[29] Aaron Boyd (22 June 2015). "OPM breach a failure on en-
     cryption, detection". Federal Times. Retrieved 17 Novem-
     ber 2015.

[30] "Watchdog accuses OPM of hindering hack investigation"
     . Retrieved 8 August 2015.

[31] "OPM's cybersecurity chief resigns in wake of massive data
     breach". Retrieved 23 February 2016.

Chapter 35

Operation Olympic Games

For The Olympic Games sport event, see Olympic Games.

Operation Olympic Games was a covert and still unacknowledged campaign of sabotage by means of cyber disruption, directed at Iranian nuclear facilities by the United States and likely Israel. As reported, it is one of the first known uses of offensive cyber weapons.*[1] Started under the administration of George W. Bush in 2006, Olympic Games was accelerated under President Obama, who heeded Bush's advice to continue cyber attacks on Iranian nuclear facility at Natanz.*[1] Bush believed that the strategy was the only way to prevent an Israeli conventional strike on Iranian nuclear facilities.*[1]

35.1 History

During Bush's second term, General James Cartwright along with other intelligence officials presented Bush with sophisticated code that would act as an offensive cyber weapon. "The goal was to gain access to the Natanz plant's industrial computer controls ... the computer code would invade the specialized computers that command the centrifuges." *[1] Collaboration happened with Israel's SIGINT intelligence service, Unit 8200. Israel's involvement was important to the United States because the former had "deep intelligence about operations at Natanz that would be vital to making the cyber attack a success." *[1] Additionally, American officials wanted to "dissuade the Israelis from carrying out their own preemptive strike against Iranian nuclear facilities." *[1] To prevent a conventional strike, Israel had to be deeply involved in Operation Olympic Games. The computer virus created by the two countries became known as "the bug," and Stuxnet by the IT community once it became public. The malicious software temporarily halted approximately 1,000 of the 5,000 centrifuges from spinning at Natanz.

A programming error in "the bug" caused it to spread to computers outside of Natanz. When an engineer "left

Natanz and connected [his] computer to the Internet, the American- and Israeli-made bug failed to recognize that its environment had changed." *[1] The code replicated on the Internet and was subsequently exposed for public dissemination. IT security firms Symantec and Kaspersky Lab have since examined Stuxnet. It is unclear whether the United States or Israel introduced the programming error.

35.2 Significance

According to the *Atlantic Monthly*, Operation Olympic Games is "probably the most significant covert manipulation of the electromagnetic spectrum since World War II, when Polish cryptanalysts*[2] broke the Enigma cipher that allowed access to Nazi codes." *[3] *The New Yorker* claims Operation Olympic Games is "the first formal offensive act of pure cyber sabotage by the United States against another country, if you do not count electronic penetrations that have preceded conventional military attacks, such as that of Iraq's military computers before the invasion of 2003." *[4] Therefore, "American and Israeli official action can stand as justification for others." *[4]

The Washington Post reported that Flame malware was also part of Olympic Games.*[5]

35.3 Leak investigation

In June 2013, it was reported that Cartwright was the target of a year-long investigation by the US Department of Justice into the leak of classified information about the operation to the US media.*[6] In March 2015, it was reported that the investigation had stalled amid concerns that necessary evidence for prosecution was too sensitive to reveal in court. *[7]

Referring to unnamed sources within CIA and NSA, the documentary film *Zero Days* claims that Stuxnet/Olympic Games malware was just a small part of a much larger mission to infiltrate and compromise Iran, "Nitro Zeus" (NZ).

35.4   See also

- Operation Merlin

35.5   References

[1] Sanger, David (1 June 2012). "Obama Order Sped Up Wave of Cyberattacks Against Iran". *The New York Times*. Retrieved 19 October 2012. President Barack Obama "secretly ordered increasingly sophisticated attacks on the computer systems that run Iran's main nuclear enrichment facilities, significantly expanding America's first sustained use of cyber weapons"

[2] Rejewski, Marian. "How Polish Mathematicians Broke the Enigma Cipher." Annals of the History of Computing 3, no. 3 (July 1981): 213–34. doi:10.1109/MAHC.1981.10033.

[3] Ambinder, Marc (5 June 2012). "Did America's Cyber Attack on Iran Make Us More Vulnerable". *The Atlantic*. Retrieved 19 October 2012.

[4] Coll, Steve (7 June 2012). "The Rewards (and Risks) of Cyber War". *The New Yorker*. Retrieved 19 October 2012.

[5] Nakashima, Ellen (June 19, 2012). "U.S., Israel developed Flame computer virus to slow Iranian nuclear efforts, officials say". *The Washington Post*. Retrieved June 20, 2012.

[6] Pete Yost (June 28, 2013). "Reports: Retired general target of leaks probe". *Associated Press*. Retrieved June 28, 2013.

[7] Ellen Nakashima and Adam Goldman (March 10, 2015). "Leak investigation stalls amid fears of confirming U.S.-Israel operation". *Associated Press*. Retrieved April 21, 2016.

35.6   Further reading

- David E. Sanger, *Confront and Conceal: Obama's Secret Wars and Surprising Use of American Power*, Crown, June 2012, ISBN 978-0307718020

Chapter 36

Operation Ababil

Operation Ababil was a series of cyber attacks starting in 2012, targeting various American financial institutions and carried out by a group calling itself the Cyber fighters of Izz Ad-Din Al Qassam.

36.1 Details

The cyber attacks, or more specifically denial of service attacks, were launched by the Cyber fighters of Izz Ad-Din Al Qassam also known as Qassam Cyber Fighters. The group announced*[1] the attacks on September 18, 2012 on Pastebin where they criticized Israel and the United States and justified the attacks as a response to the Innocence of Muslims video released by controversial American pastor Terry Jones. Their targets included the New York Stock Exchange as well as a number of banks including J.P. Morgan Chase.*[2] The result of the attacks was a limited disruption of the targeted websites. The attacks ended on Oct 23, 2012 because of the Eid al-Adha holiday*[3] at which point they offered to speak to the media through e-mail.

36.2 Name of the Group and Operation

The group's moniker, Izz ad-Din al-Qassam, was a Muslim preacher who lead in the fight against British, French and Jewish nationalist organizations in the Levant in the 1920s and 1930s. "Operation Ababil" was also the name of a failed Pakistani military operation in April 1984.

36.3 Disputed Origins of Attacks

On September 21, 2012, the Washington Post reported*[4] that the attacks originated not from a hacktivist group but from the government of Iran and cited U.S. Senator Joseph I. Lieberman as one who was a proponent of this idea.

Lieberman told C-Span that he believed the Iranian government was sponsoring the group's attacks on US banks in retaliation for Western economic sanctions.*[5] An early report by Dancho Danchev found the amateurish "outdated and virtually irrelevant technical skills" of the attack suspicious.*[6] But Michael Smith, senior security evangelist at Akamai, found the size of the attacks—65 gigabits of traffic per second—more consistent with a state actor (such as Iran) than with a typical hacktivist denial of service attack which would be less than 2 gigabits/second.*[7]

The controversial hacktivist, The Jester, claimed the Qassam Cyber Fighters had help with their attacks from the hacking group Anonymous.*[8]

36.4 Phase Two

On December 10, 2012, the Qassam Cyber Fighters announced*[9] the launching of phase two of Operation Ababil. In that statement, they specifically named U.S. Bancorp, J.P. Morgan Chase, Bank of America, PNC Financial Services and SunTrust Bank as targets and identified events such as Hurricane Sandy and the 2012 US Presidential Election as reasons for the delay of phase two. This announcement also mentioned disrespect towards the Prophet Mohammed as motivation and denied the involvement of any nation state. It was during this time that media attention increased with one journalist observing,*[10] "Operation Ababil stands out for its sophistication and focus, experts say." and allegations of involvement by Iran also increased.*[11] On January 29, 2013, an announcement*[12] was made that phase two would come to a conclusion due to the removal of the main copy of the video from YouTube. The announcement also identified additional copies of the movie also hosted on YouTube.

36.5   Phase Three

On February 12, 2013, the Qassam Cyber Fighters issued a warning[*][13] that the other copies of the movie referenced in their January 29 posting should be removed. They followed this with a "serious warning"[*][14] and then an "ultimatum"[*][15] after the additional copies of the video were not removed. On March 5, 2013, they announced[*][16] the beginning of Phase 3 of Operation Ababil on their Pastebin page. This was followed by several of the financial institutions on their target list reporting website disruptions.[*][17]

36.6   See also

- Cyber electronic warfare
- Cyberwarfare in the United States
- Cyberwarfare in Iran
- Izz ad-Din al-Qassam
- The Jester
- Anonymous
- J.P. Morgan Chase
- Bank of America
- U.S. Bancorp
- PNC Financial Services
- SunTrust Bank
- Chase Bank
- cyber attacks
- DDOS

36.7   References

[1]   "Bank of America and New York Stock Exchange under attack." . Retrieved 10 February 2013.

[2]   "Chase, NYSE Websites Targeted in Cyber Attacks." . Retrieved 10 February 2013.

[3]   "The 6th Week, Operation Ababil.". Retrieved 11 February 2013.

[4]   Nakashima, Ellen (21 September 2012). "Iran blamed for cyberattacks on U.S. banks and companies." . *The Washington Post*. Retrieved 10 February 2013.

[5]   "Deconstructing the Al-Qassam Cyber Fighters Assault on US Banks" . *2 January 2013*. Analysis Intelligence. Retrieved 19 September 2013.

[6]   Danchev, Dancho. "Dissecting 'Operation Ababil' - an OSINT Analysis" . *September 28, 2012*. Retrieved 19 September 2013.

[7]   Gonsalves, Antone. "Bank attackers more sophisticated than typical hacktivists, expert says" . *September 28, 2012*. CSO. Retrieved 19 September 2013.

[8]   "The Jester: Anonymous Hackers Helped Izz ad-Din al-Qassam DDOS US Banks." . Retrieved 11 February 2013.

[9]   "Phase 2 Operation Ababil." . Retrieved 11 February 2013.

[10] "Group halts bank cyberattacks." . Retrieved 11 February 2013.

[11] Shachtman, Noah (27 November 2012). "Bank Hackers Deny They're Agents of Iran." . *Wired*. Retrieved 11 February 2013.

[12] "Operation Ababil Suspended due to removal of insulting movie." . Retrieved 17 March 2013.

[13] "Warning, Operation Ababil" . Retrieved 17 March 2013.

[14] "Serious Warning, Operation Ababil" . Retrieved 17 March 2013.

[15] "Operation Ababil, AlQASSAM ULTIMATUM" . Retrieved 17 March 2013.

[16] "Phase 3, Operation Ababil" . Retrieved 17 March 2013.

[17] "Bank Attackers Restart Operation Ababil DDoS Disruptions" . Retrieved 17 March 2013.

36.8   External links

- Qassam Cyber Fighters Pastbin page

Chapter 37

Operation Cleaver

Operation Cleaver, as labelled in a report by American firm Cylance Inc. in late 2014, was a cyberwarfare covert operation targeting critical infrastructure organizations worldwide, allegedly planned and executed by Iran.

Cylance's report was later tacitly acknowledged in a confidential report by Federal Bureau of Investigation (FBI), though Iranian officials denied involvement in the operation.[*][1]

37.1 Cylance report

Operation Cleaver

Logo designed by Cylance

In December 2014, California-based cyber security firm Cylance Inc. published results of a 2-year investigation,[*][2] an 86-page technical report, indicating that an operation, called "Operation Cleaver", has targeted the military, oil and gas, energy and utilities, transportation, airlines, airports, hospitals and aerospace industries organizations worldwide.[*][3]

The title "Operation Cleaver" alludes to frequent uses of the word "cleaver" in the malware's coding.[*][4]

According to the report, over 50 entities in 16 countries have been hit by the campaign, based in the United States, Israel, China, Saudi Arabia, India, Germany, France and England among others.[*][5] Cylance's research does not name individual companies, but *Reuters* reports citing "a person familiar with the research" Navy Marine Corps Intranet, Calpine, Saudi Aramco, Pemex, Qatar Airlines and Korean Air were among the specific targets.[*][5]

Stuart McClure, Cylance founder and CEO believes that the hackers are sponsored by Iran and have ties to Islamic Revolutionary Guard Corps.[*][2]

37.2 FBI report

According to *Reuters*, the Federal Bureau of Investigation has filed a confidential "Flash" report, providing technical details about malicious software and techniques used in the attacks. The technical document said the hackers typically launch their attacks from two IP addresses that are in Iran, but does not attribute the attacks to the Iranian government.[*][5] FBI warned businesses to stay vigilant and to report any suspicious activity spotted on the companies' computer systems.[*][3]

37.3 Alleged victims' reaction

- A Pemex spokesman said the company had not detected any attacks from the Iranian groups but was constantly monitoring.[*][5]

- Muhammad Haneef Rana, a spokesman for Pakistan International Airlines, said he wasn't aware of any threat from hackers and "We are well secured and our firewall is in place". .*[2]

- Korean Air declined to comment.*[2]

37.4 Iran's reaction

Iran has officially denied involvement in the hacking campaign. "This is a baseless and unfounded allegation fabricated to tarnish the Iranian government image, particularly aimed at hampering current nuclear talks", said Hamid Babaei, spokesman for Permanent mission of Islamic Republic of Iran to the United Nations.*[5]

37.5 References

[1] Finkle, Jim (December 13, 2014). Christian Plumb, ed. "Exclusive: Iran hackers may target U.S. energy, defense firms, FBI warns". *Reuters*. Retrieved March 30, 2015.

[2] Riley, Michael A; Robertson, Jordan (December 2, 2014). "Iran-Backed Hackers Target Airports, Carriers: Report". *Bloomberg News*. Retrieved March 30, 2015.

[3] Plummer, Quinten (December 15, 2014). "Operation Cleaver is Bigger Threat than Previously Thought, FBI Warns US Businesses". *Tech Times*. Retrieved March 30, 2015.

[4] Bertrand, Natasha (December 8, 2014). "Iran Is Officially A Real Player In The Global Cyber War". *Business Insider*. Retrieved March 30, 2015.

[5] Finkle, Jim (December 2, 2014). Richard Valdmanis, Christian Plumb and W Simon, ed. "Iran hackers targeted airlines, energy firms: report". *Reuters*. Retrieved March 30, 2015.

37.6 See also

- Cyberwarfare in Iran

37.7 External links

- Cylance Operation Cleaver Report

Chapter 38

Operation Newscaster

Logo designed by iSIGHT Partners

"**Operation Newscaster**", as labelled by American firm *iSIGHT Partners* in 2014, is a cyber espionage covert operation directed at military and political figures using social networking, allegedly done by Iran. The operation has been described as "creative",*[1] "long-term" and "unprecedented".*[2] According to *iSIGHT Partners*, it is "the most elaborate cyber espionage campaign using social engineering that has been uncovered to date from any nation".*[2]

38.1 ISight's perceptions

On 29 May 2014, Texas-based cyber espionage research firm *iSIGHT Partners* released a report, uncovering an operation it labels "Newscaster" since at-least 2011, has targeted at least 2,000 people in United States, Israel, Britain, Saudi Arabia, Syria, Iraq and Afghanistan.*[2]*[3]

The victims who are not identified in the document due to security reasons, are senior U.S. military and diplomatic personnel, congresspeople, journalists, lobbyists, think tankers and defense contractors, including a four-star admiral.*[2]*[3]

The firm couldn't determine what data the hackers may have stolen.*[3]

According to the *iSIGHT Partners* report, hackers used 14 "elaborated fake" personas claiming to work in journalism, government, and defense contracting and were active in Facebook, Twitter, LinkedIn, Google+, YouTube and Blogger. To establish trust and credibility, the users fab-

A screenshot from NewsOnAir.org

ricated a fictitious journalism website, *NewsOnAir.org*, using content from the media like Associated Press, BBC, Reuters and populated their profiles with fictitious personal content. They then tried to befriend target victims and sent them "friendly messages"*[1] with Spear-phishing to steal email passwords*[4] and attacks and infecting them to a "not particularly sophisticated" malware for data exfiltration.*[2]*[3]

The report says *NewsOnAir.org* was registered in Tehran and likely hosted by an Iranian provider. The Persian word "Parastoo" (پرستو; meaning *swallow*) was used as a password for malware associated with the group, which appeared to work during business hours in Tehran*[2] as they took Thursday and Friday off.*[1] *iSIGHT Partners* could not confirm whether the hackers had ties to the Iranian government.*[4]

38.2 Analysis

According to *Al Jazeera*, Chinese army's cyber unit carried out scores of similar phishing schemes.[*][4]

Morgan Marquis-Boire, a researcher at the University of Toronto stated that the campaign "appeared to be the work of the same actors performing malware attacks on Iranian dissidents and journalists for at least two years" .[*][4]

Franz-Stefan Gady, a senior fellow at the EastWest Institute and a founding member of the Worldwide Cybersecurity Initiative, stated that "They're not doing this for a quick buck, to extrapolate data and extort an organization. They're in it for the long haul. Sophisticated human engineering has been the preferred method of state actors" .[*][4]

38.3 Reactions

- Facebook spokesman said the company discovered the hacking group while investigating suspicious friend requests and removed all of the fake profiles.[*][2]

- LinkedIn spokesman said they are investigating the report, though none of the 14 fake profiles uncovered were currently active.[*][2]

- Twitter declined to comment.[*][2]

- Federal Bureau of Investigation told *Al Jazeera* "it was aware of the report but that it had no comment" .[*][4]

38.4 References

[1] Nakashima, Ellen (May 29, 2014). "Iranian hackers are targeting U.S. officials through social networks, report says" . *The Washington Post*. Retrieved March 30, 2015.

[2] Finkle, Jim (May 29, 2014). Tiffany Wu, ed. "Iranian hackers use fake Facebook accounts to spy on U.S., others" . *Reuters*. Retrieved March 30, 2015.

[3] Chumley, Cheryl K. (May 29, 2014). "Iranian hackers sucker punch U.S. defense officials with creative social-media scam" . *The Washington Times*. Retrieved March 30, 2015.

[4] Pizzi, Michael (May 29, 2014). "Iran hackers set up fake news site, personas to steal U.S. secrets" . *Al Jazeera*. Retrieved March 30, 2015.

38.5 External links

- NEWSCASTER – An Iranian Threat Inside Social Media

Chapter 39

Operation Socialist

Operation Socialist is the code name given by the British signals and communications agency Government Communications Headquarters (GCHQ) to an operation in which GCHQ successfully breached the infrastructure of the Belgian telecommunications company Belgacom between 2010 and 2013.[*][1] The operations existence was first revealed in documents leaked by the former National Security Agency contractor Edward Snowden. GCHQ used a method called Quantum Insert attack [*][2] embedded in fake LinkedIn pages targeting Belgacom engineers[*][3] The breach was conducted under the code name 'OP Socialist'. The main target of the clandestine infiltration was to gain access to Belgacom's GRX Operator to enable GCHQ to obtain roaming data for mobile devices and execute what is generally referred to as Man-in-the-middle attack against targets.

When the first anomalies were detected in 2012, Belgacom's security team were unable to identify their cause.[*][4][*][5] Only in 2013 malware disguised as legitimate Microsoft software had been identified as the source of problems.[*][1]

According to the leaked documents GCHQ probed Belgacom's infrastructure for years.[*][6] According to the leaked documents 'Operation Socialist' has been qualified by the head of the GCHQ's Network Analysis Center as a success.[*][2]

Snowden subsequently described Operation Socialist as the "first documented example to show one EU member state mounting a cyber attack on another⋯"[*][7]

39.1 References

[1] Gallagher, Ryan. "The Inside Story of How British Spies Hacked Belgium's Largest Telcom". The Intercept. Retrieved 9 April 2015.

[2] "Britain's GCHQ Hacked Belgian Telecoms Firm". Der Spiegel.

[3] "Quantum Spying: GCHQ Used Fake LinkedIn Pages to Target Engineers". Der Spiegel.

[4] "Lees hier hoe de Britse geheime dienst GCHQ Belgacom aanviel". NRC.NL.

[5] "Britse geheime dienst bespioneerde jarenlang Belgacom-klanten". De Standaard.

[6] "How GCHQ hacked Belgacom". info security.

[7] "GCHQ hacked Belgium's largest telecom service". *IT Pro Portal*.

Chapter 40

OpIsrael

#OpIsrael is a coordinated cyber-attack by anti-Israel[1] groups and individuals against websites they perceived as Israeli, chiefly through denial of service assaults, database hijacking, database leaks, admin panel takeover, and defacements.[2] Timed for 7 April 2013,[3] the eve of Holocaust Remembrance Day,[4] its stated goal is to "erase Israel from the internet" in protest against claimed crimes committed against the Palestinian people on behalf of Israel.[5][6][7] The event is organized and carried out by dozens of factions associated with the Anonymous collective.[1] Websites targeted by the activists included those of banks, schools, non-profit organizations, privately owned small businesses and newspapers in Israel, as well as Israel's national Holocaust museum Yad Vashem and government agencies.[5][7][8][9]

In the leadup to the attack, Israeli organizations made preparations to defend their websites, and cyber-security experts called on home users to increase awareness and take precautions such as changing passwords, not opening strange or suspicious emails, and maintaining especial vigilance when using Facebook. The Israel Internet Association (ISOC) operated a hotline for people to report attacks and published real-time status reports on its website.[2][10]

Ultimately, #OpIsrael caused no physical damage and was assessed by the Israeli Government's National Cyber Bureau and by some security experts and journalists to have been a failure.[11][12][13][14]

40.1   Targeted websites

Larger than Life, an Israeli NGO devoted to "improving the quality of life and welfare of cancer-stricken children and their families regardless of sex, religion and nationality", stated that in the week leading up to #OpIsrael, its website was targeted repeatedly by pro-Palestinian hackers who defaced it with "flags, a skull, symbols, and all sorts of hate-related things" .[15][16][17]

Yad Vashem, Israel's national Holocaust museum, came un-

der a "fairly massive attack". Nevertheless, its website was fully operational on the day of the attack, which overlapped with Holocaust Remembrance Day.[18][19][20]

At midday, #OpIsrael activists announced on Twitter that they had defaced the website of an Israeli hair salon, Peter Hair, in Ramat HaSharon. The salon's home page showed a masked person holding a sign saying "Indonesian Security Down #OP ISRAHELL" and was signed with the message "We are Muslims, Soldier [sic] of Allah". The owner of the salon, Peter Imseis, said he had not been aware that the site had been hacked and that it had not affected his business.[20]

Government websites that experienced problems on 7 April 2013 included those of the Israeli Ministry of Education and Central Bureau of Statistics, but it was unclear whether these problems were caused by #OpIsrael.[1][21]

During the day, attackers posted numerous false and grandiose claims of successes, such as "Anonymous causes Israel to lose $5 billion" in stock market losses and "Tel Aviv loses all Internet connection" .[22]

40.2   Responses

The attack was praised by Hamas, the militant Islamist group that controls the Gaza Strip. Hamas spokesman Ihab al-Ghussain wrote: "May God protect the spirit and mission of the soldiers of this electronic war" .[7]

A statement on the website of the Tunisian Renaissance Party, signed by party leader Rashid Al-Ghannouchi, expressed "condemnation of all those who do not pursue a policy of dialogue to reach its objectives and follow the methods of terrorists to reach its goals", and threatening "to prosecute anyone involved from Tunisia in attacks on Israel on charges of compromising the security of a foreign state" . Tunisians quickly mobilized against the party, with some lawyers offering to defend hackers charged with attacking Israel free of charge. The Renaissance Party later issued a different statement saying that their website had itself been hacked and that the party does not condemn cyberattacks on Israel.*[23]

40.3 Counterattack

The attack drew a response by pro-Israel hackers, who quickly took over #OpIsrael's official*[24] website OpIsrael.com*[25]*[26] and filled it with pro-Israel content.*[27]*[28] The DNS record of opisrael.com showed a purchase made under the name 'Al Qaeda'.*[25]*[29] OpIsrael claimed after the site was hacked that it had never been their official website.*[30] Israeli Elite Force had an early start forming two days prior to the attack, taking down Iranian, Pakistani, Turkish government website and leaking information on Twitter. They received coverage in the world media.*[31]*[32]*[33]

As of 10 April, an alternate coordinating website used by the anti-Israel activists, OpIsrael.tk, had also been taken over by pro-Israel hackers and was displaying an Israeli flag.

Participants of the counter-attack are

- EhIsR - known for OpIsrael.com*[34]*[34]*[35]*[36]*[37]
- Israeli Elite Force*[31]*[32]*[38]*[39]

40.4 References

[1] As cyber-war begins, Israeli hackers hit back, Times of Israel 07-04-2013

[2] Israeli cyber activists attack anti-Israel hackers, Jerusalem Post 07-04-2013, Admin Takeover, Database Breaches and Leaks, Admin Panel Takeover, Defacement and other means.

[3] "Rival Hackers Overcome Differences For Anti-Israel Cyber Campaign". *Access ADL*. Retrieved 31 March 2015.

[4] Why did Anonymous have to attack Israel on Holocaust Memorial Day?, Forbes 08-04-2013

[5] Anonymous launches massive cyber assault on Israel, RT 07-04-2013

[6] Groups of hackers threaten to "wipe Israel off the Internet", France 24 28-03-2013 (French)

[7] Cyberwarfare: Hackers launch attacks on Israel, Der Spiegel 07-04-2013 (German)

[8] Anonymous targets Israel, JPost repels hackers, Jerusalem Post 07-04-2013

[9] Hackers target Israeli websites, fail to disrupt, CBS News 08-04-2013

[10] On eve of attack, Israel preparing for the cyber-worst, Times of Israel 05-04-2013

[11] Hackers target Israeli websites, Ynet News 07-04-2013

[12] Botched mission? #OpIsrael cyberattack fails to frustrate Israeli govt, Al-Arabiya 07-04-2013

[13] Why #OpIsrael Was an #OpFail, The Daily Beast 08-04-2013

[14] Anonymous Attacks On Israel 'Have Achieved Next To Nothing', TechWeek europe 08-04-2013

[15] Larger than Life, 04-04-2013

[16] Hackers Target Website for Children with Cancer, Israel National News 06-04-2013

[17] Anonymous Hacks Israel: Doesn't Reach Goal, But Leaks Credit Cards And Defaces NGO Website For Children With Cancer, International Business Times 08-04-2013

[18] Hacking group Anonymous launches attack on Israeli government websites on Holocaust memorial day, Daily Mail 07-04-2013

[19] Experts: Anonymous' Israel hacking 'amateur' so far, Jerusalem Post 07-04-2013

[20] Israel Says It Repelled Most Attacks on Its Web Sites by Pro-Palestinian Hackers, New York Times 07-04-2013

[21] Anonymous hacker attack on Israeli websites 'causes little real damage', The Guardian 08-04-2013

[22] Major failures, minor successes for anti-Israel hackers, Times of Israel 08-04-2013

[23] Egypt's 'war of the streets', Times of Israel 08-04-2013

[24] Anonymous Fails to 'Wipe Israel from Internet', International business Times 08-04-2013

[25] #opIsrael: Hackers launch opisrael.com website Cyber War Zone 03-16-2013

[26] Anonymous Indonesia Twitter post regarding OpIsrael.com Twitter 16-03-2013

[27] Israeli takes over OpIsrael hacktivist website, Jerusalem Post 09-04-2013

[28] #OpIsrael Backfires, Jerusalem Post (blogs) 07-04-2013

[29] Old domain records for OpIsrael.com Whois.ws

[30] OpIsrael Twitter 9-4-2013

[31] http://www.thedailybeast.com/articles/2013/04/08/why-opisrael-was-an-opfail.html

[32] http://stream.aljazeera.com/story/201304090019-0022665

[33] http://www.nytimes.com/2013/04/08/world/middleeast/
     pro-palestinian-hackers-attack-israeli-sites.html?_r=0

[34] http://blogs.jpost.com/content/opisrael-backfires

[35] http://www.israelnationalnews.com/News/Flash.aspx/
     265980#.UWrsKEZMyTM

[36] http://www.jewishaz.com/localnews_features/
     business/cyberattacks-on-israel-mainly-fail/article_
     8d26a632-a23d-11e2-89f6-0019bb30f31a.html

[37] http://www.jta.org/news/article/2013/04/07/3123651/
     israeli-websites-faceboo-pages-targeted-in-opisrael-hacking-attacks

[38] http://rt.com/news/israel-anonymous-website-hacked-577/

[39] http://nyulocal.com/national/2013/04/09/
     anonymous-launches-opisrael-attempts-unsuccessfully-to-erase-israel-from-the-internet/

Chapter 41

Presidential Policy Directive 20

Presidential Policy Directive 20 (PPD-20), provides a framework for U.S. cybersecurity by establishing principles and processes. Signed by President Barack Obama in October 2012, this directive supersedes National Security Presidential Directive NSPD-38. Integrating cyber tools with those of national security,*[1] the directive complements NSPD-54/Homeland Security Presidential Directive HSPD-23.

Classified and unreleased by the National Security Agency (NSA), NSPD-54 was authorized by George W. Bush.*[1] It gives the U.S. government power to conduct surveillance*[2] through monitoring.*[1]

Its existence was made public in June 2013 by former intelligence NSA infrastructure analyst Edward Snowden.

41.1 Background

Because of private industry, and issues surrounding international and domestic law,*[3] public-private-partnership became the, "cornerstone of America's cybersecurity strategy" .*[4] Suggestions for the private sector were detailed in the declassified 2003,*[5] National Strategy to Secure Cyberspace. Its companion document, National Security Presidential Directive (NSPD-38), was signed in secret by George W. Bush the following year.*[5]

Although the contents of NSPD 38 are still undisclosed,*[1] the U.S. military did not recognize cyberspace as a "theater of operations" until the U.S. National Defense Strategy of 2005.*[3] The report declared that the, "ability to operate in and from the global commons-space, international waters and airspace, and cyberspace is important ... to project power anywhere in the world from secure bases of operation." *[6] Three years later, George W. Bush formed the classified Comprehensive National Cybersecurity Initiative (CNCI).

Citing economic and national security, the Obama administration prioritized cybersecurity upon taking office.*[7] Af-

ter an in-depth review of the, "communications and information infrastructure," *[8] the CNCI was partially declassified and expanded under President Obama.*[9] It outlines "key elements of a broader, updated national U.S. cybersecurity strategy." *[10] By 2011, the Pentagon announced its capability to run cyber attacks.*[11]

41.2 General

After the U.S. Senate failed to pass the Cybersecurity Act of 2012 that August,*[12] Presidential Policy Directive 20 (PPD-20) was signed in secret. The Electronic Privacy Information Center (EPIC) filed a Freedom of Information Request to see it, but the NSA would not comply.*[13] Some details were reported in November 2012.*[14] The Washington Post wrote that PPD-20, "is the most extensive White House effort to date to wrestle with what constitutes an 'offensive' and a 'defensive' action in the rapidly evolving world of cyberwar and cyberterrorism." *[14] The following January,*[15] the Obama administration released a ten-point factsheet.*[16]

41.3 Controversy

On June 7, 2013, PPD-20 became public.*[15] Released by Edward Snowden and posted by *The Guardian,*[15] it is part of the 2013 Mass Surveillance Disclosures. While the U.S. factsheet claims PPD-20 acts within the law and is, "consistent with the values that we promote domestically and internationally as we have previously articulated in the International Strategy for Cyberspace" ,*[16] it doesn't reveal cyber operations in the directive.*[15]

Snowden's disclosure called attention to passages noting cyberwarfare policy and its possible consequences.*[15]*[17] The directive calls both defensive and offensive measures as Defensive Cyber Effects Operations (DCEO) and Offensive Cyber Effects Operations (OCEO), respectively.

41.4   Notable points

- "Loss of life, significant responsive actions against the United States, significant damage to property, serious adverse US foreign policy consequences, or serious economic impact on the United States."

- "OCEO can offer unique and unconventional capabilities to advance U.S. national objectives around the world with little or no warning to the adversary or target and with potential effects ranging from subtle to severely damaging. The development and sustainment of OCEO capabilities, however, may require considerable time and effort if access and tools for a specific target do not already exist."

- "The United States Government shall identify potential targets of national importance where OCEO can offer a favorable balance of effectiveness and risk as compared with other instruments of national power, establish and maintain OCEO capabilities integrated as appropriate with other U.S. offensive capabilities, and execute those capabilities in a manner consistent with the provisions of this directive."

41.5   Further reading

- 2013 Mass Surveillance Disclosures
- Comprehensive National Cybersecurity Initiative

41.6   External links

- Guardian: Presidential Policy Directive 20 (PPD)
- FAS: White House PPD-20 Factsheet

41.7   References

[1] EPIC. (n.d.). Presidential directives and cybersecurity. *EPIC.* Retrieved from http://epic.org/privacy/cybersecurity/presidential-directives/cybersecurity.html.

[2] Electronic Privacy Information Center. (n.d.). EPIC v. NSA - Cybersecurity Authority. *EPIC.* Retrieved from http://epic.org/privacy/nsa/epic_v_nsa.html.

[3] Barnard-Wills, D. & Ashenden, D. (2012). Securing virtual space cyber war, cyber terror, and risk. *Space and culture, 15*(2), p. 110-123. doi:10.1177/1206331211430016.

[4] White House. (2003, February). The National Strategy to Secure Cyberspace (Rep.). Retrieved from http://www.us-cert.gov/reading_room/cyberspace_strategy.pdf.

[5] Scahill, J. (2013). The world is a battlefield. Nation Books.

[6] The National Defense Strategy of the United States of America (Rep.) (2005, March). Retrieved from http://www.globalsecurity.org/military/library/policy/dod/nds-usa_mar2005.htm.

[7] Krebs B. (2009, May 29). Obama: Cyber security is a national priority. *Washington Post.* Retrieved from http://voices.washingtonpost.com/securityfix/2009/05/obama_cybersecurity_is_a_natio.html.

[8] White House, Office of the Press Secretary. (2009, April 17). Statement by the Press Secretary on conclusion of the cyberspace review [Press release]. Retrieved from http://www.whitehouse.gov/the_press_office/Statement-by-the-Press-Secretary-on-Conclusion-of-the-Cyberspace-Review.

[9] Vijayan, J. (2010, March 2). Obama administration partially lifts secrecy on classified cybersecurity project *Computerworld.* Retrieved from http://www.whitehouse.gov/the_press_office/Statement-by-the-Press-Secretary-on-Conclusion-of-the-Cyberspace-Review.

[10] White House. (n.d.). The Comprehensive National Cybersecurity Initiative. *The White House.* Retrieved from http://www.whitehouse.gov/issues/foreign-policy/cybersecurity/national-initiative.

[11] Nakashima, E. (2011, November 15). Pentagon: Cyber offense part of U.S. strategy. *Washington Post.* Retrieved from http://articles.washingtonpost.com/2011-11-15/news/35284321_1_cyberspace-new-report-cyberwarfare.

[12] Rizzo, J. (2012, August 02). Cybersecurity bill fails in Senate. *CNN.* Retrieved from http://www.cnn.com/2012/08/02/politics/cybersecurity-act/index.html

[13] Electronic Privacy Information Center. (n.d.). EPIC v. DHS - Defense Contractor Monitoring: Classified NSA Cybersecurity Directive Sought by EPIC Establishes NSA Cyberattack Authority. *EPIC.* Retrieved from http://epic.org/foia/dhs/defense-monitoring.html

[14] Nakashima, E. (2012, November 14). Obama signs secret directive to help thwart cyberattacks. *Washington Post.* Retrieved from http://articles.washingtonpost.com/2012-11-14/world/35505871_1_networks-cyberattacks-defense.

[15] Greenwald, G. & MacAskill, E. (2013, June 7). Obama orders US to draw up overseas target list for cyber-attacks *The Guardian.* Retrieved from http://www.theguardian.com/world/2013/jun/07/obama-china-targets-cyber-overseas

[16] Federation of American Scientists. (2013, January). Presidential Policy Directives [PPDs] Barack Obama Administration. *FAS.* Retrieved from https://www.fas.org/irp/offdocs/ppd/index.html.

[17] Schneier, B. (2013, June 18). Has U.S. started an Internet war? CNN. Retrieved from http://www.cnn.com/2013/06/18/opinion/schneier-cyberwar-policy/index.html.

Chapter 42

RockYou

Not to be confused with Roku.

RockYou is a company that developed widgets for MySpace and implemented applications for various social networks and Facebook. Since 2014, it has engaged primarily in the purchases of rights to classic video games, then incorporates in-game ads and re-distributes them.[2]

42.1 History

Based in San Francisco, California, RockYou was founded in 2005 by Lance Tokuda and Jia Shen. The company's first product, a slide show service, was designed to work as an application widget. Later applications included various forms of voice mail, text and photo stylization, and games. As of December, 2007 it is the most successful widget maker for the Facebook platform in terms of total installations.

In May, 2007, RockYou was one of the companies invited to participate in F8, the event at which Facebook announced an open platform allowing third parties to develop and operate their own software applications on the Facebook website. Applications made for Facebook include Super Wall,[3] "Hug Me", Likeness, Vampires, Slideshows, Birthdays, MyGifts, and Emote, among others.[4]

In December 2009, the company experienced a data breach resulting in the exposure of over 32 million user accounts. This resulted from storing user data in an unencrypted database and not patching a ten-year-old SQL vulnerability. RockYou failed to provide a notification of the breach to users and miscommunicated the extent of the breach.[5]

In October 2010, the company completed major layoffs.[6] In November, 2010, the company's founder and CEO, Lance Tokuda, stepped down from his position as CEO.[7] and was later replaced by Lisa Marino in April, 2011.[8]

In 2010, RockYou announced the acquisitions of two game development studios, TirNua[9] and Playdemic,[10] as well as development agreements for two new games from John Romero's social game studio Loot Drop.[11] Playdemic's first game, Gourmet Ranch, was nominated in February 2011 for a Mochi Award for Best Social Game. RockYou's investors include SoftBank, Sequoia Capital, Lightspeed Venture Partners, Partech International, and DCM.

On June 13, 2012, RockYou acquired Bingo developer Ryzing[12] and relocated its headquarters to San Francisco, CA.[13] In August 2012, RockYou launched The Walking Dead Social Game based on AMC's hit series of the same name.[14] In April 2014, RockYou purchased three Playdom social games from Disney: Gardens of Time, Words of Wonder, and City Girl, and announced it's licensing Army Attack, Crazy Penguin Wars, Millionaire City, and Zombie Lane from Digital Chocolate.[15]

In 2015 they bought The Godfather:5Families from Kabam.

42.2 Zoo World

RockYou's most played game, Zoo World is a free social media application where users try to build the best zoo they can. Participants can build on various islands, decorate their zoo with kiosks, trees, and a large variety of animals. In addition, it has features such as breeding animals, collecting objects, and visiting friend's zoo islands. The act of leveling up is based on achievements of tasks. Also, users can earn wildlife points, a bonus reward that can be used to buy special items, like ultra rare animals, and rare decorative items. Wildlife points can be earned by breeding animals, completing levels and trophies, or bought via PayPal or credit card. Lastly, around each holiday there are events, new animals, and new items to add to the zoo.

In May 2011, RockYou announced that Zoo World 2, the sequel to the original Zoo World, would be available on Facebook on June 8, 2011.

42.3 Current social games

- Bingo By Ryzing
- Bingo Blingo
- RockYou Poker
- Zoo World Classic
- City Girl Life
- Words of Wonder
- Gardens of Time
- Zombie Lane
- Millionaire City
- Kitchen Scramble
- Bakery Blitz
- Godfather: Five Families
- Edgeworld
- Glory of Rome
- Kingdoms of Camelot
- Dragons of Atlantis
- Brightwood Adventures
- Pioneer Adventures
- Gold Rush
- Lost Island
- Volcano Island
- New World
- Skull Island
- Rapid Poker
- Kahzu Slots
- PurePlay Poker
- Solitare Arena
- Solitare 3 Arena
- Lucky Slots
- Army Attack*[16]

42.4 Past social applications and games

- Pieces of Flair
- Crazy Penguin Wars
- Horoscopes
- RockYou Live
- Speed Racing
- Zoo World 2
- Birthday Cards
- Hug Me
- Hero World
- My Casino
- Toy Land
- Super Pets
- Movie Blitz
- The Walking Dead Social Game
- Jackpot Bingo
- Mall World
- Fashion Designer

42.5 References

[1] "Rockyou.com Site Info". Alexa Internet. Retrieved 2014-04-01.

[2] "Mobile-gaming ad network RockYou secures $10M in financing - GamesBeat - Games - by Jeff Grubb". *VentureBeat*.

[3] Brad Stone (October 4, 2007). "In Facebook, Investing In a Theory". New York Times. Retrieved 2007-12-23.

[4] Ellen Lee (September 3, 2007). "Widgets add flair to dress up Web sites". San Francisco Chronicle.

[5] Nik Cubrilovic. "RockYou Hack: From Bad To Worse". *TechCrunch*. AOL.

[6] Jason Kincaid. "RockYou Rocked By Layoffs As It Switches Focus To Social Games". *TechCrunch*. AOL.

[7] Jason Kincaid. "RockYou CEO Lance Tokuda Steps Down". *TechCrunch*. AOL.

[8] "Interview: New RockYou CEO Lisa Marino Talks Social Gaming, Advertising and Mobile". *insidesocialgames.com*.

[9] "TirNua acquisition". *GamesIndustry.biz*.

[10] Robin Wauters. "RockYou Buys UK-Based Social Gaming Startup Playdemic". *TechCrunch*. AOL.

[11] "RockYou signs deal with Doom creator John Romero's social game studio Loot Drop - GamesBeat - Games - by Dean Takahashi". *VentureBeat*.

[12] Mike Rose. "Gamasutra - RockYou acquires Bingo developer Ryzing". *gamasutra.com*.

[13] Anthony Ha. "RockYou Acquires Social Games Developer Ryzing, Moves to San Francisco". *TechCrunch*. AOL.

[14] "The Walking Dead Social Game's open beta lurches onto Facebook". *insidesocialgames.com*.

[15] VentureBeat, Dean Takahashi, 4/18/14, RockYou Buys Three Playdom Games from Disney to Keep Them Running http://venturebeat.com/2014/04/18/ rockyou-buys-three-playdom-games-from-disney-to-keep-them-running-for-players/

[16] Gamasutra, Christian Nutt 4/18/14, RockYou's New Strategy: Rescue Games That Other Publishers Don't Want http://www.gamasutra.com/view/news/215827/ RockYous_new_strategy_Rescue_games_that_other_ publishers_dont_want.php

42.6 External links

- Official website

Chapter 43

Shadow Network

The **Shadow Network** is a China-based computer espionage operation that stole classified documents and emails from the Indian government, the office of the Dalai Lama, and other high-level government networks.[1][2] This is the second cyber espionage operation of this sort discovered by researchers at the Information Warfare Monitor, following the discovery of GhostNet in March 2009.[3][4][5] The Shadow Network report "Shadows in the Cloud: Investigating Cyber Espionage 2.0" was released 6 April 2010, approximately one year after the publication of "Tracking GhostNet".[6]

The cyber spying network made use of Internet services,[5] such as social networking and cloud computing platforms.[4] The services included Twitter, Google Groups, Baidu, Yahoo Mail, Blogspot, and blog.com,[5] which were used to host malware[7] and infect computers with malicious software.[4]

43.1 Discovery

The Shadow Net report[8] was released following an 8-month collaborative investigation between researchers from the Canada-based Information Warfare Monitor, and the United States Shadowserver Foundation.[3][7][9] The Shadow Network was discovered during the GhostNet investigation,[3] and researchers said it was more sophisticated and difficult to detect.[3][5] Following the publication of the GhostNet report, several of the listed command and control servers went offline;[3][10] however, the cyber attacks on the Tibetan community did not cease.[10]

The researchers conducted field research in Dharamsala, India, and with the consent of the Tibetan organizations, were able to monitor the networks in order to collect copies of the data from compromised computers and identify command and control servers used by the attackers.[7][11] The field research done by the Information Warfare Monitor and the Shadowserver Foundation found that computer systems in the Office of His Holiness the Dalai Lama (OHHDL) had been compromised by multiple malware networks, one of

which was the Shadow Network.[12]

Further research into the Shadow Network revealed that, while India and the Dalai Lama's offices were the primary focus of the attacks,[5] the operation compromised computers on every continent except Australia and Antarctica.[1][13]

The research team recovered more than 1,500 e-mails from the Dalai Lama's Office[1][4] along with a number of documents belonging to the Indian government.[1] This included classified security assessments in several Indian states, reports on Indian missile systems,[10] and documents related to India's relationships in the Middle East, Africa, and Russia.[1][5] Documents were also stolen related to the movements of NATO forces in Afghanistan,[5] and from the United Nations Economic and Social Commission for Asia and the Pacific (UNESCAP).[4][5] The hackers were indiscriminate in what they took, which included sensitive information as well as financial and personal information.[4]

43.2 Origin

The attackers were tracked through e-mail addresses[4] to the city of Chengdu in the Sichuan province of China.[1][3] There was suspicion but no confirmation that one of the hackers had a connection to the University of Electronic Science and Technology in Chengdu.[2] The account of another hacker was linked to a Chengdu resident who claimed to know little about the hacking.[5]

43.3 References

[1] Anna, Cara (6 April 2010). "'Shadow Network' Of Chinese Hackers Steal Dalai Lama's Emails: REPORT". *The Huffington Post*. Retrieved 1 Nov 2014.

[2] Branigan, Tania (6 April 2010). "Cyber-spies based in China target Indian government and Dalai Lama". *The*

Guardian. Retrieved 1 Nov 2010.

[3] Zetter, Kim (6 April 2010). "Spy Network Pilfered Classified Docs From Indian Government and Others". *Wired*. Retrieved 1 Nov 2014.

[4] "Shadow cyber spy network revealed". *BBC News*. 6 April 2010. Retrieved 1 Nov 2014.

[5] Markoff, John; Barboza, David (5 April 2010). "Researchers Trace Data Theft to Intruders in China". *The New York Times*. Retrieved 1 Nov 2014.

[6] "SHADOWS IN THE CLOUD: Investigating Cyber Espionage 2.0". *Scribd*. The SecDev Group. 6 April 2010. p. 2. Retrieved 1 Nov 2010.

[7] Mills, Elinor (6 April 2010). "Report: India targeted by spy network". *CNET*. Retrieved 1 Nov 2014.

[8] "SHADOWS IN THE CLOUD: Investigating Cyber Espionage 2.0". *Scribd*. The SecDev Group. 6 April 2010. Retrieved 1 Nov 2014.

[9] Robertson, Grant (6 April 2010). "Canadian researchers reveal online spy ring based in China". *The Globe and Mail*. Retrieved 1 Nov 2014.

[10] Moore, Malcolm (6 April 2010). "Chinese hackers steal Dalai Lama's emails". *The Telegraph*. Retrieved 1 Nov 2010.

[11] "SHADOWS IN THE CLOUD: Investigating Cyber Espionage 2.0". *Scribd*. The SecDev Group. 6 April 2010. p. 9. Retrieved 1 Nov 2014.

[12] "SHADOWS IN THE CLOUD: Investigating Cyber Espionage 2.0". *Scribd*. The SecDev Group. 6 April 2010. p. 13. Retrieved 1 Nov 2014.

[13] "SHADOWS IN THE CLOUD: Investigating Cyber Espionage 2.0". *Scribd*. The SecDev Group. 6 April 2010. p. 32. Retrieved 1 Nov 2014.

43.4 External links

- Shadowserver Foundation

- Citizen Lab

- The SecDev Group

- Information Warfare Monitor

Chapter 44

Operation Shady RAT

Operation Shady RAT is an ongoing series of cyber attacks starting in mid-2006*[1] reported by Dmitri Alperovitch, Vice President of Threat Research at Internet security company McAfee in August 2011, who also led and named the Night Dragon Operation and Operation Aurora cyberespionage intrusion investigations.*[2] The attacks have hit at least 71 organizations, including defense contractors, businesses worldwide, the United Nations and the International Olympic Committee.*[3]*[4]

The operation, named by Alperovitch as a derivation of the common computer security industry acronym for Remote Access Tool, is characterized by McAfee as "a five year targeted operation by one specific actor". The report suggests that the targeting of various athletic oversight organizations around the time of the 2008 Summer Olympics "potentially pointed a finger at a state actor behind the intrusions".*[2] That state actor is widely assumed to be the People's Republic of China.*[5]

44.1 See also

- Advanced persistent threat
- DigiNotar
- Duqu
- PLA Unit 61398
- Tailored Access Operations

44.2 References

[1] Jim Finkle (2011-08-03). "State actor seen in "enormous" range of cyber attacks". Reuters. Retrieved 2011-08-03.

[2] Dmitri Alperovitch (2011-08-02). "Revealed: Operation Shady RAT" (PDF). McAfee. Retrieved 2011-08-03.

[3] "Governments, IOC and UN hit by massive cyber attack". BBC News. 2011-08-03. Retrieved 3 August 2011.

[4] Nakashima, Ellen, "Report on 'Operation Shady RAT' identifies widespread cyber-spying", *Washington Post*, 3 August 2011.

[5] Gross, Michael Joseph, "Enter the Cyber-dragon", *Vanity Fair*, September 2011.

Chapter 45

Sony Pictures Entertainment hack

45.1 Hack and perpetrators

The headquarters of Sony Pictures Entertainment in Culver City, California, United States

On November 24, 2014, a hacker group which identified itself by the name "Guardians of Peace" (GOP) leaked a release of confidential data from the film studio Sony Pictures Entertainment. The data included personal information about Sony Pictures employees and their families, e-mails between employees, information about executive salaries at the company, copies of then-unreleased Sony films, and other information.[*][1]

In December 2014, the GOP group demanded that Sony pull its film *The Interview*, a comedy about a plot to assassinate North Korean leader Kim Jong-un, and threatened terrorist attacks at cinemas screening the film. After major U.S. cinema chains opted not to screen the film in response to these threats, Sony elected to cancel the film's formal premiere and mainstream release, opting to skip directly to a digital release followed by a limited theatrical release the next day.[*][2][*][3][*][4]

United States intelligence officials, after evaluating the software, techniques, and network sources used in the hack, alleged that the attack was sponsored by North Korea.[*][5] North Korea has denied all responsibility.

The duration of the hack is yet unknown, though a purported member of the Guardians of Peace (GOP) who have claimed to have performed the hack stated that they have had access for at least a year prior to its discovery in November 2014, according to *Wired*.[*][6] The hackers involved claim to have taken more than 100 terabytes of data from Sony, but that claim has never been confirmed.[*][7] The attack was conducted using malware. Although Sony was not specifically mentioned in its advisory, US-CERT said that the attackers used a Server Message Block (SMB) Worm Tool to conduct attacks against a major entertainment company. Components of the attack included a listening implant, backdoor, proxy tool, destructive hard drive tool, and destructive target cleaning tool. The components clearly suggest an intent to gain repeated entry, extract information, and be destructive, as well as remove evidence of the attack.[*][8] The cleaning tool used on Sony's computer infrastructure, Wiper, is a malware program designed to erase data from the servers.[*][9]

Sony was made aware of the hack on Monday, November 24, 2014, as the malware previously installed rendered many Sony employees' computers inoperable by the software, with the warning by a group calling themselves the Guardians of Peace, along with a portion of the confidential data taken during the hack.[*][10] Several Sony-related Twitter accounts were also taken over.[*][6] This followed a message that several Sony Pictures executives had received via email on the previous Friday, November 21; the message, coming from a group called "God'sApstls" [*sic*], demanded "monetary compensation" or otherwise, "Sony Pictures will be bombarded as a whole".[*][10] This email message had been mostly ignored by executives, lost in the volume they had received or treated as spam email.[*][10] In addition to the activation of the malware on November 24, the message included a warning for Sony to decide on their course of action by 11pm that evening, although no apparent threat was made when that deadline passed.[*][10] In the days following this hack, the Guardians of Peace began leaking yet-unreleased films and started to release portions of the confidential data to attract the attention of social media sites, although they did not specify what they wanted in return.*[10] Sony quickly organized internal teams to try to manage the loss of data to the Internet, and contacted the FBI and the private security firm FireEye to help protect Sony employees whose personal data was exposed by the hack, repair the damaged computer infrastructure and trace the source of the leak.*[10] The first public report concerning a North Korean link to the attack was published by Re/code on November 28 and later confirmed by NBC News*[11]

"This is absurd. Yet it is exactly the kind of behavior we have come to expect from a regime that threatened to take 'merciless countermeasures' against the U.S. over a Hollywood comedy, and has no qualms about holding tens of thousands of people in harrowing gulags."

—U.S. Ambassador to the U.N. Samantha Power

On December 8, 2014, alongside the eighth large data dump of confidential information, the Guardians of Peace (GOP) threatened Sony with language relating to the September 11 attacks that drew the attention of U.S. security agencies.*[10]*[12] North Korean state-sponsored hackers are suspected by the United States of being involved in part due to specific threats made toward Sony and movie theaters showing *The Interview*, a comedy film about an assassination attempt against Kim Jong-un.*[13] North Korean officials had previously expressed concerns about the film to the United Nations, stating that "to allow the production and distribution of such a film on the assassination of an incumbent head of a sovereign state should be regarded as the most undisguised sponsoring of terrorism as well as an act of war." *[14]

In its first quarter financials for 2015, Sony Pictures set aside $15 million to deal with ongoing damages from the hack.*[15] Sony has bolstered its cyber-security infrastructure as a result, using solutions to prevent similar hacks or data loss in the future.*[10] Sony co-chairperson, Amy Pascal, announced in the wake of the hack that she would step down as of May 2015, and instead will become more involved with film production under Sony.*[16]

45.2   Information obtained

According to a notice letter dated December 8, 2014, from SPE to its employees, SPE learned on December 1, 2014, that personally identifiable information about employees and their dependents may have been obtained by unauthorized individuals as a result of a "brazen cyber-attack", including names, address, social security numbers and financial information.*[17] On December 7, 2014, C-SPAN

reported that the hackers stole 47,000 unique Social Security numbers from the SPE computer network.*[18]

Although personal data may have been stolen, early news reports focused mainly on celebrity gossip and embarrassing details about Hollywood and film industry business affairs gleaned by the media from electronic files, including private e-mail messages, released by the computer criminals. Among the information revealed in the e-mails was that Sony CEO Kazuo Hirai pressured Sony Pictures co-chairwoman Amy Pascal to "soften" the assassination scene in the upcoming Sony film *The Interview*.*[19] Many details relating to the actions of the Sony Pictures executives, including Pascal and Michael Lynton, were also released, in a manner that appeared to be intended to spur distrust between these executives and other employees of Sony.*[10]

Other e-mails released in the hack showed Pascal and Scott Rudin, a film and theatrical producer, discussing Angelina Jolie. In the e-mails, Rudin referred to Jolie as "a minimally talented spoiled brat" and criticized her wanting David Fincher to direct her film *Cleopatra*, which Rudin felt would interfere with Fincher directing a planned film about Steve Jobs.*[20] Pascal and Rudin were also noted to have had an e-mail exchange about Pascal's upcoming encounter with Barack Obama that included characterizations described as racist.*[21]*[22]*[23] The two had suggested they should mention films about African-Americans upon meeting the president, such as *Django Unchained*, *12 Years a Slave* and *The Butler*, all of which depict slavery in the United States or the pre-civil rights era.*[21]*[22]*[23] Pascal and Rudin later apologized.*[21]*[23]*[24] Details of lobbying efforts by politician Mike Moore on behalf of the Digital Citizens Alliance and FairSearch against Google were also revealed.*[25]

The leak revealed multiple details of behind-the-scenes politics on Columbia Pictures' current *Spider-Man* film series, including e-mails between Pascal and others to various heads of Marvel Studios.*[26] In addition to the emails, a copy of the script for the *James Bond* film *Spectre*, released in 2015, was obtained.*[27] Several future Sony Pictures films, including *Annie*, *Mr. Turner*, *Still Alice* and *To Write Love on Her Arms*, were also leaked.*[28]*[29]*[30] The hackers intended to release additional information on December 25, 2014,*[31] which coincided with the release date of *The Interview* in the United States.

According to *The Daily Dot*, based on the e-mail leaks, while he was at Sony, executive Charles Sipkins was responsible for following senior executives' orders to edit Wikipedia articles about them.*[32]

In December 2014, former Sony Pictures Entertainment employees filed four lawsuits against the company for not protecting their data that was released in the hack, which included Social Security numbers and medical information.*[33]

In January 2015, details were revealed of the MPAA's lobbying of the United States International Trade Commission to mandate US ISPs either at the internet transit level or consumer level internet service provider, to implement IP address blocking pirate websites as well as linking websites.*[34] WikiLeaks published over 30,000 documents that were obtained via the hack in April 2015, with founder Julian Assange stating that the document archive "shows the inner workings of an influential multinational corporation" that should be made public.*[35]

In November 2015, after Charlie Sheen revealed he was HIV positive in a television interview to Matt Lauer, it was revealed that information about his diagnosis was leaked in an email between senior Sony bosses dated March 10, 2014.*[36]*[37]

45.3 Threats surrounding *The Interview*

On December 16, for the first time since the hack, the "Guardians of Peace" mentioned the then-upcoming film *The Interview* by name, and threatened to take terrorist actions against the film's New York City premiere at Sunshine Cinema on December 18, as well as on its American wide release date, set for December 25.*[38] Sony pulled the theatrical release the following day.

Seth Rogen and James Franco, the stars of *The Interview*, responded by saying they did not know if it was definitely caused by the film,*[40] but later cancelled all media appearances tied to the film outside of the planned New York City premiere on December 16, 2014.*[41] Following initial threats made towards theaters that would show *The Interview*, several theatrical chains, including Carmike Cinemas, Bow Tie Cinemas, Regal Entertainment Group, AMC Theatres and Cinemark Theatres, announced that they would not screen *The Interview*.*[42]*[43]*[44] The same day, Sony stated that they would allow theaters to opt out of showing *The Interview*, but later decided to fully pull the national December 25 release of the film, as well as announce that there were "no further release plans" to release the film on any platform, including home video, in the foreseeable future.*[45]*[46]*[47]

On December 18, two messages (both allegedly from the Guardians of Peace) were released. One, sent in a private message to Sony executives, stated that they would not release any further information if Sony never releases the film and removed its presence from the internet. The other, posted to Pastebin, a web application used for text storage that the Guardians of Peace have used for previous messages, stated that the studio had "suffered enough" and could release *The Interview*, but only if Kim Jong-un's death scene was not "too happy". The post also stated that the company cannot "test [them] again", and that "if [Sony Pictures] makes anything else, [they] will be here ready to fight".*[48]

President Barack Obama, in an end-of-year press speech on December 19, commented on the Sony hacking and stated that he felt Sony made a mistake in pulling the film, and that producers should "not get into a pattern where you are intimidated by these acts".*[49] He also said, "We will respond proportionally and we will respond in a place and time and manner that we choose." *[50] In response to President Obama's statement, Sony Entertainment's CEO Michael Lynton said on the CNN program *Anderson Cooper 360* that the public, the press and the President misunderstood the events. Lynton said that the decision to cancel the wide release was in response to a majority of theaters pulling their showings and not to the hackers' threats. Lynton stated that they will seek other options to distribute the film in the future, and noted "We have not given in. And we have not backed down. We have always had every desire to have the American public see this movie." *[51]*[52]

On December 23, Sony opted to authorize approximately 300 mostly-independent theaters to show *The Interview* on Christmas Day, as the four major theater chains had yet to change their earlier decision not to show the film.*[53]*[54] The FBI worked with these theaters to detail the specifics of the prior threats and how to manage security for the showings, but noted that there was no actionable intelligence on the prior threats.*[55] Sony's Lynton stated on the announcement that "we are proud to make it available to the public and to have stood up to those who attempted to suppress free speech".*[56] *The Interview* was also released to Google Play, Xbox Video, and YouTube on December 24.*[57] No incidents predicated by the threats occurred with the release, and instead, the unorthodox release of the film led to it being considered a success due to increased interest in the film following the attention it had received.*[58]

On December 27, the North Korean National Defence Commission released a statement accusing Obama of being "the chief culprit who forced the Sony Pictures Entertainment to indiscriminately distribute the movie ... Obama always goes reckless in words and deeds like a monkey in a tropical forest." *[59]

45.4   U.S. accusations against North Korea

U.S. government officials stated on December 17, 2014 their belief that the North Korean government was "centrally involved" in the hacking, although there was initially some debate within the White House whether or not to make this finding public.*[5] White House officials treated the situation as a "serious national security matter",*[60] and the Federal Bureau of Investigation (FBI) formally stated on December 19 that they connected the North Korean government to the cyber-attacks.*[61]*[62] Including undisclosed evidence, these claims were made based on the use of similar malicious hacking tools and techniques previously employed by North Korean hackers—including North Korea's cyberwarfare agency Bureau 121 on South Korean targets.*[5]*[63] According to the FBI:*[64]

- "[A] technical analysis of the data deletion malware used in this attack revealed links to other malware that the FBI knows North Korea previously developed. For example, there were similarities in specific lines of code, encryption algorithms, data deletion methods, and compromised networks.

- "The FBI also observed significant overlap between the infrastructure used in this attack and other malicious cyber activity the U.S. government has previously linked directly to North Korea. For example, the FBI discovered that several Internet protocol (IP) addresses associated with known North Korean infrastructure communicated with IP addresses that were hardcoded into the data deletion malware used in this attack. The FBI later clarified that the source IP addresses were associated with a group of North Korean businesses located in Shenyang in northeastern China.*[65]

- "Separately, the tools used in the SPE attack have similarities to a cyber-attack in March of last year against South Korean banks and media outlets, which was carried out by North Korea."

The FBI later clarified more details of the attacks, attributing them to North Korea by noting that the hackers were "sloppy" with the use of proxy IP addresses that originated from within North Korea. FBI Director James Comey stated that Internet access is tightly controlled within North Korea, and as such, it was unlikely that a third party had hijacked these addresses without allowance from the North Korean government.*[66]*[67] The National Security Agency assisted the FBI in analyzing the attack, specifically in reviewing the malware and tracing its origins; NSA director Admiral Michael Rogers agreed with the FBI that the attack originated from North Korea.*[68] A disclosed NSA report published by *Der Spiegel* stated that the agency had become aware of the origins of the hack due to their own cyber-intrusion on North Korean's network that they had set up in 2010, following concerns of the technology maturation of the country.*[65]

The North Korean news agency KCNA denied the "wild rumours" of North Korean involvement, but said that "The hacking into the SONY Pictures might be a righteous deed of the supporters and sympathizers with the DPRK in response to its appeal."*[12]*[27]*[69] North Korea offered to be part of a joint probe with the United States to determine the hackers' identities, threatening consequences if the United States refused to collaborate and continued the allegation.*[70]*[71] The U.S. refused and asked China for investigative assistance instead.*[72] Some days after the FBI's announcement, North Korea temporarily suffered a nationwide Internet outage, which the country claimed to be the United States' response to the hacking attempts.*[73]

On the day following the FBI's accusation of North Korea's involvement, the FBI received an e-mail purportedly from the hacking group, linking to a YouTube video entitled "you are an idiot!", apparently mocking the organization.*[74]*[75]*[76]

On December 19, 2014, U.S. Secretary of Homeland Security Jeh Johnson released a statement saying, "The cyber attack against Sony Pictures Entertainment was not just an attack against a company and its employees. It was also an attack on our freedom of expression and way of life." He encouraged businesses and other organizations to use the Cybersecurity Framework developed by the National Institute of Standards and Technology (NIST) to assess and limit cyber risks and protect against cyber threats.*[77] On the same day, U.S. Secretary of State John Kerry published his remarks condemning North Korea for the cyber-attack and threats against movie theatres and moviegoers. "This provocative and unprecedented attack and subsequent threats only strengthen our resolve to continue to work with partners around the world to strengthen cybersecurity, promote norms of acceptable state behavior, uphold freedom of expression, and ensure that the Internet remains open, interoperable, secure and reliable," he said.*[78]

On January 2, 2015, the U.S. installed additional economic sanctions on already-sanctioned North Korea for the hack,*[79] which North Korean officials called out as "groundlessly stirring up bad blood towards" the country.*[80]

45.4.1 Doubts about accusations against North Korea

Members of the press and various cybersecurity experts have expressed doubt about the claims that North Korea was behind the hack. Cyber security experts, independently analyzing the hack separately from the FBI —including Kurt Stammberger from cyber security firm Norse,*[81]*[82] DEFCON organizer and Cloudflare researcher Marc Rogers,*[83] Sabu,*[84] and Kim Zetter, a security journalist at *Wired* magazine*[85]—have tended to agree that North Korea might not be behind the attack.

Michael Hiltzik, a *Los Angeles Times* journalist, said that all evidence against North Korea was "circumstantial" and that some cybersecurity experts were "skeptical" about accusations against the government.*[86] Cybersecurity expert Lucas Zaichkowsky said, "State-sponsored attackers don't create cool names for themselves like 'Guardians of Peace' and promote their activity to the public." *[87] Kim Zetter of *Wired* magazine called released evidence against the government "flimsy" .*[88] Former hacker Hector Monsegur, who once hacked into Sony, explained to CBS News that exfiltrating one or one hundred terabytes of data would have taken months or years, not weeks, "without anyone noticing" . Moreover, Monsegur doubted the accusations due to North Korea's possibly insufficient infrastructure to handle much data. He believed that it could have been either Chinese, Russian, or anyone else.*[89]

Stammberger provided to the FBI Norse's findings that suggest the hack was an inside job, stating, "Sony was not just hacked; this is a company that was essentially nuked from the inside. We are very confident that this was not an attack master-minded by North Korea and that insiders were key to the implementation of one of the most devastating attacks in history." *[90] Stammberger believes that the security failure may have originated from six disgruntled former Sony employees, based on their past skill sets and discussions these people made in chat rooms. Norse employees identified these people from a list of workers that were eliminated from Sony during a restructuring in May 2014, and noted that some had made very public and angry responses to their firing, and would be in appropriate positions to identify the means to access secure parts of Sony's servers.*[91]*[92]*[93] After a private briefing lasting three hours, the FBI formally rejected Norse's alternative assessment.*[94]

In response to allegations that the intrusion was the result of an inside job, or something other than a state-sponsored cyber attack, computer forensic specialist Kevin Mandia, president of the security firm FireEye, commented that there isn't a "shred of evidence" that an insider was responsible for the attack and that the evidence uncovered by his security firm supports the position of the United States government.*[95]*[96]

In February 2016, analytics firm Novetta issued a joint investigative report into the attack. The report, published in collaboration with Kaspersky Lab, Symantec, AlienVault, Invincea, Trend Micro, Carbon Black, Punch-Cyber, RiskIQ, ThreatConnect and Volexity, concluded that a well-resourced organization had committed the intrusion, and that "we strongly believe that the SPE attack was not the work of insiders or hacktivists" . The analysis said that the same group is engaged in military espionage campaigns.*[97]*[98]*[99]

> Because of the depth and scope of malware tools, structure of the analyzed code bases, TTP overlap with similar attacks, and long trail of activities attributed to the Lazarus Group, Novetta does not believe that the SPE attack was carried out by insiders or hacktivists, but rather by a more structured, resourced, and motivated organization. ... Although our analysis cannot support direct attribution of a nation-state or other specific group due to the difficulty of proper attribution in the cyber realm, the FBI's official attribution claims could be supported by our findings.*[100]

45.5 Legal responses

On January 2, 2015, U.S. President Barack Obama issued an Executive Order enacting additional sanctions against the North Korean government and a North Korean arms dealer, specifically citing the cyber attack and ongoing North Korean policies.*[101]

Obama also issued a legislative proposal to Congress to update current laws such as the Racketeer Influenced and Corrupt Organizations Act and introduce new ones to allow federal and national law enforcement officials to better respond to cybercrimes like the Sony hack, and to be able to prosecute such crimes compatibly to similar off-line crimes, while protecting the privacy of Americans.*[102]*[103]

45.6 Public discussion

45.6.1 About reporting on the hack

In December 2014, Sony requested that the media stop covering the hack.*[3] Sony also threatened legal action if the media did not comply, but according to law professor Eugene Volokh, Sony's legal threats are "unlikely to prevail" .*[104] Sony then threatened legal action against

Twitter if it did not suspend accounts of people who posted the hacked material.*[105] American screenwriter Aaron Sorkin wrote an op-ed for *The New York Times* opining that the media was helping the hackers by publishing and reporting on the leaked information.*[106] On December 18, Reddit took the unusual step of banning a subpage called "SonyGOP" that was being used to distribute the hacked files.*[107]

45.6.2 About pulling *The Interview*

The threats made directly at Sony over *The Interview* was seen by many as a threat on free speech. The decision to pull the film was criticized by several Hollywood filmmakers, actors, and television hosts, including Ben Stiller, Steve Carell, Rob Lowe, Jimmy Kimmel and Judd Apatow.*[108]*[109] Some commentators contrasted the situation to the non-controversial release of the 2004 *Team America: World Police*, a film that mocked the leadership of North Korea's prior leader, Kim Jong-il.*[110] The Alamo Drafthouse was poised to replace showings of *The Interview* with *Team America* until the film's distributor Paramount Pictures ordered the theaters to stop.*[111]

In light of the threats made to Sony over *The Interview*, New Regency cancelled its March 2015 production plans for a film adaptation of the graphic novel *Pyongyang: A Journey in North Korea*, which was set to star Steve Carell.*[112] *Hustler* announced its intentions to make a pornographic parody film of *The Interview*. *Hustler* founder Larry Flynt said, "If Kim Jong-un and his henchmen were upset before, wait till they see the movie we're going to make".*[113]

45.6.3 Outside the United States

In China, the media coverage of the hackings has been limited, including in search engines except Google, which has given out 36 million results. Hua Chunying, a spokeswoman of foreign affairs, "shied away from directly addressing" the Sony hacking situation.*[114] On December 25, 2014, Russia offered sympathy to North Korea, saying it was "quite understandable" that North Korea would be upset over the film. Russia said American threats of retaliation were "counterproductive and dangerous", and that the US did not provide any proof of who hacked Sony.*[115]

45.7 Documentary

A documentary about the Sony hacks is being developed by director Jehane Noujaim and producers Kareem Amer and Mike Lerner. Prior to November 2014, the group were already working on a documentary about international cyberattacks, and quickly switched focus after the revelation of the Sony hacks. They anticipate presenting alternative theories about the identity of the hackers in the documentary.*[116]

45.8 See also

- 2013 South Korea cyberattack
- 2015–16 SWIFT banking hack
- North Korea's illicit activities

45.9 References

[1] Gabi Siboni and David Siman-Tov, Cyberspace Extortion: North Korea versus the United States, INSS Insight No. 646, December 23, 2014.

[2] "Sony Pictures Entertainment Notice Letter" (PDF). State of California Department of Justice Office of the Attorney General. December 8, 2014. Retrieved December 20, 2014.

[3] "Sony Asks Media to Stop Covering Hacked Emails". *Time*. December 16, 2014. Retrieved December 17, 2014.

[4] Weise, Elizabeth (December 17, 2014). "Experts: Sony hackers 'have crossed the line'". *USA Today*. Retrieved December 17, 2014.

[5] Sanger, David E.; Perlroth, Nicole (December 17, 2014). "U.S. Links North Korea to Sony Hacking". *The New York Times*. Retrieved December 17, 2014.

[6] Zetter, Kim (December 3, 2014). "Sony Got Hacked Hard: What We Know and Don't Know So Far". *Wired*. Retrieved January 4, 2015.

[7] James Cook (December 16, 2014). "Sony Hackers Have Over 100 Terabytes Of Documents. Only Released 200 Gigabytes So Far". *Business Insider*. Retrieved December 18, 2014.

[8] Lennon, Mike (December 19, 2014). "Hackers Used Sophisticated SMB Worm Tool to Attack Sony". *SecurityWeek*. Retrieved February 29, 2016.

[9] Palilery, Jose (December 24, 2014). "What caused Sony hack: What we know now". CNN Money. Retrieved January 4, 2015.

[10] Seal, Mark (February 4, 2015). "An Exclusive Look at Sony's Hacking Saga". *Vanity Fair*. Retrieved February 4, 2015.

[11] Hesseldahl, Arik (November 28, 2014). "Sony Pictures Investigates North Korea Link In Hack Attack". *Recode*. Retrieved Feb 1, 2016.

[12] "Sony hack: White House views attack as security issue". BBC. December 18, 2014. Retrieved December 18, 2014.

[13] Ben Child. Hackers demand Sony cancel release of Kim Jong-un-baiting comedy, *The Guardian*. 9 December 2014.

[14] Beaumont-Thomas, Ben (July 10, 2014). "North Korea complains to UN about Seth Rogen comedy The Interview". *The Guardian*. Retrieved December 18, 2014.

[15] Frizell, Sam (February 4, 2015). "Sony Is Spending $15 Million to Deal With the Big Hack". *Time*. Retrieved February 4, 2015.

[16] Cieply, Michael; Barnes, Brooks (February 5, 2015). "Amy Pascal Leaving as Sony Studio Chief". *New York Times*. Retrieved February 5, 2015.

[17] "Submitted Breach Notification Sample, Sony Pictures Entertainment Notice Letter". *State of California Department of Justice Office of the Attorney General*. December 8, 2014. Retrieved December 20, 2014.

[18] "Washington Journal – Hacking and Cybersecurity Threats". C-SPAN. December 7, 2014. Retrieved December 22, 2014.

[19] Fackler, Martin (December 15, 2014). "Sony's International Incident: Making Kim Jong-un's Head Explode". *The New York Times*. Retrieved December 15, 2014.

[20] Stedman, Alex (December 9, 2014). "Leaked Sony Emails Reveal Nasty Exchanges and Insults". *Variety*. Retrieved March 3, 2015.

[21] Mike Fleming, Jr., Scott Rudin Apologizes After Leak Of Sony's Hacked Racially Insensitive E-Mails On Barack Obama, *Deadline.com*, December 11, 2014

[22] Variety Staff, Sony's Amy Pascal Apologizes for Obama Emails, *Variety*, December 11, 2014

[23] Christopher Rosen, Scott Rudin & Amy Pascal Apologize After Racially Insensitive Emails About Obama Leak, *The Huffington Post*, December 11, 2014

[24] "Sony Pictures' Amy Pascal and Scott Rudin's racist emails about President Obama". *Mail Online*. December 11, 2014.

[25] WINGFIELD, NICK (December 16, 2014). "Google's Detractors Take Their Fight to the States". Retrieved 1 January 2015.

[26] Fritz, Ben (December 9, 2014). "Sony, Marvel Discussed Spider-Man Movie Crossover". *The Wall Street Journal*. Retrieved December 18, 2014.

[27] Stedman, Alex (December 14, 2014). "Sony Hack: Bond Producers Say 'Spectre' Screenplay Among Stolen Material". *Variety*. Retrieved December 15, 2014.

[28] Justin McCurry. "North Korea denies hacking Sony Pictures". *the Guardian*. Retrieved December 17, 2014.

[29] "Hackers who targeted Sony invoke 9/11 attacks in warning to moviegoers". *The Guardian*. Retrieved December 17, 2014.

[30] "Sony's New Movies Leak Online Following Hack Attack". *NBC News*. Retrieved December 1, 2014.

[31] Weise, Elizabeth (December 15, 2014). "Sony fights hack damage as new threats emerge". *USA Today*. Retrieved December 15, 2014.

[32] Owens, Simon (April 23, 2015), "Sony executives ordered edits to Wikipedia pages", *The Daily Dot*

[33] Ellis, Ralph (December 20, 2014). "Lawsuits say Sony Pictures should have expected security breach". *cnn.com*. Retrieved December 21, 2014.

[34] Brandom, Russell (2 January 2015). "The MPAA has a new plan to stop copyright violations at the border". *The Verge*. Retrieved 4 January 2015.

[35] Lang, Brent (April 16, 2015). "WikiLeaks Publishes Thousands of Hacked Sony Documents". *Variety*. Retrieved April 16, 2015.

[36] Claire Rutter (November 17, 2015). "Did Sony hack disclose Charlie Sheen's HIV status in email nearly TWO years ago?". *mirror*.

[37] "Charlie Sheen HIV Positive —Sony Hack Email Discussed Open Secret - Radar Online". *Radar Online*. November 16, 2015.

[38] Rushe, Dominic (December 17, 2014). "Hackers who targeted Sony invoke 9/11 attacks in warning to moviegoers". *The Guardian*. Retrieved December 18, 2014.

[39] Boot, William (December 17, 2014). "Exclusive: Sony Emails Say State Department Blessed Kim Jong-Un Assassination in 'The Interview'". The Daily Beast. Retrieved December 19, 2014.

[40] "Seth Rogen and James Franco Address the Sony Hack". *ABC News*. December 15, 2014. Retrieved December 15, 2014.

[41] Stedman, Alex (December 16, 2014). "Seth Rogen and James Franco Cancel All Media Appearances for 'The Interview'". *Variety*. Retrieved December 16, 2014.

[42] Kilday, Gregg (December 16, 2014). "Sony Hack: Carmike Cinemas Drops 'The Interview'". *The Hollywood Reporter*. Retrieved December 17, 2014.

[43] Weise, Elizabeth (December 17, 2014). "Second theater chain pulls "The Interview" after hacker threats". *USA Today*. Retrieved December 17, 2014.

[44] Kilday, Gregg (December 17, 2014). "Top Five Theater Circuits Drop 'The Interview' After Sony Hack". *The Hollywood Reporter*. Retrieved December 17, 2014.

[45] Grow, Kory (December 17, 2014). "Sony Cancels 'Interview' New York Premiere Amid Terror Threats". *Rolling Stone*. Retrieved December 17, 2014.

[46] Lang, Brent (December 17, 2014). "Sony Cancels Theatrical Release for 'The Interview' on Christmas". *Variety*. Retrieved December 17, 2014.

[47] McNary, Dave (December 17, 2014). "Sony Has 'No Further Release Plans' for 'The Interview'". *Variety*. Retrieved December 17, 2014.

[48] Weise, Elizabeth; Johnson, Kevin (December 19, 2014). "FBI confirms North Korea behind Sony hack". *USA Today*. Retrieved December 19, 2014.

[49] "US President Barack Obama holds last news briefing of 2014". BBC. December 19, 2014. Retrieved December 19, 2014.

[50] "Obama Pledges Proportional Response to Sony Hack". ABCNews. Dec 19, 2014.

[51] Pallotta, Frank (December 19, 2014). "Sony exec fires back at President Obama". CNN Money. Retrieved December 19, 2014.

[52] "Sony 'will not drop' North Korea film The Interview". BBC. December 19, 2014. Retrieved December 19, 2014.

[53] Shaw, Lucas (December 23, 2014). "Sony to Release *The Interview* in More Than 300 Theaters on Christmas Day". *Bloomberg*. Retrieved December 26, 2014.

[54] "*The Interview*: Obama hails move to screen North Korea film." *BBC*. Retrieved December 24, 2014.

[55] Brown, Pamela (December 24, 2014). "FBI reaching out to theaters screening 'The Interview'". CNN. Retrieved December 29, 2014.

[56] Coyle, Jake (December 23, 2014). "Sony announces limited release of 'The Interview'". *Boston Globe*. Retrieved December 29, 2014.

[57] Kelsey, Eric (24 December 2014). "Sony releases 'The Interview' on Youtube, other Internet channels". *Reuters*. Retrieved 24 December 2014.

[58] Hamedy, Saba (December 28, 2014). "'The Interview' finds its audience in indie theaters, online". *Los Angeles Times*. Retrieved December 29, 2014.

[59] "North Korea berates Obama over The Interview release". BBC News. December 27, 2014. Retrieved December 30, 2014.

[60] Bacle, Ariana (December 18, 2014). "White House is treating Sony hack as 'serious national security matter'". *Entertainment Weekly*. Retrieved December 18, 2014.

[61] "FBI —Update on Sony Investigation". FBI. December 19, 2014. Retrieved December 22, 2014.

[62] Weise, Elizabeth; Johnson, Kevin (December 19, 2014). "FBI confirms North Korea behind Sony hack". *USA Today*. Retrieved December 19, 2014.

[63] "Sony cyber attack linked to North Korean government hackers, FBI says". *The Guardian*. 19 December 2014. Retrieved 19 December 2014.

[64] "Update on Sony Investigation" (Press release). Federal Bureau of Investigation. December 19, 2014. Retrieved December 19, 2014.

[65] Sanger, David E.; Fackler, Martin (January 18, 2015). "N.S.A. Tapped Into North Korean Networks Before Sony Attack, Officials Say". *New York Times*. Retrieved January 19, 2015.

[66] Brandom, Russell (January 7, 2015). "FBI Director Comey reveals new details on the Sony hack". The Verge. Retrieved January 7, 2015.

[67] "FBI details North Korean attack on Sony", *CNBC*, Jan. 8, 2014

[68] Frizeel, Sam (January 8, 2015). "NSA Director on Sony Hack: 'The Entire World is Watching'". *Time*. Retrieved January 9, 2015.

[69] http://www.kcna.co.jp/item/2014/201412/news07/20141207-12ee.html

[70] "North Korea seeks joint probe with US on Sony hack". BBC. December 20, 2014. Retrieved December 20, 2014.

[71] "North Korea demands joint inquiry with US into Sony Pictures hack". *The Guardian*. December 20, 2014. Retrieved December 20, 2014.

[72] Makinen, Julie (December 20, 2014). "North Korea decries U.S. allegations on Sony hack; U.S. turns to China." *Los Angeles Times*. Retrieved December 21, 2014.

[73] Helsel, Phil (December 26, 2014). "North Korea Insults Obama, Blames U.S. For Internet Outages". NBC News. Retrieved December 29, 2014.

[74] "Hackers 'mock' FBI investigation into Sony cyber attack." *ITV News*. December 20, 2014. Retrieved December 21, 2014.

[75] Boot, William (December 20, 2014). "Sony Hackers Guardians of Peace Troll FBI, Anonymous Convinced Hack Didn't Come From North Korea." *The Daily Beast*. Retrieved December 21, 2014.

[76] Gajewski, Ryan; Siegel, Tatiana (December 20, 2014). "Sony Hackers Appear to Mock FBI in Latest Message." *The Hollywood Reporter*. Retrieved December 21, 2014.

[77] "Statement By Secretary Johnson On Cyber Attack On Sony Pictures Entertainment". United States Department of Homeland Security. December 19, 2014. Retrieved December 24, 2014.

[78] "Condemning Cyber-Attack by North Korea". United States Department of State. December 19, 2014. Retrieved December 24, 2014.

[79] Lederman, Josh (January 2, 2015). "US slaps sanctions on North Korea after Sony hack". *Associated Press*. San Francisco Chronicle. Retrieved January 5, 2015.

[80] Siddique, Haroon (January 4, 2015). "North Korea responds with fury to US sanctions over Sony hack". *The Guardian*. Retrieved January 5, 2015.

[81] Kopan, Tal (29 December 2014). "U.S.: No alternate leads in Sony hack". Retrieved 4 January 2015.

[82] "New evidence Sony hack was "inside job", not North Korea". Retrieved 4 January 2015.

[83] Rogers, Marc. "Why the Sony hack is unlikely to be the work of North Korea." . Retrieved January 4, 2015.

[84] "Ex-Anonymous hacker questions North Korea's role in Sony hack". December 18, 2014. Retrieved January 4, 2015.

[85] Zetter, Kim. "Evidence of North Korea hack is thin". *Wired*. Retrieved January 4, 2015.

[86] Hiltzik, Michael (December 19, 2014). "The Sony hack: What if it isn't North Korea?" *Los Angeles Times*. Retrieved December 21, 2014.

[87] Mendoza, Martha (December 3, 2014). "Security experts doubt North Korea hacked into Sony; regime is angry over new Seth Rogen movie." *Associated Press* (Canada.com). Retrieved December 21, 2014.

[88] Zetter, Kim (December 17, 2014). "The Evidence That North Korea Hacked Sony Is Flimsy." *Wired*. Retrieved December 21, 2014.

[89] Monsegur, Hector (December 18, 2014). *Former Anonymous hacker doubts North Korea behind Sony attack*. CBS News. Interview with Elaine Quijano. Retrieved December 21, 2014.

[90] "Did the FBI get it wrong on North Korea?" *CBS News*. December 23, 2014. Retrieved December 24, 2014.

[91] Kiss, Jemina (December 30, 2014). "Sony hack: sacked employees could be to blame, researchers claim". *The Guardian*. Retrieved December 30, 2014.

[92] Kopan, Tal (December 29, 2014). "FBI briefed on alternate Sony hack theory". *Politico*. Retrieved December 30, 2014.

[93] Nussbaum, Daniel (December 29, 2014). "Private Intelligence Firm Briefs FBI: SONY Hack Could Have Been An Inside Job". *Breitbart News Network*. Retrieved December 30, 2014.

[94] Tal Kopan. FBI rejects alternate Sony hack theory, politico.com, December 30, 2014.

[95] Ina Fried. Sony Hack Was Not an Inside Job, Says Security Expert Kevin Mandia, recode.net, April 21, 2015.

[96] Arik Hesseldahl. FireEye's Kevin Mandia Talks About the World After the Sony Hack, recode.net, April 21, 2015.

[97] Juha Saarinen. North Korea linked to Sony hack attack: researchers, itnews.com.au, February 25, 2016.

[98] Novetta Exposes Depth of Sony Pictures Attack, novetta.com, February 24, 2016.

[99] Collaborative Operation Blockbuster aims to send Lazarus back to the dead, symantec.com, February 24, 2016.

[100] Novetta. Operation Blockbuster: Unrevealing the Long Thread of the Sony Attack, February 2016.

[101] "North Korea Sanction". *Scribd*.

[102] Daunt, Tina; Szalai, Georg (January 13, 2015). "White House Unveils Proposal for Cybersecurity Legislation in Wake of Sony Hack". *Hollywood Reporter*. Retrieved January 13, 2015.

[103] "SECURING CYBERSPACE - President Obama Announces New Cybersecurity Legislative Proposal and Other Cybersecurity Efforts". *whitehouse.gov*.

[104] Volokh, Eugene (December 15, 2014). "Can Sony sue media outlets who publish the stolen Sony documents?". *The Washington Post*. Retrieved December 15, 2014.

[105] Isidore, Chris. "Sony threatens Twitter with lawsuit over hack tweets". money.cnn.com. December 23, 2014. Retrieved December 27, 2014.

[106] Sorkin, Aaron (December 15, 2014). "The Sony Hack and the Yellow Press". *The New York Times*. Retrieved December 16, 2014.

[107] Goldman, David (December 29, 2014). "Reddit takes down Sony hack forum". Retrieved 4 January 2015.

[108] Sinha-Roy, Piya (Dec 17, 2014). "Hollywood slams Sony, movie theaters for canceling 'The Interview'". Reuters. Retrieved December 18, 2014.

[109] Marcus, Stephanie (December 7, 2014). "Celebrities React To Sony Canceling 'The Interview' Release". *The Huffington Post*. Retrieved December 18, 2014.

[110] Rife, Katie (December 18, 2014). "Alamo Drafthouse replaces The Interview with Team America: World Police — or not". A.V. Club. Retrieved December 18, 2014.

[111] Farnham, Donovan (December 18, 2014). "Paramount tells theaters no 'Team America: World Police'". *San Jose Mercury News*. Retrieved December 18, 2014.

[112] Ford, Rebecca (December 17, 2014). "Steve Carell's North Korea Thriller Dropped After Sony Hack". *The Hollywood Reporter*. Retrieved December 17, 2014.

[113] "Take That, Jong-un! Hustler Plans 'The Interview' Porn Parody". AVN. December 19, 2014. Retrieved December 20, 2014.

[114] Ripley, Will. China censors news on Sony hack. *CNN*. Retrieved December 24, 2014.

[115] "Russia offers support to North Korea amid Sony hack". *Yahoo! News*. AP. December 25, 2014. Retrieved December 25, 2014.

[116] Siegel, Tatiana (June 3, 2015). "Sony Hack Movie in the Works from Oscar-Nominated Team". *The Hollywood Reporter*. Retrieved June 3, 2015.

Chapter 46

Cybersquatting

Cybersquatting (also known as **domain squatting**), according to the United States federal law known as the Anticybersquatting Consumer Protection Act, is registering, trafficking in, or using an Internet domain name with bad faith intent to profit from the goodwill of a trademark belonging to someone else. The cybersquatter then offers to sell the domain to the person or company who owns a trademark contained within the name at an inflated price.

The term is derived from "squatting", which is the act of occupying an abandoned or unoccupied space or building that the squatter does not own, rent, or otherwise have permission to use.

46.1 Technical strategies for cybersquatters

Cybersquatters sometimes register variants of popular trademarked names, a practice known as typosquatting.

46.2 Legal resolution

Some countries have specific laws against cybersquatting beyond the normal rules of trademark law. The United States, for example, has the U.S. Anticybersquatting Consumer Protection Act (ACPA) of 1999. This expansion of the Lanham (Trademark) Act (15 U.S.C.) is intended to provide protection against cybersquatting for individuals as well as owners of distinctive trademarked names. However, even notable personalities, including rock star Bruce Springsteen and actor Kevin Spacey, failed to obtain control of their names on the internet.[1]

Jurisdiction is an issue, as shown in the case involving Kevin Spacey, in which Judge Gary A. Feess, of the United States District Court of the Central District of California, ruled that the actor would have to file a complaint in a Canadian court, where the current owner of kevinspacey.com resided.

Spacey later won the domain through the National Arbitration Forum.

46.2.1 International

Since 1999, the United Nations copyright agency, World Intellectual Property Organization (WIPO), has provided an arbitration system wherein a trademark holder can attempt to claim a squatted site. In 2006, there were 1823 complaints filed with WIPO, which was a 25% increase over the 2005 rate.[2] In 2007 it was stated that 84% of claims made since 1999 were decided in the complaining party's favor.[2]

46.3 Notable cases

46.3.1 With litigation

- Jethro Tull vs. Denny Hammerton,[3] 2000 (WIPO Case)

- Madonna vs. Parisi,[4] 2000 (WIPO Case)

- Primedia Magazine Finance Inc. (Tiger Beat) vs Next Level Productions (Benny Doro).[5]

- People for the Ethical Treatment of Animals v. Doughney, 2001

- Lamparello v. Falwell, 2005

- Lufthansa v. Future Media Architects, 2008[6]

- Microsoft vs. MikeRoweSoft

- Dennis Toeppen v . Panavision [7]

- Nissan Motors vs. Nissan Computer

153

46.3.2 Without litigation

- The White House against Whitehouse.com and Whitehouse.org

46.4 Social media

With the rising of social media websites such as Facebook and Twitter, a new form of cybersquatting involves registering trademark-protected brands or names of public figure on popular social media websites.

On June 5, 2009, Tony La Russa, the manager of the St. Louis Cardinals, filed a complaint against Twitter, accusing Twitter of cybersquatting.[8] The dispute centered on a Twitter profile that used La Russa's name, had a picture of La Russa, and had a headline that said "Hey there! Tony La Russa is now using Twitter." The profile encouraged users to "join today to start receiving Tony La Russa's updates." According to La Russa, the status updates were vulgar and derogatory. La Russa argued that the author of the profile intended, in bad faith, to divert Internet traffic away from La Russa's website and make a profit from the injury to La Russa's mark.[8] On June 26, 2009, La Russa filed a notice of voluntary dismissal after the parties settled the case.[9]

46.4.1 Efforts to curtail cybersquatting in social media

Social networking websites have attempted to curb cybersquatting, making cybersquatting a violation of their terms of service.

Twitter

Twitter's name squatting policy forbids the cybersquatting as seen in many domain name disputes, like "username for sale" accounts: "Attempts to sell or extort other forms of payment in exchange for usernames will result in account suspension.[10] " Additionally, Twitter has an "Impersonation Policy" that forbids non-parody impersonation. An account may be guilty of impersonation if it confuses or misleads others; "accounts with the clear intent to confuse or mislead may be permanently suspended." Twitter's standard for defining parody is whether a reasonable person would be aware that the fake profile is a joke.[11] Lastly, soon after the La Russa suit was filed, Twitter took another step to prevent "identity confusion" caused by squatting by unveiling "Verified Accounts.[12] " Usernames stamped with the "verified account" insignia indicate that the accounts are real and authentic.

Facebook

Facebook reserves the right to reclaim usernames on the website if they infringe on a trademark.[13] Trademark owners are responsible for reporting any trademark infringement on a username infringement form Facebook provides. Furthermore, Facebook usernames require "mobile phone authentication.[13] " In order to obtain a username, the individual needs to verify the account by phone.

46.5 See also

- Brandjacking
- Patent troll
- Domain Name System
- Michael Urvan
- John Zuccarini, convicted of violating the Truth in Domain Names Act
- Nissan Computer
- Planned Parenthood Fed'n of Am., Inc. v. Bucci
- Taubman Sucks, an intellectual property lawsuit
- Top-level domain
- Uniform Resource Locator (URL)
- Domain tasting
- Domain name front running
- Satyam Infoway Ltd. v. Sifynet Solutions Pvt. Ltd.

46.6 References

[1] "Kevin Spacey loses pivotal cybersquatting court case" . *Theregister.co.uk*. Retrieved 2016-09-27.

[2] "U.N: Cybersquatting complaints rise" . Yahoo! News. March 12, 2007. Archived from the original on March 21, 2007.

[3] ""The Independent'" July 30, 2000: A hit for Jethro Tull in domain name dispute" . Independent.co.uk. 2000-07-31. Retrieved 2013-09-22.

[4]

[5] Arbitration and Mediation Center. "WIPO Arbitration and Mediation Center ADMINISTRATIVE PANEL DECISION Primedia Magazine Finance Inc. v. Next Level Productions" . Wipo.int. Retrieved 2013-09-22.

[6] "Deutsche Lufthansa AG v Future Media Architects, Inc"
     . *Adrforum.com*. Retrieved 2016-09-27.

[7] "Panavision Int'l, L.P. v. Toeppen | Internet Trademark
     Case Summaries" . *Finnegan.com*. Retrieved 2016-09-27.

[8] ""see"La Russa Complaint, La Russa v. Twitter, Inc., No.
     CGC-09-488101, 2009 WL 1569936" . Citmedialaw.org.
     Retrieved 2013-09-22.

[9] ""see"La Russa Notice of Voluntary Dismissal, La Russa v.
     Twitter, Inc., No. CGC-09-488101, 2009 WL 1569936" .
     Citmedialaw.org. Retrieved 2013-09-22.

[10] "Twitter   Support: Name   Squatting   Policy" .
     Help.twitter.com. Retrieved 2013-09-22.

[11] "Twitter   Support: Impersonation   Policy" .
     Help.twitter.com. Retrieved 2013-09-22.

[12] "About verified accounts | Twitter Help Center" . Twitter.
     Retrieved 2016-09-27.

[13] "Help Center, FACEBOOK" . Facebook.com. Retrieved
     2013-09-22.

46.7 External links

- Disputed Domain Names at DMOZ

Chapter 47

Stuxnet

Stuxnet is a malicious computer worm believed to be a jointly built American-Israeli cyberweapon.[1] Although neither state has confirmed this openly,[2] anonymous US officials speaking to *The Washington Post* claimed the worm was developed during the Bush administration to sabotage Iran's nuclear program with what would seem like a long series of unfortunate accidents.[3]

Stuxnet specifically targets programmable logic controllers (PLCs), which allow the automation of electromechanical processes such as those used to control machinery on factory assembly lines, amusement rides, or centrifuges for separating nuclear material. Exploiting four zero-day flaws,[4] Stuxnet functions by targeting machines using the Microsoft Windows operating system and networks, then seeking out Siemens Step7 software. Stuxnet reportedly compromised Iranian PLCs, collecting information on industrial systems and causing the fast-spinning centrifuges to tear themselves apart.[5] Stuxnet's design and architecture are not domain-specific and it could be tailored as a platform for attacking modern SCADA and PLC systems (e.g., in automobile or power plants), the majority of which reside in Europe, Japan and the US.[6] Stuxnet reportedly ruined almost one fifth of Iran's nuclear centrifuges.[7]

Stuxnet has three modules: a worm that executes all routines related to the main payload of the attack; a link file that automatically executes the propagated copies of the worm; and a rootkit component responsible for hiding all malicious files and processes, preventing detection of the presence of Stuxnet.[8]

Stuxnet is typically introduced to the target environment via an infected USB flash drive. The worm then propagates across the network, scanning for Siemens Step7 software on computers controlling a PLC. In the absence of either criterion, Stuxnet becomes dormant inside the computer. If both the conditions are fulfilled, Stuxnet introduces the infected rootkit onto the PLC and Step7 software, modifying the codes and giving unexpected commands to the PLC while returning a loop of normal operations system values feedback to the users.[9][10]

In 2015, Kaspersky Labs' research findings on another highly sophisticated espionage platform created by what they called the Equation Group, noted that the group had used two of the same zero-day attacks used by Stuxnet, before they were used in Stuxnet, and their use in both programs was similar. The researchers reported that "the similar type of usage of both exploits together in different computer worms, at around the same time, indicates that the Equation Group and the Stuxnet developers are either the same or working closely together".[11]:13 Costin Raiu, the director of Kaspersky Lab's global research and analysis team, believes that the Equation Group cooperates with them only from a position of clear superiority, giving them their "bread crumbs".[12]

47.1 Discovery

Stuxnet, discovered by Sergey Ulasen, initially spread via Microsoft Windows, and targeted Siemens industrial control systems. While it is not the first time that hackers have targeted industrial systems,[13] nor the first publicly known intentional act of cyberwarfare to be implemented, it is the first discovered malware that spies on and subverts industrial systems,[14] and the first to include a programmable logic controller (PLC) rootkit.[15][16]

The worm initially spreads indiscriminately, but includes a highly specialized malware payload that is designed to target only Siemens supervisory control and data acquisition (SCADA) systems that are configured to control and monitor specific industrial processes.[17][18] Stuxnet infects PLCs by subverting the Step-7 software application that is used to reprogram these devices.[19][20]

Different variants of Stuxnet targeted five Iranian organizations,[21] with the probable target widely suspected to be uranium enrichment infrastructure in Iran;[20][22][23] Symantec noted in August 2010 that 60% of the infected computers worldwide were in Iran.[24] Siemens stated that the worm has not caused any damage to its customers,[25] but the Iran nuclear program, which uses embargoed Siemens equipment procured secretly, has been damaged by Stuxnet.*[26]*[27] Kaspersky Lab concluded that the sophisticated attack could only have been conducted "with nation-state support".*[28] This was further supported by the F-Secure's chief researcher Mikko Hyppönen who commented in a Stuxnet FAQ, "That's what it would look like, yes".*[29]

In May 2011, the PBS program *Need To Know* cited a statement by Gary Samore, White House Coordinator for Arms Control and Weapons of Mass Destruction, in which he said, "we're glad they [the Iranians] are having trouble with their centrifuge machine and that we – the US and its allies – are doing everything we can to make sure that we complicate matters for them", offering "winking acknowledgement" of US involvement in Stuxnet.*[30] According to *The Daily Telegraph*, a showreel that was played at a retirement party for the head of the Israel Defense Forces (IDF), Gabi Ashkenazi, included references to Stuxnet as one of his operational successes as the IDF chief of staff.*[31]

On 1 June 2012, an article in *The New York Times* said that Stuxnet is part of a US and Israeli intelligence operation called "Operation Olympic Games", started under President George W. Bush and expanded under President Barack Obama.*[32]

On 24 July 2012, an article by Chris Matyszczyk from CNET*[33] reported how the Atomic Energy Organization of Iran e-mailed F-Secure's chief research officer Mikko Hyppönen to report a new instance of malware.

On 25 December 2012, an Iranian semi-official news agency announced there was a cyberattack by Stuxnet, this time on the industries in the southern area of the country. The virus targeted a power plant and some other industries in Hormozgan province in recent months.*[34]

According to expert Eugene Kaspersky, the worm also infected a nuclear powerplant in Russia. Kaspersky noted, however, that since the powerplant is not connected to the public Internet, the system should remain safe.*[35]

47.2 History

The worm was at first identified by the security company VirusBlokAda in mid-June 2010.*[19] Journalist Brian Krebs's blog posting on 15 July 2010 was the first widely read report on the worm.*[36]*[37] The original name given by VirusBlokAda was "Rootkit.Tmphider";*[38] Symantec however called it "W32.Temphid", later changing to "W32.Stuxnet".*[39] Its current name is derived from a combination of some keywords in the software (".stub" and "mrxnet.sys").*[40]*[41] The reason for the discovery at this time is attributed to the virus accidentally

spreading beyond its intended target (the Natanz plant) due to a programming error introduced in an update; this led to the worm spreading to an engineer's computer that had been connected to the centrifuges, and spreading further when the engineer returned home and connected his computer to the internet.*[32]

Kaspersky Lab experts at first estimated that Stuxnet started spreading around March or April 2010,*[42] but the first variant of the worm appeared in June 2009.*[19] On 15 July 2010, the day the worm's existence became widely known, a distributed denial-of-service attack was made on the servers for two leading mailing lists on industrial-systems security. This attack, from an unknown source but likely related to Stuxnet, disabled one of the lists and thereby interrupted an important source of information for power plants and factories.*[37] On the other hand, researchers at Symantec have uncovered a version of the Stuxnet computer virus that was used to attack Iran's nuclear program in November 2007, being developed as early as 2005, when Iran was still setting up its uranium enrichment facility.*[43]

The second variant, with substantial improvements, appeared in March 2010, apparently because its authors believed that Stuxnet was not spreading fast enough; a third, with minor improvements, appeared in April 2010.*[37] The worm contains a component with a build time-stamp from 3 February 2010.*[44] In the United Kingdom on 25 November 2010, Sky News reported that it had received information from an anonymous source at an unidentified IT security organization that Stuxnet, or a variation of the worm, had been traded on the black market.*[45]

47.3 Affected countries

A study of the spread of Stuxnet by Symantec showed that the main affected countries in the early days of the infection were Iran, Indonesia and India:*[46]

Iran was reported to have "beefed up" its cyberwar capabilities following the Stuxnet attack, and has been suspected of retaliatory attacks against US banks.*[47]

47.4 Operation

Unlike most malware, Stuxnet does little harm to computers and networks that do not meet specific configuration requirements; "The attackers took great care to make sure that only their designated targets were hit... It was a marksman's job."*[48] While the worm is promiscuous, it makes itself inert if Siemens software is not found on infected computers, and contains safeguards to prevent each infected computer from spreading the worm to more than three others, and to erase itself on 24 June 2012.[*][37]

For its targets, Stuxnet contains, among other things, code for a man-in-the-middle attack that fakes industrial process control sensor signals so an infected system does not shut down due to detected abnormal behavior.[*][37][*][48][*][49] Such complexity is very unusual for malware. The worm consists of a layered attack against three different systems:

1. The Windows operating system,

2. Siemens PCS 7, WinCC and STEP7 industrial software applications that run on Windows and

3. One or more Siemens S7 PLCs.

47.4.1   Windows infection

Stuxnet attacked Windows systems using an unprecedented four zero-day attacks (plus the CPLINK vulnerability and a vulnerability used by the Conficker worm[*][50]). It is initially spread using infected removable drives such as USB flash drives,[*][20][*][44] and then uses other exploits and techniques such as peer-to-peer RPC to infect and update other computers inside private networks that are not directly connected to the Internet.[*][51][*][52][*][53] The number of zero-day exploits used is unusual, as they are highly valued and malware creators do not typically make use of (and thus simultaneously make visible) four different zero-day exploits in the same worm.[*][22] Amongst these exploits were remote code execution on a computer with Printer Sharing enabled,[*][54] and the LNK/PIF vulnerability,[*][55] in which file execution is accomplished when an icon is viewed in Windows Explorer; negating the need for user interaction.[*][56] Stuxnet is unusually large at half a megabyte in size,[*][51] and written in several different programming languages (including C and C++) which is also irregular for malware.[*][14][*][19][*][49] The Windows component of the malware is promiscuous in that it spreads relatively quickly and indiscriminately.[*][44]

The malware has both user-mode and kernel-mode rootkit capability under Windows,[*][53] and its device drivers have been digitally signed with the private keys of two certificates that were stolen from separate well-known companies, JMicron and Realtek, both located at Hsinchu Science Park in Taiwan.[*][44][*][51] The driver signing helped it install kernel-mode rootkit drivers successfully without users being notified, and therefore it remained undetected for a relatively long period of time.[*][57] Both compromised certificates have been revoked by VeriSign.

Two websites in Denmark and Malaysia were configured as command and control servers for the malware, allowing it to be updated, and for industrial espionage to be conducted by

uploading information. Both of these websites have subsequently been taken down as part of a global effort to disable the malware.[*][53][*][37]

47.4.2   Step 7 software infection

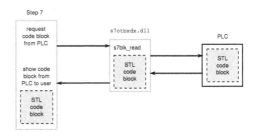

Overview of normal communications between Step 7 and a Siemens PLC

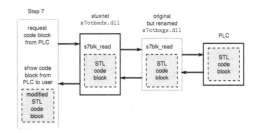

Overview of Stuxnet hijacking communication between Step 7 software and a Siemens PLC

According to researcher Ralph Langner,[*][58][*][59] once installed on a Windows system Stuxnet infects project files belonging to Siemens' WinCC/PCS 7 SCADA control software[*][60] (Step 7), and subverts a key communication library of WinCC called s7otbxdx.dll. Doing so intercepts communications between the WinCC software running under Windows and the target Siemens PLC devices that the software is able to configure and program when the two are connected via a data cable. In this way, the malware is able to install itself on PLC devices unnoticed, and subsequently to mask its presence from WinCC if the control software attempts to read an infected block of memory from the PLC system.[*][53]

The malware furthermore used a zero-day exploit in the WinCC/SCADA database software in the form of a hardcoded database password.[*][61]

Siemens Simatic S7-300 PLC CPU with three I/O modules attached

47.4.3 PLC infection

The entirety of the Stuxnet code has not yet been disclosed, but its payload targets only those SCADA configurations that meet criteria that it is programmed to identify.[37]

Stuxnet requires specific slave variable-frequency drives (frequency converter drives) to be attached to the targeted Siemens S7-300 system and its associated modules. It only attacks those PLC systems with variable-frequency drives from two specific vendors: Vacon based in Finland and Fararo Paya based in Iran.[62] Furthermore, it monitors the frequency of the attached motors, and only attacks systems that spin between 807 Hz and 1210 Hz. The industrial applications of motors with these parameters are diverse, and may include pumps or gas centrifuges.

Stuxnet installs malware into memory block DB890 of the PLC that monitors the Profibus messaging bus of the system.[53] When certain criteria are met, it periodically modifies the frequency to 1410 Hz and then to 2 Hz and then to 1064 Hz, and thus affects the operation of the connected motors by changing their rotational speed.[62] It also installs a rootkit – the first such documented case on this platform – that hides the malware on the system and masks the changes in rotational speed from monitoring systems.

47.5 Removal

Siemens has released a detection and removal tool for Stuxnet. Siemens recommends contacting customer support if an infection is detected and advises installing Microsoft updates for security vulnerabilities and prohibiting the use of third-party USB flash drives.[63] Siemens also advises immediately upgrading password access codes.[64]

The worm's ability to reprogram external PLCs may com-plicate the removal procedure. Symantec's Liam O'Murchu warns that fixing Windows systems may not completely solve the infection; a thorough audit of PLCs may be necessary. Despite speculation that incorrect removal of the worm could cause damage,[65] Siemens reports that in the first four months since discovery, the malware was successfully removed from the systems of 22 customers without any adverse impact.[63][66]

47.6 Control system security

Main article: Control system security

Prevention of control system security incidents,[67] such as from viral infections like Stuxnet, is a topic that is being addressed in both the public and the private sector.

The US Department of Homeland Security National Cyber Security Division (NCSD) operates the Control System Security Program (CSSP).[68] The program operates a specialized computer emergency response team called the Industrial Control Systems Cyber Emergency Response Team (ICS-CERT), conducts a biannual conference (ICSJWG), provides training, publishes recommended practices, and provides a self-assessment tool. As part of a Department of Homeland Security plan to improve American computer security, in 2008 it and the Idaho National Laboratory (INL) worked with Siemens to identify security holes in the company's widely used Process Control System 7 (PCS 7) and its software Step 7. In July 2008, INL and Siemens publicly announced flaws in the control system at a Chicago conference; Stuxnet exploited these holes in 2009.[48]

Several industry organizations[69][70] and professional societies[71][72] have published standards and best practice guidelines providing direction and guidance for control system end-users on how to establish a control system security management program. The basic premise that all of these documents share is that prevention requires a multi-layered approach, often referred to as "defense-in-depth".[73] The layers include policies and procedures, awareness and training, network segmentation, access control measures, physical security measures, system hardening, e.g., patch management, and system monitoring, anti-virus and intrusion prevention system (IPS). The standards and best practices also all recommend starting with a risk analysis and a control system security assessment.[74][75]

47.7   Target and origin

Experts believe that Stuxnet required the largest and costliest development effort in malware history.[37] Developing its many capabilities would have required a team of highly capable programmers, in-depth knowledge of industrial processes, and an interest in attacking industrial infrastructure.[14][19] Eric Byres, who has years of experience maintaining and troubleshooting Siemens systems, told *Wired* that writing the code would have taken many man-months, if not years.[51] Symantec estimates that the group developing Stuxnet would have consisted of anywhere from five to thirty people, and would have taken six months to prepare.[76][37] *The Guardian*, the BBC and *The New York Times* all claimed that (unnamed) experts studying Stuxnet believe the complexity of the code indicates that only a nation-state would have the capabilities to produce it.[22][76][77] The origin is unknown beyond rumour, however. The self-destruct and other safeguards within the code could imply that a Western government was responsible, or at least is responsible in the development of it.[37] Software security expert Bruce Schneier initially condemned the 2010 news coverage of Stuxnet as hype, however, stating that it was almost entirely based on speculation.[78] But after subsequent research, Schneier stated in 2012 that "we can now conclusively link Stuxnet to the centrifuge structure at the Natanz nuclear enrichment lab in Iran".[79]

47.7.1   Iran as target

Ralph Langner, the researcher who identified that Stuxnet infected PLCs,[20] first speculated publicly in September 2010 that the malware was of Israeli origin, and that it targeted Iranian nuclear facilities.[80] However Langner more recently, in a TED Talk recorded in February 2011, stated that, "My opinion is that the Mossad is involved, but that the leading force is not Israel. The leading force behind Stuxnet is the cyber superpower – there is only one; and that's the United States." [81] Kevin Hogan, Senior Director of Security Response at Symantec, reported that the majority of infected systems were in Iran (about 60%),[82] which has led to speculation that it may have been deliberately targeting "high-value infrastructure" in Iran[22] including either the Bushehr Nuclear Power Plant or the Natanz nuclear facility.[51][83][84] Langner called the malware "a one-shot weapon" and said that the intended target was probably hit,[85] although he admitted this was speculation.[51] Another German researcher and spokesman of the German-based Chaos Computer Club, Frank Rieger, was the first to speculate that Natanz was the target.[37]

Natanz nuclear facilities

Anti-aircraft guns guarding Natanz Nuclear Facility

According to the Israeli newspaper *Haaretz*, in September 2010 experts on Iran and computer security specialists were increasingly convinced that Stuxnet was meant "to sabotage the uranium enrichment facility at Natanz – where the centrifuge operational capacity has dropped over the past year by 30 percent." [87] On 23 November 2010 it was announced that uranium enrichment at Natanz had ceased several times because of a series of major technical problems.[88][89] A "serious nuclear accident" (supposedly the shutdown of some of its centrifuges[90]) occurred at the site in the first half of 2009, which is speculated to have forced the head of Iran's Atomic Energy Organization Gholam Reza Aghazadeh to resign.[91] Statistics published by the Federation of American Scientists (FAS) show that the number of enrichment centrifuges operational in Iran mysteriously declined from about 4,700 to about 3,900 beginning around the time the nuclear incident WikiLeaks mentioned would have occurred.[92] The Institute for Science and International Security (ISIS) suggests, in a report published in December 2010, that Stuxnet is a reasonable explanation for the apparent damage[93] at Natanz, and may have destroyed up to 1000 centrifuges (10 percent) sometime between November 2009 and late January 2010. The authors conclude:

> The attacks seem designed to force a change in the centrifuge's rotor speed, first raising the speed and then lowering it, likely with the intention of inducing excessive vibrations or distortions that would destroy the centrifuge. If its goal was to quickly destroy all the centrifuges in the FEP [Fuel Enrichment Plant], Stuxnet failed. But if the goal was to destroy a more limited number of centrifuges and set back Iran's progress in operating the FEP, while making detection diffi-

cult, it may have succeeded, at least temporarily.[*][93]

The ISIS report further notes that Iranian authorities have attempted to conceal the breakdown by installing new centrifuges on a large scale.[*][93][*][94]

The worm worked by first causing an infected Iranian IR-1 centrifuge to increase from its normal operating speed of 1,064 hertz to 1,410 hertz for 15 minutes before returning to its normal frequency. Twenty-seven days later, the worm went back into action, slowing the infected centrifuges down to a few hundred hertz for a full 50 minutes. The stresses from the excessive, then slower, speeds caused the aluminum centrifugal tubes to expand, often forcing parts of the centrifuges into sufficient contact with each other to destroy the machine.[*][95]

According to *The Washington Post*, IAEA cameras installed in the Natanz facility recorded the sudden dismantling and removal of approximately 900–1000 centrifuges during the time the Stuxnet worm was reportedly active at the plant. Iranian technicians, however, were able to quickly replace the centrifuges and the report concluded that uranium enrichment was likely only briefly disrupted.[*][96]

On 15 February 2011, ISIS released a report concluding that:

> Assuming Iran exercises caution, Stuxnet is unlikely to destroy more centrifuges at the Natanz plant. Iran likely cleaned the malware from its control systems. To prevent re-infection, Iran will have to exercise special caution since so many computers in Iran contain Stuxnet.
>
> Although Stuxnet appears to be designed to destroy centrifuges at the Natanz facility, destruction was by no means total. Moreover, Stuxnet did not lower the production of LEU during 2010. LEU quantities could have certainly been greater, and Stuxnet could be an important part of the reason why they did not increase significantly. Nonetheless, there remain important questions about why Stuxnet destroyed only 1,000 centrifuges. One observation is that it may be harder to destroy centrifuges by use of cyber attacks than often believed.[*][97]

Iranian reaction

The Associated Press reported that the semi-official Iranian Students News Agency released a statement on 24 September 2010 stating that experts from the Atomic Energy Organization of Iran met in the previous week to discuss how Stuxnet could be removed from their systems.[*][18] According to analysts, such as David Albright, Western intelligence agencies have been attempting to sabotage the Iranian nuclear program for some time.[*][98][*][99]

The head of the Bushehr Nuclear Power Plant told Reuters that only the personal computers of staff at the plant had been infected by Stuxnet and the state-run newspaper *Iran Daily* quoted Reza Taghipour, Iran's telecommunications minister, as saying that it had not caused "serious damage to government systems".[*][77] The Director of Information Technology Council at the Iranian Ministry of Industries and Mines, Mahmud Liaii, has said that: "An electronic war has been launched against Iran... This computer worm is designed to transfer data about production lines from our industrial plants to locations outside Iran." [*][100]

In response to the infection, Iran has assembled a team to combat it. With more than 30,000 IP addresses affected in Iran, an official has said that the infection is fast spreading in Iran and the problem has been compounded by the ability of Stuxnet to mutate. Iran has set up its own systems to clean up infections and has advised against using the Siemens SCADA antivirus since it is suspected that the antivirus is actually embedded with codes which update Stuxnet instead of eradicating it.[*][101][*][102][*][103][*][104]

According to Hamid Alipour, deputy head of Iran's government Information Technology Company, "The attack is still ongoing and new versions of this virus are spreading." He reports that his company had begun the cleanup process at Iran's "sensitive centres and organizations." [*][102] "We had anticipated that we could root out the virus within one to two months, but the virus is not stable, and since we started the cleanup process three new versions of it have been spreading", he told the Islamic Republic News Agency on 27 September 2010.[*][104]

On 29 November 2010, Iranian president Mahmoud Ahmadinejad stated for the first time that a computer virus had caused problems with the controller handling the centrifuges at its Natanz facilities. According to Reuters he told reporters at a news conference in Tehran, "They succeeded in creating problems for a limited number of our centrifuges with the software they had installed in electronic parts." [*][105][*][106]

On the same day two Iranian nuclear scientists were targeted in separate, but nearly simultaneous car bomb attacks near Shahid Beheshti University in Tehran. Majid Shahriari, a quantum physicist was killed. Fereydoon Abbasi, a high-ranking official at the Ministry of Defense was seriously wounded. *Wired* speculated that the assassinations could indicate that whoever was behind Stuxnet felt that it was not sufficient to stop the nuclear program.[*][107] That same *Wired* article suggested the Iranian government could have been behind the assassinations.[*][107] In January 2010, another Iranian nuclear scientist, a physics professor at Tehran University, had been killed in a similar bomb explosion.*[107] On 11 January 2012, a Director of the Natanz nuclear enrichment facility, Mostafa Ahmadi Roshan, was killed in an attack quite similar to the one that killed Shahriari.*[108]

An analysis by the FAS demonstrates that Iran's enrichment capacity grew during 2010. The study indicates that Iran's centrifuges appear to be performing 60% better than in the previous year, which would significantly reduce Tehran's time to produce bomb-grade uranium. The FAS report was reviewed by an official with the IAEA who affirmed the study.*[109]*[110]*[111]

European and US officials, along with private experts, have told Reuters that Iranian engineers were successful in neutralizing and purging Stuxnet from their country's nuclear machinery.*[112]

Given the growth in Iranian enrichment capability in 2010, the country may have intentionally put out misinformation to cause Stuxnet's creators to believe that the worm was more successful in disabling the Iranian nuclear program than it actually was.*[37]

Israel

Israel, through Unit 8200,*[113]*[114] has been speculated to be the country behind Stuxnet in many media reports*[76]*[90]*[115] and by experts such as Richard A. Falkenrath, former Senior Director for Policy and Plans within the US Office of Homeland Security.*[116]*[77] Yossi Melman, who covers intelligence for the Israeli daily newspaper *Haaretz* and is writing a book about Israeli intelligence, also suspected that Israel was involved, noting that Meir Dagan, the former (up until 2011) head of the national intelligence agency Mossad, had his term extended in 2009 because he was said to be involved in important projects. Additionally, Israel now expects that Iran will have a nuclear weapon in 2014 or 2015 – at least three years later than earlier estimates – without the need for an Israeli military attack on Iranian nuclear facilities; "They seem to know something, that they have more time than originally thought", he added.*[27]*[48] Israel has not publicly commented on the Stuxnet attack but confirmed that cyberwarfare is now among the pillars of its defense doctrine, with a military intelligence unit set up to pursue both defensive and offensive options.*[117]*[118]*[119] When questioned whether Israel was behind the virus in the fall of 2010, some Israeli officials broke into "wide smiles", fueling speculation that the government of Israel was involved with its genesis.*[120] American presidential advisor Gary Samore also smiled when Stuxnet was mentioned,*[48] although American officials have indicated that the virus orig-

inated abroad.*[120] According to *The Telegraph*, Israeli newspaper *Haaretz* reported that a video celebrating operational successes of Gabi Ashkenazi, retiring IDF Chief of Staff, was shown at his retirement party and included references to Stuxnet, thus strengthening claims that Israel's security forces were responsible.*[121]

In 2009, a year before Stuxnet was discovered, Scott Borg of the United States Cyber-Consequences Unit (US-CCU)*[122] suggested that Israel might prefer to mount a cyber-attack rather than a military strike on Iran's nuclear facilities.*[99] And, in late 2010 Borg stated, "Israel certainly has the ability to create Stuxnet and there is little downside to such an attack, because it would be virtually impossible to prove who did it. So a tool like Stuxnet is Israel's obvious weapon of choice." *[123] Iran uses P-1 centrifuges at Natanz, the design for which A. Q. Khan stole in 1976 and took to Pakistan. His black market nuclear-proliferation network sold P-1s to, among other customers, Iran. Experts believe that Israel also somehow acquired P-1s and tested Stuxnet on the centrifuges, installed at the Dimona facility that is part of its own nuclear program.*[48] The equipment may be from the United States, which received P-1s from Libya's former nuclear program.*[124]*[48]

Some have also referred to several clues in the code such as a concealed reference to the word "MYRTUS", believed to refer to the Myrtle tree, or Hadassah in Hebrew. Hadassah was the birth name of the former Jewish queen of Persia, Queen Esther.*[125]*[126] However, it may be that the "MYRTUS" reference is simply a misinterpreted reference to SCADA components known as *RTUs* (Remote Terminal Units) and that this reference is actually "My RTUs"–a management feature of SCADA.*[127] Also, the number 19790509 appears once in the code and might refer to the date "1979 May 09", the day Habib Elghanian, a Persian Jew, was executed in Tehran.*[53]*[128]*[129] Another date that appears in the code is "24 September 2007", the day that Iran's president Mahmoud Ahmadinejad spoke at Columbia University and made comments questioning the validity of the Holocaust.*[37] Such data is not conclusive, since, as written by Symantec, "Attackers would have the natural desire to implicate another party" with a false flag.*[37]*[53]

United States

There has also been testimony on the involvement of the United States and its collaboration with Israel,*[130]*[131] with one report stating that "there is vanishingly little doubt that [it] played a role in creating the worm." *[37] It has been reported that the United States, under one of its most secret programs, initiated by the Bush administration and accelerated by the Obama administration, has sought to destroy Iran's nuclear program by novel methods such as undermining Iranian computer systems. A diplomatic cable obtained by WikiLeaks showed how the United States was advised to target Iran's nuclear capabilities through 'covert sabotage'.*[132] A New York Times article as early as January 2009 credited a then unspecified program with preventing an Israeli military attack on Iran where some of the efforts focused on ways to destabilize the centrifuges.*[133] A *Wired* article claimed that Stuxnet "is believed to have been created by the United States" .*[134] The fact that John Bumgarner, a former intelligence officer and member of the United States Cyber-Consequences Unit (US-CCU), published an article prior to Stuxnet being discovered or deciphered, that outlined a strategic cyberstrike on centrifuges*[135] and suggests that cyber attacks are permissible against nation states which are operating uranium enrichment programs that violate international treaties gives some credibility to these claims. Bumgarner pointed out that the centrifuges used to process fuel for nuclear weapons are a key target for *cybertage* operations and that they can be made to destroy themselves by manipulating their rotational speeds.*[136]

In a March 2012 interview with CBS News' "60 Minutes", retired USAF General Michael Hayden – who served as director of both the Central Intelligence Agency and National Security Agency – while denying knowledge of who created Stuxnet said that he believed it had been "a good idea" but that it carried a downside in that it had legitimized the use of sophisticated cyberweapons designed to cause physical damage. Hayden said, "There are those out there who can take a look at this... and maybe even attempt to turn it to their own purposes" . In the same report, Sean McGurk, a former cybersecurity official at the Department of Homeland Security noted that the Stuxnet source code could now be downloaded online and modified to be directed at new target systems. Speaking of the Stuxnet creators, he said, "They opened the box. They demonstrated the capability... It's not something that can be put back." *[137]

Joint effort and other states and targets

In April 2011 Iranian government official Gholam Reza Jalali stated that an investigation had concluded that the United States and Israel were behind the Stuxnet attack.*[138] Frank Rieger stated that three European countries' intelligence agencies agreed that Stuxnet was a joint United States-Israel effort. The code for the Windows injector and the PLC payload differ in style, likely implying collaboration. Other experts believe that a US-Israel cooperation is unlikely because "the level of trust between the two countries' intelligence and military establishments is not high." *[37]

A Wired magazine article about US General Keith B. Alexander stated: "And he and his cyberwarriors have already launched their first attack. The cyberweapon that came to be known as Stuxnet was created and built by the NSA in partnership with the CIA and Israeli intelligence in the mid-2000s." *[139]

China,*[140] Jordan, and France are other possibilities, and Siemens may have also participated.*[37]*[130] Langner speculated that the infection may have spread from USB drives belonging to Russian contractors since the Iranian targets were not accessible via the Internet.*[20]*[141]

Sandro Gaycken from the Free University Berlin argued that the attack on Iran was a ruse to distract from Stuxnet's real purpose. According to him, its broad dissemination in more than 100,000 industrial plants worldwide suggests a field test of a cyber weapon in different security cultures, testing their preparedness, resilience, and reactions, all highly valuable information for a cyberwar unit.*[142]

The United Kingdom has denied involvement in the worm's creation.*[143]

Stratfor Documents released by Wikileaks suggest that the International Security Firm 'Stratfor' believe that Israel is behind Stuxnet - "But we can't assume that because they did stuxnet that they are capable of doing this blast as well" .*[144]

In July 2013, Edward Snowden claimed that Stuxnet was cooperatively developed by the United States and Israel.*[145]

47.7.2 Deployment in North Korea

According to a report by Reuters, the NSA also tried to sabotage North Korea's nuclear program using a version of Stuxnet. The operation was reportedly launched in tandem with the attack that targeted Iranian centrifuges in 2009–10. The North Korean nuclear program shares many similarities with the Iranian, both having been developed with technology transferred by Pakistani nuclear scientist A.Q. Khan. The effort failed, however, because North Korea's extreme secrecy and isolation made it impossible to introduce Stuxnet into the nuclear facility.*[146]

47.8 Related malware

47.8.1 "Stuxnet's Secret Twin"

A November 2013 article*[147] in Foreign Policy magazine claims existence of an earlier, much more sophisticated attack on centrifuge complex at Natanz, focused on increasing centrifuge failure rate over long time period via stealthily inducing uranium hexafluoride gas overpressure incidents. This malware was capable of spreading only by being physically installed, probably by previously contaminated field equipment used by contractors working on Siemens control systems within the complex. It is not clear whether this attack attempt was successful, but it being followed by a different, simpler and more conventional attack is indicative.

47.8.2 Duqu

Main article: Duqu

On 1 September 2011, a new worm was found, thought to be related to Stuxnet. The Laboratory of Cryptography and System Security (CrySyS) of the Budapest University of Technology and Economics analyzed the malware, naming the threat **Duqu**.[148][149] Symantec, based on this report, continued the analysis of the threat, calling it "nearly identical to Stuxnet, but with a completely different purpose", and published a detailed technical paper.[150] The main component used in Duqu is designed to capture information[49] such as keystrokes and system information. The exfiltrated data may be used to enable a future Stuxnet-like attack. On 28 December 2011, Kaspersky Lab's director of global research and analysis spoke to Reuters about recent research results showing that the platform Stuxnet and Duqu both originated from in 2007, and is being referred to as Tilded due to the ~d at the beginning of the file names. Also uncovered in this research was the possibility for three more variants based on the Tilded platform.[151]

47.8.3 Flame

Main article: Flame (malware)

In May 2012, the new malware "Flame" was found, thought to be related to Stuxnet.[152] Researchers named the program "Flame" after the name of one of its modules.[152] After analysing the code of Flame, Kaspersky Lab said that there is a strong relationship between Flame and Stuxnet. An early version of Stuxnet contained code to propagate infections via USB drives that is nearly identical to a Flame module that exploits the same vulnerability.[153]

47.9   Media coverage

Since 2010, there has been extensive international media coverage on Stuxnet and its aftermath. In early commentary, *The Economist* pointed out that Stuxnet was "a new

kind of cyber-attack." [154] On 8 July 2011, *Wired* then published an article detailing how network security experts were able to decipher the origins of Stuxnet. In that piece, Kim Zetter claimed that Stuxnet's "cost–benefit ratio is still in question." [155] Later commentators tended to focus on the strategic significance of Stuxnet as a cyber weapon. Following the Wired piece, Holger Stark called Stuxnet the "first digital weapon of geopolitical importance, it could change the way wars are fought." [156] Meanwhile, Eddie Walsh referred to Stuxnet as "the world's newest high-end asymmetric threat." [157] Ultimately, some claim that the "extensive media coverage afforded to Stuxnet has only served as an advertisement for the vulnerabilities used by various cybercriminal groups." [158] While that may be the case, the media coverage has also increased awareness of cyber security threats.

Alex Gibney's 2016 documentary *Zero Days* covers the phenomenon around Stuxnet.

47.10   In popular culture

- In *Castle* season 8, episode 18 "Backstabber" Stuxnet is revealed to have been (fictionally) created by MI-6, and a version of it is used to take down the London power grid.

- Zero Days is a 2016 American documentary film about Stuxnet

47.11   See also

- Advanced persistent threat

- Cyber electronic warfare

- Cyber security standards

- Cyber-attack

- Cyberterrorism

- Cyberwarfare in the United States

- DigiNotar

- Killer poke

- List of cyber attack threat trends

- Mahdi (malware)

- Operation High Roller

- Operation Merlin

- Operation Olympic Games

- Proactive cyber defence

- Stars virus

- Tailored Access Operations

- United States Cyber Command

- Vulnerability of nuclear plants to attack

47.12 References

[1] "Confirmed: US and Israel created Stuxnet, lost control of it". *Ars Technica*.

[2] Razvan, Bogdan. "Win32.Worm.Stuxnet.A". Retrieved 28 March 2014.

[3] Ellen Nakashima (2 June 2012). "Stuxnet was work of U.S. and Israeli experts, officials say". *The Washington Post*.

[4] "Stuxnet attackers used 4 Windows zero-day exploits". ZDNet. 14 September 2010.

[5] Kushner, David. "The Real Story of Stuxnet". *ieee.org*. IEEE Spectrum. Retrieved 25 March 2014.

[6] S. Karnouskos: "Stuxnet Worm Impact on Industrial Cyber-Physical System Security". In: "37th Annual Conference of the IEEE Industrial Electronics Society (IECON 2011), Melbourne, Australia", 7–10 November 2011. Retrieved 20 April 2014.

[7] "The Stuxnet Attack On Iran's Nuclear Plant Was 'Far More Dangerous' Than Previously Thought". *Business Insider*. 20 November 2013.

[8] "STUXNET Malware Targets SCADA Systems". Trend Micro. January 2012.

[9] "A Declaration of Cyber-War". *Vanity Fair*. April 2011.

[10] "Exploring Stuxnet's PLC Infection Process". Symantec. 23 January 2014.

[11] https://securelist.com/files/2015/02/Equation_group_questions_and_answers.pdf

[12] Equation: The Death Star of Malware Galaxy, *SecureList*, Costin Raiu (director of Kaspersky Lab's global research and analysis team): "It seems to me Equation Group are the ones with the coolest toys. Every now and then they share them with the Stuxnet group and the Flame group, but they are originally available only to the Equation Group people. Equation Group are definitely the masters, and they are giving the others, maybe, bread crumbs. From time to time they are giving them some goodies to integrate into Stuxnet and Flame."

[13] "Building a Cyber Secure Plant". Siemens. 30 September 2010. Retrieved 5 December 2010.

[14] Robert McMillan (16 September 2010). "Siemens: Stuxnet worm hit industrial systems". Computerworld. Retrieved 16 September 2010.

[15] "Last-minute paper: An indepth look into Stuxnet". Virus Bulletin.

[16] "Stuxnet worm hits Iran nuclear plant staff computers". BBC News. 26 September 2010.

[17] Nicolas Falliere (6 August 2010). "Stuxnet Introduces the First Known Rootkit for Industrial Control Systems". Symantec.

[18] "Iran's Nuclear Agency Trying to Stop Computer Worm". Tehran. Associated Press. 25 September 2010. Archived from the original on 25 September 2010. Retrieved 25 September 2010.

[19] Gregg Keizer (16 September 2010). "Is Stuxnet the 'best' malware ever?". Infoworld. Retrieved 16 September 2010.

[20] Steven Cherry; with Ralph Langner (13 October 2010). "How Stuxnet Is Rewriting the Cyberterrorism Playbook". IEEE Spectrum.

[21] "Stuxnet Virus Targets and Spread Revealed". BBC News. 15 February 2011. Retrieved 17 February 2011.

[22] Fildes, Jonathan (23 September 2010). "Stuxnet worm 'targeted high-value Iranian assets'". BBC News. Retrieved 23 September 2010.

[23] Beaumont, Claudine (23 September 2010). "Stuxnet virus: worm 'could be aimed at high-profile Iranian targets'". London: The Daily Telegraph. Retrieved 28 September 2010.

[24] MacLean, William (24 September 2010). "UPDATE 2-Cyber attack appears to target Iran-tech firms". *Reuters*.

[25] ComputerWorld (14 September 2010). "Siemens: Stuxnet worm hit industrial systems". Computerworld. Retrieved 3 October 2010.

[26] "Iran Confirms Stuxnet Worm Halted Centrifuges". *CBS News*. 29 November 2010.

[27] Ethan Bronner & William J. Broad (29 September 2010). "In a Computer Worm, a Possible Biblical Clue". *NYTimes*. Retrieved 2 October 2010. "Software smart bomb fired at Iranian nuclear plant: Experts". Economictimes.indiatimes.com. 24 September 2010. Retrieved 28 September 2010.

[28] "Kaspersky Lab provides its insights on Stuxnet worm". *Kaspersky*. Russia. 24 September 2010.

[29] "Stuxnet Questions and Answers – F-Secure Weblog". *F-Secure*. Finland. 1 October 2010.

[30] Gary Samore speaking at the 10 December 2010 Washington Forum of the Foundation for Defense of Democracies in Washington DC, reported by C-Span and contained in the PBS program Need to Know ("Cracking the code: Defending against the superweapons of the 21st century cyberwar", 4 minutes into piece)

[31] Williams, Christopher (15 February 2011). "Israel video shows Stuxnet as one of its successes". London: Telegraph.co.uk. Retrieved 14 February 2012.

[32] Sanger, David E. (1 June 2012). "Obama Order Sped Up Wave of Cyberattacks Against Iran". The New York Times. Retrieved 1 June 2012.

[33] Matyszczyk, Chris (24 July 2012). "Thunderstruck! A tale of malware, AC/DC, and Iran's nukes". CNET. Retrieved 8 July 2013.

[34] "Iran 'fends off new Stuxnet cyber attack'". BBC NEWS. 25 December 2012. Retrieved 28 May 2015.

[35] Shamah, David (11 November 2013). "Stuxnet, gone rogue, hit Russian nuke plant, space station". *The Times of Israel*. Retrieved 12 November 2013.

[36] Krebs, Brian (17 July 2010). "Experts Warn of New Windows Shortcut Flaw". *Krebs on Security*. Retrieved 3 March 2011.

[37] Gross, Michael Joseph (April 2011). "A Declaration of Cyber-War". *Vanity Fair*. Condé Nast.

[38] "Rootkit.TmpHider". *wilderssecurity.com*. Wilders Security Forums. Retrieved 25 March 2014.

[39] Shearer, Jarrad (13 July 2010). "W32.Stuxnet". *symantec.com*. Symantec. Retrieved 25 March 2014.

[40] Zetter, Kim (11 July 2011). "How digital detectives deciphered Stuxnet, the most menacing malware in history". *arstechnica.com*. Retrieved 25 March 2014.

[41] Karl. "Stuxnet opens cracks in Iran nuclear program". *abc.net.au*. ABC. Retrieved 25 March 2014.

[42] Alexander Gostev (26 September 2010). "Myrtus and Guava: the epidemic, the trends, the numbers". Retrieved 22 January 2011.

[43] Finkle, Jim (26 February 2013). "Researchers say Stuxnet was deployed against Iran in 2007". *Reuters*.

[44] Aleksandr Matrosov; Eugene Rodionov; David Harley & Juraj Malcho. "Stuxnet Under the Microscope" (PDF). Retrieved 24 September 2010.

[45] Sam Kiley. "Super Virus A Target For Cyber Terrorists". Retrieved 25 November 2010.

[46] "W32.Stuxnet". Symantec. 17 September 2010. Retrieved 2 March 2011.

[47] "Iran denies hacking into American banks" Reuters, 23 September 2012

[48] Broad, William J.; Markoff, John; Sanger, David E. (15 January 2011). "Israel Tests on Worm Called Crucial in Iran Nuclear Delay". *New York Times*. Retrieved 16 January 2011.

[49] Steven Cherry; with Larry Constantine (14 December 2011). "Sons of Stuxnet". IEEE Spectrum.

[50] "Conficker Worm: Help Protect Windows from Conficker". Microsoft. 10 April 2009. Retrieved 6 December 2010.

[51] Kim Zetter (23 September 2010). "Blockbuster Worm Aimed for Infrastructure, But No Proof Iran Nukes Were Target". Wired. Retrieved 24 September 2010.

[52] Liam O Murchu (17 September 2010). "Stuxnet P2P component". Symantec. Retrieved 24 September 2010.

[53] "W32.Stuxnet Dossier" (PDF). Symantec Corporation.

[54] Microsoft (14 September 2010). "Microsoft Security Bulletin MS10-061 – Critical". Microsoft. Retrieved 20 August 2015.

[55] Microsoft (2 August 2010). "Microsoft Security Bulletin MS10-046 – Critical". Microsoft. Retrieved 20 August 2015.

[56] Gostev, Alexander (14 September 2010). "Myrtus and Guava, Episode MS10-061". Kaspersky Lab. Retrieved 20 August 2015.

[57] "Kaspersky Lab provides its insights on Stuxnet worm". Kaspersky Lab. 24 September 2010. Retrieved 27 September 2010.

[58] Michael Joseph Gross (April 2011). "A Declaration of Cyber-War". *Vanity Fair*. Retrieved 4 March 2011.

[59] Ralph Langner (14 September 2010). "Ralph's Step-By-Step Guide to Get a Crack at Stuxnet Traffic and Behaviour". Retrieved 4 March 2011.

[60] Nicolas Falliere (26 September 2010). "Stuxnet Infection of Step 7 Projects". Symantec.

[61] "Vulnerability Summary for CVE-2010-2772". National Vulnerability Database. 22 July 2010. Retrieved 7 December 2010.

[62] Eric Chien (12 November 2010). "Stuxnet: A Breakthrough". Symantec. Retrieved 14 November 2010.

[63] "SIMATIC WinCC / SIMATIC PCS 7: Information concerning Malware / Virus / Trojan". Siemens. Retrieved 24 September 2010.

[64] Tom Espiner (20 July 2010). "Siemens warns Stuxnet targets of password risk". CNET. Retrieved 17 September 2010.

[65] "Siemens: Stuxnet Worm Hit Industrial Systems". IDG News.

[66] crve (17 September 2010). "Stuxnet also found at industrial plants in Germany". The H. Retrieved 18 September 2010.

[67] "Repository of Industrial Security Incidents". Security Incidents Organization. Retrieved 14 October 2010.

[68] "DHS National Cyber Security Division's CSSP". DHS. Retrieved 14 October 2010.

[69] "ISA99, Industrial Automation and Control System Security". International Society of Automation. Retrieved 14 October 2010.

[70] "Industrial communication networks – Network and system security – Part 2-1: Establishing an industrial automation and control system security program". International Electrotechnical Commission. Retrieved 14 October 2010.

[71] "Chemical Sector Cyber Security Program". ACC ChemITC. Retrieved 14 October 2010.

[72] "Pipeline SCADA Security Standard" (PDF). API. Retrieved 19 November 2010.

[73] Marty Edwards (Idaho National Laboratory) & Todd Stauffer (Siemens). *2008 Automation Summit: A User's Conference* (PDF). United States Department of Homeland Security. p. 35.

[74] "The Can of Worms Is Open-Now What?". controlglobal.com. Retrieved 14 October 2010.

[75] Byres, Eric & Cusimano, John (16 February 2012). "The 7 Steps to ICS Security". Tofino Security and exida Consulting LLC. Retrieved 3 March 2011.

[76] Halliday, Josh (24 September 2010). "Stuxnet worm is the 'work of a national government agency'". London: The Guardian. Retrieved 27 September 2010.

[77] Markoff, John (26 September 2010). "A Silent Attack, but Not a Subtle One". New York Times. Retrieved 27 September 2010.

[78] Schneier, Bruce (6 October 2010). "The Story Behind The Stuxnet Virus". *Forbes*.

[79] Schneier, Bruce (23 February 2012). "Another Piece of the Stuxnet Puzzle". Schneier on Security. Retrieved 4 March 2012.

[80] Bright, Arthur (1 October 2010). "Clues Emerge About Genesis of Stuxnet Worm". Christian Science Monitor. Retrieved 4 March 2011.

[81] Langner, Ralph (February 2011). "Ralph Langner: Cracking Stuxnet, a 21st-century cyber weapon".

[82] Robert McMillan (23 July 2010). "Iran was prime target of SCADA worm". Computerworld. Retrieved 17 September 2010.

[83] Paul Woodward (22 September 2010). "Iran confirms Stuxnet found at Bushehr nuclear power plant". Warincontext.org. Retrieved 28 September 2010.

[84] "6 mysteries about Stuxnet". Blog.foreignpolicy.com. Retrieved 28 September 2010.

[85] Clayton, Mark (21 September 2010). "Stuxnet malware is 'weapon' out to destroy ... Iran's Bushehr nuclear plant?". Christian Science Monitor. Retrieved 23 September 2010.

[86] Pike, John. "Satellite Imagery of the Nantanz Enrichment Facility". *globalsecurity.org*. GlobalSecurity.org. Retrieved 25 March 2014.

[87] Yossi Melman (28 September 2010). "'Computer virus in Iran actually targeted larger nuclear facility'". Retrieved 1 January 2011.

[88] "Iranian Nuclear Program Plagued by Technical Difficulties". Globalsecuritynewswire.org. 23 November 2010. Retrieved 24 November 2010.

[89] "Iran pauses uranium enrichment at Natanz nuclear plant". Haaretz.com. 24 November 2010. Retrieved 24 November 2010.

[90] "The Stuxnet worm: A cyber-missile aimed at Iran?". The Economist. 24 September 2010. Retrieved 28 September 2010.

[91] "Serious nuclear accident may lay behind Iranian nuke chief%27s mystery resignation". wikileaks. 16 July 2009. Retrieved 1 January 2011.

[92] "IAEA Report on Iran" (PDF). Institute for Science and International Security. 16 November 2010. Retrieved 1 January 2011.

[93] "Did Stuxnet Take Out 1,000 Centrifuges at the Natanz Enrichment Plant?" (PDF). Institute for Science and International Security. 22 December 2010. Retrieved 27 December 2010.

[94] "Stuxnet-Virus könnte tausend Uran-Zentrifugen zerstört haben". Der Spiegel. 26 December 2010. Retrieved 27 December 2010.

[95] Stark, Holger (8 August 2011). "Mossad's Miracle Weapon: Stuxnet Virus Opens New Era of Cyber War". Der Spiegel.

[96] Warrick, Joby, "Iran's Natanz nuclear facility recovered quickly from Stuxnet cyberattack", *The Washington Post*, 16 February 2011, retrieved 17 February 2011.

[97] "Stuxnet Malware and Natanz: Update of ISIS December 22, 2010 Report". Institute for Science and International Security. 15 February 2011.

[98] "Signs of sabotage in Tehran's nuclear programme". Gulf News. 14 July 2010.

[99] Dan Williams (7 July 2009). "Wary of naked force, Israel eyes cyberwar on Iran". Reuters.

[100] Aneja, Atul (26 September 2010). "Under cyber-attack, says Iran". Chennai, India: The Hindu.

[101] "شبکه خبر :: راه های مقابله با ویروس"استاکس نت"" (in Iranian).Irinn.ir. Retrieved 28 September 2010.

[102] "Stuxnet worm rampaging through Iran: IT official". AFP. Archived from the original on 28 September 2010.

[103] "IRAN: Speculation on Israeli involvement in malware computer attack". Los Angeles Times. 27 September 2010. Retrieved 28 September 2010.

[104] Erdbrink, Thomas; Nakashima, Ellen (27 September 2010). "Iran struggling to contain 'foreign-made' 'Stuxnet' computer virus". The Washington Post. Retrieved 28 September 2010.

[105] "Ahmadinedschad räumt Virus-Attacke ein". Der Spiegel. 29 November 2010. Retrieved 29 December 2010.

[106] "Stuxnet: Ahmadinejad admits cyberweapon hit Iran nuclear program". The Christian Science Monitor. 30 November 2010. Retrieved 29 December 2010.

[107] Zetter, Kim (29 November 2010). "Iran: Computer Malware Sabotaged Uranium Centrifuges | Threat Level". Wired.com. Retrieved 14 February 2012.

[108] "US Denies Role In Iranian Scientist's Death". Fox News. 7 April 2010. Retrieved 14 February 2012.

[109] Monica Amarelo (21 January 2011). "New FAS Report Demonstrates Iran Improved Enrichment in 2010". Federation of American Scientists.

[110] "Report: Iran's nuclear capacity unharmed, contrary to U.S. assessment". Haaretz. 22 January 2011.

[111] Jeffrey Goldberg (22 January 2011). "Report: Report: Iran's Nuclear Program Going Full Speed Ahead". The Atlantic.

[112] "Experts say Iran has "neutralized"Stuxnet virus". Reuters. 14 February 2012.

[113] Beaumont, Peter (30 September 2010). "Stuxnet worm heralds new era of global cyberwar". London: Guardian.co.uk.

[114] Sanger, David E. (1 June 2012). "Obama Order Sped Up Wave of Cyberattacks Against Iran". The New York Times. Retrieved 1 June 2012.

[115] Hounshell, Blake (27 September 2010). "6 mysteries about Stuxnet". Foreign Policy. Retrieved 28 September 2010.

[116] "Falkenrath Says Stuxnet Virus May Have Origin in Israel: Video. Bloomberg Television". 24 September 2010.

[117] Williams, Dan (15 December 2009). "Spymaster sees Israel as world cyberwar leader". Reuters. Retrieved 29 May 2012.

[118] Dan Williams. "Cyber takes centre stage in Israel's war strategy". Reuters, 28 September 2010.

[119] Antonin Gregoire. "Stuxnet, the real face of cyber warfare". Iloubnan.info, 25 November 2010.

[120] Broad, William J.; Sanger, David E. (18 November 2010). "Worm in Iran Can Wreck Nuclear Centrifuges". The New York Times.

[121] Williams, Christoper (16 February 2011). "Israeli security chief celebrates Stuxnet cyber attack". The Telegraph. London. Retrieved 23 February 2011.

[122] U.S. Cyber Consequences Unit. "The U.S. Cyber Consequences Unit". usccu.us.

[123] "A worm in the centrifuge: An unusually sophisticated cyber-weapon is mysterious but important". The Economist. 30 September 2010.

[124] David Sanger (25 September 2010). "Iran Fights Malware Attacking Computers". New York Times. Retrieved 28 September 2010.

[125] "Iran/Critical National Infrastructure: Cyber Security Experts See The Hand Of Israel's Signals Intelligence Service In The "Stuxnet" Virus Which Has Infected Iranian Nuclear Facilities". Mideastsecurity.co.uk. 1 September 2010.

[126] Riddle, Warren (1 October 2010). "Mysterious 'Myrtus' Biblical Reference Spotted in Stuxnet Code". SWITCHED. Retrieved 6 October 2010.

[127] "SCADA Systems Whitepaper" (PDF). Motorola.

[128] "Symantec Puts 'Stuxnet' Malware Under the Knife". PC Magazine.

[129] Zetter, Kim (1 October 2010). "New Clues Point to Israel as Author of Blockbuster Worm, Or Not". Wired.

[130] Reals, Tucker (24 September 2010). "Stuxnet Worm a U.S. Cyber-Attack on Iran Nukes?". CBS News.

[131] "Snowden Der Spiegel Interview" (in English and German). Der Spiegel. Retrieved 3 October 2015.

[132] Halliday, Josh (18 January 2011). "WikiLeaks: US advised to sabotage Iran nuclear sites by German thinktank". The Guardian. London. Retrieved 19 January 2011.

[133] David E. Sanger (10 January 2009). "U.S. Rejected Aid for Israeli Raid on Iranian Nuclear Site". The New York Times. Retrieved 12 October 2013.

[134] Kim Zetter (17 February 2011). "Cyberwar Issues Likely to Be Addressed Only After a Catastrophe". Wired. Retrieved 18 February 2011.

[135] Chris Carroll (18 October 2011). "Cone of silence surrounds U.S. cyberwarfare". Stars and Stripes. Retrieved 30 October 2011.

[136] John Bumgarner (27 April 2010). "Computers as Weapons of War" (PDF). IO Journal. Retrieved 30 October 2011.

[137] Kroft, Steve (4 March 2012). "Stuxnet: Computer worm opens new era of warfare". 60 Minutes (CBS News). Retrieved 9 March 2012.

[138] CBS News staff (16 April 2011). "Iran blames U.S., Israel for Stuxnet malware" (SHTML). CBS News. Retrieved 15 January 2012.

[139] James Balford (12 June 2013). "THE SECRET WAR". Wired. Retrieved 2 June 2014.

[140] Carr, Jeffrey (14 December 2010). "Stuxnet's Finnish-Chinese Connection". Forbes. Retrieved 19 April 2011.

[141] Clayton, Mark (24 September 2010). "Stuxnet worm mystery: What's the cyber weapon after?". Christian Science Monitor. Retrieved 21 January 2011.

[142] Gaycken, Sandro (26 November 2010). "Stuxnet: Wer war's? Und wozu?". Die ZEIT. Retrieved 19 April 2011.

[143] Hopkins, Nick (31 May 2011). "UK developing cyber-weapons programme to counter cyber war threat". *The Guardian*. United Kingdom. Retrieved 31 May 2011.

[144] "The Global Intelligence Files – Re: [alpha] S3/G3* IS-RAEL/IRAN – Barak hails munitions blast in Iran". Wikileaks. 14 November 2011. Retrieved 4 March 2012.

[145] Iain Thomson (8 July 2013). "Snowden: US and Israel Did Create Stuxnet Attack Code". The Register. Retrieved 8 July 2013.

[146] Menn, Joseph (29 May 2015). "Exclusive: U.S. tried Stuxnet-style campaign against North Korea but failed – sources". Reuters. Retrieved 31 May 2015.

[147] "Stuxnet's Secret Twin". Foreign Policy. 19 November 2013.

[148] "Duqu: A Stuxnet-like malware found in the wild, technical report" (PDF). Laboratory of Cryptography of Systems Security (CrySyS). 14 October 2011.

[149] "Statement on Duqu's initial analysis". Laboratory of Cryptography of Systems Security (CrySyS). 21 October 2011. Retrieved 25 October 2011.

[150] "W32.Duqu – The precursor to the next Stuxnet (Version 1.2)" (PDF). Symantec. 20 October 2011. Retrieved 25 October 2011.

[151] Jim Finkle (28 December 2011). "Stuxnet weapon has at least 4 cousins: researchers". Reuters.

[152] Zetter, Kim (28 May 2012). "Meet 'Flame,' The Massive Spy Malware Infiltrating Iranian Computers". *Wired*. Archived from the original on 30 May 2012. Retrieved 29 May 2012.

[153] "Resource 207: Kaspersky Lab Research Proves that Stuxnet and Flame Developers are Connected". Kaspersky Lab. 11 June 2012.

[154] "The Meaning of Stuxnet". The Economist. 30 September 2010.

[155] Kim Zetter (8 July 2011). "How Digital Detectives Deciphered Stuxnet, the Most Menacing Malware in History". *Wired*.

[156] Holger Stark (8 August 2011). "Mossad's Miracle Weapon: Stuxnet Virus Opens New Era of Cyber War". *Der Spiegel*.

[157] Eddie Walsh (1 January 2012). "2011: The year of domestic cyber threat". Al Jazeera English.

[158] Vyacheslav Zakorzhevsky (5 October 2010). "Sality & Stuxnet – Not Such a Strange Coincidence". Kaspersky Lab.

47.13 Further reading

- Langner, Ralph (March 2011). "Ralph Langner: Cracking Stuxnet, a 21st-century cyber weapon". TED. Retrieved 13 May 2011.

- "The short path from cyber missiles to dirty digital bombs". Blog. Langner Communications GmbH. 26 December 2010. Retrieved 13 May 2011.

- Ralph Langner's Stuxnet Deep Dive

- Langner, Ralph (November 2013). "To Kill a Centrifuge: A Technical Analysis of What Stuxnet's Creators Tried to Achieve" (PDF).

- Falliere, Nicolas (21 September 2010). "Exploring Stuxnet's PLC Infection Process". Blogs: Security Response. Symantec. Retrieved 13 May 2011.

- "Stuxnet Questions and Answers". News from the Lab (blog). F-Secure. 1 October 2010. Retrieved 13 May 2011.

- Mills, Elinor (5 October 2010). "Stuxnet: Fact vs. theory". CNET News. Retrieved 13 May 2011.

- Dang, Bruce; Ferrie, Peter (28 December 2010). "27C3: Adventures in analyzing Stuxnet". Chaos Computer Club e.V. Retrieved 13 May 2011.

- Russinovich, Mark (30 March 2011). "Analyzing a Stuxnet Infection with the Sysinternals Tools, Part 1". Mark's Blog. Microsoft Corporation. MSDN Blogs. Retrieved 13 May 2011.

- Zetter, Kim (11 July 2011). "How Digital Detectives Deciphered Stuxnet, the Most Menacing Malware in History". Threat Level Blog. *Wired*. Retrieved 11 July 2011.

- Kroft, Steve (4 March 2012). "Stuxnet: Computer worm opens new era of warfare". *60 Minutes*. CBS News. Retrieved 4 March 2012.

- Sanger, David E. (1 June 2012). "Obama Order Sped Up Wave of Cyberattacks Against Iran". *The New York Times*. Retrieved 1 June 2012.

- Kim Zetter, *Countdown to Zero Day: Stuxnet and the Launch of the World's First Digital Weapon*. New York: Crown Publishing Group, 2014. ISBN 978-0-7704-3617-9.

47.14   External links

- Ralph Langner: Cracking Stuxnet, a 21st-century cyber weapon – video at TED

- Stuxnet code – at Internet Archive

Chapter 48

Titan Rain

Lockheed Martin Aeronautics Discussion

Titan Rain was the designation given by the federal government of the United States to a series of coordinated attacks on American computer systems since 2003; they were known to have been ongoing for at least three years.[*][1] The attacks were labeled as Chinese in origin, although their precise nature, e.g., state-sponsored espionage, corporate espionage, or random hacker attacks, and their real identities – masked by proxy, zombie computer, spyware/virus infected – remain unknown. The activity known as "Titan Rain" is believed to be associated with an Advanced Persistent Threat.

In early December 2005 the director of the SANS Institute, a security institute in the United States, said that the attacks were "most likely the result of Chinese military hackers attempting to gather information on U.S. systems."[*][2]

Titan Rain hackers gained access to many United States defense contractor computer networks who were targeted for their sensitive information,[*][1] including those at Lockheed Martin, Sandia National Laboratories, Redstone Arsenal, and NASA.

48.1 Attackers

The series of attacks are believed by some to be the actions of the People's Liberation Army (PLA), rather than some freelance Chinese hackers. These hackers attacked both the American (*Defense Intelligence Agency* – DOD) and British Government Departments (Ministry of Defence – MOD). The British government had an incident in 2006 where a part of the House of Commons computer system was shut down by - initially thought to be an individual – an "organised Chinese hacking group."[*][3] Although most of the evidence has pointed to the Chinese government as the attackers, China have claimed that it was not them who attacked the United States, leading to another possibility that it was hackers using Chinese computers. See Alternative Cases

48.2 Consequences

'Titan Rain' has caused friction between the U.S. and Chinese governments as, although with little evidence, the U.S. government has blamed the Chinese government for the attacks of 2004 on the unclassified, although potentially fatal information. Adam Paller, SANS Institute research director, stated that the attacks came from individuals with "intense discipline," and that, "no other organisation could do this if they were not a military". Such sophistication and evidence has pointed toward the Chinese military (People's Liberation Army) as the attackers.[*][4]

'Titan Rain' reportedly attacked multiple high-end political systems, such as NASA and the FBI. Although no sensitive and classified information was reported stolen, the hackers were however able to steal unclassified information (e.g. information from a home computer). The fact that the information was classified or not was somewhat irrelevant; when it all comes together it could reveal the strengths and weaknesses of the U.S., making such an attack very damaging.[*][5]

'Titan Rain' has caused distrust between other countries (such as the United Kingdom and Russia – other superpowers) and China. Such distrust has occurred because these countries were likely attacked, but either did not detect an attack or have not released statements that they were at-

The U.S. Department of the Treasury, Washington, D.C.

tacked. The United Kingdom have stated officially that their governmental offices were attacked by hackers of a Chinese source. The events of 'Titan Rain' have caused the rest of the world to be more cautious of attacks; not just from China, but from other countries as well, thereby causing, however small, a slight distrust between other countries. This distrust between them may affect future agreements and dealings and as such further affect their relationship with China.

48.3   Alternative cases

One of the alternative to the People's Liberation Army carrying out the attacks is: hackers using Chinese computers and websites to carry out the attack. It has been long known that many Chinese computers and websites are very insecure. Hackers use the website/system to attack a targeted system. This makes it look as if it was a Chinese system attacking the target, and not the hacker. This method allows a hacker to attack a system without his/her location being revealed. People's Republic of China (PRC) have argued that this method had been used to attack the U.S. and other locations targeted by 'Titan Rain'. This has, however, sparked controversy as to who actually cause the events of 'Titan Rain' – the Chinese or a bored hacker?*[6]

In addition, to support Adam Paller's idea of the attackers having to be a large, organised body with "intense discipline," it is possible such an organisation could have exploited these insecure computers, servers and websites to attempt to steal sensitive information from the United States and other targets. A rogue state and/or a large, sophisticated collection of hackers could have used these insecurities in China's computers to attack the targets, rather than China themselves being the attacker. Using this method of using China's computers means that this organisation can hide themselves while making an effective attack, all with rela-

tive ease. Such a plot protects the hackers but put the Chinese government in a predicament where they cannot prove that they did not do the attack, causing tensions between the United States and China.

48.4   See also

- Shawn Carpenter
- Moonlight Maze
- Operation Aurora
- Cyberwarfare
- Advanced Persistent Threat
- Computer network operations
- Stakkato

48.5   References

[1] Bodmer, Kilger, Carpenter, & Jones (2012). Reverse Deception: Organized Cyber Threat Counter-Exploitation. New York: McGraw-Hill Osborne Media.   ISBN 0071772499, ISBN 978-0071772495

[2] "Hacker attacks in US linked to Chinese military" at the Wayback Machine (archived December 22, 2006)

[3] Richard Norton-Taylor (2007) Titan Rain - how Chinese hackers targeted Whitehall The Guardian

[4] Homeland Security News Wire (2005) The lesson of Titan Rain

[5] Dvice (2010) The 7 worst cyberattacks in history (that we know about)

[6] Nathan Thornburgh (2005) The Invasion of the Chinese Cyberspies (And the Man Who Tried to Stop Them) Time

48.6   External links

- Graham, Bradley (2005-08-25). "Hackers Attack Via Chinese Web Sites". *Washington Post.*

- Espiner, Tom (2005-11-23). "Security experts lift lid on Chinese hack attacks". *ZDNet News.* Archived from the original on 2006-12-11.

- Thornburgh, Nathan (2005-08-25).   "Inside the Chinese Hack Attack". *Time.com.*

- Thornburgh, Nathan (2005-08-29). "The Invasion of the Chinese Cyberspies (And the Man Who Tried to Stop Them)". *Time*.

- Brenner, Bill (2005-08-31). "Myfip's Titan Rain connection". *SearchSecurity.com*.

- Onley, Dawn S.; Wait, Patience (2007-08-21). "Red Storm Rising". *Government Computing News*.

- Norton-Taylor, Richard (2007-09-05). "Titan Rain - how Chinese hackers targeted Whitehall". *the-guardian.com*.

- Winkler, Ian (2005-10-20). "Guard against Titan Rain hackers". *computerworld.com*.

Chapter 49

Operation Tunisia

Operation Tunisia refers to the actions by internet group Anonymous during the Tunisian revolution.

49.1 Tactics

In their traditional manner; Anonymous launched a series of DDoS attacks against government websites.[1][2] Additionally, Anonymous provided protesters with documents required to take down the incumbent government as well as distributing a care package, among other things, including Tor, and a greasemonkey script to avoid proxy interception by the government.[3] The providing of information was considered by some a part of Operation Leakspin. They also aided in passing information about the protests in and out of the country.[3]

49.2 Aftermath

At first Anonymous posted a video on YouTube declaring their intentions. Anonymous begun DDoS attacks.[4] It wasn't long before multiple government websites in Tunisia were taken offline as a result of the attacks.[1][5] Anonymous supplied protesters, through Tunisian blogger Slim Amamou, with anonymising software such as Tor.[6] While the group did wage its online, a large-scale professional strikes by Tunisia's professional class of lawyers and teachers, culminating in the fleeing of President Ben Ali on January 14, 2011.

49.3 Tunisian Involvement

Some Anonymous members in the #OpTunisia channel were Tunisians, one of them called 'slim404', whose real name was Slim Amamou, a Tunisian blogger. He aided in passing software between Anonymous and protestors. Amamou was arrested on Jan. 6, 2011. He was later re-leased from jail and went on to become the secretary of state for sport and youth, he resigned in May to protest the transitional government's censorship of the web.[3]

49.4 See also

- Tunisian Revolution
- Arab Spring

49.5 References

[1] "Anonymous Operation Tunisia rages, US Govt grows worried | MyCE – My Consumer Electronics". Myce.com. Retrieved 2011-05-01.

[2] Yasmine Ryan (2011-01-06). "Tunisia's bitter cyberwar - Features". Al Jazeera English. Retrieved 2011-05-01.

[3] Norton, Quinn (2012-01-11). "2011: The Year Anonymous Took On Cops, Dictators and Existential Dread". *Wired*.

[4] "Anonymous - Operation Tunisia - A Press Release". YouTube. Retrieved 2011-05-01.

[5] "Brian's Coffeehouse: Operation Tunisia". Bjulrich.blogspot.com. 2011-01-03. Retrieved 2011-05-01.

[6] "The new media: Between revolution and repression – Net solidarity takes on censorship - Reporters Without Borders". En.rsf.org. Retrieved 2011-05-01.

49.6 External links

- https://www.anonymoustunisie.com/ Website of Anonymous TN

Chapter 50

TV5Monde

This article is about the European TV network. For the related French-Canadian TV channel, see TV5 Québec Canada.

TV5Monde (French pronunciation: [te ve sɛ̃k mɔ̃d]; formerly known as **TV5**) is a global television network, broadcasting several channels of French language programming. It is an approved participant member of the European Broadcasting Union.*[1]

50.1 Summary

TV5 started on 2 January 1984 and was under the management of Serge Adda until his death in November 2004; the new director, named on 6 April 2005 is Jean-Jacques Aillagon, former French Minister for Culture and Communication. The present Director-General is Marie-Christine Saragosse.

In January 1992 TV5 underwent a major overhaul including re-branding as "TV5MONDE" to stress its focus as a global network ("**Monde**" is French for "**World**"). Also part of the changes are a new schedule and new program line-up. Since 1993, "**TV5 Monde**" is part of the channel's corporate name. Its Canadian operations are branded "TV5 Québec Canada", however, though the shorter version TV5 is also used.

TV5MONDE claims to be one of the top three most available global television networks available around the world with CNN and MTV.

50.2 History

TV5 was formed on 2 January 1984, under the guidance of Claude Cheysson, French Minister for Foreign Affairs, and by TV5 President Serge Adda by five public television channels: TF1, Antenne 2, and FR3 from France, the Swiss Television Suisse Romande and the Belgian RTBF. The "5"

from the name TV5 comes from these five public broadcasters. On 18 December 1985, TV5 was amongst the first four channels carried by cable television in France, inaugurated in Cergy-Pontoise.

Following its privatisation in 1987, TF1 retired from the TV5 consortium, although it continued to supply its programmes to the channel up until 1995. On 1 September 1988 TV5 Québec Canada was created, then TV5 Afrique in 1991. The following year TV5 transmitted using digital compression towards Latin America and the Caribbean. Its coverage was expanded in 1996 with the launch of its Asian-Pacific signal with TV5 Asie-Pacifique and its subscription channel TV5 États-Unis in the United States. Two years later, the Middle East feed was launched with TV5 Moyen-Orient in 1998.

In early 1999, TV5 split its European signal into two, with the launch of TV5 France Belgique Suisse, a signal specific to Francophone Europe (France, Belgium, Switzerland, Monaco, Luxembourg etc.). TV5 Europe continued to serve the wider continental audience.

A consortium formed by public channels Arte and La Cinquième entered into the capital of the channel, which brought with it new sources of programming. A new schedule was constructed, centred around news programmes such as news flashes on the hour, two TV5 bulletins and rebroadcasts of its partners' main news programmes (*20 Heures* from France 2; *Soir 3* from France 3; *Le Journal* Switzerland; *13 Heures* from Belgium).

A meeting with ministers from TV5 in Vevey, Switzerland, gave a mandate to the channel's council of cooperation in order to reform the structure of the channel, in view of creating a unique worldwide channel. The national governments in charge of the five participants gave an agreement to turn management of TV5-Etats-Unis and TV5 Amerique-Latine over to TV5 Monde, the new name for the channel's head operations in Paris.

Following the September 2001 terrorist attacks and the period leading up to the 2003 Iraq War, the subsequent media coverage put the spotlight on TV5's particular way of broadcasting news bulletins from its member public broadcasters. International conflicts arising from the decision to go to war by the United States and the United Kingdom (in which France, notably had refused to participate) had relaunched the debate over whether to create an international news channel from a French perspective, resulting in the 2006 launch of France 24.

With the creation of France 24 placing TV5's own existence in doubt, its new CEO Jean-Jacques Aillagon decided that, from 1 January 2006 to rename the channel **TV5Monde** to better underline its status as the only international Francophone channel available on-air (France 24 at this stage was only available in Europe, the Middle East, Africa and in the United States' cities of New York and Washington DC in French). Aillagon stepped down from his post on 3 March 2006.

The name TV5Monde only applies to its eight different signals, broadcast from its Paris headquarters. In Canada and in French-speaking Quebec, TV5 Quebec Canada is managed from Montreal, which keeps the original name **TV5**, as it is operated by an independent company distinct from TV5MONDE. As well as being part of the TV5 'family', TV5 Quebec Canada has its own management and its schedule is made with the Canadian viewer in mind (and to conform to Canadian broadcast regulations, amongst which, sets domestic production quotas and limits foreign investors to a minority stake).

In 2007 a new programme schedule saw the reduction of programming from France Télévisions (France 2, 3 and 5), for example, one daily news bulletin from France 2 (abandoning France 3's midday news programme). In 2008, TV5Monde became part of holding company France Monde.

In 2009, TV5Monde launched TV5Monde Asie, a feed for territories located between GMT+8 (Hong Kong) and GMT+12 (New Zealand). TV5Monde's Pacific signal is an adaptation of its existing Asian signal which has been adopted to its time zones to better serve its viewers.

On 25 February 2015, a new signal called TV5Monde Brésil was launched, broadcasting its programming with Portuguese subtitles.[2]

50.2.1 April 2015 cyber-attack and resulting disruption

On the evening of 8 April 2015, TV5Monde was the victim of a cyberattack by the hacker group "CyberCaliphate", which claimed to have ties to the terrorist organization Islamic State of Iraq and the Levant (ISIL). The hackers breached the broadcaster's internal systems in what director Yves Bigot described as an "unprecedented" attack, over-

riding TV5Monde's broadcast programming for over three hours, with service only partially restored in the early hours of the following morning.[3] Normal broadcasting services were still disrupted late into 9 April.[3] Various computerised internal administrative and support systems including e-mail were also still shut down or otherwise inaccessible due to the attack.[3][4] The hackers also hijacked TV5Monde's Facebook and Twitter pages to post the personal information of relatives of French soldiers participating in actions against the organization, along with messages critical of President François Hollande, arguing that the January 2015 terrorist attacks were "gifts" for his "unforgivable mistake" of partaking in conflicts that "[serve] no purpose".[3][5]

As part of the official response to the attack, the French Minister of Culture and Communications, Fleur Pellerin, called for an emergency meeting of the heads of various major media outlets and groups. The meeting took place on 10 April at an undisclosed location.[4] The French Prime Minister Manuel Valls called the attack "an unacceptable insult to freedom of information and expression".[4] His cabinet colleague, the Interior Minister Bernard Cazeneuve attempted to allay public concern by stating that France "had already increased its anti-hacking measures to protect against cyber-attacks" following the aforementioned terrorist attacks on January earlier that year, which had left a total of 20 people dead.[4]

French investigators later discounted the theory that the attack was connected to ISIL, instead suspecting the APT28 or *Pawn Storm*, a hacking group with alleged links to the Russian government.[6]

50.3 Content

Most of its content is taken from mainstream networks in the French-speaking world, notably France Télévisions from France, RTBF from Belgium, RTS from Switzerland, and the Radio-Canada and TVA networks in Canada. In addition to international news, TV5MONDE broadcasts Ligue 1, Coupe de France, Coupe de la Ligue, Trophée des Champions, films and music magazines.

50.4 Ownership

The number "5" in the name is the number of founding networks: Télévision Française 1 (TF1), Antenne 2 (France 2), FR 3 (France 3), TSR (RTS Un) and RTBF (La Une). Today, the partnership making up the TV5MONDE consortium are France Télévisions, Arte France, Institut national de l'audiovisuel, CBC/Radio-Canada, Télé-Québec, RTBF and RTS. This consortium owns 51% of the service, while the other 49% is owned by France Médias Monde, a holding company that manages France's international broadcasting services.

50.5 Channels

As of 2015, ten feeds are being transmitted:

- **TV5MONDE FBS** (France, Belgium, Switzerland, Monaco and Luxembourg)

- **TV5MONDE Europe** (rest of Europe)

- **TV5MONDE Afrique** (Africa, except Maghreb)

- **TV5MONDE Maghreb–Orient** (Maghreb, Middle East) with occasional Arabic subtitles

- **TV5MONDE India** (rest of Asia) and all India

- **TV5MONDE États-Unis** (United States) with occasional English subtitles

- **TV5MONDE Amérique Latine & Caraïbes** (Latin America and the Caribbean) with Spanish and Portuguese subtitles

- **TV5MONDE Pacifique** (Japan – South Korea – Southeast Asia - Oceania)

- **TV5 Québec Canada** (Canada)

(*)TV5MONDE États-Unis has certain programs subtitled in English. Particularly some newscasts and most movies are subtitled in English language. It is unusual to watch a French movie without English language subtitles on TV5MONDE États-Unis.
(**)TV5 Québec Canada is produced in Montreal.
(***) in Brazil, the French network has partnered with Brazilian National Cine Agency to stimulate the production of independent content in Brazilian pay TV.*[7]

50.6 Logos

From 1984, for this television network, there are five different logos. The first logo of television network is used from 1984 to 1988, the second logo is used from 1988 to 1990, the third logo is used from 1990 to 1995, the fourth logo is used from 1995 to 2006, and the fifth and current logo is in use from 2006.

From 1991 to 2003, the digital on-screen graphic was located on the upper right corner of the screen. From 2003 onwards, it has been moved to the upper left corner of the screen.

- TV5 logo, 1995–present. Logo is still in use by TV5 Québec Canada.

- TV5MONDE logo since 2006–present.

50.7 Network availability

50.7.1 Europe

TV5MONDE FBS and TV5MONDE Europe are Free-To-Air and can be received by satellite. Additionally:

- Albania: TV5MONDE Europe can be found on analogue broadcasting in some Albanian municipalities on channels 43, 35, 50, 39, 25, 56 UHF.

- Croatia: TV5MONDE Europe can be found on digital cable.

- Denmark: TV5MONDE Europe can be found on digital cable.

- Germany: TV5MONDE Europe can be found on analogue or digital cable.

- Greece: TV5MONDE Europe can be found on ERT channel 22, 46.

- Israel: TV5MONDE Europe can be found on Yes channel 131.

- Italy: TV5MONDE Europe can be found on SKY Italia channel 540 and on IPTV Infostrada TV, Tiscali TV and Alice Home TV on the same channel number and on TV di FASTWEB channel 68.

- Netherlands: TV5MONDE Europe can be found on satellite: CanalDigitaal channel 194, on Cable television: Ziggo channel 71 and all other small cable companies, on IPTV: KPN channel 70 and Glashart Media channel 421. TV5MONDE FBS can be found on satellite: CanalDigitaal channel 195.

- Norway: TV5MONDE Europe can be found on Canal Digital channel 152.

- Republic of Ireland: TV5MONDE Europe can be found on Virgin Media Ireland channel 825 and Sky channel 796

- Romania: TV5MONDE Europe can be found on Dolce channel 116. On UPC Romania in digital, it is available on channel 721, on mediabox or LCN.

- Spain: TV5MONDE Europe can be found on ONO (Spain) cable channel 402.

- Turkey: TV5MONDE Europe can be found on Digiturk channel 102 and Turkish Cable Television.

- United Kingdom: TV5MONDE Europe can be found with English subtitles on Sky satellite channel 796; on Virgin Media cable channel 825; and free-to-air satellite via Astra 1L at 19.2°E and Eutelsat Hotbird at 13°E.

50.7.2   North America

Neither TV5MONDE nor its supplementary services are Free-To-Air in North America.

Canada

Main article: TV5 Québec Canada

TV5 Canada is a French Canadian version of TV5MONDE. It offers largely the same programming schedule, with the exception that programming from Radio-Canada, which is already available across Canada, is replaced with content from the provincial educational networks Télé-Québec and TFO. As with TV5MONDE, TV5 Québec Canada is also a cooperative effort, though involving French Canadian networks and producers through l'Association des producteurs de films et de télévision du Québec. The Canadian license also includes *Unis*, a channel focused on francophone communities outside Quebec.

United States

In the United States, **TV5MONDE États-Unis** is one of several foreign-language premium channels offered through International Media Distribution. Broadcast is in standard definition only. The channel is offered nationwide on Dish Network, AT&T U-verse, and Verizon FiOS, and offered in most major markets on traditional cable systems such as Time Warner Cable, Cox Communications, Xfinity and Bright House Networks. TV5MONDE is offered on cable and satellite as an a la carte selection for $9.99 a month. On most systems, a subscription to another programming tier or a digital cable package may be required. Purportedly due to underfunding, TV5MONDE cannot yet offer accurate advance scheduling or on-time programming, but progress is being made in these fronts.

In addition, TV5MONDE USA offers a French-language children's channel, **TiVi5MONDE**, which offers a selection of Children's and young adult programming in French.

The channel is currently available on Dish Network, as part of the TV5MONDE subscription. Daily blocks of TiVi5MONDE programming is also seen on the main TV5MONDE channel.*[8]

TV5MONDE launched **TV5MONDE Cinema on Demand**, a video on demand service available to Xfinity subscribers in July 2013 that features a selection of francophone films.*[9]

Mexico, Central America and Caribbean

In Mexico and most countries of Central America and The Caribbean, TV5MONDE Amérique Latine & Caraïbes is available SKY México, a satellite television platform, on Channel 277.

50.7.3   South America

Brazil

In Brazil is transmitted with subtitles in Portuguese on their schedule, currently negotiations are being held to launch the first original channel productions in the country. TV5MONDE Brésil is available on SKY Brasil on channel 108, Claro TV on channel 132, Net on channel 141, as well as Vivo TV.

Others countries

TV5MONDE Amérique Latine & Caraïbes is not Free-To-Air in South America, The channel is present in the main TV operators pay of Hispanic countries, the half programming is displayed with Spanish subtitles.

In French Guiana, territory located in northern South America and is a French overseas territory, the channel is free and displayed with programming entirely in French.

50.7.4   Asia, Australia and New Zealand

It is free to air from the AsiaSat 3S satellite, covering most of Asia and Australia. Triangle TV in Auckland, Nepal (Everest) and Wellington rebroadcasts some news programmes. In Nepal (Everest), TiVi5 Monde is broadcast by Dish Home on Channel no D-864. In Singapore, StarHub TV service broadcasts it on Channel 152 for its digital service customers on MediaCorp TV Channel 5 and MediaCorp TV HD5. In India, Zee Network provides this channel for its Dish Network DTH services subscribers. Also, many others like Hathway cable TV and local cable TV operators offer TV5Monde free of cost. The channel is also available in Japan on Fuji Television platform (as TV5MONDE Pacifique, though Japan is a part of the Asian continent) and Television New Zealand in New Zealand.

In South Korea, ISP provider Qrix offers TV5 on its premium HD cable package and will begin offering it via IPTV from 16 Feb..

- India: TV5MONDE Asie used to be available on Dish TV channel 731 but it has been withdrawn now. Currently, it is available in Airtel Digital TV channel no 157 and Tata Sky channel no 537.

- Indonesia - Southeast Asia: TV5MONDE Asia can be found on channel 62 UHF in Jakarta.

- Pakistan: TV5MONDE Asie is available on demand by requesting the local cable operator.

- Philippines: TV5MONDE Asie can be found on SkyCable Channel 134 (Digital), Destiny Cable Channel 134 (Digital) through digital platform.

- Singapore: TV5MONDE Asie can be found on StarHub TV channel 152.

- Sri Lanka: TV5MONDE Asie can be found on Peo TV Channel 90

- Taiwan: TV5MONDE Asie can be found on CHT MOD channel 111.

- Thailand: TV5MONDE Asie can be found on TrueVisions channel 166.

- Vietnam: TV5MONDE Asie can be found on VTV-Cab, SCTV, HTVC, MyTV, FPT Play HD, AVG.

50.7.5 Middle East and North Africa

In most of the region, TV5MONDE Maghreb-Orient is available on Nilesat 101 and Badr 4 under the frequencies of 11900.00 V 27500 3/4 and 12073.00 H 27500 3/4, respectively. In Lebanon, it is also available on Cablevision (a cable television platform serving the country), and via Tele Liban's French channel, Tele Liban Le Neuf.

50.8 References

[1] "TV5MONDE". *EBU*. Retrieved 7 June 2011.

[2] "TV5Monde in Brazil". Retrieved 27 February 2015.

[3] "Isil hackers seize control of France's TV5Monde network in 'unprecedented' attack". *Daily Telegraph*. 9 April 2015. Retrieved 10 April 2015.

[4] "French media groups to hold emergency meeting after Isis cyber-attack". *Guardian (online edition)*. 9 April 2015. Retrieved 10 April 2015.

[5] "French TV network TV5Monde 'hacked by cyber caliphate in unprecedented attack' that revealed personal details of French soldiers". *The Independent*. 9 April 2015. Retrieved 9 April 2015.

[6] "France probes Russian lead in TV5Monde hacking: sources". *Reuters*. 10 June 2015. Retrieved 9 July 2015.

[7] "TV5Monde has partnered with Ancine". Retrieved 27 February 2015.

[8] TV5MONDE USA: TiVi5MONDE

[9] Facebook: TV5MONDE Cinema on Demand

50.9 External links

- Official Site (French)

- TV5 Québec Canada (French)

- TV5Monde US

- TV5Monde Asia

- TV5Monde Charter (French)

Chapter 51

2008 cyberattack on United States

The **2008 Cyberattack on the United States** was the "worst breach of U.S. military computers in history". The defense against the attack was named "Operation Buckshot Yankee". It led to the creation of the United States Cyber Command.*[1]*[2]*[3]

51.1 History

It started when a USB flash drive infected by a foreign intelligence agency was left in the parking lot of a Department of Defense facility at a base in the Middle East. It contained malicious code and was put into a USB port from a laptop computer that was attached to United States Central Command.*[1]*[2]

The Pentagon spent nearly 14 months cleaning the worm, named agent.btz, from military networks. Agent.btz, a variant of the SillyFDC worm, has the ability "to scan computers for data, open backdoors, and send through those backdoors to a remote command and control server." *[4]It was suspected that Russian hackers were behind it because they had used the same code that made up agent.btz before in previous attacks. In order to try and stop the spread of the worm, the Pentagon banned USB drives, and disabled Windows autorun feature.*[5]

51.2 References

[1] "Defense Department Confirms Critical Cyber Attack". *Eweek*. August 25, 2010. Retrieved 2010-08-25. A senior Pentagon official has revealed details of a previously-classified malware attack he declared "the most significant breach of U.S. military computers ever." In an article for Foreign Affairs, Deputy Defense Secretary William J. Lynn III writes that in 2008, a flash drive believed to have been infected by a foreign intelligence agency uploaded malicious code onto a network run by the military's Central Command. ...

[2] William J. Lynn III. "Defending a New Domain". *Foreign Affairs (journal)*. Retrieved 2010-08-25. In 2008, the U.S. Department of Defense suffered a significant compromise of its classified military computer networks. It began when an infected flash drive was inserted into a U.S. military laptop at a base in the Middle East. The flash drive's malicious computer code, placed there by a foreign intelligence agency, uploaded itself onto a network run by the U.S. Central Command. That code spread undetected on both classified and unclassified systems, establishing what amounted to a digital beachhead, from which data could be transferred to servers under foreign control. It was a network administrator's worst fear: a rogue program operating silently, poised to deliver operational plans into the hands of an unknown adversary.

[3] Knowlton, Brian (August 25, 2010). "Military Computer Attack Confirmed". *New York Times*. Retrieved 2010-08-26.

[4] Shachtman, Noah. "Insiders Doubt 2008 Pentagon Hack Was Foreign Spy Attack", The Brookings Institution, 25 August 2010.

[5] Shachtman, Noah. "Insiders Doubt 2008 Pentagon Hack Was Foreign Spy Attack (Updated)". Retrieved 2016-10-04.

51.3 Further reading

- Nakashima, Ellen; Julie Tate (8 Dec 2011), "Cyber-intruder sparks massive federal response —and debate over dealing with threats", *The Washington Post*, washingtonpost.com, retrieved 9 Dec 2011, This article, which contains previously undisclosed information on the extent of the infection, the nature of the response and the fractious policy debate it inspired, is based on interviews with two dozen current and former U.S. officials and others with knowledge of the operation.

Chapter 52

Vietnamese airports hackings

On 29 July 2016, a group suspected coming from China launched hacker attacks on the website of Vietnam Airlines with client information leaked and on flight information screens at Vietnam's 2 biggest airports, Tan Son Nhat International Airport and Noi Bai International Airport, posting derogatory messages against Vietnam and the Philippines in their territorial row against China in the South China Sea.*[1]*[2]*[3]*[4]

52.1 Background

On 12 July 2016, the Permanent Court of Arbitration ruled in favor of the Philippines against China over an arbitration case concerning the disputes in the South China Sea;*[5]*[6] in its major ruling, the tribunal ruled that China has "no historical rights" based on the "nine-dash line" map.*[5]*[6] Within hours of the Permanent Court of Arbitration's unanimous rebuke of China's territorial claims in the South China Sea last week, at least 68 national and local government websites in the Philippines were knocked offline in a massive distributed denial of service (DDoS) attack.*[7]

This hack comes days after a row involving a Chinese tourist at one of the hacked airports, Tan Son Nhat International Airport. A Chinese visitor complained, that her passport was handed back with obscenities written on the page that contains a map including China's "nine-dash line", that marks China's claim to territories in the South China Sea.*[8]

52.2 Incidents

According to the Civil Aviation Administration of Vietnam, at 13h46 on 29 July the IT-systems of VietJet, Vietnam Airlines to do the flight check-ins at the Tan Son Nhat International Airport were attacked and had to stop working. At 16h07', A team of self-proclaimed Chinese Hackers attacked flight information screens at Noi Bai International Airport, posting notices that state media said criticized the Philippines and Vietnam and their claims in the South China Sea.,*[9]*[10] The hackers also took control of the speaker system at Noi Bai airport for a few minutes, during which the speakers broadcast a male voice distorting Viet Nam's claims over the East Sea in English.*[11] The check-ins system of Vietnam Airlines there was also attacked and had to switch to manual procedure completion, which lead to flight delays.*[12] altogether, Noi Bai airport has 30 flight, and Tan Son Nhat more than 60 flight delayed from 15 til more than an hour, affect about 2.000 passengers.*[9]

The official website of Vietnam Airlines, vietnamairlines.com, was also hacked by the same group at about 4pm the same day. The website page was replaced by the same picture that appeared on the airports' screens. The website was back to normal at 18.30pm, however, the airlines' customer database was stolen and made public on the internet, according to a press release from Vietnam Airlines. The airlines advised its members to change their account passwords as soon as the network system is recovered.*[11]

Another 2 webpages were also compromised, are the webpage from Vietnam Football Federation on the same day *[13] and from National Economics University (Vietnam) the next day.*[14]

On next day, 50% of the computers can check in again, but the flight information screens are still off at Noi Bai airport. The speaker system is also still not working again. At Tan Son Nhat airport the situation is similar to Noi Bai with no flight information screens and no speaker system.*[9]

52.3 Perpetrators

The hackers claimed to be the 1937CN from China, which is one of the biggest hacker groups in the country and has a history of hacking Viet Nam's and the Philippines' websites in 2013 and 2015, respectively.*[11]

52.4   References

[1] Flight Info Screens at Vietnam's 2 Major Airports Hacked, nytimes, 29.7.2016

[2] Cyber-terrorists attack flight info screens at Vietnam's 2 major airports, vnexpress, 29.7.2016

[3] Flight information screens in two Vietnam airports hacked, theguardian, 29.7.2016

[4] Hackers target flight info screens at Vietnam's airports, dw, 29.7.2016

[5] "PCA Press Release: The South China Sea Arbitration (The Republic of the Philippines v. The People's Republic of China) | PCA-CPA". *pca-cpa.org*. Retrieved 2016-07-12.

[6] Perlez, Jane (2016-07-12). "Tribunal Rejects Beijing's Claims in South China Sea". *The New York Times*. ISSN 0362-4331. Retrieved 2016-07-12.

[7] China's Secret Weapon in the South China Sea: Cyber Attacks, thediplomat, 22.7.2016

[8] South China Sea: Vietnam airport screens hacked, bbc, 29.7.2016

[9] Hơn 100 chuyến bay bị chậm vì tin tặc tấn công sân bay, vnexpress, 30.7.2016

[10] Hackers hit Vietnam airports with South China Sea messages, reuters, 29.7.2016

[11] Chinese hackers attack VN's airports and Vietnam Airlines' website, vietnamnews, 29.7.2016

[12] Alleged Chinese hackers compromise Vietnam's airports, airline website, tuoitrenews, 29.7.2016

[13] Website của Liên đoàn bóng đá Việt Nam bị tấn công Minh Minh, VnExpress 29/7/2016 | 23:15 GMT+7

[14] Hacker TQ 'phủ nhận cáo buộc tấn công VN' BBC 30 tháng 7 2016

Chapter 53

Vulcanbot

Vulcanbot is the name of a botnet predominantly spread in Vietnam. The botnet began to spread after the website of the Vietnamese Professionals Society (vps.org) was hacked and the legitimate Vietnamese keyboard driver (VPSKeys) hosted on the site was replaced with a backdoored version. Google posted on its blog that it believed the botnet thus created was used predominantly to DDoS bloggers critical of the bauxite mining in Vietnam, thus making it a politically motivated attack.*[1]

53.1   See also

- Operation Aurora

53.2   References

[1] http://www.theregister.co.uk/2010/03/31/vietnam_botnet/

Chapter 54

World of Hell

World of Hell (or simply **WoH**) was a grey hat computer hacker group that claims to be responsible for several high profile attacks in the year 2001. It gained attention due to its high profile targets and the lighthearted messages it has posted in the aftermath of its attacks.

54.1 Overview

World of Hell first emerged in March 2001, and has successfully attacked the websites of several major corporations.[*][1][*][2] It specializes in finding websites with poor security, and then defacing it with an advice message. It has used well-known zero day exploits in that period of time.

The group has used the motto "Kiss my a$$ because I 0wn3d yours" in several cases but also used funny political pictures against war, corruption or any kind of thing against hackers.

World of Hell was also involved in the cyberwarfare "Project-China".[*][3][*][4]

54.2 Members

Cowhead2000, RaFa, FonE_TonE, foney, nold, dawgyg, Messiah-x, Azap, Rubix, goof-athon, delta-x, d1ckw33d, Divine, Apocalypse, gl0b4l.

54.3 Supposed attacks

Defense Information Systems Agency, ROLEX, FOIA CIA, PFIZER, Hard Rock Cafe, Virginia State, Microsoft, 700 sites in one minute, etc.[*][5]

54.4 Convictions

In 2001 Robert Junior aka Cowhead2000 was arrested. On June 12, 2002 Thomas DeVoss aka dawgyg was arrested. In 2005 Rafael Núñez aka RaFa was arrested. The fate of the other members is currently unknown.

54.5 References

[1] "Internet Archive Wayback Machine". Web.archive.org. 2001-07-21. Archived from the original on July 21, 2001. Retrieved 2011-07-15.

[2] "World of Hell hackers on rampage - IT News from". V3.co.uk. Retrieved 2011-07-15.

[3] "Internet Archive Wayback Machine". Web.archive.org. 2001-11-01. Archived from the original on November 1, 2001. Retrieved 2011-07-15.

[4] "Internet Archive Wayback Machine". Web.archive.org. 2001-11-01. Archived from the original on November 1, 2001. Retrieved 2011-07-15.

[5] "Internet Archive Wayback Machine". Web.archive.org. 2001-11-29. Archived from the original on November 29, 2001. Retrieved 2011-07-15.

54.6 External links

- World of Hell hackers on rampage
- Hell is 700 sites hacked in one minute
- Time's up for Rolex website
- Over 200 websites defaced in minutes
- World of Hell back on the warpath
- Hacking group spills the beans
- Campaign seeks to defang Rafa's hacker image

- The hacker diaries: confessions of teenage hackers By
  Dan Verton

Chapter 55

Zombie Zero

Zombie Zero[*][1] is an attack vector where a cyber attacker utilized malware that was clandestinely embedded in NEW barcode readers which were manufactured overseas.

It remains unknown if this attack was promulgated by organized crime or a nation state. Clearly there was significant planning and investment in order to design the malware, and then embed it into the hardware within the bar code scanner. Internet of things (IoT) devices may be similarly preinstalled with malware that can capture the network passwords and then open a backdoor to attackers. Given the high volume of these devices manufactured overseas high caution is to be exercised before placing these devices on corporate or government networks.

Detailed data on the attack follows:

A malware embedded scanner was installed on a wireless network. An attack against the internal network initiated automatically using a server message block protocol.

The stolen data which was scanned included every piece of information about the item, destination address, source and more. This was sent clandestinely to a command and control connection back to a botnet in China. This botnet connected to the Lanxiang Vocational School located in the China Unicom Shandong province network. This school in China has been connected to previous attacks including Google and the Operation AURORA attack. The manufacturer of the scanner was located just a few blocks away from the school.

The botnet then downloaded an additional, second payload that broadened the command and control which now extended to the target company's corporate servers in finance. Now the attackers had detailed financial data on all customers and shipments. The attacker was looking for logistics data on all shipping on a worldwide basis and succeeded in stealing this data.

Detection of Zombie Zero

Zombie Zero can be detected using deception technology.[*][2][*][3][*][4][*][5][*][6][*][7]

55.1 References

[1] "How a Scanner Infected Corporate Systems and Stole Data: Beware Trojan Peripherals" . *Forbes.com*. Retrieved 2016-09-09.

[2] Antone Gonsalves (2014-07-10). "Shipping companies' computers compromised by malware-infected Chinese scanners" . CSO Online. Retrieved 2016-09-09.

[3] "Chinese Hackers Target Logistics & Shipping Firms With Poisoned Inventory Scanners" . *Darkreading.com*. Retrieved 2016-09-09.

[4] Lucian Constantin (2014-07-10). "Malware hidden in Chinese inventory scanners targeted logistics, shipping firms" . Network World. Retrieved 2016-09-09.

[5] Anand, Priya (2014-07-10). "Hackers know who is shipping what, and to where" . MarketWatch. Retrieved 2016-09-09.

[6] "How a Scanner Infected Corporate Systems and Stole Data: Beware Trojan Peripherals" . *Forbes.com*. Retrieved 2016-09-09.

[7] "Hacker Traps: Fake Computers Used as Bait in Hunt for Cyber Criminals" . *Sputniknews.com*. Retrieved 2016-09-09.

55.2 Text and image sources, contributors, and licenses

55.2.1 Text

- **Cyber-attack** *Source:* https://en.wikipedia.org/wiki/Cyber-attack?oldid=741887283 *Contributors:* Andrewman327, Tpbradbury, Antandrus, Scriberius, Dadu~enwiki, Tenebrae, Morphh, Malcolma, Arthur Rubin, Philippschaumann, JustAGal, Dawnseeker2000, Manionc, PhilKnight, Malik Shabazz, Philip Trueman, Farcaster, WereSpielChequers, Flyer22 Reborn, Trivialist, NeuralDream, Addbot, MrOllie, Yobot, AnomieBOT, Jim1138, FrescoBot, MenoBot II, I dream of horses, LizzieBabes419, RjwilmsiBot, Josve05a, Bamyers99, AndrewOne, Gsarwa, GermanJoe, Senator2029, ClueBot NG, Doyna Yar, BG19bot, Hz.tiang, Adeelyounas53, BattyBot, Teammm, Cyberbot II, Mogism, 93, Me, Myself, and I are Here, Ian.Kovac, Wikiuser13, Kevin Gunaratna, Karinera, Germtimer, DaVgunter, Poiuytrewqvtaatv123321, Thenickman100, Luis150902, Peculiarwanderlust, Paultimothyjones714, Nickhui7 and Anonymous: 54

- **List of cyber-attacks** *Source:* https://en.wikipedia.org/wiki/List_of_cyber-attacks?oldid=743802383 *Contributors:* Ceyockey, Ruud Koot, Bgwhite, Econterms, Ark25, Yobot, Materialscientist, Hessamnia, GoingBatty, BG19bot, Pahlevun, Me, Myself, and I are Here, Fixuture, Ceannlann gorm, Eurocus47, Dan3141592653 and Anonymous: 4

- **2010 Japan–South Korea cyberwarfare** *Source:* https://en.wikipedia.org/wiki/2010_Japan%E2%80%93South_Korea_cyberwarfare?oldid=711452499 *Contributors:* Rpyle731, Bgwhite, Philip Trueman, Bentogoa, Niceguyedc, Boneyard90, Arjayay, Yobot, BattyBot, Kanghuitari, Stamptrader, Fixuture, 8068joshua, Kurousagi and Anonymous: 2

- **2011 PlayStation Network outage** *Source:* https://en.wikipedia.org/wiki/2011_PlayStation_Network_outage?oldid=739287833 *Contributors:* Ihcoyc, Slark, Tpbradbury, Jeffq, Graeme Bartlett, Cloud200, Mckaysalisbury, Golbez, DmitryKo, Bender235, Jtalledo, Btornado, RHaworth, Rjwilmsi, XP1, Yug, Benlisquare, Bgwhite, Hydrargyrum, Voidxor, BorgQueen, CWenger, John Broughton, Mardus, SmackBot, Ggctuk, Nahald, Prodego, C.Fred, Vorophobe, W Tanoto, Portillo, Victorgrigas, The359, Modest Genius, Muboshgu, Alphathon, Jasca Ducato, GVnayR, Cybercobra, NickPenguin, DMacks, Bob Castle, Ser Amantio di Nicolao, Axem Titanium, AGK, Mnemnoch, Mika1h, Stevo1000, Mrrightguy10, Mato, Mr. XYZ, UberMan5000, DumbBOT, X201, Nick Number, Yellowdesk, Lfstevens, Dreaded Walrus, Sonicsuns, Hello32020, Magioladitis, Cadsuane Melaidhrin, Keith D, Frontin, Little Professor, Ohms law, Uhai, Gemini1980, Gellender, Ajcadoo, Wraithdart, Addit, Rockstone35, Erier2003, Svick, JenniferHeartsU, Escape Orbit, Mild Bill Hiccup, Uncle Milty, Aria1561, Excirial, Estemshorn, Subcelestial, FaithLehaneTheVampireSlayer, M.O.X, Darkcat1, Badmachine, Ost316, Tool-apc, Addbot, Chris TC01, Protonk, Execute Robot, LuK3, Swarm, TheSuave, Yobot, EdwardLane, Fraggle81, Amirobot, JDC808, Dmarquard, AnomieBOT, Danno uk, TheRealNightRider, Trut-hurts man, RadiX, Transpar3nt, Jwojdylo, Alvin Seville, Chaheel Riens, FrescoBot, Louperibot, Shardok, TedderBot, GWPSP090, Tbhotch, Jackass2009, SEA-VAC, RjwilmsiBot, Ripchip Bot, Noommos, Elium2, CR4ZE, EmausBot, Word Logix, John of Reading, WikitanvirBot, EclecticEnnui, Gfoley4, Heymid, Dewritech, RenamedUser01302013, Rike255, Hounder4, Joker264, Funnysheep, Brandmeister, Eddievhfan1984, BrandonsLe, ChuispastonBot, ThePowerofX, BulbaThor, Rusted AutoParts, ResidentAnthropologist, ClueBot NG, Awesomeness95, Another n00b, Abdellatif Samiky, Pillow2011, Alexhch, Widr, Tblack93, Helpful Pixie Bot, M0ment0m, Kc2545, Rogington2, Wahmae, Ceradon, Imgaril, TomJackson95, Alexander Borgia, BattyBot, Cyberbot II, EuroCarGT, Dexbot, Mogism, Formenthos, Balletro, PrivateMasterHD, Frenzie23, James1345, Second Skin, Vieque, Ppeerii, Droustt, Js2008068, Jannabear, CAPTAIN RAJU, Anna.cruz676, GreenC bot and Anonymous: 92

- **2013 Singapore cyberattacks** *Source:* https://en.wikipedia.org/wiki/2013_Singapore_cyberattacks?oldid=743331881 *Contributors:* Bender235, Woohookitty, Nikkimaria, Ohconfucius, Mgiganteus1, Dl2000, Zhanzhao, Funandtrvl, Serols, Bonkers The Clown, ChrisGualtieri, DoctorKubla, Fixuture, StandNThrow and Anonymous: 10

- **2014 JPMorgan Chase data breach** *Source:* https://en.wikipedia.org/wiki/2014_JPMorgan_Chase_data_breach?oldid=722054965 *Contributors:* Rpyle731, DarTar, Ocdcntx, Yobot, VanEman and Fixuture

- **2015–16 SWIFT banking hack** *Source:* https://en.wikipedia.org/wiki/2015%E2%80%9316_SWIFT_banking_hack?oldid=732655643 *Contributors:* Chrisvls, QuackGuru, Soccer-holic, Yobot, Everymorning, Finnusertop, Parsley Man and Anonymous: 1

- **Anonplus** *Source:* https://en.wikipedia.org/wiki/Anonplus?oldid=744414839 *Contributors:* Lquilter, Klemen Kocjancic, Koavf, Ondenc, David Mörike, Brianga, Trivialist, Aj00200, Addbot, Nedim Ardoğa, Weliopark, Winner 42, ZéroBot, Status, Wbm1058, Met358, BattyBot, Dexbot, Monkbot, InternetArchiveBot and Anonymous: 7

- **Anonymous (group)** *Source:* https://en.wikipedia.org/wiki/Anonymous_(group)?oldid=744415555 *Contributors:* The Anome, Caltrop, Leandrod, Clintp, Ixfd64, Lquilter, GTBacchus, Ronabop, Ahoerstemeier, Glenn, WhisperToMe, Abscissa, Nv8200pa, Thomasedavis, Kenatipo, Mirv, Markewilliams, Bkell, Xanzzibar, Alan Liefting, DocWatson42, Ævar Arnfjörð Bjarmason, HangingCurve, Michael Devore, Nomad~enwiki, Micru, Ofus, BigBen212, Kainaw, SWAdair, SoWhy, OverlordQ, Jossi, Phil Sandifer, Phil1988, Mpesce, Ulmanor, Running, Jayjg, Discospinster, Rich Farmbrough, KillerChihuahua, FT2, Vapour, Ibagli, Bender235, Nabla, Generic~enwiki, Adambro, Themarcuscreature, John Vandenberg, Enric Naval, Wisdom89, Giraffedata, Chirag, VBGFscJUn3, Alansohn, Jhertel, Gargaj, Retran, Babajobu, Apoc2400, Sligocki, Titanium Dragon, Danhash, Geraldshields11, Jtrainor, Ron Ritzman, Natalya, ReelExterminator, DarTar, Firsfron, Muftak, Woohookitty, Digx, Theoriste, Sburke, NotSuper, Pol098, The Wordsmith, Tabletop, Hbdragon88, Scootey, El Mariachi, BD2412, Rjwilmsi, Nightscream, Jake Wartenberg, Vary, Miserlou, Bubba73, Boccobrock, Yug, DoubleBlue, Bratch, Yamamoto Ichiro, Fish and karate, Titoxd, Figs, SchuminWeb, RobertG, Nogburt, Vsion, Jw21, Katerg, Ayla, Billybobfred, Czar, Alexjohnc3, 8q67n4tqr5, TravisBatos, Spriteless, Kri, Sharkface217, Bgwhite, Gwernol, Dadu~enwiki, Wavelength, Personman, Sceptre, Hairy Dude, Jachin, Arzel, RussBot, Petrus4, TheDoober, Leftofftheark, Splette, Hydrargyrum, NawlinWiki, Rjensen, RazorICE, Genin~enwiki, Brandon, Weirdperson11, Moe Epsilon, Leotohill, Deku-shrub, BOT-Superzerocool, Jverkoey, Nlu, Intershark, FF2010, Show no mercy, LamontCranston, Joshmaul, Chase me ladies, I'm the Cavalry, Closedmouth, Th1rt3en, Nessuno834, Andjam, Smurfy, ViperSnake151, JDspeeder1, Rwwww, Karora, SmackBot, Nahald, MattieTK, YellowMonkey, Kellen, Malkinann, InverseHypercube, CompuHacker, Hydrogen Iodide, McGeddon, Verne Equinox, Stifle, Spadly, HalfShadow, Xaosflux, Kudzu1, CyberSpork, Portillo, Carbon-16, Tyciol, Chris the speller, Ziiv, Miquonranger03, SchfiftyThree, Renamed user Sloane, Farry, ZyMOS, Ned Scott, Gsp8181, WDGraham, Frap, Neo139, Addshore, Grover cleveland, Nahum Reduta, Tonerman, PiMaster3, Flyguy649, JudahH, Gabi S., Tronicum, Cybercobra, Ne0Freedom, BullRangifer, WereWolf, Kleuske, Jeremyb, Kendrick7, Can Not, Armitage~enwiki, Ohconfucius, Will Beback, Deepred6502, Llxwarbirdxll, Cast, Mukadderat, Eliyak, Robomaeyhem, MegA, JzG, Drieux,

Kuru, John, Zaphraud, DavidCooke, ZEROmegster, Thanos5150, Gobonobo, Almkglor, InsaneZeroG, VirtualDave, Tktktk, YdoUask, Scetoaux, MaximusBrood, IronGargoyle, Camilo Sanchez, Ckatz, Hanii Puppy, Slakr, Hvn0413, Beetstra, Superorange, Meco, Andyroo316, Ryulong, Manifestation, Caiaffa, Asforoneday, Stephenjudge, BranStark, Iridescent, Kencf0618, 293.xx.xxx.xx, Kernow, Stripedtiger, Elgaroo, Exander, Josh a brewer, Pjbflynn, Nephrastar, Piepie, Rdunn, Spartan948265, Weedbag, Tar7arus, The Haunted Angel, ERAGON, J Milburn, Karibou, NinjaKid, GhostStalker, KnightLago, Ferdiaob, FlyingToaster, SuperAntx, Penfish, Penbat, Necrat, Mattbuck, Equendil, Creek23, Marcuscalabresus, Jkokavec, Bellerophon5685, Ahawowow, Soetermans, Benjiboi, Synergy, Krator, DumbBOT, Ike-bana, Ebrahim, Zalgo, Satori Son, Mtijn, Epbr123, Héous, Billy Bishop, N5iln, Ace ofgabriel, Derek328, Missvain, Second Quantization, RickinBaltimore, JustAGal, Roninbk, The Fat Man Who Never Came Back, Heroeswithmetaphors, Haha169, Luna Santin, Jj137, Smartse, Danger, Credema, Wisl, Zadernet, David Shankbone, Ghmyrtle, Dorotheou, Skomorokh, Sonicsuns, Mcrfan44, Avaya1, Nthep, Hypnometal, Fetchcomms, Awilley, Bread2, Some thing, PhilKnight, Rothorpe, JDCAce, Kerotan, GoodDamon, Guy0307, Acroterion, Repku, Io Katai, Magioladitis, Bongwarrior, VoABot II, Dentren, Thatpalechick, Brandt Luke Zorn, Xb2u7Zjzc32, Khaled Khalil, Wtstar, Emptyandgray, Catgut, Giggy, Seleucus, Sno777, Little Jimmy, Mkdw, Squingynaut, Exiledone, Derilyct, Jimothy scrye, Youdummy, Coffeepusher, Connor Behan, Kayau, Thompson.matthew, CeeWhy2, Chugsworth, Ztobor, Qweniden, Adlerschloß, Rzrscm, Dorchester83, InnocuousPseudonym, Keith D, Mad Drunk, Beofan, CommonsDelinker, AlexiusHoratius, EvilHom3r, Juventas, RockMFR, J.delanoy, Captain panda, Aaron Bongart, Richiekim, Discott, C.A.T.S. CEO, Nigholith, Ymirfrostgiant, Neon white, Patronise, Dkendr, Shawn in Montreal, McSly, Peblairman, Crakkpot, P4k, Anonywiki, Kaylahawk, Es187, Aar, Knulclunk, DadaNeem, Fongyun, Flatterworld, Mufka, Steve Murray, Dragonbutt120, Joshua Issac, Juliancolton, Toxic Ninja, Kidlittle, Cometstyles, S02178, Jevansen, Noah Benham, Supervegeta37, Ajfweb, Wikimandia, Useight, Ruukasu2005, Priceman86, Nikthestunned, UnicornTapestry, VolkovBot, ABF, Riraito, Jeff G., Indubitably, Jedravent, Philip Trueman, Af648, Xtoothxpastex, Oshwah, Thomas d stewart, GDonato, Bozonessinc, Vi Veri Veniversum Vivus Vici, Jason C.K., Seraphim, Supertask, AllGloryToTheHypnotoad, LeaveSleaves, JayMaslar, TaborG, Redmagemp3, Maxim, Anyquestions, Billinghurst, Michaeldsuarez, Haseo9999, Benchilada, Roman619, Bahamut0013, Gojira87, Seresin, C45207, Justmeherenow, Sardaka, Edkollin, Dessymona, Gamsbart, Bitbut, Nagy, DarthBotto, Munci, Jitenya, De1337, Korosuke, DigitalC, EJF, Coffee, CotyXD, Caulde, Jim E. Black, Jauerback, Gerakibot, Mungo Kitsch, Yuefairchild, X-Fi6, Crash Underride, Starius, Keilana, Toddst1, Tiptoety, Arbor to SJ, Boston Prodigy, Jc-SOCO, Cyberjaz, Oxymoron83, Lightmouse, Techman224, Hobartimus, Alex.muller, AngelTrigger, RiseDarthVader, Ahangar-e-Gaz, Apavlides24, Dillard421, Svick, RDVoDkA, Capitalismojo, AlexCatlin, Tesi1700, Hamiltondaniel, RedmonkeyVII, Yair rand, Geoff Plourde, Akldawgs, Troy 07, MaxwellHansen, Linkednet, RobinHood70, Cjhard, Wikipedian-Marlith, Kakama5, Martarius, Sfan00 IMG, FlamingSilmaril, ClueBot, Classic Fan, Artichoker, Hutcher, Snigbrook, Infoeco, Starkiller88, Ice-Unshattered, Leopedia2, Mx3, Fixingit, Arakunem, Sfiga, L.cash.m, Liekmudkipz, Frmorrison, Mild Bill Hiccup, Zeldageekchannel, TBustah, Razor Ramon, Niceguyedc, Bokan, Fendue, Marselan, Trivialist, ZerglingChamp, William Ortiz, Rprpr, Cirt, Luckyhalo, Adjustdis, The Scarlet Letter, Sirius85, DragonBot, Butthax, Stepshep, Alexbot, Mack-the-random, CrazyChemGuy, MantisEars, Inthenameofmine, Ottre, Eeekster, John Nevard, Vivio Testarossa, Dr DBW, Rhododendrites, Sun Creator, Anonymous reader, NuclearWarfare, Ice Cold Beer, Arjayay, Lacelotte, Chicagomusicfan, GiantMidget, Joseph Leito, Eleven Special, H7a, La Pianista, Thingg, Advanstra, Dance With The Devil, Versus22, Simon Villeneuve, Belchfire, Tommosimmo, Wnt, Goodvac, Vanished user uih38riiw4hjlsd, Psychcf, Bearsona, BarretB, XLinkBot, Watchman Rorschach, Chairsenses, AnotherSolipsist, Cremington, Poison Pen, Z00r, WikHead, Netrat, Galzigler, Mifter, Ziggy Sawdust, Arabik, Mm40, Colliric, Saltyfishinc, MystBot, Tchalvakspam, Swytch1990, Truthseeq, Good Olfactory, WPjcm, RyanCross, Belfunk, TWMM91, T3hpaul33n2, Otterathome, Mortense, Nashez, Grayfell, Wickford, Kelly, Imeriki al-Shimoni, Twaz, Vidber, Anon031408, RobBarr, Bomblol, SUSA ltd, Sairith, VCHunter, Nohomers48, Chris19910, Fieldday-sunday, Nathrael, FrunkSpace, Wikigodz, MrOllie, Protonk, Proxima Centauri, Iwasamap, Lulzwut, Paulfetchisfail, LAAFan, Bfair2mychurch, Dyaa, Bassbonerocks, LULZEPIXHAHAHAHAHA, Evilawesome, Avazelda13, Vespa-Girl64, Tehdewd, Ninja9, Roux, Teirriblechan, Lotharsrevenge, George Gastin, CuteHappyBrute, Taopman, 84user, Evildeathmath, R3ap3R, Captain Obvious and his crime-fighting dog, Shaqadim, Ivanov id, SasiSasi, Balabiot, Jarble, Nonary, Gravelz, Ableapart, Ben Ben, Zell65, Luckas-bot, Yobot, 2D, Themfromspace, Monk1andahalf, Kroova, Cflm001, II MusLiM HyBRiD II, Zenkaizer, Amirobot, SyntheticProsthetic, LisaKachold, THEN WHO WAS PHONE?, Reenem, Blackfish711, Kwacka, Ningauble, DrFleischman, Guypimpin, Munchenoriginal, Againme, Vörös, IcemanCrogonk, Sepan, Dmarquard, Danielspencer2, Clayton on Crack, Bility, AnomieBOT, Dendiphi, VanishedUser sdu9aya9fasdsopa, Destroyer666, Arkbg, Sagaci, Damngoths, Umbrellanon, Placemanan, Name that hasnt been used, Six words, Galoubet, Cptnono, Piano non troppo, M15t3r53xy, Wealliekmudkipz, Quispiam, Joel Amos, Tehori, L3lackEyedAngels, Law, Ulric1313, Rulesoneand2, -Butthurt Miscavige-, Flewis, Squeakurs, Dfgdsfgasggsdf, Nobalss, Materialscientist, Soonr34, Are you ready for IPv6?, Ritualistic1986, Fear 2 Stop, Henceearly, Ninjasaif, McrashLog, Fourgreatlulz, Deliafcipe, Ploploplop, Legionzim, ArthurBot, Impoverished Flour, LilHelpa, The Firewall, Execoot, Gurgle528, Carturo222, Xqbot, S h i v a (Visnu), Spidern, Tomot010, Wutudidthere...isawit, Capricorn42, Theliesofmistera, EvenBetter, Xxblackhawkxxx, Joshuaingram, Toa Nidhiki05, Tad Lincoln, Delehaye, Mechanic1c, PsuedoName, Julle, Srich32977, Cazza157, Doctorx0079, LVAustrian, GrouchoBot, The will shall be done, StealthCopyEditor, Wonderflonium, Smurdah, Corruptie-van-lulz, Y1ff1nH3ll, CalmCalamity, Witticism, Multixfer, Houghcon, JediMaster362, Irisred, Raining Zeppelins, Xiuhtecutli, Seventests777, Smallman12q, Richard BB, Yevrowl, Stiepan Pietrov, Aaron Kauppi, JonIsaksen, Green Cardamom, Tktru, GTNz, LucienBOT, Amuletxheart, Megapeen, D'ohBot, Cs32en, Citation bot 1, Mimzy1990, Vicenarian, 5Celcious, GatorSlayerFSU, Deunick, Scoundr3l, Half price, ReneJohnsen, Reanimated X, RedBot, Gingermint, Σ, ScottMHoward, Swalgal, Kevintampa5, Alexey Izbyshev, Xeworlebi, Dy2007, SIbuff, Arbero, Indexme, Tuxedage, Trappist the monk, Itsmaec, MorbidChid, 122589423KM, Lotje, Dinamik-bot, Roy McCoy, Shagyman, Zpconn, Purplepox01, Merlinsorca, Diannaa, Stephen MUFC, Tbhotch, ArishiaNishi, Jfmantis, RjwilmsiBot, Xaltotun, TjBot, Ripchip Bot, Phlegat, Lopifalko, Becritical, AnAbsolutelyOriginalUsername42, Knoxjeff, Chibby0ne, Nihola, DASHBot, Makassarpanassekali, PcGnome, EmausBot, Acather96, WikitanvirBot, Semperlibre, Ghostofnemo, Surlyduff50, Sophie, Gigrantula, Physics16, GoingBatty, Jadeslair, Zagoury, RenamedUser01302013, Toonmonk, Qrsdogg, TuneyLoon, Captain Ran, Elvenmuse, TeleComNasSprVen, Rkononenko, JoshuaGolbez, Wcpeterson, AvicBot, HiW-Bot, ZéroBot, QuentinUK, NathanielTheBold, Shuipzv3, Jaydiem, Rainbowofpeace, AOC25, H3llBot, Francis York Morgan, Wagner, May Cause Dizziness, Ocaasi, Moomoopashoo, Xsahilx, Demiurge1000, Labnoor, Kawadri, TheProphet1993, Wiggles007, Podgod, Brandmeister, Rostz, Xsythe, Conwilcon, QWERTY531, Inswoon, XRiamux, BadaBoom, Cymbelmineer, Sugar-Baby-Love, ChuispastonBot, ThePowerofX, EdoBot, Kartasto, JohnnyLurg, Woolfy123, ClueBot NG, Dager2345, TT-97976, WIERDGREENMAN, Tschis, Shrewmania, Drwwht, Kleio, DokReggar, BiLlYpItZeR, Tejasrnbr, TehAnonymous, Levdr1, Dru of Id, TacfuJecan, Jamesmax01, Night Ranger, Tr00rle, Hakermania, Puppynose, Tblack93, Educatedseacucumber, Miros 0571, Dougmcdonell, Penyulap, North Atlanticist Usonian, Helpful Pixie Bot, Thisthat2011, Levardi, Kondi, Wbm1058, Fancyflyboy, BG19bot, DrJimothyCatface, Hodeken, Skullcandle, Tuxmascot, Northamerica1000, Puramyun31, ZombieRamen, I7laseral, ComputerJA, Graham11, Malnormalulo, Wiki13, Nathan2055, Cometcaster, AvocatoBot, Badon, A Dirty Watermelon, Compfreak7, FutureTrillionaire, Dainomite, Turnhout, Jeancey, North911, Smmmaniruzzaman, Peboki, Sumit8158, Minsbot, Angelina Souren, Shaun, Dreambeaver, BattyBot, Mdann52, Ben525, Gazkthul, Cyberbot II, ChrisGualtieri, Blue Eagle 21063, Arrivalatheathrowairport, Khazar2, Ciaran Sinclair, Dobie80, Marek3571, Rezonansowy, Mogism, Kbog, Kephir, KingBrooke, Cerabot~enwiki, NFLisAwesome, Yoshiman6464, Megaminxwin, ProfessorTofty, AldezD, Eleventhblock, Sowlos, Mfwnoface, Zziccardi, Death35, ChristophThomas, Vrave98, TheBlueCanoe, Epicgenius, Kap 7, Toksoz, Soffredo, Leaxe, Drspidr100, Hexatekin, IranitGreenberg, Buffbills7701, D Eaketts, Seriouslyonlyusernameleft, Bboppy, Noyster, Liz, Scaniaman188, Fixture, Second Skin, Learjet60guy, Ejaz92, DFVV92, Bilorv, Jaqoc, Mquantum, Dobrate0831, Csbisbee, Seen a Mike, KBH96, Insertcleverphrasehere, Wikiguys12, ChamithN, CitiV, Hollth, Zppix, Kidsankyran, Rosonolicts'sk, Salvebrutta, Evan.foote, Wikia6969, Gary dah bookw0rm, Grammarian3.14159265359, KasparBot, Wikisbyjulie, Funny648, The Professor123, JoshBM16, Deranged economist, InternetArchiveBot, Floyd M. Bunsen, JJMC89 bot, Invisible Guy, Electricbees, GreenC bot, 0x5849857, StaedtlerTheOnLy, Pyotr Luzhin and Anonymous: 356

- **Antisec Movement** *Source:* https://en.wikipedia.org/wiki/Antisec_Movement?oldid=739045802 *Contributors:* Edward, IceKarma, Secretlondon, Pmsyyz, Alansohn, RichardWeiss, Vegaswikian, Miserlou, Ground Zero, Benlisquare, Welsh, Slicing, Ninly, E Wing, SmackBot, Rtc, Mauls, Thumperward, Frap, Flyguy649, Derek R Bullamore, Robofish, Gogo Dodo, Marek69, Jazzeur, Destynova, Fbi04, Largoplazo, Michaeldsuarez, Bentogoa, Jojalozzo, ClueBot, John Nevard, Bearsona, Fastily, Addbot, MrOllie, Download, OlEnglish, Skippy le Grand Gourou, Yobot, AnomieBOT, PabloCastellano, DSisyphBot, Amaury, DrilBot, Nowayover, Jdou, Whiteh8, Antisec, Manfromthemoon, Lotje, Nandi1986, EugeneKay, Tremaster, DASHBot, Wikitoov, VorSec, Gamepro127, ClueBot NG, Widr, Helpful Pixie Bot, Guydmann, Cyberbot II, Fixture, Saectar, AKS.9955, SantiLak, Orthogonal1, NotaDick, Frightsec, GreenC bot and Anonymous: 60

- **Ashley Madison data breach** *Source:* https://en.wikipedia.org/wiki/Ashley_Madison_data_breach?oldid=744226517 *Contributors:* Bueller 007, Fuzheado, Bender235, MarnetteD, Intgr, Deku-shrub, ViperSnake151, Greenshed, Bilby, Dl2000, Kencf0618, Gaijin42, Spudst3r, KConWiki, JMyrleFuller, Connor Behan, 97198, Wikimandia, Drmargi, Flounder19, RJaguar3, Niceguyedc, JasonAQuest, Another Believer, Callinus, Editorofthewiki, XLinkBot, Dsimic, TotientDragooned, FreeRangeFrog, Jsharpminor, PM800, Green Cardamom, Arfed, MrX, Schwede66, Jim Michael, ClueBot NG, BG19bot, Brustopher, Biosthmors, Thebuck093, Cwobeel, AldezD, Corn cheese, Glencoco8995, FiredanceThroughTheNight, Fixture, 22merlin, Carriebranch, Strongjam, Eon2004, FivePillarPurist, NewHikaru07, Romancerc, Cagepanes, Elyot89 and Anonymous: 30

- **Operation Aurora** *Source:* https://en.wikipedia.org/wiki/Operation_Aurora?oldid=739503708 *Contributors:* Julesd, Conti, Echarp, DHN, Neutrality, Avenue, Richwales, Firsfron, Apokrif, BD2412, Vegaswikian, Benlisquare, JoltinJoe, Bdell555, Arthur Rubin, Modify, JLaTondre, SmackBot, Midway, Cla68, Skizzik, Telempe, Cattus, Frap, Underbar dk, Ohconfucius, DavidBailey, Jesse Viviano, Cydebot, Odysseus654, JohnInDC, Bobby fletcher, Strausszek, PhiLiP, Widefox, DagosNavy, Ian Bailey, Jiguso, Andareed, Emergentchaos, Psyche825, Hac13, Flwyd, ClueBot, Eegorr, Ottawahitech, Rprpr, Socrates2008, SF007, XLinkBot, Addbot, Louperivois, Drpickem, Luckas-bot, Yobot, DeltaSPARTAN003, AnomieBOT, VanishedUser sdu9aya9fasdsopa, Pm4Gn, Arilang1234, LilHelpa, Carrag, Tomwsulcer, Thorenn, Gene-va, Swalgal, December21st2012Freak, Pownerus, RjwilmsiBot, Look2See1, Gscarp12, 632eb412137f2a08d72f2372cc95c7ce, Cybercitizen123, Tenomk, Jeffrey Hiday, Homunculus, Sabres87, Mumbojumbo 101, ZéroBot, TomCaines, EneMsty12, Erianna, Brandmeister, Erget2005, Tijfo098, Catlemur, Widr, Timlograsso, Gyrotooka, M0rphzone, SoledadKabocha, And16kmsouth, Derkommander0916, Monkbot, Limestoneforest, ICPSGWU, Star72, Prinsgezinde, Yasuo Miyakawa, QuantumBogosort and Anonymous: 54

- **Aurora Generator Test** *Source:* https://en.wikipedia.org/wiki/Aurora_Generator_Test?oldid=736969662 *Contributors:* IceKarma, Vsmith, Nikkimaria, Arthur Rubin, Fromeout11, Widefox, Hugo999, Johnfos, Josejuan05, Erier2003, MatthewVanitas, Maslen, Yobot and Anonymous: 9

- **2016 Bangladesh Bank heist** *Source:* https://en.wikipedia.org/wiki/2016_Bangladesh_Bank_heist?oldid=742868153 *Contributors:* Kaldari, Chrisvls, Gcbirzan, Patl, The Rambling Man, Mauls, Jayanta Sen, Tdl1060, Howard the Duck, Iridescent, Gogo Dodo, Fconaway, Joshua Issac, Gene93k, Faizul Latif Chowdhury, Yobot, Worldbruce, AnomieBOT, Supergabbyshoe, I dream of horses, Hariboneagle927, BG19bot, Dubk, Bagoto, David.moreno72, RioHondo, Shhhhwwww!!, Wbakeriii, Fuebaey, TagaSanPedroAko, SomeRandomPasserby, Boss RA, JoshMuir-Wikipedia, ESAD-Hooker, Sorrc, RakeshAsh, DispostableEE, Randall Tor and Anonymous: 19

- **2010 cyberattacks on Myanmar** *Source:* https://en.wikipedia.org/wiki/2010_cyberattacks_on_Myanmar?oldid=739234916 *Contributors:* Koavf, Mikeblas, Cydebot, Heroeswithmetaphors, DagosNavy, Kumioko (renamed), Fadesga, Dthomsen8, DASHBot, Dondervogel 2, Phyo WP, Muffin Wizard, BattyBot, Sawol, Sociorobot, Bravesirrobinranaway, GreenC bot and Anonymous: 4

- **Cellphone surveillance** *Source:* https://en.wikipedia.org/wiki/Cellphone_surveillance?oldid=740171234 *Contributors:* BD2412, RadioFan, Deku-shrub, Gogo Dodo, Doug Weller, LuckyLouie, JamesBWatson, Tokyogirl79, Flyer22 Reborn, Elassint, Ehrenkater, TracyMcClark, GoingBatty, Dcirovic, Josve05a, Palosirkka, ClueBot NG, Northamerica1000, Wuerzele, Flat Out, Dannyruthe, Filedelinkerbot, Ruhrcools, Brutemenu, Oisecycle, Angieclick, Meterclassification, Dirtyelecto99, Wefliwehjfliwhelfh, Ghosts556, Briankennethswain, Geny S. Soboes and Anonymous: 17

- **Commission on Elections data breach** *Source:* https://en.wikipedia.org/wiki/Commission_on_Elections_data_breach?oldid=733024983 *Contributors:* Kkmurray, WayKurat, Heran et Sang'gres, LilHelpa, Steve Quinn, SkyHigher, Hariboneagle927, BG19bot, Fixture, Boss RA, BSrap, Kevin Trawma and Anonymous: 2

- **Cyber attack during the Paris G20 Summit** *Source:* https://en.wikipedia.org/wiki/Cyber_attack_during_the_Paris_G20_Summit?oldid=538973833 *Contributors:* TiMike, Millelacs and Sociorobot

- **Cyberattacks during the Russo-Georgian War** *Source:* https://en.wikipedia.org/wiki/Cyberattacks_during_the_Russo-Georgian_War?oldid=739134189 *Contributors:* Gadfium, Mzajac, KNewman, Vsmith, YUL89YYZ, MBisanz, John Vandenberg, Jeodesic, Anthony Appleyard, Kober, Woohookitty, Ardfern, Flamingspinach, Cuchullain, Friejose, Koavf, Russavia, Black Falcon, Nikkimaria, SmackBot, Hmains, Meco, Cydebot, DumbBOT, DagosNavy, Pleckaitis, JaGa, Hodja Nasreddin, Nug, Digwuren, Dans, Mayalld, Kanonkas, ImageRemovalBot, Niceguyedc, Nymf, XLinkBot, Good Olfactory, Yobot, Extremepro, AnomieBOT, FeelSunny, FrescoBot, FriscoKnight, Jandalhandler, Lotje, RjwilmsiBot, Dixtosa, H3llBot, Zabanio, Nearearth, PussBroad, UA Victory, Elysans, GreenC bot and Anonymous: 14

- **CyberBerkut** *Source:* https://en.wikipedia.org/wiki/CyberBerkut?oldid=742374586 *Contributors:* Rpyle731, Vsmith, Dennis Brown, Rwxrwxrwx, Arthur Rubin, Jprg1966, Yulia Romero, Bejnar, General Ization, Cydebot, Nick Number, Johnpacklambert, Capsot, Lvivske, Niceguyedc, MilNwsCurator, Rhododendrites, AnomieBOT, Yevrowl, Hell in a Bucket, GoingBatty, Zezen, Catlemur, BG19bot, EdwardRech, RGloucester, Anidaat, B01010100, Dctrzl, Cryptingnet, Monplait, Stewi101015, JJMC89 bot and Anonymous: 12

- **Cyberterrorism** *Source:* https://en.wikipedia.org/wiki/Cyberterrorism?oldid=741839143 *Contributors:* Delirium, Goatasaur, Jeejee, Ronz, GCarty, WhisperToMe, Furrykef, Fvw, Jamesday, Francs2000, Sdedeo, Lowellian, Sverdrup, Meelar, Hadal, GreatWhiteNortherner, Alan Liefting, David Gerard, Dbenbenn, Sinned, Xinoph, AlistairMcMillan, Golbez, Piotrus, Jossi, AndrewKeenanRichardson, Klemen Kocjancic, Twinxor, Pmsyyz, Zappaz, Antaeus Feldspar, Bender235, Loren36, RoyBoy, Alansohn, Eleland, Walter Görlitz, MattWade, Velella, Tony Sidaway, LFaraone, H2g2bob, Johntex, Firsfron, Woohookitty, Stefanomione, Peatoneil, Descendall, Sjakkalle, Rjwilmsi, Jbamb, JamesEG, FlaBot, Vsion, RexNL, Gurch, Chobot, Benvenuto, Dadu~enwiki, YurikBot, Seegoon, Nlu, FlooK, Emijrp, Closedmouth, Vicarious, 7Train, Anticrash, John Broughton, IslandHopper973, SmackBot, Richardkselby, Gilliam, Betacommand, Lakshmin, Chris the speller, Bluebot, H2ppyme, MK8, Can't sleep, clown will eat me, Nixeagle, Edivorce, Abmac, John, Gobonobo, Accurizer, Nobunaga24, Mr. Vernon, NJMauthor, Hu12, HisSpaceResearch, Joseph Solis in Australia, James pic, Trocisp, Abdullahzzam, Themightyquill, Cydebot, Thijs!bot, RisingStar, A3RO, Ludde23, Luminarie, Dawnseeker2000, Tennisuser123, AntiVandalBot, Luna Santin, Aniyochanan, Cjs2111, Modernist, Falconleaf, Qwerty Binary, Dreaded Walrus, Magioladitis, JamesBWatson, Garygoldstein, Esanchez7587, CliffC, Sjjupadhyay~enwiki, Anaxial, Srielity, J.delanoy, Athaenara, Octopus-Hands, AntiSpamBot, NewEnglandYankee, Olegwiki, STBotD, Burzmali, SoCalSuperEagle, AlnoktaBOT, Colarik, Fences and windows, Lunadesign, Aesopos, Philip Trueman, Porjo, Dchall1, Pmedema, Martin451, Kcraten, Fletcherman, Kurowoofwoof111, Rsnbrgr, Oth, Tachikoma's All Memory, Glenjenvey, SieBot, Ostap R, Grieferhate, Ractive1, Flyer22 Reborn, Toryblue, Steven Crossin, Miyokan, Dc3tech, ClueBot, Zeerak88, The Thing That Should Not Be, Mookie25, Laudak, Stfun00bs, Alexbot, Erebus Morgaine, Suttonmas214, Rhododendrites, Islaammaged126, Tnxman307, Joshua 1 16, Light show, DumZiBoT, Kgcoleman, Gabeten, Archie888, Bamford, Scostigan, WikiDao, Jaanusele, Addbot, Willking1979, Melab-1, Proxima Centauri, Tyw7, CuteHappyBrute, Luckas-bot, Yobot, Fraggle81, Brushed clean, AnomieBOT, Jim1138, Bluerasberry, Materialscientist, SanjayTilaiyan, Citation bot, ChrisGilb, LilHelpa, Xqbot, Zad68, DBCubix, Capricorn42, DJScias, Shadowjams, FrescoBot, Bobbymax12, Sidna, Citation bot 1, Pinethicket, I dream of horses, Yotna, A412, MastiBot, Serols, Mentmic, Cnwilliams, Thejokerface, Lotje, Callanecc, Mean as custard, RjwilmsiBot, HeinzzzderMannn, Belomorkanal, Blade8603, Rayman60, Life in General, Natesagirl, Cogiati, George-lt, Aeonx, Techsciences, SporkBot, Erianna, Qao-bou, Dylan Flaherty, Zabanio, Cat10001a, ClueBot NG, Cwmhiraeth, Gareth Griffith-Jones, Jack Greenmaven, Silv the Something, Rawkage, GoldenGlory84, Snotbot, Frietjes, Biosketch, Marechal Ney, Widr, Ximar, Helpful Pixie Bot, Titodutta, Dukes08, BG19bot, BendelacBOT, AvocatoBot, Mark Arsten, BattyBot, David.moreno72, Bcb3-NJITWILL, Justincy, MadGuy7023, FoCuSandLeArN, Guijoocho, Jackninja5, Riverstogo, Frosty, Buterchiken, Ansdub, 069952497a, Me, Myself, and I are Here, Cowie97, Chantastique, Dr Dinosaur IV, Zordsthrone, A.sky245, Futuregray, Amanda.kowalek, ArchPope Sextus VI, JaconaFrere, Germtimer, Monkbot, Jbowne29, StaceyHutter, AJFU, DirkvVeldhuizen, Some Gadget Geek, Pblowry, GeneralizationsAreBad, Amccann421, Tejalpatel, Tpdwkouaa, Imiăriet, Blackdevil 69, Rudra Protap Chackraborty and Anonymous: 288

- **Cyberwarfare in China** *Source:* https://en.wikipedia.org/wiki/Cyberwarfare_in_China?oldid=739405211 *Contributors:* Julesd, Tpbradbury, Altenmann, Xanzzibar, Icairns, Vsmith, Bender235, Art LaPella, Woohookitty, John Hill, Cantorman, Arthur Rubin, SmackBot, Cla68, Hmains, Skizzik, Cattus, Snori, Ohconfucius, Cydebot, Hcobb, Fayenatic london, Smartse, DagosNavy, Richard1990, KathleenSeidel, GrahamHardy, Hugo999, Dillard421, Nolelover, Yobot, AnomieBOT, FeelSunny, Vreelacj, RjwilmsiBot, Vco123, GoingBatty, Rigley, GermanJoe, Xanchester, BrekekekexKoaxKoax, Intelgirl5, Helpful Pixie Bot, Cyberbot II, Codename Lisa, Wetrace, TheBlueCanoe, Evano1van, New worl, ICPSGWU, GreenC bot and Anonymous: 40

- **Cyxymu** *Source:* https://en.wikipedia.org/wiki/Cyxymu?oldid=742374687 *Contributors:* Mingwangx, Pmsyyz, Grutness, Alansohn, Gargaj, BanyanTree, Ekem, Koavf, Teiladnam, DMS, Mahdiislam, Meco, Cydebot, Tocino, Waacstats, Moscvitch, Colchicum, Secleinteer, VolkovBot, Swliv, NiggardlyNorm, Thorncrag, Martarius, Muro Bot, Addbot, Jfry3, Caio Brandão Costa, Pantz12, Gddoe, RjwilmsiBot, Snotbot, KasparBot, JJMC89 bot and Anonymous: 8

- **2007 cyberattacks on Estonia** *Source:* https://en.wikipedia.org/wiki/2007_cyberattacks_on_Estonia?oldid=731530714 *Contributors:* Conti, Greenrd, Lysy, BigHaz, Rich Farmbrough, Vsmith, Vecrumba, Ency, Richard Arthur Norton (1958-), Woohookitty, Ardfern, Pehlakas, Vanished user 05, Rjwilmsi, Frlejose, Koavf, Naraht, John Baez, Russavia, RussBot, Alex Bakharev, ExRat, Suva, Mysid, Arthur Rubin, Elfalem, SmackBot, Taavi2302, Darius Dhlomo, Veni Markovski, Ohconfucius, JLogan, Mukadderat, Mathiasrex, Robofish, EdC~enwiki, Sander Säde, Borism, Bwoodcock, Cydebot, Otto4711, MLWilson, DagosNavy, Magioladitis, Pleckaitis, Cdiasoh, Pfleegerc, Hodja Nasreddin, Hillock65, Nug, Una Smith, Rsnbrgr, Oth, Kevinfromhk, Digwuren, Alexia Death, Ptrt, RJ CG, CaptainIron555, Treekids, Miyokan, ClueBot, Alexbot, John Nevard, Acabashi, MystBot, Good Olfactory, Jaanusele, Addbot, KnowledgeHegemonyPart2, Rejectwater, Luckas-bot, Yobot, AnomieBOT, 1exec1, Jim1138, Thedeadcow, Xqbot, AudeBot, Tyrol5, Arni.leibovits, Twirligig, Leavit2stever, Kyng, MerlLinkBot, Airborne84, Citation bot 1, FriscoKnight, Theissue, RjwilmsiBot, AsceticRose, Zabanio, Jnorthdur, Groberts1980, Cerabot~enwiki and Anonymous: 48

- **GhostNet** *Source:* https://en.wikipedia.org/wiki/GhostNet?oldid=727435631 *Contributors:* William Avery, Caltrop, Michael Hardy, EdH, Adam Bishop, Tempshill, Nurg, Jondel, JerryFriedman, Ancheta Wis, Piotrus, Canterbury Tail, Vsmith, Jnestorius, Rammer, Sukiari, Jonathunder, Dismas, Jackhynes, Camw, Laneb2005, Cbdorsett, Rjwilmsi, Bob A, Toby Douglass, AySz88, Mahlon, Benlisquare, Bgwhite, NawlinWiki, Mysid, Arthur Rubin, BorgQueen, ViperSnake151, SmackBot, Midway, Nil Einne, Mauls, Skizzik, GoldDragon, Cattus, Thumperward, J. Spencer, Rrburke, Andrei Stroe, Ohconfucius, Loadmaster, HongQiGong, Jim101, Old Guard, Cydebot, Studerby, Difluoroethene, Joowwww, Nick Number, Widefox, Seaphoto, Leuqarte, Sanchom, Andreas Toth, Rainpat, JaGa, WLU, Atulsnischal, Sm8900, Lilac Soul, J.delanoy, All Is One, Nineteenninetyfour, WLRoss, Saibod, Broadbot, UnitedStatesian, Bearian, ARUNKUMAR P.R, Kbrose, Calliopejen1, Techman224, SimonTrew, LarRan, Tomdobb, ClueBot, Artichoker, Pi zero, Blanchardb, Alexbot, M4gnum0n, Ottre, Human.v2.0, Netanel h, Lx 121, Wnt, XLinkBot, AgnosticPreachersKid, Addbot, Alsoam, MrOllie, Green Squares, Tide rolls, Zorrobot, Frehley, DisillusionedBitterAndKnackered, Goodmorningworld, AnomieBOT, Chedorlaomer, Choij, Rjanag, Lapost, Xqbot, Dilyn, SixBlueFish, SD5, TenuredProfessorAtPrivateUniversity, Yotomak, CoachPE, MidiWhisk, FreeWilliam, M Haoran, HKcitizen1, Bchern, Moldycrow, Shirley-BK, PorkchopLarue, Metaluscorp, HamburgerRadio, Citation bot 1, Miracle Pen, ZhBot, RjwilmsiBot, Lopifalko, Scarp12, TuHan-Bot, H3llBot, EneMsty12, Bradleyjefferson, BG19bot, Gyrotooka, PhnomPencil, Cyberbot II, ChrisGualtieri, TheBlueCanoe, Toksoz, Fixuture, Monkbot, Mstelfox, Bootvito2423 and Anonymous: 91

- **Great Hacker War** *Source:* https://en.wikipedia.org/wiki/Great_Hacker_War?oldid=737907323 *Contributors:* Modster, Dysprosia, Raul654, Tesseract~enwiki, Pengo, Everyking, Mboverload, Long John Silver~enwiki, Chmod007, Thedangerouskitchen, Adrian~enwiki, InShaneee, Circuitloss, H2g2bob, Recury, Markaci, Mindmatrix, Professor Ninja, Myleslong, Amatus, Kbdank71, Josh Parris, Quale, Collins.mc, Evil Eccentric, Fish and karate, Conscious, CambridgeBayWeather, Rwwww, Snottily, SmackBot, Amcbride, Rtc, 6Akira7, TrancedOut, Durova, Bluebot, Renamed user Sloane, Frap, Edivorce, Gimbij, Xionbox, SubSeven, Twas Now, Rokstr, Vanisaac, CmdrObot, Cameron Roy, Cydebot,

Miss Dark, Mdawg728, Netw1z, Spartaz, DagosNavy, Midderwe, Chromancer, Chahax, WereSpielChequers, Matt Brennen, Sephiroth storm, Sensible matters, Micron713, Download, Lightbot, Jarble, AnomieBOT, Mark abene, Dewritech, Foodlegs, LWG, ClueBot NG, St4rh4kr, The Last Arietta, Lordtennyson, Ksauh2o, Woowoosec and Anonymous: 59

- **July 2009 cyber attacks** *Source:* https://en.wikipedia.org/wiki/July_2009_cyber_attacks?oldid=739044881 *Contributors:* Petersam, Art LaPella, Nsaa, Alansohn, Tiger Khan, LjL, Benlisquare, Geg, Bullzeye, RUL3R, FlyingPenguins, Intershark, Malekhanif, BorgQueen, Smack-Bot, Midway, Skizzik, Fredvanner, Smallbones, Cesium 133, Mgiganteus1, PRRfan, Aeternus, The editor1, Bellerophon5685, Maziotis, Louis Waweru, Colin MacLaurin, DagosNavy, J.delanoy, Truthanado, AdRock, Jerryobject, Kys951, Autumn Wind, LarRan, Phyte, ClueBot, Bearsona, Addbot, Roaring Siren, Protonk, Nguoimay, Debresser, Numbo3-bot, عبد الفتاح أحمد محمد, Yobot, Seloloving, AnomieBOT, Yeshua-David, Galoubet, Daviessimo, Mark Schierbecker, Phillipe Israel, Javert, John Kronenwetter, Casimirpo, Anonauthor, Odessaukrain2, Urbanus et instructus, HP Lovecraft The Second, BoBoIsGod, Mayor of Gotham City, JimDiller, Whywhenwhohow, Wikipelli, H3llBot, Bomazi, Snotbot, Cyberbot II, Soda drinker, GreenC bot and Anonymous: 47

- **June 25 cyber terror** *Source:* https://en.wikipedia.org/wiki/June_25_cyber_terror?oldid=693583862 *Contributors:* Davidcannon, Niceguyedc, Frietjes, Kurousagi and German pop music

- **Lazarus Group** *Source:* https://en.wikipedia.org/wiki/Lazarus_Group?oldid=741568042 *Contributors:* Bearcat, CommonsDelinker, Yobot, SwisterTwister, ThePowerofX, Finnusertop, Jake6767 and Anonymous: 5

- **Lizard Squad** *Source:* https://en.wikipedia.org/wiki/Lizard_Squad?oldid=742809293 *Contributors:* Xanzzibar, Nsh, WikiPediaAid, Macaddct1984, MZMcBride, Deku-shrub, Nick-D, Frap, Only, Majora4, Gogo Dodo, Mazaru, OhanaUnited, Swpb, Jessicapierce, Keith D, Jack007, TrueCRaysball, Artichoker, Gene93k, Doloco, Rhododendrites, Dthomsen8, Ronhjones, Mjsa, DerM, Yobot, AnomieBOT, Materialscientist, Cullen328, Lotje, Vaypertrail, NameIsRon, ThePowerofX, ClueBot NG, Satellizer, Chjb, BG19bot, Faissaloo, 3hunna, Mogism, GabeIglesia, Corn cheese, Superusergeneric, Everymorning, Haminoon, Crou, Finnusertop, D Eaketts, Fixuture, Dizzyzane, Foia req, EoRdE6, Rubbish computer, SwiGGish, F7020, Lizard Script Kid, Scranton16, Okimnotcool, Anonymous0192837465, Anonymous643267, L.J. Bolton, McEC16, L1T5YAZXBF OP4D1ULI7L NB4DJ265Z5 MQ9YI10E0V 9VSKAIZQT2, TheTMOBGaming2, Anarchyte, Srednuas Lenoroc, Keira1996, SummerPhDv2.0, RaymondBrown and Anonymous: 6

- **LulzRaft** *Source:* https://en.wikipedia.org/wiki/LulzRaft?oldid=702353371 *Contributors:* Hydrargyrum, Eptin, BlindWanderer, Magioladitis, Oshwah, Ragingcamel, Addbot, Materialscientist, ArticCynda, Qrsdogg, ZéroBot, Wagner, AndyTheGrump, Helpsome, FlyingAce015, NZSNIPER, Phantomlordy and Anonymous: 3

- **Moonlight Maze** *Source:* https://en.wikipedia.org/wiki/Moonlight_Maze?oldid=740379693 *Contributors:* Danski14, RJFJR, Dismas, Nuggetboy, Rjwilmsi, Milo99, ChrisHibbert, SmackBot, Skookum1, Timothy Clemans, Frap, Evenfiel, NathanDahlin, Fayenatic london, Fennessy, Tinucherian, Crakkpot, Sephiroth storm, AuthorAuthor, Addbot, Willking1979, Lightbot, OlEnglish, AnomieBOT, Omaha DBA, 4twenty42o, New traffic pattern, Chaheel Riens, FrescoBot, LucienBOT, Savonneux, Throwaway85, Diannaa, Gscarp12, Mz7, Yulli67, Wikiuser13, Odd12348 and Anonymous: 17

- **Night Dragon Operation** *Source:* https://en.wikipedia.org/wiki/Night_Dragon_Operation?oldid=715520736 *Contributors:* Robofish, Nikthestunned, CAPTAIN RAJU, MMXVI and Anonymous: 1

- **Office of Personnel Management data breach** *Source:* https://en.wikipedia.org/wiki/Office_of_Personnel_Management_data_breach?oldid=740541595 *Contributors:* Beland, Neutrality, Pmsyyz, Vsmith, Elvey, Hydrargyrum, MarkAb, Muboshgu, Loadmaster, Zzsql, Yellowdesk, Yobot, AnomieBOT, Jim1138, RevelationDirect, Salvidrim!, Mochaman69, GoingBatty, Anita5192, Toploftical, Everymorning, Nephx, Ilovemylife9, MissPiggysBoyfriend, Lr0^^k, CosmicAdventure, Searien and Anonymous: 20

- **Operation Olympic Games** *Source:* https://en.wikipedia.org/wiki/Operation_Olympic_Games?oldid=743755379 *Contributors:* PaulinSaudi, Bearcat, Thincat, Klemen Kocjancic, Jantangring, Koavf, Gareth E. Kegg, Guanxi, Wavelength, Alexbrennen, Erudy, Yamaguchi 先生, Jprg1966, Nbarth, Cydebot, Buckshot06, Vikizh, Katharineamy, DadaNeem, Kaiketsu, Addbot, Debresser, Webmgr, AnomieBOT, Materialscientist, Tiller54, ElNuevoEinstein, Innotata, Mvk608, ZéroBot, 978fesfv, Th4n3r, Y.khedar, Timothysandole, Artavasdes, Pahlevun, 93, Nithin.danday, Amerifat, Finesga and Anonymous: 11

- **Operation Ababil** *Source:* https://en.wikipedia.org/wiki/Operation_Ababil?oldid=724131182 *Contributors:* BoogaLouie, Niceguyedc, Addbot, Yobot, RjwilmsiBot, ZxxZxxZ, Martinsrp, BG19bot, Pahlevun, Tanweer Khan and Anonymous: 5

- **Operation Cleaver** *Source:* https://en.wikipedia.org/wiki/Operation_Cleaver?oldid=739637045 *Contributors:* Art LaPella, Choess, Pro translator, Brandmeister, DaltonCastle, Pahlevun, Missionedit and Anonymous: 4

- **Operation Newscaster** *Source:* https://en.wikipedia.org/wiki/Operation_Newscaster?oldid=724130705 *Contributors:* Egsan Bacon, Fuddle, John of Reading, ZxxZxxZ, Klbrain, Pahlevun, DoomCult and Anonymous: 1

- **Operation Socialist** *Source:* https://en.wikipedia.org/wiki/Operation_Socialist?oldid=709065024 *Contributors:* Gareth E. Kegg, Ser Amantio di Nicolao, Cydebot, Arjayay, Yobot, BG19bot, ChristophThomas, Whizz40, Fixuture, EChastain and Anonymous: 1

- **OpIsrael** *Source:* https://en.wikipedia.org/wiki/OpIsrael?oldid=743398669 *Contributors:* Mike Rosoft, Shrike, WadeSimMiser, Sjö, Bgwhite, Neitherday, Dbfirs, Nickst, Andy M. Wang, Kathovo, Seektrue, Learrus, Laval, BloodDoll, Flyer22 Reborn, Mr. Granger, XLinkBot, Staticshakedown, Legobot, Yobot, Reenem, AnomieBOT, Jim1138, Ulric1313, JimVC3, Jalapenos do exist, Joaquin008, FrescoBot, John of Reading, Jaydiem, Xsythe, ClueBot NG, Gilderien, Hitcher9211, All Rows4, Kndimov, The Almighty Drill, Wickedcat14, Pratyya Ghosh, IdanElh, Faizan, Tentinator, Anarcho-syndikalist101, IranitGreenberg, Dr.nein, Dafuki, LieutenantLatvia, Michael Zeev, HammerKinFan, Manul, Wlglunight93, Matthewfisher09, BlankZ404, Vieque, SEIGNOT, CoolHand Logan, AnonHQ, Vítor, Security07, Averysoda, MildlyKnowledgeable, Kkajakhjkah, Akjhak, Rhaut and Anonymous: 82

- **Presidential Policy Directive 20** *Source:* https://en.wikipedia.org/wiki/Presidential_Policy_Directive_20?oldid=667727868 *Contributors:* LindsayH, Pol098, Ground Zero, Whoisjohngalt, Aldis90, Vanjagenije, Yobot, LilHelpa, MenoBot II, Skakkle, BG19bot, BattyBot, Kahtar, Monyprice and Anonymous: 1

- **RockYou** *Source:* https://en.wikipedia.org/wiki/RockYou?oldid=735761234 *Contributors:* Gary, Geraldshields11, Scratchy, ZacBowling, Markavian, Meco, Magioladitis, CAN, Wikidemon, OKBot, Winterheat, Seth.illgard, XLinkBot, Yobot, AnomieBOT, CorporateM, Lotje, Mean as custard, RjwilmsiBot, STATicVapor, Dewritech, Djembayz, Alpha Quadrant, SkNs, Ego White Tray, ClueBot NG, Hellokitkathello, Goalloverhere, Timur9008, Wikimarcos26, Me, Myself, and I are Here, Lemnaminor, Oh Blah Dee, Hoho24, Strawberryfields4ever, Tribute-fromdistrict12, Themixagency, SSTflyer, Themediaman, The Green Arrow1 and Anonymous: 28

- **Shadow Network** *Source:* https://en.wikipedia.org/wiki/Shadow_Network?oldid=724828449 *Contributors:* Davidcannon, DocWatson42, Arthur Rubin, Yobot, Dexbot, Deyoungisthan, Danies91 and Anonymous: 2

- **Operation Shady RAT** *Source:* https://en.wikipedia.org/wiki/Operation_Shady_RAT?oldid=715520813 *Contributors:* Timrollpickering, Gracefool, Morphh, Johnsemlak, Arthur Rubin, Modify, Cla68, Cattus, Robofish, Altonbr, Cydebot, DagosNavy, NapoliRoma, Speciate, Alexbot, TedderBot, RjwilmsiBot, EmausBot, GoingBatty, ZéroBot, Ipsign, Fbacchin, Helpful Pixie Bot, Zackmann08, Someone not using his real name and Anonymous: 12

- **Sony Pictures Entertainment hack** *Source:* https://en.wikipedia.org/wiki/Sony_Pictures_Entertainment_hack?oldid=744070155 *Contributors:* Julesd, Beland, Brianhe, Vsmith, Bender235, Zaslav, Smalljim, Eric Kvaalen, Philip Cross, Drbogdan, Scartol, MarnetteD, Gareth E. Kegg, Rsrikanth05, Deku-shrub, Nikkimaria, Jack Upland, ViperSnake151, Cumbiagermen, Kintetsubuffalo, Yamaguchi 先生, Gilliam, George Ho, Muboshgu, Ahess247, Derek R Bullamore, DMacks, Masem, Kencf0618, Briancua, Jesse Viviano, CuriousEric, N2e, Bellerophon5685, Yellowdesk, Ericoides, Y2kcrazyjoker4, Cartoon Boy, KConWiki, Elinruby, Ontarioboy, Hammersoft, Oshwah, Emigdioofmiami, Natg 19, Malcolmxl5, Haberstr, Dppvt, Niceguyedc, Ottawahitech, Excirial, Arjayay, Light show, XLinkBot, Prayer for the wild at heart, TriiipleThreat, Favonian, Issyl0, LuK3, Yobot, AnomieBOT, Cybersecurityczar, Materialscientist, Anonymous from the 21st century, PM800, Green Cardamom, Sock, Lipsquid, Jersey92, Galatz, Tony414, Absurdist1968, Alcea setosa, Ylight42, RRabbit42, Thewolfchild, ThePowerofX, Clue-Bot NG, Somedifferentstuff, Davprince97, Marloweperel, BG19bot, Kndimov, Brustopher, MusikAnimal, Elisfkc, BattyBot, Sfarney, LightandDark2000, Mogism, Fireflyfanboy, Febetsh23, AbstractIllusions, 93, Athomeinkobe, Corn cheese, Renommé04122015, TheBlueCanoe, Cawhee, Epicgenius, Everymorning, Rolf h nelson, Finnusertop, Noyster, Jeremyb-phone, Fixuture, ShawntheGod, Mrkaijik, Keiiri, Kitty-Carmichael, Signedzzz, Inthefastlane, Adyaman, Mr. Magoo and McBarker, HafizHanif, NotUnusual, 09I500, Nysrtup, Hiyaimtruth, PI909, RadarRedsox, Adlhgeo1990, Djkobyone, Cirripedia, MusikBot, Kgarcia28, Qzd, Bobbyboy391, Searien and Anonymous: 80

- **Cybersquatting** *Source:* https://en.wikipedia.org/wiki/Cybersquatting?oldid=741925202 *Contributors:* Eloquence, Heron, Frecklefoot, Michael Hardy, Vera Cruz, Graue, Julesd, Corixidae, Furrykef, K1Bond007, Shantavira, SD6-Agent, Paul W, Robbot, Chocolateboy, Altenmann, Postdlf, Rfc1394, Rasmus Faber, Trevor Johns, Xanzzibar, Beardo, Jason Quinn, Antandrus, Taka, Rdsmith4, Vishahu, Zondor, Kate, Smyth, Crypticfirefly, El C, Marcok, The Noodle Incident, Stesmo, Ejrrjs, Polylerus, Amcl, Andrewpmk, Gblaz, DreamGuy, Fourthords, Henry W. Schmitt, Kusma, Japanese Searobin, Brianwc, Mindmatrix, Staphylococcus, Isnow, Stefanomione, Betsythedevine, Gettingtoit, Rjwilmsi, Nightscream, Azalero, Margosbot~enwiki, TheDJ, Subversive, WhyBeNormal, Nicholasink, Chobot, YurikBot, Wavelength, Rapido, Jimp, Open4D, Hede2000, Pigman, Kyorosuke, Purodha, RattleMan, Test-tools~enwiki, Korny O'Near, Irishguy, Kkronenb, 7Train, Some guy, Rwwww, WolfWings, Errickfoxy, SmackBot, ReidarM, Reedy, Basseq, Ohnoitsjamie, Jcc1, Jerome Charles Potts, UNV, FrankWilliams, Derek R Bullamore, Just plain Bill, Amartyabag, Hbachus, PseudoSudo, Ckatz, Moroveus, Iridescent, Beno1000, Leebert, Courcelles, Radiant chains, HMishkoff, Doug Nelson, Franks1, Fordmadoxfraud, Tawkerbot4, DumbBOT, Technodollarz, Arbitrary username, Thijs!bot, Dawnseeker2000, Natalie Erin, Malvineous, Dr who1975, Kennard2, PaulOD, EECavazos, Erxnmedia, Yale s, .anacondabot, Repku, Bongwarrior, Rich257, Adrian J. Hunter, Johnsalomon, InvertRect, Patstuart, Flowanda, CliffC, CommonsDelinker, Jmccormac, TommieDrash, Kimse, Mbeatty, Octopus-Hands, GeveraBert, AntiSpamBot, Gwen Gale, Nawulf, Num1dgen, Philip Trueman, TXiKiBoT, Enrico1999, Mjlissner, Sherdor, Guest9999, Wykypydya, Softtest123, Myavantssoslow, Koolaboola, Kbrose, SieBot, Troublecat, Pxma, Arthur Smart, Culture-Drone, Maitreg, ClueBot, NickIre, Trotline, Mild Bill Hiccup, Mr. Laser Beam, Socrates2008, CurtisNeeley, Johnuniq, Sqpatrol, Delicious carbuncle, Feinoha, Pouletetanc, Addbot, Dogdane2000, Eedlee, Nuozgroup, Americanfreedom, Numbo3-bot, Lightbot, HerculeBot, Ben Ben, AnomieBOT, ThaddeusB, Galoubet, Timtenza, Briansalle, MohitSingh, Reece111, Ericgoldman, ArkinAardvark, Green Cardamom, 白布飘扬, Tom Photos, Kez1304, Peacock486, EmausBot, WikitanvirBot, Avenue X at Cicero, LisaFowler, GoingBatty, Checkingfax, Army777, Pgolobish, Helpful Pixie Bot, BG19bot, Chmarkine, Lastrosestudios, Yaj57, Cyberbot II, Mr. Guye, Liediqiya0, Epicgenius, Jonnymaceachern, Quadbook, Gamebuster19901, Callmeskelly and Anonymous: 157

- **Stuxnet** *Source:* https://en.wikipedia.org/wiki/Stuxnet?oldid=741373572 *Contributors:* The Anome, Nealmcb, Pnm, Lousyd, Liftarn, KAMiKAZOW, Julesd, GCarty, PaulinSaudi, WhisperToMe, Markhurd, Tpbradbury, Thue, AnonMoos, Pigsonthewing, HaeB, Xanzzibar, DocWatson42, Cattac, Richards1052, Jason Quinn, Stay, Golbez, Piotrus, Ulmanor, Now3d, Thorwald, Mernen, Discospinster, Rich Farmbrough, FT2, Pmsyyz, Smyth, Bender235, Kms, Ylee, Shrike, Jantangring, John Vandenberg, Kjkolb, Brainy J, Jonathunder, Spitzl, Alansohn, Gargaj, Nsd, Arthena, Penwhale, Kocio, Danhash, Dismas, Hq3473, Woohookitty, Mindmatrix, YuriBCN, Ekem, Pol098, Trödel, MONGO, Tabletop, Wikiklrsc, Choas~enwiki, Tickle me, Teemu Leisti, Lawrence King, Tim!, Koavf, Brighterorange, Flarn2006, Caek, Nihiltres, Error9900, Ahunt, DVdm, Bgwhite, Vmenkov, Noclador, Wavelength, Eraserhead1, Hydrargyrum, FFLaguna, Gillis, Tony1, Mysid, Slicing, ReCover, Thnidu, Arthur Rubin, BorgQueen, Whaa?, Allens, Bluezy, Phr en, Ozzmosis, SmackBot, Cthompson, Verne Equinox, Cla68, Pascalvanhecke, Xaosflux, Gilliam, Skizzik, Fintler, Autarch, Audacity, Thumperward, Snori, Skygawker, Nbarth, Emurphy42, Duerra, Gyrobo, Audriusa, Simpsons contributor, Tamfang, Frap, Caspermilktoast, Madman2001, Cybercobra, Lambiam, Zaxius, Atkinson 291, Khazar, Gobonobo, Bonzi, Xofc, Shattered, Loadmaster, Illythr, Kvng, Dl2000, Hu12, JHP, Chetvorno, Chris55, FleetCommand, Jesse Viviano, Location, Future Perfect at Sunrise, Quibik, Christian75, Silver Sonic Shadow, Mojo Hand, Iviney, Bowerster, Heroeswithmetaphors, Lajsikonik, Dawnseeker2000, BMB, Marokwitz, Esbjörn, Byornski, Smartse, Yellowdesk, Rico402, Msm10, Sanchom, TonyChanYT, PatriotX, Hifrommike65, Seleucus, LorenzoB, NMaia, Fconaway, RockMFR, Shellwood, CFCF, Mattnad, Maurice Carbonaro, Vision3001, Ben Skála, Zero Serenity, Knight of BAAWA, Sigmundur, Bonadea, Alterrabe, Sgeureka, TreasuryTag, Johnfos, BoogaLouie, Philip Trueman, GroveGuy, Timhogs, Gilisa, Softtest123, Nikosgreencookie, Dick Kimball, Lerdthenerd, Michaeldsuarez, Edkollin, NPguy, Michael Frind, Foxmajik, AH-Martin, AdRock, Techtonic, Sephiroth storm, Marmotdan, Yerpo, RMB1987, Wellifitisntsamphippen, Rhsimard, Escape Orbit, Joel Rennie, ImageRemovalBot, Beeblebrox, Apuldram, XenonofArcticus, Kennvido, Helenabella, Carthu15, Supertouch, Dlabtot, Drmies, Mild Bill Hiccup, Niceguyedc, Nanobear~enwiki, Trivialist, Supergodzilla2090, Ktr101, Excirial, Socrates2008, Art-top, MaSt, 7&6=thirteen, B.Zsolt, Daniel-Pharos, Freelion, Expertjohn, XLinkBot, Ost316, Avoided, Addbot, Fyrael, Fluffernutter, CactusWriter, Download, Buster7, Lihaas, Debresser, Maslen, Jasper Deng, AgadaUrbanit, 84user, OlEnglish, דוד שי, Matěj Grabovský, Zorrobot, חובבשירה, Snaily, StraSSenBahn, Luckas-bot, Yobot, BayuAH, Lerichard, Bryan.burgers, DiverDave, AnomieBOT, Wikieditoroftoday, Spyderbane, 1exec1, Idanpl, Citation bot, ArthurBot,

Kevin chen2003, Xqbot, Intelati, Andrewmin, Druiffic, Leon3289, Buckeyebrett, Mcfrag, Colorred, Bugefun, Chaheel Riens, PM800, Jsp722, Thehelpfulbot, Plot Spoiler, Green Cardamom, Captain-n00dle, TastyChikan, Geleto, Surv1v4l1st, LucienBOT, Doremo, Gire 3pich2005, I dream of horses, Tóraí, ElNuevoEinstein, Cusimanoja, Enemenemu, Trappist the monk, Manfromthemoon, Talencar, Lotje, Comet Tuttle, Nataev, Postal2600, Reaper Eternal, Rram321, Makki98, Sigwald, DARTH SIDIOUS 2, Obankston, Christoph hausner, RjwilmsiBot, Hbirjand, Slon02, EmausBot, Tuankiet65, WikitanvirBot, Lunaibis, Clark42, GoingBatty, ZxxZxxZ, Rbaleksandar, Mo ainm, TreacherousWays, Arrto, Dcirovic, K6ka, Jasonanaggie, The Blade of the Northern Lights, ZéroBot, Alcea setosa, Contribute23, Druzhnik, Midas02, Ebrambot, H3llBot, 1Veertje, MajorVariola, Ewa5050, L1A1 FAL, Glennconti, Coasterlover1994, L Kensington, Mayur, Bulwersator, ChuispastonBot, Ihardlythinkso, Pastore Italy, Uzi4upal, Paperthing, Zabanio, SilverFox93, Kebmebms, Rams132, Vesuviuz, Rnotakid, Are23421, Paddingtonbaer, Jsnsoft, Pymansorl, Gastonlagaffe~enwiki, SochenZar, ClueBot NG, SecurityMeister, Antonin33, Malleus Felonius, InfoNetting, Gnume, BrekekekexKoaxKoax, Kazemita1, Loginnigol, XorXLNC, Quaber, NPz1, Thompn4, Frietjes, Jasperwebster, Eli778, Widr, Dms77, Helpful Pixie Bot, Eric.Byres, Ramaksoud2000, Bonvallite, BG19bot, DallasSecurity, Frodoxe, Gyrotooka, Raudive, Kendall-K1, Ucflap, Mobmation, Luizpuodzius, Marcusdunlap, WebHorizon, Ugncreative Usergname, Thetruthofwords, MRC37, 220 of Borg, Benjitheijneb, RavelTwig, MeanMotherJr, BattyBot, Proslayer999, Joshthomas1233456, Cyberbot II, ChrisGualtieri, Fijianz, Rezonansowy, Rokr zep, Hellowns, Jakob-Steenberg, Pahlevun, Clovis3321, JCN9000, Geau, Armanschwarz, TheBlueCanoe, Canuttle1956, Barzane, American In Brazil, Soffredo, Reaskyz, Davis4K5, Joeyseal, Comp.arch, IranitGreenberg, A Certain Lack of Grandeur, Jfps, Ginsuloft, Michael Zeev, Someone not using his real name, Kwal0203, FockeWulf FW 190, Juhuyuta, Thatonewikiguy, Armaan Ladak, Unrealmimimi, Rft123456789, Gnirre, Monkbot, P-123, Sean308255, Dsprc, Macofe, Iamahashtag, ChamithN, Eurodyne, Keramiton, GrammarFixeroni, Eteethan, User000name, TQuentin, Prinsgezinde, Anarchyte, WoziSSL, JeremiahY, CaseyMillerWiki, Heetbeet, Amerifat, Boopbopbip, Gulumeemee, DucttapeloverXDXDXD, Thebasketballer, Commander2006 and Anonymous: 370

- **Titan Rain** *Source:* https://en.wikipedia.org/wiki/Titan_Rain?oldid=743453216 *Contributors:* Tzaquiel, Itai, Shizhao, Geni, Ylee, Freyr, Bobrayner, Stefanomione, RadioActive~enwiki, Rschen7754, TheMidnighters, Imrehg, Srleffler, Bgwhite, RussBot, Hydrargyrum, Daveswagon, Alynna Kasmira, Retired username, Tiger888, Cm205, SmackBot, Xaosflux, Ohnoitsjamie, Cattus, Snori, Mukadderat, Publicus, VoxLuna, Cydebot, NathanDahlin, Thijs!bot, RobotG, DagosNavy, Magioladitis, Buckshot06, Tinucherian, KConWiki, Airfinance, Bytecount, KylieTastic, Enviroboy, PixelBot, Sweeper tamonten, Addbot, LaaknorBot, Tassedethe, Lightbot, Yobot, Quantumseven, LilHelpa, New traffic pattern, Ranaenc, Epp, DexDor, Gscarp12, Doelleri, ZéroBot, AndrewOne, Frietjes, Gyrotooka, Ugncreative Usergname, ArmbrustBot, The One And Only Group 18, Ghaaz B, 65jes89, GreenC bot and Anonymous: 29

- **Operation Tunisia** *Source:* https://en.wikipedia.org/wiki/Operation_Tunisia?oldid=732032451 *Contributors:* Timrollpickering, Klemen Kocjancic, Bender235, Stefanomione, RussBot, Hydrargyrum, Cydebot, Silver Sonic Shadow, Heroeswithmetaphors, DagosNavy, Squids and Chips, Gold1618, Niceguyedc, Rhododendrites, Good Olfactory, Addbot, Matthew.Dimashki, Xqbot, Swalgal, RjwilmsiBot, Helmoony, AvicBot, Wagner, Widr, Helpful Pixie Bot, Wbm1058, A Dirty Watermelon, Jeancey, Ciaran Sinclair, Dexbot, Kephir, Sharmin.h, Juhuyuta, Bashtn and Anonymous: 10

- **TV5Monde** *Source:* https://en.wikipedia.org/wiki/TV5Monde?oldid=743674832 *Contributors:* Tregoweth, Gabriel, Kwekubo, Shizhao, Mr-Weeble, Denelson83, Bearcat, Gidonb, Rdash, Xyzzyva, DocWatson42, Utcursch, OwenBlacker, Liberlogos, Valmi, Grstain, Tolo, Rich Farmbrough, Xezbeth, Quiensabe, Bender235, CanisRufus, Väsk, Hinotori, Mrmiscellanious~enwiki, Gpvos, Eleusis, Ikescs, Eyreland, Marudubshinki, BD2412, Sjakkalle, Nanami Kamimura, Viakenny, Vegaswikian, ApprenticeFan, RasputinAXP, Tlitic, YurikBot, Rapido, Ronald20, Joshdboz, Robert Moore, Kiwidude, JSH-alive, CLW, Arthur Rubin, NYArtsnWords, AntL, ViperSnake151, Thomas Blomberg, NeilN, Luk, SmackBot, Estoy Aquí, Godgoddingham333, Eskimbot, Steam5, AWeenieMan, Alphathon, Chlewbot, Kanabekobaton, Azumanga1, Iam4Lost, Kevlar67, The Toad, Zonux, WayKurat, WikiWitch, Rialbbe, Gobonobo, AxG, Dl2000, Hu12, Iridescent, Courcelles, Skyisthebest, Picaroon, Krikorianshant, Alaibot, Northwest, Piccolo Modificatore Laborioso, Thijs!bot, Matt69er, JustAGal, MichaelT1979, Tobibln, Husond, Andonic, Jimmy, Suduser85, Geniac, Magioladitis, Musimax, Enaidmawr, Cvac1, Garkbit, Jasmeet 181, VolkovBot, RingtailedFox, AlnoktaBOT, AMAPO, Neasden Villa, TXiKiBoT, Orielglassstudio, Rei-bot, Alphaios~enwiki, Dougal18, McM.bot, Peeperman, Synthebot, SieBot, Bot-Multichill, Gerakibot, Scarlatine, Oahiyeel, Aspects, Werldwayd, Kjtobo, Ken123BOT, Laurentiu Popa, ImageRemovalBot, De Boni 2007, Malpass93, Farras Octara, Viplux, ElSaxo, Bbb2007, Arjayay, Pioelad, Donegal92, A.h. king, Cheque 02, SilvonenBot, Addbot, Dancetrance, Muddycrutchboy, AndersBot, Chzz, Tide rolls, WuBot, -iNu-, Michaello, Shikuesi3, Luckas-bot, Yobot, Bunnyhop11, Ngagnebin, AnomieBOT, Vic201401, Film-DekPakChong, Mahmudmasri, TheTechieGeek63, LilHelpa, Marcosrom, Cthuang, RibotBOT, 789123j, Thehelpfulbot, PatriciaV, FrescoBot, Wikiaide, The GateKeeper07, ProcEnforce, LittleWink, MondalorBot, Full-date unlinking bot, Loginfeatlog, Digimon Adventure, Fappah, EmausBot, John of Reading, RA0808, C0re1980, Jenks24, EWVGN3T0, Ὁ οἶστρος, KARom, TheA5, ClueBot NG, Mishukdero, MerlIwBot, BG19bot, PhnomPencil, Geraldo Perez, Glorious 93, Gazkthul, Ngoquangduong, Codename Lisa, Sajithsameera, Cmdireland, Eric abiog, George23820, EvergreenFir, Fanofbfolders, Narutzy, Siégégé Ctable, IC-AJ, Thibaut120094, Libertarian12111971, ClassicOnAStick, Manzilkonepse20, Jai51, प्रशान्त पाण्डेय, XPanettaa, Ceannlann gorm, Cableboy30, Utkarshshah6, Onlyraffael, Issimo 15, Oussama miyamoto and Anonymous: 171

- **2008 cyberattack on United States** *Source:* https://en.wikipedia.org/wiki/2008_cyberattack_on_United_States?oldid=742559903 *Contributors:* SC, Ceyockey, Richard Arthur Norton (1958-), Woohookitty, SmackBot, Ser Amantio di Nicolao, Meco, DagosNavy, Adamdaley, Addbot, Trappist the monk, RjwilmsiBot, ZéroBot, Jt9855, Rms5175 and Anonymous: 10

- **Vietnamese airports hackings** *Source:* https://en.wikipedia.org/wiki/Vietnamese_airports_hackings?oldid=737494139 *Contributors:* ImageRemovalBot, Yobot, I dream of horses, Hariboneagle927, DanGong and Anonymous: 3

- **Vulcanbot** *Source:* https://en.wikipedia.org/wiki/Vulcanbot?oldid=625335426 *Contributors:* Green Giant, Niceguyedc, DanielPharos, Ironholds, Tassedethe, Tijfo098 and Enfcer

- **World of Hell** *Source:* https://en.wikipedia.org/wiki/World_of_Hell?oldid=713022784 *Contributors:* Lquilter, Varlaam, Klemen Kocjancic, JHCaufield, Magioladitis, CommonsDelinker, NYCRuss, SchreiberBike, XLinkBot, Yobot, AnomieBOT, Anna Frodesiak, Buddy23Lee, Wbm1058, Rsotillo, Epist, 220 of Borg, Cyberbot II, Rezonansowy and Anonymous: 13

- **Zombie Zero** *Source:* https://en.wikipedia.org/wiki/Zombie_Zero?oldid=740414732 *Contributors:* Derek R Bullamore, Zackmann08, DaltonCastle, MRD2014, TechnoChief2011 and 20JacksonP

55.2.2   Images

- **File:270_Park_Avenue_(WTM_by_official-ly_cool_100).jpg** *Source:* https://upload.wikimedia.org/wikipedia/commons/5/56/270_Park_ Avenue_%28WTM_by_official-ly_cool_100%29.jpg *License:* CC BY-SA 3.0 *Contributors:* Contributed by author. *Original artist:* This photo was taken by participant/team *official-ly cool* as part of the Commons:Wikipedia Takes Manhattan project on April 4, 2008.

- **File:33_Liberty_Street_IMG_9062_stitched.jpg** *Source:* https://upload.wikimedia.org/wikipedia/commons/a/a7/33_Liberty_Street_IMG_ 9062_stitched.jpg *License:* CC BY-SA 3.0 *Contributors:* File:33 Liberty Street IMG 9062.JPG *Original artist:* Gryffindor

- **File:A_coloured_voting_box.svg** *Source:* https://upload.wikimedia.org/wikipedia/en/0/01/A_coloured_voting_box.svg *License:* Cc-by-sa-3.0 *Contributors:* ? *Original artist:* ?

- **File:Ambox_current_red.svg** *Source:* https://upload.wikimedia.org/wikipedia/commons/9/98/Ambox_current_red.svg *License:* CC0 *Contributors:* self-made, inspired by Gnome globe current event.svg, using Information icon3.svg and Earth clip art.svg *Original artist:* Vipersnake151, penubag, Tkgd2007 (clock)

- **File:Ambox_important.svg** *Source:* https://upload.wikimedia.org/wikipedia/commons/b/b4/Ambox_important.svg *License:* Public domain *Contributors:* Own work, based off of Image:Ambox scales.svg *Original artist:* Dsmurat (talk · contribs)

- **File:Ambox_wikify.svg** *Source:* https://upload.wikimedia.org/wikipedia/commons/e/e1/Ambox_wikify.svg *License:* Public domain *Contributors:* Own work *Original artist:* penubag

- **File:Anonymous-Bruxelles.jpg** *Source:* https://upload.wikimedia.org/wikipedia/commons/6/67/Anonymous-Bruxelles.jpg *License:* CC BY-SA 3.0 *Contributors:* Own work *Original artist:* Morburre

- **File:Anonymous-hacked-straits-times-blog-post.jpg**   *Source:*   https://upload.wikimedia.org/wikipedia/en/9/9f/ Anonymous-hacked-straits-times-blog-post.jpg *License:* Fair use *Contributors:*
The Straits Times
Original artist: ?

- **File:Anonymous.svg** *Source:* https://upload.wikimedia.org/wikipedia/commons/e/e0/Anonymous.svg *License:* Public domain *Contributors:* clipart-rahmen.de *Original artist:* Clipart Guru

- **File:AnonymousOccupy.jpg** *Source:* https://upload.wikimedia.org/wikipedia/commons/3/31/AnonymousOccupy.jpg *License:* CC BY 2.0 *Contributors:* http://www.flickr.com/photos/shankbone/6157303489/ *Original artist:* david_shankbone

- **File:Anonymous_Flag.svg** *Source:* https://upload.wikimedia.org/wikipedia/commons/5/51/Anonymous_Flag.svg *License:* Public domain *Contributors:* Own work *Original artist:* Anonymous

- **File:Anonymous_Fox_11.jpg** *Source:* https://upload.wikimedia.org/wikipedia/en/8/8b/Anonymous_Fox_11.jpg *License:* Fair use *Contributors:*
KTTV Fox 11
Original artist: ?

- **File:Anonymous_Scientology_1_by_David_Shankbone.JPG** *Source:* https://upload.wikimedia.org/wikipedia/commons/c/c6/Anonymous_ Scientology_1_by_David_Shankbone.JPG *License:* CC-BY-SA-3.0 *Contributors:* David Shankbone *Original artist:* David Shankbone

- **File:Anonymous_at_Scientology_in_Los_Angeles.jpg** *Source:* https://upload.wikimedia.org/wikipedia/commons/b/b0/Anonymous_at_ Scientology_in_Los_Angeles.jpg *License:* CC BY-SA 2.0 *Contributors:* originally posted to **Flickr** as Anonymous at Scientology in Los Angeles *Original artist:* Vincent Diamante

- **File:Anonymous_emblem.svg** *Source:* https://upload.wikimedia.org/wikipedia/commons/a/a6/Anonymous_emblem.svg *License:* Public domain *Contributors:* This file has been **extracted** from another file: Anonymous Flag.svg
Original artist: Kephir at English Wikipedia

- **File:Anti-sec_manifesto.png** *Source:* https://upload.wikimedia.org/wikipedia/commons/b/b7/Anti-sec_manifesto.png *License:* Public domain *Contributors:* Wikipedia *Original artist:* Brian_Eetar

- **File:Aurora_generator_starting_to_smoke.png** *Source:* https://upload.wikimedia.org/wikipedia/commons/5/5a/Aurora_generator_ starting_to_smoke.png *License:* Public domain *Contributors:* https://muckrock.s3.amazonaws.com/foia_files/aurora_high_res.wmv *Original artist:* Department of Homeland Security

- **File:Blank_television_set.svg** *Source:* https://upload.wikimedia.org/wikipedia/commons/8/8c/Blank_television_set.svg *License:* CC-BY-SA-3.0 *Contributors:* en:Image:Aus tv.png (among others) *Original artist:* Traced by User:Stannered

- **File:Commons-logo.svg** *Source:* https://upload.wikimedia.org/wikipedia/en/4/4a/Commons-logo.svg *License:* CC-BY-SA-3.0 *Contributors:* ? *Original artist:* ?

- **File:Copyright-problem.svg** *Source:* https://upload.wikimedia.org/wikipedia/en/c/cf/Copyright-problem.svg *License:* PD *Contributors:* ? *Original artist:* ?

- **File:Crystal_Clear_app_Login_Manager_2.png** *Source:* https://upload.wikimedia.org/wikipedia/en/c/c2/Crystal_Clear_app_Login_ Manager_2.png *License:* ? *Contributors:* ? *Original artist:* ?

- **File:Crystal_Clear_app_browser.png** *Source:* https://upload.wikimedia.org/wikipedia/commons/f/fe/Crystal_Clear_app_browser.png *License:* LGPL *Contributors:* All Crystal icons were posted by the author as LGPL on kde-look *Original artist:* Everaldo Coelho and YellowIcon

- **File:Crystal_Clear_app_kspread.png** *Source:* https://upload.wikimedia.org/wikipedia/commons/6/6f/Crystal_Clear_app_kspread.png *License:* LGPL *Contributors:* All Crystal Clear icons were posted by the author as LGPL on kde-look; *Original artist:* Everaldo Coelho and YellowIcon;

- **File:CyberBerkut.png** *Source:* https://upload.wikimedia.org/wikipedia/en/9/95/CyberBerkut.png *License:* Fair use *Contributors:* http://www.cyber-berkut.org/img/logo.png *Original artist:* ?
- **File:Defaced_Air_Botswana_Website.JPG** *Source:* https://upload.wikimedia.org/wikipedia/en/0/0f/Defaced_Air_Botswana_Website.JPG *License:* Fair use *Contributors:*
www.airbotswana.co.bw/ (September 7, 2010)
Original artist: ?
- **File:Dr._Atiur_Rahman,_Governor_of_Bangladesh_Bank_cropped.jpg** *Source:* https://upload.wikimedia.org/wikipedia/en/1/13/Dr._Atiur_Rahman%2C_Governor_of_Bangladesh_Bank_cropped.jpg *License:* GFDL *Contributors:*
Wikipedia, File:Dr. Atiur Rahman, Governor of Bangladesh Bank.jpg *Original artist:*
Mirza Salman Hossain Beg
- **File:Edit-clear.svg** *Source:* https://upload.wikimedia.org/wikipedia/en/f/f2/Edit-clear.svg *License:* Public domain *Contributors:* The *Tango! Desktop Project. Original artist:*
The people from the Tango! project. And according to the meta-data in the file, specifically: "Andreas Nilsson, and Jakub Steiner (although minimally)."
- **File:Flag_of_Abkhazia.svg** *Source:* https://upload.wikimedia.org/wikipedia/commons/2/27/Flag_of_Abkhazia.svg *License:* Public domain *Contributors:* Own work , see URL http://www.abkhaziagov.org/ru/state/sovereignty/flag_b.jpg *Original artist:* Drawn by User:Achim1999
- **File:Flag_of_Georgia.svg** *Source:* https://upload.wikimedia.org/wikipedia/commons/0/0f/Flag_of_Georgia.svg *License:* Public domain *Contributors:* Own work based on File:Brdzanebuleba 31.pdf *Original artist:* User:SKopp
- **File:Flag_of_Iran.svg** *Source:* https://upload.wikimedia.org/wikipedia/commons/c/ca/Flag_of_Iran.svg *License:* Public domain *Contributors:* URL http://www.isiri.org/portal/files/std/1.htm and an English translation / interpretation at URL http://flagspot.net/flags/ir'.html *Original artist:* Various
- **File:Flag_of_North_Korea.svg** *Source:* https://upload.wikimedia.org/wikipedia/commons/5/51/Flag_of_North_Korea.svg *License:* Public domain *Contributors:* Own work *Original artist:* Zscout370
- **File:Flag_of_Russia.svg** *Source:* https://upload.wikimedia.org/wikipedia/en/f/f3/Flag_of_Russia.svg *License:* PD *Contributors:* ? *Original artist:* ?
- **File:Flag_of_Singapore.svg** *Source:* https://upload.wikimedia.org/wikipedia/commons/4/48/Flag_of_Singapore.svg *License:* Public domain *Contributors:* The drawing was based from http://app.www.sg/who/42/National-Flag.aspx. Colors from the book: *(2001). The National Symbols Kit. Singapore: Ministry of Information, Communications and the Arts. pp. 5. ISBN 8880968010* Pantone 032 shade from http://www.pantone.com/pages/pantone/colorfinder.aspx?c_id=13050 *Original artist:* Various
- **File:Flag_of_South_Ossetia.svg** *Source:* https://upload.wikimedia.org/wikipedia/commons/1/12/Flag_of_South_Ossetia.svg *License:* Public domain *Contributors:* The law on State flag of South Ossetia *Original artist:* Various
- **File:Flag_of_Tunisia.svg** *Source:* https://upload.wikimedia.org/wikipedia/commons/c/ce/Flag_of_Tunisia.svg *License:* Public domain *Contributors:* http://www.w3.org/ *Original artist:* entraîneur: BEN KHALIFA WISSAM
- **File:Flag_of_the_People'{}s_Republic_of_China.svg** *Source:* https://upload.wikimedia.org/wikipedia/commons/f/fa/Flag_of_the_People%27s_Republic_of_China.svg *License:* Public domain *Contributors:* Own work, http://www.protocol.gov.hk/flags/eng/n_flag/design.html *Original artist:* Drawn by User:SKopp, redrawn by User:Denelson83 and User:Zscout370
- **File:Flag_of_the_United_States.svg** *Source:* https://upload.wikimedia.org/wikipedia/en/a/a4/Flag_of_the_United_States.svg *License:* PD *Contributors:* ? *Original artist:* ?
- **File:Folder_Hexagonal_Icon.svg** *Source:* https://upload.wikimedia.org/wikipedia/en/4/48/Folder_Hexagonal_Icon.svg *License:* Cc-by-sa-3.0 *Contributors:* ? *Original artist:* ?
- **File:Georgia,_Ossetia,_Russia_and_Abkhazia_(en).svg** *Source:* https://upload.wikimedia.org/wikipedia/commons/c/cd/Georgia%2C_Ossetia%2C_Russia_and_Abkhazia_%28en%29.svg *License:* CC-BY-SA-3.0 *Contributors:* Own work + Image:Caucasus-ethnic en.svg. Image renamed from Image:Georgia, Ossetia, Russia and Abkhazia.svg *Original artist:* Ssolbergj & creator of source map.
- **File:IllegalFlowerTribute1.jpg** *Source:* https://upload.wikimedia.org/wikipedia/commons/9/9c/IllegalFlowerTribute1.jpg *License:* CC BY-SA 3.0 *Contributors:* Own work *Original artist:* Xhacker
- **File:Increase_Negative.svg** *Source:* https://upload.wikimedia.org/wikipedia/commons/5/59/Increase_Negative.svg *License:* Public domain *Contributors:*
- Increase2.svg *Original artist:* Increase2.svg: Sarang
- **File:Industry5.svg** *Source:* https://upload.wikimedia.org/wikipedia/commons/2/2a/Industry5.svg *License:* CC0 *Contributors:* https://openclipart.org/detail/237859/factory *Original artist:* Tsaoja
- **File:Internet_map_1024.jpg** *Source:* https://upload.wikimedia.org/wikipedia/commons/d/d2/Internet_map_1024.jpg *License:* CC BY 2.5 *Contributors:* Originally from the English Wikipedia; description page is/was here. *Original artist:* The Opte Project
- **File:Internet_map_1024_-_transparent,_inverted.png** *Source:* https://upload.wikimedia.org/wikipedia/commons/3/3f/Internet_map_1024_-_transparent%2C_inverted.png *License:* CC BY 2.5 *Contributors:* Originally from the English Wikipedia; description page is/was here. *Original artist:* The Opte Project
- **File:Intrusion_Kill_Chain_-_v2.png** *Source:* https://upload.wikimedia.org/wikipedia/commons/1/1d/Intrusion_Kill_Chain_-_v2.png *License:* Public domain *Contributors:* http://www.public.navy.mil/spawar/Press/Documents/Publications/03.26.15_USSenate.pdf *Original artist:* U.S. Senate Committee on Commerce, Science, and Transportation

- **File:KLatin_icon.png** *Source:* https://upload.wikimedia.org/wikipedia/commons/5/5d/KLatin_icon.png *License:* CC-BY-SA-3.0 *Contributors:* ? *Original artist:* ?

- **File:Lockheed_Martin_Aeronautics_Discussion.jpg** *Source:* https://upload.wikimedia.org/wikipedia/commons/e/ed/Lockheed_Martin_ Aeronautics_Discussion.jpg *License:* CC BY 2.0 *Contributors:* https://www.flickr.com/photos/atkeison/7143525321 *Original artist:* Charles Atkeison

- **File:Malware_logo.svg** *Source:* https://upload.wikimedia.org/wikipedia/commons/f/ff/Malware_logo.svg *License:* LGPL *Contributors:* Skull and crossbones.svg (valid SVG)

  Original artist: Skull and crossbones.svg: Silsor

- **File:Message_to_Scientology.ogv** *Source:* https://upload.wikimedia.org/wikipedia/commons/7/73/Message_to_Scientology.ogv *License:* Public domain *Contributors:* http://www.youtube.com/watch?v=JCbKv9yiLiQ
  Video footage: File:Timelapse Clouds Compilation.ogv
  Music: File:The Rise of Satan by kingj4life3.ogg *Original artist:* Anonymous (group). Originally uploaded January 21, 2008 to YouTube under YouTube user account: "Church0fScientology"

- **File:Monitor_padlock.svg** *Source:* https://upload.wikimedia.org/wikipedia/commons/7/73/Monitor_padlock.svg *License:* CC BY-SA 3.0 *Contributors:* Own work (Original text: *self-made*) *Original artist:* Lunarbunny (talk)

- **File:Natanz_nuclear.jpg** *Source:* https://upload.wikimedia.org/wikipedia/commons/3/3a/Natanz_nuclear.jpg *License:* CC BY 2.0 *Contributors:* http://www.flickr.com/photos/hamed/237790717 *Original artist:* Hamed Saber

- **File:National_Park_Service_9-11_Statue_of_Liberty_and_WTC_fire.jpg** *Source:* https://upload.wikimedia.org/wikipedia/commons/f/ fd/National_Park_Service_9-11_Statue_of_Liberty_and_WTC_fire.jpg *License:* Public domain *Contributors:* https://web.archive.org/web/ 20021019052836/http://www.nps.gov/remembrance/statue/index.html *Original artist:* National Park Service

- **File:New-Map-Francophone_World.PNG** *Source:* https://upload.wikimedia.org/wikipedia/commons/5/50/New-Map-Francophone_ World.PNG *License:* Public domain *Contributors:* Own work *Original artist:* aaker

- **File:NewsOnAir.org.jpg** *Source:* https://upload.wikimedia.org/wikipedia/en/d/dd/NewsOnAir.org.jpg *License:* Fair use *Contributors:* http://www.hotforsecurity.com/wp-content/uploads/2014/05/newsonair.jpeg *Original artist:* ?

- **File:Newscaster.jpg** *Source:* https://upload.wikimedia.org/wikipedia/en/8/8c/Newscaster.jpg *License:* Fair use *Contributors:* http://www.isightpartners.com/wp-content/uploads/2014/05/Newscaster-Blog-Image.jpg *Original artist:* ?

- **File:Noynoy_Aquino.jpg** *Source:* https://upload.wikimedia.org/wikipedia/commons/a/af/Noynoy_Aquino.jpg *License:* CC BY-SA 2.0 *Contributors:* Aquino *Original artist:* Jeffrey Avellanosa from Makati, Philippines

- **File:Operation_Cleaver.png** *Source:* https://upload.wikimedia.org/wikipedia/en/a/a2/Operation_Cleaver.png *License:* Fair use *Contributors:* www.cylance.com/assets/Cleaver/Cylance_Operation_Cleaver_Report.pdf
  Original artist: ?

- **File:Peace_sign.svg** *Source:* https://upload.wikimedia.org/wikipedia/commons/d/d2/Peace_sign.svg *License:* Public domain *Contributors:* Transferred from en.wikipedia to Commons. *Original artist:* The original uploader was Schuminweb at English Wikipedia

- **File:PlayStation_Network_logo.png** *Source:* https://upload.wikimedia.org/wikipedia/commons/f/f2/PlayStation_Network_logo.png *License:* Public domain *Contributors:* http://www.scei.co.jp/corporate/release/150129a_c.html *Original artist:* Sony Computer Entertainment

- **File:Portal-puzzle.svg** *Source:* https://upload.wikimedia.org/wikipedia/en/f/fd/Portal-puzzle.svg *License:* Public domain *Contributors:* ? *Original artist:* ?

- **File:Ps3-fat-console.png** *Source:* https://upload.wikimedia.org/wikipedia/commons/9/91/Ps3-fat-console.png *License:* Public domain *Contributors:* Own work *Original artist:* Evan-Amos

- **File:Question_book-new.svg** *Source:* https://upload.wikimedia.org/wikipedia/en/9/99/Question_book-new.svg *License:* Cc-by-sa-3.0 *Contributors:*
  Created from scratch in Adobe Illustrator. Based on Image:Question book.png created by User:Equazcion *Original artist:*
  Tkgd2007

- **File:RegisteredTM.svg** *Source:* https://upload.wikimedia.org/wikipedia/commons/2/2b/RegisteredTM.svg *License:* Public domain *Contributors:* This vector image was created with Inkscape. *Original artist:* Roman Tworkowski

- **File:Rockyou_logo.png** *Source:* https://upload.wikimedia.org/wikipedia/commons/d/d5/Rockyou_logo.png *License:* Public domain *Contributors:* www.rockyou.com *Original artist:* RockYou

- **File:S7300.JPG** *Source:* https://upload.wikimedia.org/wikipedia/commons/1/1f/S7300.JPG *License:* CC BY-SA 2.5 *Contributors:* Own work *Original artist:* Ulli1105

- **File:Searchtool.svg** *Source:* https://upload.wikimedia.org/wikipedia/en/6/61/Searchtool.svg *License:* ? *Contributors:* ? *Original artist:* ?

- **File:Sonypicturesentertainmentoffices.jpg** *Source:* https://upload.wikimedia.org/wikipedia/commons/e/ea/ Sonypicturesentertainmentoffices.jpg *License:* CC-BY-SA-3.0 *Contributors:* Photographed on May 10, 2008 by user Coolcaesar. (Transferred from en.wikipedia) *Original artist:* Coolcaesar at en.wikipedia

- **File:Standard_legirons_taiwan01.jpg** *Source:* https://upload.wikimedia.org/wikipedia/commons/b/b8/Standard_legirons_taiwan01.jpg *License:* CC-BY-SA-3.0 *Contributors:* Own work *Original artist:* User:Klaus with K

- **File:Step7_communicating_with_plc.svg** *Source:* https://upload.wikimedia.org/wikipedia/commons/9/9b/Step7_communicating_with_plc. svg *License:* CC BY-SA 3.0 *Contributors:* Own work *Original artist:* Grixlkraxl

55.2.3 Content license

www.ingramcontent.com/pod-product-compliance
Lightning Source LLC
LaVergne TN
LVHW060122070326
832902LV00019B/3081